INSTANT POT PRESSURE COOKER COOKBOOK

by: Katherine Rice

Contents

INTRODUCTION

When memory takes me back to my childhood, I can clearly remember a pressure cooker, one of the most impressive cookware from a grandma's kitchen. Grandma's old-school recipes such as refried beans, tender beef roasts, perfect turkey drumsticks, hearty stews and nourishing soups are all part of my wonderful memories. These exceptional pressure cooker meals are timeless and they make you feel cozy time after time.

This stunning kitchen gear is returning in a very big way! Inspired by an old-fashioned way of cooking and a modern-day life, manufacturers develop innovative cookware where the newest technologies and futuristic design go hand in hand. In other words, an electric pressure cooker, such as an Instant Pot, is a "fusion" of a grandma's timeless cookware and third-generation technology. The Instant Pot makes your cooking easy, fast, convenient and most importantly – amazingly healthy. The boiling point of water increases as the pressure rises so you can cook your food faster, preserving more heat-sensitive nutrients and saving energy. The Instant Pot is a multifunctional electric cooker – it can boil, sauté, bake, and steam a wide variety of foods, including meats, seafood, vegetables, fruits, beans, grains, and even deserts. Rediscover grandma's comforting recipes with your Instant Pot and you will be pleasantly suppressed what this multi-cooker can do for you!

Needless to say, food is essential to human life; it can fulfill different needs in our body so we should care about where our food comes from. A number of studies have shown that more nutrients are retained by pressure cooking food as opposed to standard cooking, simmering, and boiling. In addition, pressure cooking does not produce harmful compounds such as acrylamide. The Instant Pot and this recipe collection can drastically improve your cooking and your health. Embrace this super-sophisticated technology, break poor eating habits and start living your best life!

Why Everyone Is Talking About the Instant Pot?

As society around us develops, smart kitchen gadgets such as an electric pressure cooker become more than a trend. The Instant Pot is an electric pressure cooker that can replace multiple kitchen appliances. It works as a sauté pan, warming pot, slow cooker, steamer, yogurt maker, convection oven, and rice maker. All in One! Thus, it's worth a closer look. Your Instant Pot includes a base unit with the control panel and heating element; an insert (inner pot), which can be removed; a cooker's lid with a gasket and valve; other accessories include racks, trivet, steaming basket, measuring cups and so on.

How does the Instant Pot work? It utilizes the power of hot, trapped steam that helps foods to cook faster than ever before. This steam also helps force liquid and moisture into the food so tough meats, dry beans and grains get very tender in the shortest possible time. With all of this information, we can start using out Instant Pot. Here are three basic steps.

Step 1: Place ingredients in a removable inner pot. The content should never exceed the maximum level marking of the pot (be careful when cooking foods such as grains and legumes, since they will expand during the cooking process). Keep all ingredients in the inner pot to prevent contact from heating elements.

Step 2: Seal the lid and press the desired button; the cooking cycle will start automatically in 10 seconds. Turn the steam release knob to the sealed position; the valve should always flutter a little.

Step 3: Once your cooker completes its cooking cycle, release the pressure and remove the cooker's lid carefully. Remember – never force the cooker's lid open!

As for accessories, steamer insert pans are great for pot-in-pot cooking, re-heating foods, and baking casseroles and lasagnas. Furthermore, you can reheat two dishes at once. They can be used as containers for storing food as well. Then, a silicone lid is one of the greatest accessories for your Instant Pot. It allows you to store your leftovers right in the inner pot. Gripper clips are also one of the must haves for your Instant Pot. They are coated with silicone so you can easily clip and lift a hot inner pot or steamer basket without hurting yourself. Other useful accessories include mesh strainer basket, vegetable steamer insert, egg basket, silicone handle, pasta strainer, removable dividers, silicone cupcake liners, and so on.

How Cooking Programs Work?

MANUAL – this is a multifunctional, all-purpose button; you can adjust the time and temperature to suit your recipe.

RICE – this program works as a standard rice cooker. For long-grain white rice like Jasmine or Basmati, cook time is only 3 minutes. White rice takes 8 minutes, brown rice takes 22 minutes. Wild rice requires 30 minutes. Just make sure to rinse your rice before pressure cooking (it's important to get rid of excess starches). You should measure a 1:1 ratio of water-to-rice because every kind of rice needs to absorb its own volume in water.

STEAM – you can steam delicate foods such as vegetables, fish, and selfish, by using a metal trivet or steamer basket. A steaming rack is a secret weapon to cook vegetables that are colorful, tender and crisp at the same time. When it comes to the seafood, you can pour in a little wine to improve the tastes of natural juices. It is very popular to cook fish and shellfish "en papillote" i.e. "in foil packets".

You can skip the microwave ovens and reheat your meals in the Instant Pot. Place water in the inner pot. Place your leftovers in steamer insert pans. Your cooker will heat the water, secure-fitting lid traps in heat, which will reheat your food.

BEAN/CHILI – this is one of the most favorite programs because you can cook dry beans in less than 30 minutes. In addition, your beans are tastier with the Instant Pot thanks to its revolutionary flavor-infusion technology. In general, you should place 1 pound of dried beans and about 8 cups of water in the inner pot. Almost all beans take 30 minutes to cook (for softer beans, cook for 40 minutes). Never fill the inner pot more than 1/2 full.

SOUP – it cooks soups gently and slowly without boiling too heavily. The perfect function for home-style stocks, meaty soups, as well as creamy chowders.

MEAT/STEW – with this program, you can cook inexpensive cuts just like grandma used to make. Adjust the settings depending on the texture you want to achieve ("More" or "Less").

POULTRY – It will default for 15 minutes on high pressure, which is great for small portions. Larger pieces of poultry will take up to 25 minutes. Frozen chicken will take between 30 to 35 minutes.

MULTIGRAIN – this setting is great for cooking brown rice, wild rice, cereal, and whole grains.

PORRIDGE – if you tend to make a porridge with a softer texture, this is the perfect program. Use natural pressure release with this function.

SLOW COOK – your Instant Pot can work as a typical slow cooker. Four-hour cook time is a default time but you can adjust the cook time by using the "+/-" button. You can select either the cooking duration (30 minutes to 20 hours) or a cooking mode (Normal, More and Less). Inexpensive cuts of meat, dry beans, grains, and root vegetables are well suited for slow cooking.

YOGURT – this function is a true game changer. Making homemade yogurt is time-consuming but with this two-step program, it is nearly fail-safe and effortless. Do not forget to clean the inner pot with boiling water before adding the milk. As for a yogurt starter, you can use 1 tablespoon of prepared yogurt for every quart of milk.

SAUTÉ – your Instant Pot redefines one-pot meals with its possibilities for searing, browning, simmering, and thickening. Sauté your vegetables, brown meat or thicken the sauce just as you would in a standard skillet or saucepan. Here is a pro top – use this function to speed up "come to pressure" time! Simply pour a small amount of liquid and press the "Sauté" button.

KEEP WARM / CANCEL – Once your Instant Pot completes its cooking cycle, you should press the "Cancel" button; otherwise, the "Keep Warm" function will be activated automatically to keep your food warm until ready to serve.

NATURAL RELEASE and QUICK RELEASE – You can use two ways to release the pressure. Press the "Cancel" button or unplug your device to perform a natural pressure release. Release the steam manually in order to perform a quick pressure release. Make sure your Instant Pot is fully depressurized when you try to open it.

Although your Instant Pot has built-in modes with preset times and pressure levels, it offers the range of cooking options. In addition, you can control the cook time, temperature, and pressure level. A control panel consists of 3 mode indicators, 3 operation buttons, and 13 function buttons. It also includes the "+", "-", and "Adjust" buttons. Luckily, you can cancel the cooking process at any time. Furthermore, a new Instant Pot can be controlled by your mobile device. You can boil your food in the Instant Pot – just add enough liquid to the inner pot in order to cover the ingredients by half. Further, you can cook Bain Marie in the Instant Pot – it is a water bath or pan-in-pot method; this is the perfect cooking method for delicate sweet or savory dishes that require gentle cooking. You can make poached eggs, fish, puddings, and a wide range of desserts. It is also a great way to reheat your meals while keeping the authentic texture (for instance, potato mash or chowder). Canning is one of the greatest functions of electric pressure cookers; you can make marmalade or jam by using a hot-water bath or you can use a pressure canning and perform the natural pressure release at the end. Last but not least, you can extract juices by using a steamer basket and a bowl underneath.

8 Things You Need to Know
Before Using the Instant Pot

Doubtlessly, learning to use the Instant Pot opens up new possibilities in the kitchen. From hearty soups to holiday roast and desserts, you have a card up your sleeve for getting the best food on the table in no time. Here are eight common things you need to know when using the Instant Pot.

The manufacturer's directions should be read thoroughly before using a new device. I know you can't wait to start cooking with your Instant Pot, but first of all, read manufacturer's directions.

Pay attention to the amount of water. Is this a big deal? Your Instant Pot works by trapping steam inside the sealed environment under an airtight lid. The liquid creates the steam pressure that cooks your food faster. Your Instant Pot requires a minimum of 1 cup of liquid in order to function properly; it can be water, broth, cooking wine, tomato juice or fruit juice. The liquid won't evaporate under an airtight lid; thus, do not add too much liquid if you do not want to end up with a finished dish that lacks flavor or a thin, tasteless sauce.

You can always use a thickener such as cornstarch, arrowroot powder, all-purpose flours after pressure cooking. Simply choose the "Sauté" function and let the cooking liquid simmer until it reaches your desired consistency.

Never force a pressure lid open. Regardless of the pressure release method, be sure to release any remaining pressure before removing the cooker's lid. The float valve will drop down so you can safely remove the cooker's lid.

Avoid temptation to cook all foods at the same time. Just as with regular cooking, your ingredients have different cook times. You can cook in phases. For instance, you can start by browning meats and cook them under pressure for a certain amount of time. Then, release the pressure and add in the vegetables. Seal the lid again, bring your Instant Pot back to pressure and let it cook for a few minutes longer.

What size Instant Pot should your purchase? The simplest explanation is – 5-Quart IP can feed up to 5 people, and an 8-Quart IP can feed up to 8 people, and so forth. When in doubt, purchase a bigger model. Seriously, I prefer to have an extra space in the inner pot rather than cook in batches and waste my time.

Instant Pot allows you to easily double your recipe. Keep in mind that a larger amount of food does not mean longer cook times; the Instant Pot cooks everything at the same rate. So clever!

A well-stocked pantry can be a lifesaver. Be pantry smart when cooking with your Instant Pot. This is a basic list but it can differ depending on what type of diet you follow.

<u>Stocks and canned goods</u> on hand are always a must. They include tomato juice, pumpkin purée, pasta sauce, chicken broth, vegetable broth, and so forth.

<u>Dry goods</u> such as rice, beans, lentils, and grains can be a true lifesaver.

<u>Oils, vinegar, herbs, and spices</u> are pantry staples that make cooking at home really easy.

<u>Frozen items</u> such as fruits, vegetables, fresh or precooked meats can be your best friends when you get home late. Just remember that frozen meats require 50% more of the recommended cooking time. Firstly, cook your food on the "Sauté" function for 5 minutes to start thawing it. As for frozen vegetables, you can follow cooking time tables. For instance, fresh Brussel sprouts take 2 to 3 minutes to cook; on the other hand, frozen Brussel sprouts take about 4 minutes. Fresh mixed vegetables take 3 to 4 minutes to cook; frozen vegetables will take 4 to 6 minutes. You can also reheat pre-prepared freezer meals in your Instant Pot; use the "Steam" function for 5 to 10 minutes and quick release pressure.

Do not be afraid to make mistakes. Mistakes are a big part of how we learn to cook. Embrace new cooking methods and do not be afraid to experiment in your kitchen.

4 Main Reasons We Love the Instant Pot

A genius way to improve your mental and physical health.

Not surprisingly, cooking at home has a strong part in many cultures all over the world. There are numerous benefits of home-cooked meals in the Instant Pot. First, and most practical, cooking at home is cheaper than going out and it can help you control your eating. It can help you build a good relationship with your family members and improve your social life.

Home-cooked meals go hand in glove with good physical and mental health. The Instant Pot utilizes super-heated steam and sealed environment to cook your food, retaining more nutrients. The longer your food is cooked, the more nutrients are destroyed. Pressure cooking locks in essential nutrients in food, enhancing the amazing flavors of your meals. Moreover, you can always save and reuse cooking liquid. This is a unique opportunity to include healthy foods such as high-fiber vegetables, beans, grains, and seafood into your diet. Our recipes call for natural and wholesome ingredients so the Instant Pot may change the way you eat forever!

Further, the Instant Pot uses less oil. As you probably already know, the consumption of saturated fat and trans-fat may cause serious problems such as obesity, cardiovascular disease, diabetes, and cancer. The worst fats for you are partially hydrogenated vegetable oils. You might find them in fried foods, fast foods, cakes, pastries, and processed snack foods. To avoid trans-fat, you should check food labels or cook at home, it's up to you. Nutritionists consider monounsaturated fat and polyunsaturated fat good fats for your health. You can find them in fatty fish, nuts, olive oil, and so forth. And remember – healthy fats are a big part of a balanced diet! To sum up, it's a good idea to use your Instant Pot to cook foods that contain good (monounsaturated and polyunsaturated) fats.

How can you start eating healthier? Steam or bake fish and seafood instead of frying it. Opt for lean and skinless meat and trim visible fat from meat. Snack smart and choose nuts, fresh fruits, and salads.

Unlike many other high-heat cooking techniques, the Instant Pot can help you lose weight and feel better in your skin. There are numerous weight loss diets out there; unfortunately, most of them do not work. Overly-restrictive diets do not lead to long-term results. Instead of that, you need a lifestyle change and a good, healthy eating plan. Above all, the right kitchen equipment is a must! When you're cooking in your Instant Pot, there are many effective ways to cut extra calories. Pressure cooking is well known as a lower calorie cooking method since it requires very little added fat. It makes meat and root vegetables very tender; in addition, you can choose only lean proteins. Sautéing is a great way to boost flavors and you need very minimal amounts of added fats to cook the foods in the Instant Pot. Steaming helps vegetables to retain their color and nutrients; digging a little deeper, you can eliminate all forms of oil. Simply spritz the bottom of the inner pot with non-stick oil.

Every recipe in this book is followed by the nutritional information, which can help you keep track of your calories. It can also help you count your macronutrients and start an effective meal planning. It's a good strategy that can help you improve your quality of life. Last but not least, pressure cookers have the ability to sterilize food and kill bacteria such as E.Coli, Salmonella, or Listeria.

You can make perfect one-pot meals with a touch of a button.
Let's say you want to cook pasta. You will need a pot, pan, and strainer to make a conventional pasta recipe or you can make pasta and sauce directly in the Instant Pot. You can brown meat, de-glaze the pot, boil pasta and thicken the sauce with your Instant Pot. By the same token, you don't have to dirty another cookware to make potato casserole. You can boil potatoes, sauté vegetables, sweat onions, and bake your casserole directly in the Instant Pot. Despite the simplicity of this cooking method, your dishes turn out perfect every time!

The Instant Pot can jazz up any dish so well that it could compete with any fancy meal at a Michelin star restaurant. For vegan, ketoers, meat eaters, and the pickiest eaters ever, the Instant Pot is a common ground. It means lots of distinct flavors and vibrant aromas! You can download an Instant Pot's app and get direct control over your cooker. These smart kitchen appliances could revolutionize how food gets on the table!

You can save your time.
Imagine that you can get home from work and have dinner on the table in 30 minutes. This is one of the biggest advantages the Instant Pot offers. You can caramelize onions, brown meats, steam your food, bake cakes, and sauté the vegetables in this super-sophisticated machine.

Your Instant Pot is able to drastically reduce the cooking time of your food. Foods cook approximately 70 % faster in the Instant Pot. For instance, beans can be done in 20 minutes while white rice will take only 10 minutes from start to finish; homemade, grandma-style chicken stock can be done in 30 minutes. You can cook whole frozen chicken in 45 minutes; ordinarily, a whole chicken would take several hours to thaw and about an hour to cook. Cooking on the stove requires your attention; you have to check your food now and then to see if something is done yet; it also requires stirring to ensure even cooking. You don't have to do that with your Instant Pot! Your Instant pot will turn off when the cooking cycle is completed. Moreover, if you want a hot meal when you come home, you can delay the cook start time. It is good to know that most recipes in this collection take about 20 minutes from prep to plate. Fast and delicious!

You can save your money.

Thanks to this intelligent device, you can make a hearty meal in a flash and feed your family with just five common ingredients. Your Instant Pot cooks economical dishes such as cheap cuts of meat, grains, bread puddings, beans, and soups to absolute perfection. Most recipes in this collection call for budget-friendly and affordable ingredients that are available everywhere. With its futuristic design, the Instant Pot will save a ton of space in your kitchen. Then, your Instant Pot is energy efficient because it uses less energy than traditional cooking methods. The Instant Pot promotes minimalism so you can save money on cookware and boost your savings overall. It can help save Mother Earth, so go green!

How You Can Benefit From our Recipe Collection

With your Instant Pot, you can take a "shortcut" in preparing the best family meals ever! Each recipe in this collection includes suggested serving sizes, the ingredient list, detailed directions, approximate cook time, and nutritional analysis. From authentic and old-fashioned meals to the hottest culinary trends, these recipes will help you unlock the mysteries of a successful pressure cooking. The more you use your Instant Pot, the more you'll realize what a great kitchen device it is! You will love it!

With 575 carefully picked recipes, this collection is your go-to source for the best Instant Pot meals. Get started with the great recipes that follow and enjoy!

CHICKEN

1. Classic Buffalo Wings

(Ready in about 40 minutes | Servings 4)

Per serving: 408 Calories; 22.1g Fat; 8.8g Carbs; 41.6g Protein; 2.8g Sugars

INGREDIENTS

2 pounds chicken wings
2 garlic cloves, halved
1 teaspoon sea salt
1/2 teaspoon ground black pepper

1/2 teaspoon cayenne pepper flakes
4 tablespoons butter, melted
1/2 cup roasted vegetable broth
1/2 cup Cholula hot sauce

1 tablespoon brown sugar
1 teaspoon barbecue sauce
1 teaspoon corn starch, dissolved in 1 tablespoon of water

DIRECTIONS

Rub the chicken legs with the garlic halves; then, season with salt, black pepper, and cayenne pepper. Press the "Sauté" button.

Once hot, melt 2 tablespoons of the melted butter and sear the chicken wings approximately 4 minutes, turning them once during the cooking time. Add a splash of vegetable broth to deglaze the bottom of the pan.

Now, add the remaining broth and secure the lid. Choose the "Manual" mode and High pressure; cook for 12 minutes. Once the cooking is complete, use a quick pressure release; carefully remove the lid.

Remove the chicken wings from the Instant Pot, reserving the cooking liquid. Place the chicken wings on a lightly greased baking sheet.

Turn your oven on to High Broil. Broil the chicken wings approximately 15 minutes until it is crisp and golden brown; make sure to turn them over halfway through the cooking time.

Press the "Sauté" button and add the remaining 2 tablespoons of butter. Once hot, add the hot sauce, sugar, and barbecue sauce; pour in the reserved cooking liquid.

Let it simmer for 4 minutes; add the corn starch slurry and continue to simmer until the cooking liquid has reduced and concentrated. Pour the prepared sauce over the reserved chicken and serve warm. Bon appétit!

2. Cheesy Chicken Tenders with Potatoes

(Ready in about 25 minutes | Servings 6)

Per serving: 377 Calories; 12.3g Fat; 28.3g Carbs; 37.3g Protein; 2.3g Sugars

INGREDIENTS

2 tablespoons olive oil
2 pounds chicken tenders
2 pounds Yukon Gold potatoes, peeled and diced
2 cloves garlic, smashed

1/4 teaspoon ground black pepper
1 teaspoon red pepper flakes
Pink Himalayan salt, to taste
1 teaspoon shallot powder
1 teaspoon dried basil

1 teaspoon dried rosemary
1 ½ cups chicken stock
6 tablespoons Romano cheese, grated

DIRECTIONS

Press the "Sauté" button to preheat your Instant Pot. Now, heat the olive oil and sear the chicken tenders for 3 to 4 minutes.

Add the potatoes and garlic; sprinkle with black pepper, red pepper, salt, shallot powder, basil, and rosemary.

Pour in the chicken stock and secure the lid. Choose the "Poultry" mode and High pressure; cook for 15 minutes. Once cooking is complete, use a quick pressure release; carefully remove the lid.

Top with the grated Romano cheese and serve warm. Enjoy!

3. 20-minute Ground Chicken Tacos

(Ready in about 20 minutes | Servings 6)

Per serving: 502 Calories; 22.5g Fat; 39.4g Carbs; 36.3g Protein; 6.9g Sugars

INGREDIENTS

1 tablespoon olive oil
1 pound ground chicken
1 pound ground turkey
2 cloves garlic, minced
1 onion, chopped
2 sweet peppers, deseeded and chopped
1 serrano pepper, deseeded and

chopped
1/3 cup hoisin sauce
1 cup water
1 tablespoon tamari sauce
Salt, to taste
1/2 teaspoon freshly ground black pepper
1 teaspoon Mexican oregano

6 (approx. 6-inch diameter) tortillas
1 cup sweet corn kernels, cooked
1 cup canned black beans, drained
1 tablespoon Dijon mustard
1 teaspoon jalapeno pepper, minced
2 tomatoes, sliced
1 head butter lettuce

DIRECTIONS

Press the "Sauté" button. Once hot, heat the olive oil until sizzling. Now, brown the ground meat for 2 to 3 minutes, stirring continuously.

Add the garlic, onion, peppers, hoisin sauce, water, tamari sauce, salt, black pepper, and Mexican oregano.

Secure the lid. Choose the "Manual" mode and High pressure; cook for 6 minutes. Once cooking is complete, use a quick pressure release; carefully remove the lid.

Assemble the tortillas with the ground chicken filling, corn, beans, mustard, jalapeno pepper, tomatoes, and lettuce. Enjoy!

4. Sticky Asian Glazed Chicken

(Ready in about 25 minutes | Servings 4)

Per serving: 394 Calories; 18.9g Fat; 30.6g Carbs; 26g Protein; 27.2g Sugars

INGREDIENTS

2 tablespoons sesame seed oil

4 chicken drumsticks

1/4 teaspoon fresh ground pepper, or more to taste

Sea salt, to taste

1 tablespoon Chinese rice vinegar

6 tablespoons honey

2 tablespoons sweet chili sauce

3 cloves garlic, minced

1/3 cup low-sodium soy sauce

1/3 cup no salt ketchup

1/2 cup water

1 tablespoon fresh cilantro, chopped

Small bunch scallions, chopped

DIRECTIONS

Press the "Sauté" button to preheat your Instant Pot.

Heat the sesame seed oil and sear the chicken for 5 minutes, stirring periodically. Season with black pepper and salt.

After that, stir in the vinegar, honey, chili sauce, garlic, soy sauce, ketchup, water, and cilantro; stir well to combine.

Secure the lid and choose the "Poultry" mode. Cook for 15 minutes. Afterwards, use a natural release and carefully remove the lid.

Garnish with chopped scallions. Bon appétit!

5. Creamed Chicken Cutlets with Herbs

(Ready in about 25 minutes | Servings 6)

Per serving: 422 Calories; 8.5g Fat; 41.5g Carbs; 45.6g Protein; 2g Sugars

INGREDIENTS

2 pounds chicken cutlets

Kosher salt and ground black pepper, to taste

1 teaspoon dried oregano

1 teaspoon dried basil

1 teaspoon dried rosemary

1 teaspoon dried parsley flakes

1/4 cup dry white wine

2 cups vegetable broth

2 garlic cloves, minced

1/2 cup double cream

2 tablespoons cornstarch

6 cups pasta, cooked

DIRECTIONS

Season the chicken cutlets with salt, black pepper, oregano, basil, rosemary, and parsley. Press the "Sauté" button to preheat your Instant Pot.

Once hot, cook the seasoned chicken cutlets for 5 minutes, turning once during cooking. Add the white wine and scrape the bottom of the pan to deglaze.

Pour in the vegetable broth. Add the garlic and secure the lid.

Choose the "Manual" mode and High pressure; cook for 8 minutes. Once cooking is complete, use a quick release and remove the lid.

Reserve the chicken cutlets, keeping them warm.

Stir the double cream and cornstarch into the cooking liquid.

Press the "Sauté" button and simmer for 6 minutes or until the cooking liquid has reduced by half. Serve with warm pasta. Bon appétit!

6. Greek-Style Chicken Fillets

(Ready in about 20 minutes | Servings 6)

Per serving: 268 Calories; 10.1g Fat; 7g Carbs; 35.9g Protein; 4.4g Sugars

INGREDIENTS

2 pounds chicken fillets

2 garlic cloves, halved

1 ½ tablespoons olive oil

1/2 cup tamari sauce

1/2 cup tomato puree

1/2 cup chicken broth

1 tablespoon molasses

Sea salt and freshly ground black pepper, to taste

1/2 teaspoon red pepper flakes

1 bay leaf

1 rosemary sprig

1/2 cup Kalamata olives, pitted and halved

DIRECTIONS

Rub the chicken fillets with the garlic halves on all sides. Press the "Sauté" button to preheat your Instant Pot.

Heat the olive oil and sear the chicken fillets for 2 minutes per side.

Add the tamari sauce, tomato puree, broth, molasses, salt, black pepper, red pepper, bay leaf and rosemary sprig.

Secure the lid. Choose the "Manual" mode and High pressure; cook for 9 minutes. Once cooking is complete, use a quick release; remove the lid.

Serve garnished with Kalamata olives. Enjoy!

7. Sunday Chicken Salad *- not good*

(Ready in about 10 minutes + chilling time | Servings 4)

Per serving: 386 Calories; 26.5g Fat; 3.1g Carbs; 34.3g Protein; 0.6g Sugars

INGREDIENTS

1 pound chicken breasts, skinless and boneless
1 cup chicken stock
2 garlic cloves, crushed
2 tablespoons fresh basil leaves, roughly chopped
4 tablespoons sour cream
1/2 cup mayonnaise

1 tablespoon yellow mustard
1 tablespoon fresh lime juice
1 Lebanese cucumber, sliced
1/2 cup scallions, chopped
Coarse sea salt and ground black pepper, to taste

DIRECTIONS

Place the chicken breasts, stock, and garlic in the Instant Pot.

Secure the lid. Choose the "Manual" mode and High pressure; cook for 8 minutes. Once cooking is complete, use a quick release.

Shred the chicken breasts with 1/2 cup of cooking liquid and transfer to a salad bowl; add the remaining ingredients and gently stir to combine.

Place in your refrigerator until ready to serve. Bon appétit!

8. Authentic Chicken Taco Meat

(Ready in about 35 minutes | Servings 6)

Per serving: 412 Calories; 27.8g Fat; 1.1g Carbs; 36.9g Protein; 0.4g Sugars

INGREDIENTS

2 pounds whole chicken, meat and skin
1 Old El Paso Taco spice mix
1 tablespoon canola oil
1 fresh jalapeño chili, seeded and finely chopped

Kosher salt and ground black pepper, to taste
Fresh juice of 1 orange
1 cup chicken broth
A small handful of coriander, roughly chopped

DIRECTIONS

Toss the chicken in the Taco spice mix to coat. Press the "Sauté" button to preheat your Instant Pot.

Heat the canola oil and sear the chicken, stirring periodically, for 3 to 4 minutes or until golden brown.

Add the jalapeño chili, salt, black pepper, fresh orange juice, and chicken broth; stir to combine. Secure the lid.

Choose the "Poultry" mode and High pressure; cook for 30 minutes. Once cooking is complete, use a quick release.

Shred the chicken and garnish with fresh coriander leaves. Enjoy!

9. Cheesy Chicken and Pasta Casserole

(Ready in about 20 minutes | Servings 5)

Per serving: 544 Calories; 21.8g Fat; 39.7g Carbs; 44.9g Protein; 1.1g Sugars

INGREDIENTS

2 tablespoons olive oil
2 garlic cloves, minced
2 strips bacon, diced
1 ½ pounds chicken legs, boneless skinless, cubed

2 ounces vermouth
7 ounces Ricotta cheese, crumbled, at room temperature
1 cup water
4 cups elbow pasta

1 onion, sliced
2 sweet peppers, seeded and thinly sliced
1 cup chicken broth

DIRECTIONS

Press the "Sauté" button to preheat your Instant Pot.

Once hot, heat the olive oil. Now, cook the garlic and bacon until they are fragrant.

Stir in the cubed chicken and cook for 3 minutes more or until it is no longer pink. Use vermouth to scrape the remaining bits of meat off the bottom of the inner pot.

Add the softened Ricotta cheese and water. Secure the lid. Choose the "Poultry" mode and High pressure; cook for 5 minutes. Once cooking is complete, use a quick release.

Add the elbow pasta, onion, and peppers. Pour in the chicken broth; gently stir to combine.

Secure the lid and choose the "Manual" mode. Cook for 4 minutes longer. Afterwards, use a quick release and carefully remove the lid. Bon appétit!

10. Saucy Chicken with Root Vegetables

(Ready in about 20 minutes | Servings 5)

Per serving: 300 Calories; 8g Fat; 16.1g Carbs; 40.1g Protein; 4.3g Sugars

INGREDIENTS

2 pounds whole chicken, boneless, skinless, and cubed

1 celery stalk, trimmed and sliced

2 carrots, trimmed and sliced

2 parsnips, trimmed and sliced

1 bell pepper, seeded and thinly sliced

1 habanero pepper, seeded and thinly sliced

1 cup vegetable broth

2 garlic cloves, smashed

1/2 teaspoon ginger, grated

1 teaspoon smoked paprika

1 tablespoon sesame seed oil

1 tablespoon arrowroot powder

2 tablespoons toasted sesame seeds

DIRECTIONS

Place the chicken pieces in the inner pot. Place the vegetables on the top. Pour in the vegetable broth.

Add the remaining ingredients, except for the toasted sesame seeds.

Secure the lid. Choose the "Poultry" mode and High pressure; cook for 15 minutes. Once cooking is complete, use a quick release.

Transfer the chicken and veggies to serving plates using a slotted spoon. Press the "Sauté" button to preheat the Instant Pot. Stir the arrowroot powder into the cooking liquid to thicken the sauce.

Spoon the sauce over the warm chicken and vegetables. Garnish with the toasted sesame seeds. Bon appétit!

11. Ranch Chicken Thighs

(Ready in about 25 minutes | Servings 5)

Per serving: 435 Calories; 33.1g Fat; 1.4g Carbs; 30.1g Protein; 0.1g Sugars

INGREDIENTS

1 tablespoon butter, melted

2 pounds chicken thighs, bone-in, skin-on

2 garlic cloves, minced

1 yellow onion, sliced

1 packet dry ranch salad dressing mix

1 teaspoon paprika

1/2 teaspoon ground bay leaf

1/2 teaspoon ground black pepper

Sea salt, to taste

2 tablespoons champagne vinegar

1 cup chicken bone broth

DIRECTIONS

Press the "Sauté" button and melt the butter.

Now, sear the chicken thighs for 4 to 5 minutes or until browned on all sides.

Add the remaining ingredients in the order listed above.

Secure the lid. Choose the "Poultry" setting and cook for 15 minutes at High pressure. Once cooking is complete, use a natural release and carefully remove the lid.

You can thicken the sauce on the "Sauté" mode. Serve over hot cooked rice if desired. Enjoy!

12. Spanish Arroz con Pollo

(Ready in about 20 minutes | Servings 5)

Per serving: 537 Calories; 23.1g Fat; 44.4g Carbs; 36.9g Protein; 6.1g Sugars

INGREDIENTS

1 tablespoon olive oil

1/2 cup brown onion, chopped

1 pound chicken breasts, trimmed and cut into bite-sized pieces

2 tablespoons Rueda

1 cup short-grain white rice

1 ½ cups chicken broth

1 cup tomato puree

1 teaspoon dried oregano

Sea salt and ground black pepper, to taste

1/2 teaspoon saffron threads

5 ounces seafood mix

5 ounces chorizo sausage, casings removed and crumbled

1 lemon, juiced and zested

2 tablespoons fresh parsley, roughly chopped

DIRECTIONS

Press the "Sauté" button and heat the olive oil.

Now, cook the brown onion and chicken until the onion is translucent and the chicken is no longer pink or about 4 minutes. Deglaze the pot with the Rueda wine.

Stir in the rice, broth, tomato puree, oregano, salt, black pepper, and saffron.

Secure the lid and choose the "Manual" mode. Cook for 5 minutes at High pressure. Afterwards, use a quick release and carefully remove the lid.

Add the seafood mix and sausage. Secure the lid and choose the "Manual" mode. Cook for 4 to 5 minutes at High pressure; use a quick release and carefully remove the lid.

Add the lemon and parsley and serve immediately. Bon appétit!

13. Easy Millet and Chicken Bowl

(Ready in about 25 minutes | Servings 4)

Per serving: 440 Calories; 12.8g Fat; 47.1g Carbs; 34g Protein; 4.6g Sugars

INGREDIENTS

4 chicken drumsticks, skinless and boneless

Sea salt and ground black pepper, to taste

1/2 teaspoon red pepper flakes, crushed

1/2 teaspoon dried basil

1/2 teaspoon dried oregano

1/2 teaspoon ground cumin

1 ½ tablespoons olive oil

1/2 cup shallots, chopped

2 garlic cloves, finely chopped

1 bell pepper, deseeded and chopped

1 cup millet

1 cup vegetable broth

1 cup tomato puree

1 bay leaf

1 cup green beans

DIRECTIONS

Season the chicken drumsticks with salt, black pepper, red pepper, basil, oregano, and cumin.

Press the "Sauté" button and heat the olive oil. Sear the chicken drumsticks for 5 minutes, turning them to ensure even cooking.

Add the shallots, garlic, pepper, millet, broth, tomato puree, and bay leaf to the Instant Pot.

Secure the lid and choose the "Poultry" mode. Cook for 15 minutes at High pressure. Once cooking is complete, use a quick pressure release; carefully remove the lid.

Add the green beans and secure the lid again; let it sit in the residual heat until wilts. Enjoy!

14. Chicken and Kidney Bean Casserole

(Ready in about 25 minutes | Servings 4)

Per serving: 352 Calories; 17.7g Fat; 7.8g Carbs; 38.7g Protein; 1.8g Sugars

INGREDIENTS

2 tablespoons olive oil

1 pound chicken drumettes, cut into bite-sized pieces

1 onion, chopped

1 cup chicken bone broth

1 teaspoon granulated garlic

1 teaspoon cayenne pepper

Salt and ground black pepper, to taste

1 teaspoon Sriracha sauce

16 ounces canned kidney beans, drained

1 tablespoon fresh cilantro, chopped

DIRECTIONS

Press the "Sauté" button and heat the olive oil.

Now, cook the chicken drumettes until no longer pink or about 4 minutes.

Add the onion, chicken broth, garlic, cayenne pepper, salt, black pepper, and Sriracha sauce to the inner pot; gently stir to combine.

Secure the lid and choose the "Poultry" mode. Cook for 15 minutes at High pressure. Once cooking is complete, use a quick pressure release; carefully remove the lid.

Stir in the kidney beans; secure the lid and let it sit in the residual heat until thoroughly heated. Serve garnished with fresh cilantro. Enjoy!

15. Tender Chicken with Garden Vegetables

(Ready in about 20 minutes | Servings 4)

Per serving: 447 Calories; 21.5g Fat; 24.5g Carbs; 40.1g Protein; 9.5g Sugars

INGREDIENTS

2 tablespoons lard, at room temperature

1 pound chicken breasts, sliced into serving-size pieces

1 teaspoon dried marjoram

1/2 teaspoon dried sage

1/2 teaspoon ground black pepper

Sea salt, to taste

1/2 cup leeks, sliced

2 garlic cloves, sliced

1 cup chicken bone broth

2 cups butternut squash, diced

1 eggplant, diced

1/2 head cabbage, diced

1/4 cup fresh chives, chopped

DIRECTIONS

Press the "Sauté" button and melt the lard until sizzling.

Then, sear the chicken breasts until it is lightly browned or about 5 minutes. Add the spices and stir to combine.

Add the leeks and garlic. Pour in the chicken bone broth. Afterwards, add the vegetables and secure the lid.

Choose the "Manual" mode. Cook for 8 minutes at High pressure. Once cooking is complete, use a quick pressure release; carefully remove the lid.

Using a slotted spoon, remove the chicken and vegetables to a serving platter.

Press the "Sauté" button and simmer the cooking liquid for about 3 minutes until slightly thickened. Serve garnished with fresh chives. Bon appétit!

16. Famous New Orleans Gumbo

(Ready in about 25 minutes | Servings 4)

Per serving: 592 Calories; 29.2g Fat; 30.2g Carbs; 52.1g Protein; 6.2g Sugars

INGREDIENTS

4 tablespoons olive oil
1 onion, chopped
2 sweet peppers, deseeded and chopped
1 ½ pounds chicken breasts, boneless, skinless, and cubed
8 ounces Andouille sausage, sliced
1 red chili pepper, deseeded and chopped

2 celery stalks, trimmed and diced
2 carrots, trimmed and diced
2 cloves garlic, sliced
2 large ripe tomatoes, pureed
1 teaspoon basil, dried
1 teaspoon paprika
Kosher salt and ground black pepper, to taste
2 bay leaves, dried

1 tablespoon gumbo file
1 tablespoon chicken bouillon granules
6 cups water
1/3 cup all-purpose flour
1/2 pound okra, cut into bite-sized pieces

DIRECTIONS

Press the "Sauté" button and heat 2 tablespoons of oil until sizzling. Now, sweat the onion and peppers until tender and aromatic or about 3 minutes; reserve.
Then, heat the remaining 2 tablespoons of olive oil and cook the chicken and sausage until no longer pink, about 4 minutes. Make sure to stir periodically to ensure even cooking.
Stir the chili pepper, celery, carrot, garlic, tomatoes, basil, paprika, salt, black pepper, bay leaves, gumbo file, and chicken bouillon granules into the inner pot. Add the reserved onion/pepper mixture. Pour in 6 cups of water.
Secure the lid. Choose the "Manual" mode. Cook for 7 minutes at High pressure. Once cooking is complete, use a quick pressure release; carefully remove the lid.
Mix the flour with 1 cup of cooking liquid and reserve. Afterwards, stir in the okra and flour mixture into the inner pot.
Secure the lid. Choose "Manual" mode. Cook for 3 minutes at High pressure. Once cooking is complete, use a natural pressure release; carefully remove the lid.
Serve in individual bowls, garnished with garlic croutons if desired. Bon appétit!

17. Creamy Lemon Chicken

(Ready in about 25 minutes | Servings 4)

Per serving: 388 Calories; 25.2g Fat; 5.4g Carbs; 33.1g Protein; 2g Sugars

INGREDIENTS

2 tablespoons sesame oil
4 chicken drumsticks, boneless and skinless
2/3 cup chicken broth
1 teaspoon garlic powder

1/2 teaspoon cayenne pepper
1/4 teaspoon ground black pepper, or more to taste
1 teaspoon oregano
1 teaspoon basil

1/2 teaspoon thyme
1 onion, chopped
1 lemon, juiced and zested
1/3 heavy cream

DIRECTIONS

Press the "Sauté" button and heat the oil until sizzling. Sear the chicken drumsticks, stirring occasionally, for about 4 minutes.
Add a few tablespoons of broth to deglaze the bottom of the pan. Stir in the spices, onion, and chicken broth; stir to combine well.
Secure the lid. Choose the "Poultry" mode. Cook for 15 minutes at High pressure. Once cooking is complete, use a quick pressure release; carefully remove the lid.
Remove the chicken from the Instant Pot using a slotted spoon.
Add the lemon and heavy cream to the cooking liquid; stir to combine. Press the "Sauté" button and let it simmer until the sauce has thickened slightly.
Spoon the sauce over the reserved chicken and serve warm. Enjoy!

18. Christmas Roast Chicken

(Ready in about 35 minutes | Servings 4)

Per serving: 376 Calories; 18.2g Fat; 2g Carbs; 49.1g Protein; 0.7g Sugars

INGREDIENTS

4 tablespoons butter, softened
1 head of garlic, crushed
Salt and ground black pepper, to taste

1 tablespoon paprika
2 rosemary sprigs, crushed
2 thyme sprigs, crushed

2 quarts water
1 (3 ½ pounds) whole chicken

DIRECTIONS

In a small mixing dish, thoroughly combine the butter, garlic, salt, black pepper, paprika, rosemary, and thyme.
Pour the water into the inner pot.
Pat the chicken dry. Then, rub the butter mixture all over the chicken to season well. Place the chicken in the inner pot.
Secure the lid. Choose "Manual" mode. Cook for 20 minutes at High pressure. Once cooking is complete, use a natural pressure release; carefully remove the lid.
Afterwards, place the chicken under the broiler for 10 minutes until the skin is lightly crisped. Bon appétit!

19. Mom's Orange Chicken

(Ready in about 15 minutes | Servings 4)

Per serving: 337 Calories; 26g Fat; 8.8g Carbs; 18.9g Protein; 2g Sugars

INGREDIENTS

1 tablespoon olive oil
2/3 pound ground chicken
1/3 pound bacon, chopped
2 tablespoons sherry wine

1 medium red onion, chopped
2 garlic cloves, minced
1 jalapeno pepper, chopped
Sea salt and ground black pepper, to taste

1 teaspoon paprika
Fresh juice and zest of 1/2 orange
1 tablespoon arrowroot powder

DIRECTIONS

Press the "Sauté" button and heat the oil until sizzling. Sear the chicken and bacon until they are slightly brown.

Add the sherry wine and stir with a wooden spoon, scraping up the browned bits on the bottom of the pan. Add the red onion, garlic, and jalapeno pepper; stir to combine.

Season with salt, black pepper, and paprika. Pour in 1 cup of water.

Secure the lid. Choose "Poultry" mode. Cook for 5 minutes at High pressure. Once cooking is complete, use a quick pressure release; carefully remove the lid.

Add the orange juice and zest; stir in the arrowroot powder. Press the "Sauté" button and simmer, stirring occasionally, until it thickens. Bon appétit!

20. Chinese-Style Chicken Congee

(Ready in about 20 minutes | Servings 6)

Per serving: 471 Calories; 20.8g Fat; 41.1g Carbs; 28.2g Protein; 12.7g Sugars

INGREDIENTS

3 tablespoons sesame oil
6 chicken drumsticks
4 garlic cloves, minced
2 tablespoons Worcestershire sauce

2 tablespoons champagne vinegar
2 cups vegetable broth
2 cups water
1/4 cup honey

Salt and ground black pepper, to taste
1 teaspoon Wuxiang powder
1 cup rice
2 tablespoons flaxseed meal

DIRECTIONS

Press the "Sauté" button and heat 2 tablespoons of the sesame oil. Sear the chicken drumsticks until slightly brown on all sides. Add the garlic and cook for 1 minute or so, until aromatic.

Add the remaining ingredients, except for the flaxseed meal.

Secure the lid. Choose "Poultry" mode. Cook for 15 minutes at High pressure. Once cooking is complete, use a quick pressure release; carefully remove the lid.

Afterwards, stir in the flaxseed meal; stir until everything is well combined. Press the "Sauté" button and cook until the cooking liquid is reduced by about half. Bon appétit!

21. French-Style Creamy Mustard Chicken

(Ready in about 20 minutes | Servings 4)

Per serving: 413 Calories; 27.2g Fat; 3.3g Carbs; 37.5g Protein; 1.2g Sugars

INGREDIENTS

2 tablespoons olive oil, divided
1 pound chicken breasts, boneless
1 teaspoon dried basil
1/2 teaspoon dried oregano

1/2 teaspoon dried sage
1 teaspoon paprika
1 teaspoon garlic powder
Sea salt and ground black pepper, to taste

1 tablespoon Dijon mustard
1 cup chicken bone broth
1/2 cup heavy cream

DIRECTIONS

Press the "Sauté" button and heat the olive oil. Sear the chicken breasts until they are no longer pink.

Add the seasonings, mustard, and chicken bone broth.

Secure the lid. Choose "Manual" mode and cook for 8 minutes at High pressure. Once cooking is complete, use a natural pressure release; carefully remove the lid.

Lastly, add the heavy cream, cover with the lid, and let it sit in the residual heat for 6 to 8 minutes. Serve in individual bowls. Enjoy!

22. Fiesta Chicken Bake

(Ready in about 20 minutes | Servings 4)

Per serving: 756 Calories; 34.9g Fat; 66g Carbs; 45.2g Protein; 4.7g Sugars

INGREDIENTS

2 tablespoons olive oil
1 pound chicken breast, boneless, cut into chunks
2 cups cream of celery soup
2 cups spiral pasta
1 cup Cotija cheese, crumbled

1 cup queso fresco, crumbled
1 ½ cups spiral pasta
1 cup salsa
1 cup fresh breadcrumbs

DIRECTIONS

Press the "Sauté" button and heat the olive oil. Now, brown the chicken breasts for 3 to 4 minutes.
Add the remaining ingredients in the order listed above.
Secure the lid. Choose "Manual" mode and cook for 6 minutes at High pressure. Once cooking is complete, use a natural pressure release; carefully remove the lid.
Serve warm.

23. Chicken Tenders with Cottage Cheese

(Ready in about 25 minutes | Servings 4)

Per serving: 305 Calories; 13.1g Fat; 2.8g Carbs; 41.9g Protein; 1.7g Sugars

INGREDIENTS

2 tablespoons butter, softened
1 ½ pounds chicken tenders
1 cup vegetable broth
1 teaspoon shallot powder
1 teaspoon garlic powder

1/2 teaspoon smoked paprika
Sea salt and freshly ground black pepper, to taste
1 cup Cottage cheese, crumbled
2 heaping tablespoons fresh chives, roughly chopped

DIRECTIONS

Press the "Sauté" button and melt the butter. Sear the chicken tenders for 2 to 3 minutes.
Add the vegetable broth, shallot powder, garlic powder, paprika, salt, and black pepper.
Secure the lid. Choose "Manual" mode and cook for 8 minutes at High pressure. Once cooking is complete, use a natural pressure release; carefully remove the lid.
Stir in the cheese; cover with the lid and let it sit in the residual heat for 5 minutes. Garnish with fresh chives and serve immediately.

24. Sicilian-Style Chicken Wings

(Ready in about 25 minutes | Servings 4)

Per serving: 457 Calories; 26.3g Fat; 13.7g Carbs; 39.8g Protein; 3.1g Sugars

INGREDIENTS

2 tablespoons butter, room temperature
4 chicken drumsticks, boneless
1/4 cup all-purpose flour
1 teaspoon Italian seasoning mix

Sea salt and ground black pepper, to taste
2 bell peppers, deseeded and sliced
1 cup scallions, chopped
4 cloves garlic, smashed

1/4 cup Marsala wine
1 cup chicken broth
1/4 cup cream cheese

DIRECTIONS

Press the "Sauté" button to preheat your Instant Pot. Melt 1 tablespoon of the butter.
Dredge your chicken in the flour; season with spices and cook until slightly brown; reserve.
Melt the remaining tablespoon of butter and sauté the peppers, scallions, and garlic. Pour in the wine, scraping up any browned bits from the bottom of the pan. Add the chicken broth and secure the lid.
Choose the "Manual" mode and cook for 10 minutes at High pressure. Once cooking is complete, use a natural pressure release; carefully remove the lid.
Press the "Sauté" button to preheat your Instant Pot one more time. Add the cream cheese and cook for a further 4 to 5 minutes or until everything is thoroughly heated.
To serve, spoon the sauce over the chicken drumsticks. Bon appétit!

25. Chicken with Couscous and Haloumi Cheese

(Ready in about 20 minutes | Servings 4)

Per serving: 444 Calories; 12.2g Fat; 45.1g Carbs; 37g Protein; 4.5g Sugars

INGREDIENTS

2 teaspoons butter, at room temperature
1 pound chicken fillets, diced
1 onion, diced
1 sweet pepper, deseeded and sliced
1 red chili pepper, deseeded and sliced

3 cloves garlic, minced
1 teaspoon dried rosemary
1 teaspoon dried oregano
Kosher salt and ground black pepper,
to taste

2 cups vegetable broth
1 cup dry couscous
4 ounces halloumi cheese, crumbled

DIRECTIONS

Press the "Sauté" button to preheat your Instant Pot. Melt 1 teaspoon of the butter. Cook the chicken fillets until golden brown. Set aside.
Then, melt the remaining 1 teaspoon of butter. Now, sauté the onion, peppers, and garlic until tender and aromatic.
Add the rosemary, oregano, salt, pepper, and vegetable broth.
Secure the lid. Choose the "Poultry" mode and cook for 5 minutes at High pressure. Once cooking is complete, use a quick pressure release; carefully remove the lid.
Add the couscous and stir to combine. Secure the lid. Choose the "Manual" mode and cook for 2 minutes at High pressure. Once cooking is complete, use a quick pressure release; carefully remove the lid.
Divide between four serving plates; garnish each serving with halloumi cheese and enjoy!

26. Easy Teriyaki Chicken

(Ready in about 30 minutes | Servings 4)

Per serving: 294 Calories; 13.3g Fat; 15.1g Carbs; 27g Protein; 9.8g Sugars

INGREDIENTS

2 tablespoons sesame oil
1 pound chicken drumettes, skinless,
boneless, cut into bite-sized chunks
2 garlic cloves, minced
1/4 cup soy sauce

1/2 cup water
1/2 cup rice vinegar
1/4 cup brown sugar
1 teaspoon ground ginger
2 tablespoons rice wine

3 tablespoons Mirin
1 pound broccoli florets
1 teaspoon arrowroot powder

DIRECTIONS

Press the "Sauté" button to preheat your Instant Pot. Heat the sesame oil and cook the chicken drumettes for 3 to 4 minutes.
Then, add the garlic and cook for 30 seconds more or until fragrant. Add the soy sauce, water, vinegar, sugar, ginger, rice wine, and Mirin. Secure the lid.
Choose the "Manual" mode and cook for 10 minutes at High pressure. Once cooking is complete, use a quick pressure release; carefully remove the lid.
Add the broccoli florets and secure the lid. Choose the "Manual" mode and cook for 2 minutes at High pressure. Once cooking is complete, use a quick pressure release; carefully remove the lid.
Transfer the chicken and broccoli to a nice serving platter.
Press the "Sauté" button to preheat your Instant Pot again. Add the arrowroot powder and stir until it is completely dissolved. Cook for 5 to 6 minutes or until the sauce thickens slightly. Spoon over the chicken and serve.

27. Chicken Enchilada Sliders

(Ready in about 25 minutes | Servings 4)

Per serving: 504 Calories; 17.2g Fat; 49.1g Carbs; 36.3g Protein; 6.7g Sugars

INGREDIENTS

1 pound chicken breasts, boneless and skinless
Kosher salt and freshly ground black pepper, to taste
1 cup chicken broth

8 ounces canner red enchilada sauce
1 cup spring onions, sliced
8 slider buns

DIRECTIONS

Place the chicken breasts in the inner pot. Season with salt and pepper; pour in the chicken broth and enchilada sauce.
Secure the lid. Choose the "Manual" mode and cook for 9 minutes at High pressure. Once cooking is complete, use a quick pressure release; carefully remove the lid.
Place the bottom half of the slider buns on a baking sheet. Top with layers of the chicken mixture and spring onions. Put on the top buns and spritz with cooking spray.
Bake about 10 minutes in the preheated oven until buns are golden. Enjoy!

28. Favorite Chicken Sandwiches

(Ready in about 25 minutes | Servings 4)

Per serving: 452 Calories; 27.1g Fat; 25.2g Carbs; 26.1g Protein; 4.5g Sugars

INGREDIENTS

2 tablespoons butter, at room temperature
1 pound whole chicken, skinless and boneless
2 garlic cloves, crushed
1 yellow onion, chopped

Sea salt and ground black pepper, to your liking
1 teaspoon cayenne pepper
4 hamburger buns
1 tablespoons mustard

1 large tomato, sliced
1 Lebanese cucumber, sliced
1 tablespoon fresh cilantro, chopped
2 tablespoons fresh green onions, chopped

DIRECTIONS

Press the "Sauté" button to preheat your Instant Pot. Melt the butter and cook the chicken for 3 to 4 minutes or until slightly brown.
Add the garlic, onion, salt, black pepper, and cayenne pepper.
Secure the lid. Choose the "Poultry" mode and cook for 15 minutes at High pressure. Once cooking is complete, use a quick pressure release; carefully remove the lid.
Shred the chicken with two forks.
Spread the mustard on the bottom half of each hamburger bun. Top with the tomato, cumber, chicken, cilantro, and green onions; top with the remaining bun halves. Serve immediately.

29. Cholula Chicken Meatballs

(Ready in about 15 minutes | Servings 4)

Per serving: 532 Calories; 30.7g Fat; 26.5g Carbs; 37.6g Protein; 4.6g Sugars

INGREDIENTS

4 tablespoons olive oil
1 carrot, finely chopped
1 celery stalk, finely chopped
1 shallot, minced
2 garlic cloves, minced
1 ½ pounds ground chicken

1 egg, beaten
1/2 cup buttermilk
1 teaspoon celery seeds
1/2 teaspoon mustard seeds
Sea salt and ground black pepper, to taste

1 cup fine panko crumbs
1 cup chicken broth
1/2 cup Cholula's hot sauce
1 tablespoon arrowroot powder

DIRECTIONS

Press the "Sauté" button and heat 1 tablespoon of olive oil. Cook the carrot, celery, shallot, and garlic until tender and fragrant.
Stir in the ground chicken, egg, buttermilk, celery seeds, mustard seeds, salt, pepper, and panko crumbs. Mix to combine well and shape the chicken/vegetable mixture into 1-inch balls.
Heat 1 tablespoon of olive oil and sear the meatballs until golden brown on all sides.
Add 2 tablespoons of olive oil, chicken broth, Cholula's hot sauce, and arrowroot to the inner pot; stir to combine. Fold in the prepared meatballs.
Secure the lid. Choose the "Poultry" mode and cook for 5 minutes at High pressure. Once cooking is complete, use a quick pressure release; carefully remove the lid. Serve warm.

30. Favorite BBQ Meatloaf

(Ready in about 45 minutes | Servings 5)

Per serving: 450 Calories; 27.8g Fat; 15.6g Carbs; 34.2g Protein; 5.9g Sugars

INGREDIENTS

2 tablespoons olive oil
1 tablespoon Worcestershire sauce
1 pound ground chicken
1/2 pound ground beef
1/2 cup crackers, crushed
1/4 cup Parmesan cheese, grated

1 medium carrot, grated
2 sweet peppers, deseeded and chopped
1 chili pepper, deseeded and finely chopped
1 onion, finely chopped

2 garlic cloves, minced
1 egg, beaten
1/2 cup BBQ sauce
Smoked salt flakes and freshly ground black pepper, to taste

DIRECTIONS

Place a steamer rack inside the inner pot; add 1/2 cup water. Cut 1 sheet of heavy-duty foil and brush with cooking spray.
In large mixing dish, thoroughly combine all ingredients until mixed well.
Shape the meat mixture into a loaf; place the meatloaf in the center of the foil. Wrap your meatloaf in the foil and lower onto the steamer rack.
Secure the lid. Choose the "Poultry" mode and cook for 30 minutes at High pressure. Once cooking is complete, use a quick pressure release; carefully remove the lid.
Then, transfer your meatloaf to a cutting board. Let it stand for 10 minutes before cutting and serving. To serve, brush with some extra BBQ sauce, if desired. Bon appétit!

TURKEY

31. The Best Thanksgiving Turkey Ever

(Ready in about 45 minutes | Servings 5)

Per serving: 449 Calories; 24.4g Fat; 3.7g Carbs; 50.6g Protein; 0.8g Sugars

INGREDIENTS

3 tablespoons olive oil
1 teaspoon sage, chopped
1 teaspoon basil, chopped
1 teaspoon rosemary, chopped

Sea salt and freshly cracked black pepper, to taste
1 teaspoon paprika
2 pounds turkey breasts, boneless
1 splash dry white wine

1 cup chicken bone broth
1 tablespoon mustard
2 tablespoons half-and-half
1 tablespoon cornstarch, dissolved in 1 tablespoon of water

DIRECTIONS

Mix the olive oil with the spices; brush the mixture all over the turkey breasts. Press the "Sauté" button to preheat your Instant Pot.

Add the turkey breasts, skin side down and cook until slightly brown on all sides. Add a splash of wine to deglaze the pot.

Pour the chicken bone broth into the inner pot. Add the mustard and half-and-half.

Secure the lid. Choose the "Poultry" mode and cook for 30 minutes at High pressure. Once cooking is complete, use a natural pressure release; carefully remove the lid.

Afterwards, place the turkey breast under the broiler until the outside is crisp.

Meanwhile, press the "Sauté" button to preheat your Instant Pot again; add the cornstarch slurry and whisk to combine well. Let it cook until the sauce is slightly thickened. Slice the turkey breasts and serve with the pan juices. Enjoy!

32. Herbed Turkey Meatloaf

(Ready in about 40 minutes | Servings 5)

Per serving: 365 Calories; 19.8g Fat; 14.6g Carbs; 33.3g Protein; 9.1g Sugars

INGREDIENTS

1 tablespoon olive oil
1 shallot, minced
1 ½ pounds ground turkey
1/2 cup Romano cheese, grated
1/3 cup fine breadcrumbs

1 egg, whisked
Sea salt and ground black pepper, to taste
1 tablespoon garlic and herb seasoning blend

1/2 cup ketchup
1 teaspoon molasses
1 teaspoon Dijon mustard
1 tablespoon soy sauce

DIRECTIONS

Press the "Sauté" button to preheat your Instant Pot. Heat the oil and sauté the shallot until tender and aromatic.

Add the ground turkey, cheese, breadcrumbs, egg, salt, pepper, and herb seasoning blend. Shape the mixture into a meatloaf and wrap it into a piece of foil.

Mix the ketchup, molasses, mustard and soy sauce in a small bowl. Pour the mixture on top of the meatloaf, spreading it into an even layer.

Place a steamer rack and 1/2 cup of water inside the inner pot. Lower your meatloaf onto the steamer rack.

Secure the lid. Choose the "Poultry" mode and cook for 30 minutes at High pressure. Once cooking is complete, use a quick pressure release; carefully remove the lid.

Let your meatloaf stand for 10 minutes before cutting and serving. Bon appétit!

33. Turkey Breasts with Bacon and Gravy

(Ready in about 35 minutes | Servings 4)

Per serving: 392 Calories; 16.3g Fat; 14.4g Carbs; 45.9g Protein; 4.9g Sugars

INGREDIENTS

1 tablespoon butter, melted
1 ½ pounds turkey breasts, boneless and skinless
4 rashers smoked bacon
2 garlic cloves, minced

1 teaspoon onion powder
Salt, to taste
1/2 teaspoon mixed peppercorns, crushed
2 sweet peppers, sliced

1 cup cherry wine
1 cup chicken stock
1 tablespoon arrowroot powder

DIRECTIONS

Press the "Sauté" button to preheat your Instant Pot. Melt the butter and cook the turkey breasts for 4 to 6 minutes until golden brown on both sides.

Top with the bacon; add the garlic, onion powder, salt, and crushed peppercorns. Add the sweet peppers.

Pour in the wine and chicken stock and secure the lid.

Choose the "Manual" mode and cook for 25 minutes at High pressure. Once cooking is complete, use a quick pressure release; carefully remove the lid.

Press the "Sauté" button again and thicken the pan juices with the arrowroot powder. Spoon the gravy over the turkey breasts and serve immediately. Bon appétit!

34. Turkey and Barley Tabbouleh

(Ready in about 20 minutes | Servings 4)

Per serving: 426 Calories; 14.5g Fat; 43.6g Carbs; 30.1g Protein; 2.4g Sugars

INGREDIENTS

1 pound turkey breast fillet, slice into bite-sized pieces
1 cup pearl barley
1 bay leaf
2 carrots, trimmed and thinly sliced
2 ½ cups vegetable broth

1 bunch spring onions, thinly sliced
1 medium cucumber, sliced
2 medium vine-ripened tomatoes, sliced
1 garlic clove, crushed
1 tablespoon harissa paste

2 limes, freshly squeezed
4 tablespoons extra-virgin olive oil
1/4 teaspoon freshly ground black pepper
Pink salt, to taste

DIRECTIONS

Add the turkey breast fillets, barley, bay leaf, carrots, and vegetable broth to the inner pot.
Secure the lid. Choose the "Manual" mode and cook for 9 minutes at High pressure. Once cooking is complete, use a quick pressure release; carefully remove the lid.
Drain, chill and transfer to a serving bowl. Add the spring onions, cucumber, tomatoes, and garlic to the bowl.
In a small mixing dish, thoroughly combine the remaining ingredients. Drizzle this dressing over your salad and serve immediately. Bon appétit!

35. Greek-Style Turkey Salad

(Ready in about 25 minutes + chilling time | Servings 4)

Per serving: 473 Calories; 32.2g Fat; 13.2g Carbs; 33.1g Protein; 3.5g Sugars

INGREDIENTS

1 pound turkey breast, skinless and boneless, slice into bite-sized pieces
1 cup chicken bone broth
1 red onion
2 sweet peppers, deseeded and thinly sliced
1 serrano pepper, deseeded and thinly sliced
1 tablespoon mustard
1 tablespoon fresh lime juice

1 tablespoon champagne vinegar
1/4 cup extra-virgin olive oil
1/2 teaspoon dried dill
1/2 teaspoon dried oregano
Sea salt and ground black pepper, to taste
1 cup feta cheese, cubed
1/2 cup Kalamata olives, pitted and sliced

DIRECTIONS

Place the turkey breasts in the inner pot; pour in the chicken bone broth.
Secure the lid. Choose the "Manual" mode and cook for 12 minutes at High pressure. Once cooking is complete, use a quick pressure release; carefully remove the lid. Transfer to a big tray and allow it to cool.
Place the chilled turkey breast in a serving bowl. Add the red onion and peppers. In a small dish, whisk the mustard, lime juice, vinegar, olive oil, dill, oregano, salt, and black pepper.
Dress the salad and serve topped with feta cheese and Kalamata olives. Serve well chilled and enjoy!

36. Copycat Panera Turkey Sandwich

(Ready in about 35 minutes | Servings 4)

Per serving: 560 Calories; 29.1g Fat; 22.5g Carbs; 49g Protein; 3.1g Sugars

INGREDIENTS

1 ½ pounds turkey breast
1 clove garlic
Salt and ground black pepper, to taste
1 teaspoon thyme
1 teaspoon marjoram

1 teaspoon basil
2 tablespoons butter, at room temperature
1 cup vegetable broth
8 slices walnut bread

2 tablespoons Dijon mustard
8 lettuce leaves
4 (1-ounce) slices white cheddar cheese

DIRECTIONS

Place the turkey breasts, garlic, salt, black pepper, thyme, marjoram, basil, and butter in the inner pot; pour in the vegetable broth.
Secure the lid. Choose the "Manual" mode and cook for 25 minutes at High pressure. Once cooking is complete, use a natural pressure release; carefully remove the lid.
Spread the mustard on 4 slices of bread. Layer the slices of bread with the turkey, lettuce, and cheese.
Place remaining 4 slices of bread on top of the sandwiches and serve immediately.

37. Turkey with Peppers and Gravy

(Ready in about 35 minutes | Servings 6)

Per serving: 458 Calories; 26.1g Fat; 4.1g Carbs; 49g Protein; 1.3g Sugars

INGREDIENTS

2 ½ pounds turkey breasts

2 bell peppers, deseeded and chopped

1 serrano pepper, deseeded and chopped

2 garlic cloves, minced

1 cup turkey stock

3 tablespoons olive oil

2 thyme sprigs

1 teaspoon dried sage

1/2 teaspoon dried dill

Sea salt and ground black pepper, to taste

2 tablespoons butter

1 tablespoon flour

1/4 cup dry white wine

Sea salt and ground black pepper, to taste

DIRECTIONS

Add the turkey, peppers, garlic, turkey stock, olive oil, thyme, sage, dried dill, salt, and black pepper to the inner pot.

Secure the lid. Choose the "Manual" mode and cook for 25 minutes at High pressure. Once cooking is complete, use a natural pressure release; carefully remove the lid.

Press the "Sauté" button again and melt the butter. Now, add the flour, wine, salt, and pepper; let it cook until the sauce has thickened.

Spoon the gravy over the turkey breasts and serve warm. Bon appétit!

38. Cheese Stuffed Turkey Meatballs in Sauce

(Ready in about 15 minutes | Servings 4)

Per serving: 485 Calories; 23.3g Fat; 14.7g Carbs; 54.1g Protein; 6.4g Sugars

INGREDIENTS

2 slices bacon, chopped

1 pound ground turkey

1/2 pound ground beef

1 shallot, finely minced

1 bell pepper, deseeded and finely minced

2 garlic cloves, minced

1 cup crushed saltines

Sea salt and freshly cracked black pepper, to taste

1 teaspoon dried basil

1 teaspoon dried rosemary

1 teaspoon dried parsley flakes

1/2 cup buttermilk

4 ounces Fontina cheese, cut into 16 pieces

1 teaspoon mustard

1 cup marinara sauce

DIRECTIONS

Press the "Sauté" button to preheat your Instant Pot. Cook the chopped bacon until crisp; reserve. Cook the ground turkey, beef, shallot, pepper, and garlic until the meat is no longer pink.

Add the crushed saltines, salt, black pepper, basil, rosemary, parsley, and buttermilk. Stir in the reserved bacon. Shape the meat mixture into 16 meatballs. Insert 1 cube of Fontina cheese into the center of each meatball.

Add the mustard and marinara sauce to the inner pot; stir to combine and fold in the meatballs.

Secure the lid. Choose the "Poultry" mode and cook for 5 minutes at High pressure. Once cooking is complete, use a quick pressure release; carefully remove the lid. Serve warm.

39. Caribbean-Style Saucy Turkey Drumsticks

(Ready in about 30 minutes | Servings 5)

Per serving: 394 Calories; 17.3g Fat; 3.7g Carbs; 50.1g Protein; 0.7g Sugars

INGREDIENTS

2 pounds turkey drumsticks, boneless

1 (12-ounce) bottle beer

2 carrots, sliced

1 medium-sized leek, sliced

2 garlic cloves, sliced

1/2 teaspoon ground allspice

2 sprigs rosemary, chopped

2 bay leaves

Sea salt and freshly ground black pepper, to taste

DIRECTIONS

Add all ingredients to the inner pot.

Secure the lid. Choose the "Manual" mode and cook for 20 minutes at High pressure. Once cooking is complete, use a natural pressure release; carefully remove the lid.

You can thicken the pan juices if desired. Enjoy!

40. Turkey with Harvest Vegetable Bowl

(Ready in about 30 minutes | Servings 6)

Per serving: 391 Calories; 5.9g Fat; 11.2g Carbs; 69.9g Protein; 3.9g Sugars

INGREDIENTS

3 pounds whole turkey breasts
1 cup cream of celery soup
1 celery stalk, cut into bite-sized chunks
2 medium carrots, cut into bite-sized chunks
2 bell pepper, cut into bite-sized chunks

1 onion, quartered
4 cloves garlic, halved
1/4 cup tomato paste
1 tablespoon Italian spice blend
1 tablespoon arrowroot powder

DIRECTIONS

Place the turkey breasts and cream of celery soup in the inner pot.
Secure the lid. Choose the "Manual" mode and cook for 20 minutes at High pressure. Once cooking is complete, use a natural pressure release; carefully remove the lid.
Add the vegetables and tomato paste; sprinkle with the Italian spice blend.
Secure the lid. Choose the "Manual" mode and cook for 3 minutes at High pressure. Once cooking is complete, use a quick pressure release; carefully remove the lid.
Transfer the turkey and vegetables to a serving bowl.
Press the "Sauté" button; add the arrowroot powder and cook until the cooking liquid is reduced by about half. Bon appétit!

41. Spring Turkey Salad with Apples

(Ready in about 20 minutes + chilling time | Servings 4)

Per serving: 391 Calories; 5.9g Fat; 11.2g Carbs; 69.9g Protein; 3.9g Sugars

INGREDIENTS

1 ½ pounds turkey breasts, boneless and skinless
1 cup water
2 celery stalks, diced
1 apple, cored and diced
1/2 cup spring onions, chopped
1 head butterhead lettuce, shredded

1/2 cup cream cheese
1 cup mayonnaise
1 tablespoon fresh lemon juice
1 teaspoon sage
Kosher salt and white pepper, to taste

DIRECTIONS

Place the turkey breasts and water in the inner pot.
Secure the lid. Choose the "Manual" mode and cook for 9 minutes at High pressure. Once cooking is complete, use a natural pressure release; carefully remove the lid.
Add the remaining ingredients; gently stir to combine. Serve well chilled and enjoy!

42. Honey-Glazed Turkey Thighs

(Ready in about 25 minutes | Servings 4)

Per serving: 479 Calories; 25g Fat; 20.5g Carbs; 41.7g Protein; 17.2g Sugars

INGREDIENTS

2 pounds turkey thighs
Sea salt and freshly ground black pepper, to taste
1 teaspoon red pepper flakes
1 teaspoon dried parsley flakes
4 tablespoons olive oil

1 orange, sliced
1/2 cup water
1/2 cup turkey stock
4 tablespoons honey
2 tablespoons all-purpose flour

DIRECTIONS

Rub the salt, black pepper, red pepper, and parsley flakes all over the turkey thighs.
Press the "Sauté" button and heat the olive oil. Sear the turkey thighs for 3 minutes per side. Then, add the orange, water, stock, and honey.
Secure the lid. Choose the "Manual" mode and cook for 15 minutes at High pressure. Once cooking is complete, use a quick pressure release; carefully remove the lid.
Then, add the flour to thicken the cooking liquid. Spoon the sauce over the turkey thighs and serve warm. Bon appétit!

43. Herbed Mayonnaise Roast Turkey

(Ready in about 35 minutes | Servings 8)

Per serving: 393 Calories; 25g Fat; 1.9g Carbs; 39.2g Protein; 0.4g Sugars

INGREDIENTS

3 pounds turkey breasts
4 garlic cloves, smashed
2 thyme sprigs
2 rosemary sprigs

1 cup mayonnaise
2 teaspoons coarse salt
1 teaspoon mixed peppercorns, crushed

2 tablespoons ghee, softened
1 lemon, sliced

DIRECTIONS

Pat the turkey dry. In a mixing dish, thoroughly combine the garlic, thyme, rosemary, mayonnaise, salt, peppercorns, and ghee. Rub the mayonnaise mixture all over the turkey breasts.

Add a steamer rack and 1/2 cup of water to the bottom of your Instant Pot. Throw in the lemon slices.

Secure the lid. Choose the "Manual" mode and cook for 20 minutes at High pressure. Once cooking is complete, use a natural pressure release; carefully remove the lid.

Let your turkey stand for 5 to 10 minutes before slicing and serving. Bon appétit!

44. Ground Turkey and Cabbage Casserole

(Ready in about 20 minutes | Servings 4)

Per serving: 385 Calories; 19.1g Fat; 19g Carbs; 37.1g Protein; 8.6g Sugars

INGREDIENTS

1 tablespoon lard
1 ½ pounds ground turkey
1 (1 ½-pound) head of cabbage, shredded
2 ripe tomatoes, pureed

1 sweet pepper, sliced
1 red chili pepper, minced
1 yellow onion, chopped
3 garlic cloves, smashed

2 tablespoons fresh parsley, roughly chopped
1 bay leaf
Salt and ground black pepper, to taste

DIRECTIONS

Press the "Sauté" button and melt the lard. Now, brown the ground turkey until no longer pink, about 3 minutes.

Add the remaining ingredients and secure the lid.

Secure the lid. Choose the "Manual" mode and cook for 10 minutes at High pressure. Once cooking is complete, use a natural pressure release; carefully remove the lid.

Divide between individual bowls and serve warm. Enjoy!

45. Turkey Meatball Sliders

(Ready in about 15 minutes | Servings 4)

Per serving: 502 Calories; 15.8g Fat; 52.9g Carbs; 37.3g Protein; 5.5g Sugars

INGREDIENTS

Meatballs:
1 pound ground turkey
1/2 cup seasoned breadcrumbs
2 tablespoons fresh cilantro, chopped
1 egg, whisked
2 cloves garlic, minced
Sea salt, to taste

1/2 teaspoon freshly cracked black pepper
Sauce:
1 tablespoon butter, at room temperature
2 cloves garlic, minced
1 cup tomatoes puree

1 onion, minced
1/4 cup fresh basil, chopped
Salt, to taste
1 teaspoon hot sauce
Meatball Sliders:
1/2 cup mozzarella, shredded
8 honey wheat slider buns, toasted

DIRECTIONS

Mix all ingredients for the meatballs until everything is well incorporated; form the mixture into small balls.

Spritz the sides and bottom of the inner pot with cooking spray. Press the "Sauté" button and cook your meatball until they are golden brown on all sides.

Add all ingredients for the sauce to the inner pot. Fold in the meatballs.

Secure the lid. Choose the "Poultry" mode and cook for 5 minutes at High pressure. Once cooking is complete, use a quick pressure release; carefully remove the lid. Serve warm.

Preheat your oven to broil.

To assemble the slider, place 1 meatball and a spoonful of sauce on the bottom of each bun. Top with mozzarella. Place under the broiler and bake until the cheese has melted about 2 minutes.

Top with another bun half and serve immediately. Bon appétit!

DUCK

46. Thai Red Duck

(Ready in about 50 minutes | Servings 4)

Per serving: 467 Calories; 27.8g Fat; 6.8g Carbs; 47.6g Protein; 2.5g Sugars

INGREDIENTS

1 tablespoon Thai red curry paste
Zest and juice of 1 fresh lime
2 pounds duck breast
1 tablespoon olive oil
1/2 teaspoon black peppercorns, crushed

1 teaspoon cayenne pepper
1 teaspoon sea salt
4 garlic cloves, minced
2 thyme sprigs, chopped
2 rosemary sprigs, chopped
1 cup light coconut milk

1/2 cup chicken broth, preferably homemade
1/4 small pack coriander, roughly chopped

DIRECTIONS

Combine the red curry paste with the lime zest and juice; rub the mixture all over the duck breast and leave it to marinate for 30 minutes. Press the "Sauté" button and heat the oil until sizzling. Cook the duck breast until slightly brown on both sides.

Then, season the duck breasts with the peppercorns, cayenne pepper, and salt. Add the garlic, thyme, rosemary, coconut milk, and chicken broth. Secure the lid. Choose the "Poultry" mode and cook for 15 minutes at High pressure. Once cooking is complete, use a quick pressure release; carefully remove the lid.

Garnish with chopped coriander and serve warm. Bon appétit!

47. Duck with Sticky Cranberry Sauce

(Ready in about 35 minutes | Servings 6)

Per serving: 517 Calories; 36.7g Fat; 3.3g Carbs; 40.6g Protein; 1.7g Sugars

INGREDIENTS

3 pounds whole duck
Kosher salt, to taste
1/2 teaspoon freshly ground black pepper
1/2 teaspoon red pepper flakes

1/2 teaspoon smoked paprika
1 teaspoon onion powder
2 cloves garlic, minced
1 cup chicken stock
1 tablespoon butter

1/2 cup cranberries, halved
1 tablespoon brown sugar
1/4 cup raspberry vinegar
1 teaspoon wholegrain mustard

DIRECTIONS

Press the "Sauté" button and melt the butter; place the duck skin-side down in the inner pot and sear until the skin is crisp and brown. Turn and cook the other side for about 4 minutes.

Pour away all but a tablespoon of the fat. Add the salt, black pepper, red pepper, paprika, onion powder, garlic, and chicken stock to the inner pot. Secure the lid. Choose the "Manual" mode and cook for 25 minutes at High pressure. Once cooking is complete, use a natural pressure release; carefully remove the lid.

Now, remove the duck from the inner pot.

Press the "Sauté" button and add the remaining ingredients to the cooking liquid.

Continue to cook for 5 to 6 minutes, until the cranberries start to slightly break down and soften. Spoon over the reserved duck and serve immediately. Bon appétit!

48. Asian Ginger-Glazed Duck Breast

(Ready in about 25 minutes | Servings 4)

Per serving: 411 Calories; 14.5g Fat; 22.1g Carbs; 47.6g Protein; 18.5g Sugars

INGREDIENTS

1 teaspoon sesame oil
2 pounds duck breasts
1 teaspoon red pepper flakes
Sea salt and freshly ground black pepper, to taste
1 teaspoon dry mustard
1 tablespoon paprika

1 teaspoon ground star anise
1 teaspoon ground ginger
Kosher salt and ground black pepper, to taste
1 cup chicken broth
Ginger Glaze:
1 tablespoon peanut oil

1-inch piece ginger, finely chopped
3 cloves garlic, finely chopped
1 tablespoon Sriracha sauce
1/4 cup low-sodium soy sauce
1/4 cup honey

DIRECTIONS

Press the "Sauté" button to preheat your Instant Pot.

Heat the sesame seed oil and sear the duck breasts for 5 minutes, stirring periodically. Sprinkle your spices all over the duck breasts. Add the chicken broth.

Secure the lid and choose the "Poultry" mode. Cook for 15 minutes. Afterwards, use a quick release and carefully remove the lid. Remove the duck breasts from the inner pot.

After that, stir in the other ingredients for the ginger glaze; stir well to combine.

Press the "Sauté" button to preheat your Instant Pot. Cook until thoroughly heated. Place the duck breasts in the serving plates and brush with the ginger glaze. Serve warm and enjoy!

49. Xiang Su Ya (Szechuan Duck)

(Ready in about 35 minutes | Servings 6)

Per serving: 525 Calories; 37.2g Fat; 4.5g Carbs; 40.5g Protein; 2.9g Sugars

INGREDIENTS

2 tablespoons Szechuan peppercorns
1 teaspoon Chinese 5-spice powder
2 tablespoons salt
3 pounds whole duck

4 cloves garlic, sliced
2 star anise
1/4 cup soy sauce
1/4 cup Shaoxing rice wine

1 red chili pepper, chopped
1 tablespoon dark brown sugar
1 cup water

DIRECTIONS

Press the "Sauté" button to preheat your Instant Pot. Then, add the Szechuan peppercorn to the inner pot and roast until really fragrant. Remove it to a spice grinder and ground into a powder.

Add the Chinese 5-spice powder and salt. Rub the duck with the spice mixture. Leave it to marinate overnight.

Press the "Sauté" button to preheat your Instant Pot. Now, place the duck skin-side down in the inner pot and sear until the skin is crisp and brown. Turn and cook the other side for 4 to 5 minutes.

Stir in the other ingredients.

Secure the lid and choose the "Manual" mode. Cook for 25 minutes at High pressure. Afterwards, use a quick release and carefully remove the lid. Serve warm.

50. Braised Duck with Mixed Vegetables

(Ready in about 30 minutes | Servings 4)

Per serving: 554 Calories; 38g Fat; 9.3g Carbs; 41.9g Protein; 5.2g Sugars

INGREDIENTS

2 pounds whole duck
1 cup chicken stock
Kosher salt and ground black pepper,
to taste
1 teaspoon smoked paprika
1 bay leaf

1 tablespoon butter, melted
1 onion, quartered
1 red bell pepper, deseeded and sliced
1 green bell pepper, deseeded and
sliced
2 carrots, sliced

1 celery stalk, sliced
4 cloves garlic, sliced
2 rosemary sprigs
1 thyme sprig
2 tablespoons balsamic vinegar
2 tablespoons Worcestershire sauce

DIRECTIONS

Press the "Sauté" button to preheat your Instant Pot. Now, place the duck skin-side down in the inner pot and sear until the skin is crisp and brown. Turn and cook the other side for 4 to 5 minutes.

Add the chicken stock, salt, black pepper, smoked paprika, and bay leaf to the inner pot.

Secure the lid and choose the "Manual" mode. Cook for 20 minutes at High pressure. Afterwards, use a quick release and carefully remove the lid.

Add the remaining ingredients in the order listed above.

Secure the lid. Choose the "Manual" mode and cook for 3 minutes at High pressure. Once cooking is complete, use a quick pressure release; carefully remove the lid. Serve immediately.

51. Aromatic Duck Salad

(Ready in about 25 minutes | Servings 6)

Per serving: 349 Calories; 11.3g Fat; 12.3g Carbs; 48.6g Protein; 6.3g Sugars

INGREDIENTS

3 pounds duck breasts
1 cup water
Salt and black pepper, to taste
2 heads romaine lettuce, torn into small pieces
2 tomatoes, diced
2 red onions, sliced diagonally

2 tablespoons balsamic vinegar
1 garlic clove, minced
1 teaspoon fresh ginger, grated
2 tablespoons tamari sauce
2 tablespoons peanut butter

DIRECTIONS

Put the duck breasts and water into the inner pot.

Secure the lid and choose the "Poultry" mode. Cook for 15 minutes at High pressure. Afterwards, use a quick release and carefully remove the lid.

Now, slice the meat into strips and place in a salad bowl. Season with salt and pepper. Add the romaine lettuce, tomatoes, and onion.

In a small mixing dish, whisk the balsamic vinegar, garlic, ginger, tamari sauce, and peanut butter. Dress the salad and serve well chilled. Bon appétit!

52. Duck with Hoisin Sauce

(Ready in about 40 minutes | Servings 6)

Per serving: 385 Calories; 14.6g Fat; 17.5g Carbs; 43.8g Protein; 8.1g Sugars

INGREDIENTS

3 pounds whole duck
Salt and ground black pepper, to your liking
1 cup roasted vegetable broth
2 carrots, chopped

1 head broccoli, chopped into florets
1 leek, white part only, chopped
1 small bunch of fresh coriander stalks, roughly chopped
2 cloves garlic, sliced

1 bay leaf
1/2 cup Hoisin sauce
1 lemon, cut into wedges

DIRECTIONS

Press the "Sauté" button to preheat your Instant Pot.
Now, cook the duck for 4 to 5 minutes or until the skin turns golden brown. Pour in the roasted vegetable broth.
Secure the lid and choose the "Manual" mode. Cook for 25 minutes at High pressure. Afterwards, use a quick release and carefully remove the lid. Add the vegetables, coriander, garlic, and bay leaf.
Secure the lid. Choose the "Manual" mode and cook for 3 minutes at High pressure. Once cooking is complete, use a quick pressure release; carefully remove the lid.
Remove the duck to a chopping board and rest for 5 minutes before cutting and serving.
Lastly, slice the duck and serve with the braised vegetables, Hoisin sauce, and lemon wedges. Bon appétit!

53. Japanese Duck and Rice Bowl

(Ready in about 20 minutes + marinating time | Servings 4)

Per serving: 631 Calories; 31.2g Fat; 28.8g Carbs; 56.6g Protein; 3.6g Sugars

INGREDIENTS

2 pounds duck breasts, skinless and boneless
2 tablespoons orange juice
2 tablespoons Mirin
2 tablespoons tamari
1 tablespoon sesame oil
1 cup vegetable broth
2 garlic cloves, grated

1 teaspoon honey
Sea salt and freshly ground pepper, to taste
1 shallot, chopped
1/4 cup loosely packed fresh parsley leaves, roughly chopped
1 fresh lemon, juiced
2 tablespoons extra-virgin oil

1 cup Chinese cabbage, shredded
2 tablespoons sesame seeds, toasted
1 red chili, finely chopped
2 cups cooked rice
1 tablespoon olive oil
4 eggs

DIRECTIONS

Place the duck breasts, orange juice, Mirin, and tamari sauce in a ceramic dish. Let it marinate for 1 hour in your refrigerator.
Press the "Sauté" button and heat the oil until sizzling. Cook the duck for about 5 minutes or until it is no longer pink.
Add the vegetable broth and secure the lid.
Choose the "Manual" mode and cook for 10 minutes at High pressure. Once cooking is complete, use a quick pressure release; carefully remove the lid.
Slice the duck and transfer to a nice serving bowl. Add the garlic, honey, salt, black pepper, shallot, fresh parsley, lemon, oil, cabbage, sesame seeds, chili pepper, and cooked rice.
Heat the olive oil in a skillet over medium-high flame. Fry the eggs until the whites are completely set. Place the fried eggs on the top and serve immediately.

54. Duck with Balsamic Cherry Sauce

(Ready in about 30 minutes | Servings 5)

Per serving: 454 Calories; 28.2g Fat; 14.6g Carbs; 34.1g Protein; 7.5g Sugars

INGREDIENTS

2 pounds whole duck
1/2 teaspoon curry paste
Salt and ground black pepper, to taste
1 onion, finely chopped

2 garlic cloves, minced
6 ounces canned red tart cherries
1 tablespoon lemon rind, grated
2 tablespoons dry white wine

2 tablespoons balsamic vinegar
1 cup vegetable broth

DIRECTIONS

Place all ingredients in the inner pot.
Secure the lid. Choose the "Manual" mode and cook for 20 minutes at High pressure. Once cooking is complete, use a quick pressure release; carefully remove the lid.
Remove the duck from the inner pot.
Press the "Sauté" button and cook the cooking liquid until it is reduced by about half. Bon appétit!

55. Father's Day Duck Ragù

(Ready in about 30 minutes | Servings 4)

Per serving: 496 Calories; 23.2g Fat; 26.1g Carbs; 45.5g Protein; 7.8g Sugars

INGREDIENTS

1 pound fettuccine
1 pound duck legs
2 cloves garlic, crushed
1 onion, chopped
1 red chili pepper, minced

2 sweet peppers, deseeded and finely chopped
Sea salt and freshly ground black pepper, to taste
1/2 cup tomato purée
1/2 cup chicken bone broth
2 tablespoons dry cooking wine

DIRECTIONS

Bring a pot of salted water to a boil. Cook the fettuccine, stirring occasionally, until al dente. Drain, reserving 1 cup of the pasta water; set aside. Add the reserved pasta water along with the duck legs to the Instant Pot.

Secure the lid. Choose the "Manual" mode and cook for 20 minutes at High pressure. Once cooking is complete, use a quick pressure release; carefully remove the lid.

Shred the meat with two forks. Add the meat back to the Instant Pot. Add the remaining ingredients and press the "Sauté" button.

Let it cook for 5 to 7 minutes more or until everything is heated through. Serve with the reserved pasta and enjoy!

56. Exotic Duck Masala

(Ready in about 35 minutes | Servings 6)

Per serving: 539 Calories; 38.2g Fat; 5.2g Carbs; 45.1g Protein; 2.7g Sugars

INGREDIENTS

2 tablespoons butter, melted at room temperature
3 pounds duck thighs
Sea salt, to taste
1/4 teaspoon crushed black peppercorns, or more to taste
1 teaspoon ginger powder
1/2 teaspoon chili powder
1 tablespoon rosemary

1 tablespoon sage
1/2 teaspoon allspice berries, lightly crushed
2 garlic cloves, sliced
1/2 cup tomato paste
1/2 cup bone broth
1 tablespoon Garam masala
1 small bunch of fresh coriander, roughly chopped

DIRECTIONS

Press the "Sauté" button and melt the butter. Now, cook the duck thighs until golden brown on both sides. Add all seasonings.

Next, stir in the garlic, tomato paste, broth, and Garam masala.

Secure the lid. Choose the "Manual" mode and cook for 25 minutes at High pressure. Once cooking is complete, use a quick pressure release; carefully remove the lid.

Serve with fresh coriander. Enjoy!

57. Duck Breasts in Blood Orange Sauce

(Ready in about 35 minutes | Servings 4)

Per serving: 472 Calories; 14.2g Fat; 42.8g Carbs; 42.4g Protein; 9.7g Sugars

INGREDIENTS

1 tablespoon olive oil
1 ½ pounds duck breast
2 blood oranges, juiced
Sea salt and ground black pepper, to taste
1/2 teaspoon cayenne pepper

1 teaspoon dried dill weed
1 cup chicken bone broth
1/2 cup dry white wine
2 tablespoons apricot jam
2 tablespoons potato starch

DIRECTIONS

Press the "Sauté" button and heat the oil until sizzling. Then, cook the duck breasts for 4 minutes per side.

Add the oranges, salt, black pepper, cayenne pepper, dill, and broth.

Secure the lid. Choose the "Poultry" mode and cook for 15 minutes at High pressure. Once cooking is complete, use a quick pressure release; carefully remove the lid.

Remove the duck from the cooking liquid using a slotted spoon. Add the remaining ingredients to the cooking liquid and press the "Sauté" button again.

Let it simmer for 5 to 7 minutes or until slightly thickened. Spoon the sauce onto the duck and serve immediately. Bon appétit!

BEEF

58. Sticky Beef with Brown Sauce

(Ready in about 40 minutes | Servings 4)

Per serving: 460 Calories; 18.7g Fat; 22.5g Carbs; 51.3g Protein; 15.7g Sugars

INGREDIENTS

2 tablespoons olive oil
2 pounds beef stew meat, cubed
1/4 cup Syrah wine
1/2 cup dark brown sugar

6 cloves garlic, sliced
1 cup beef bone broth
1/4 cup soy sauce
1 teaspoon red pepper flakes

1 bay leaf
2 tablespoons arrowroot powder
1/4 cup scallions, roughly chopped

DIRECTIONS

Press the "Sauté" button and heat the oil until sizzling. Then, brown the beef in batches.

Add a splash of red wine to deglaze the pot. Add the remaining wine, sugar, garlic, broth, soy sauce, red pepper, and bay leaf.

Secure the lid. Choose the "Meat/Stew" mode and cook for 35 minutes at High pressure. Once cooking is complete, use a quick pressure release; carefully remove the lid.

Press the "Sauté" button again and add the arrowroot powder. Let it cook until the sauce has reduced slightly and the flavors have concentrated. Serve garnished with fresh scallions and enjoy!

59. Creamy Beef and Mushroom Stroganoff

(Ready in about 50 minutes | Servings 5)

Per serving: 474 Calories; 28.1g Fat; 12.5g Carbs; 43.1g Protein; 5.4g Sugars

INGREDIENTS

2 tablespoons cornstarch
Coarse sea salt, to taste
1/2 teaspoon ground black pepper
1/2 teaspoon cayenne pepper
1 teaspoon smoked paprika

2 pounds beef sirloin, cut into bite-sized chunks
1 tablespoon lard, melted
1 teaspoon dried basil
1/2 teaspoon dried marjoram
2 cloves garlic, peeled and halved

2 cups beef broth
1 ½ pounds button mushrooms, quartered
1 red onion, quartered
2 tablespoons tomato paste
1/2 cup double cream

DIRECTIONS

In a shallow dish, combine the cornstarch with the salt, black pepper, cayenne pepper, and smoked paprika.

Dredge the beef pieces in the seasoned mixture to coat on all sides.

Press the "Sauté" button to preheat your Instant Pot. Melt the lard and brown the beef until no longer pink.

Add the basil, marjoram, garlic, and beef broth.

Secure the lid. Choose the "Meat/Stew" mode and cook for 35 minutes at High pressure. Once cooking is complete, use a quick pressure release; carefully remove the lid.

Add the button mushrooms, onions and tomato paste.

Secure the lid. Choose the "Manual" mode and cook for 3 minutes at High pressure. Once cooking is complete, use a quick pressure release; carefully remove the lid.

Stir in the double cream; seal the lid and let it sit in the residual heat for 5 to 7 minutes. Serve warm.

60. One Pot Beef Enchilada Pasta

(Ready in about 15 minutes | Servings 4)

Per serving: 693 Calories; 18.1g Fat; 90.1g Carbs; 40.1g Protein; 6.1g Sugars

INGREDIENTS

1 tablespoon olive oil
1 pound ground chuck
1 pound elbow macaroni
8 ounces canned enchilada sauce

1 cup beef bone broth
1 cup water
Sea salt and ground black pepper, to taste

1 bay leaf
1 teaspoon paprika
1/2 cup Cotija cheese, crumbled

DIRECTIONS

Press the "Sauté" button to preheat your Instant Pot. Heat the oil and brown the ground chuck for 2 to 3 minutes.

Add the other ingredients, except for the cheese, to the Instant Pot.

Secure the lid. Choose the "Manual" mode and cook for 5 minutes at High pressure. Once cooking is complete, use a natural pressure release; carefully remove the lid.

Serve in individual bowls topped with the crumbled cheese. Enjoy!

61. Classic Ground Beef Tacos

(Ready in about 30 minutes | Servings 4)

Per serving: 618 Calories; 37.8g Fat; 21g Carbs; 47.1g Protein; 4.4g Sugars

INGREDIENTS

1 tablespoon canola oil
1 ½ pounds ground beef
1 onion, chopped
2 sweet peppers, deseeded and sliced
1 chili pepper, minced
4 garlic cloves, minced

1 teaspoon marjoram
1 teaspoon Mexican oregano
Kosher salt and ground black pepper, to taste
1 teaspoon cumin powder
1/2 teaspoon red pepper flakes

1 teaspoon mustard seeds
12 small taco shells
1 head lettuce
1/2 cup chunky salsa
1/2 cup sour cream

DIRECTION

Press the "Sauté" button to preheat your Instant Pot. Heat the oil and sear the ground chuck for 2 to 3 minutes or until mostly brown. Add the onion, peppers, garlic, and spices to the inner pot.

Secure the lid. Choose the "Manual" mode and cook for 10 minutes at High pressure. Once cooking is complete, use a natural pressure release; carefully remove the lid.

Press the "Sauté" button and cook, stirring continuously, until the liquid has almost evaporated or about 10 minutes.

To assemble your tacos, layer the beef mixture and lettuce in each taco shell. Serve with the salsa and sour cream. Enjoy!

62. Easy Ground Beef Bowl

(Ready in about 20 minutes | Servings 4)

Per serving: 535 Calories; 31.2g Fat; 16.9g Carbs; 48.1g Protein; 6.7g Sugars

INGREDIENTS

1 teaspoon olive oil
1 ½ pounds lean ground chuck
1 (1-ounce) packet taco seasoning mix
1 cup vegetable broth
1 onion, chopped
2 garlic cloves, minced

1 red bell pepper, deseeded and sliced
1 green bell pepper, deseeded and sliced
1 cup tomato puree
1 tablespoon chipotle paste
1 (15-ounce) can black beans, drained and rinsed

1 ½ cups Monterey-Jack cheese, shredded
2 tablespoons fresh cilantro leaves, chopped

DIRECTIONS

Press the "Sauté" button to preheat your Instant Pot. Heat the oil and cook the ground chuck for 2 to 3 minutes or until mostly brown. Next, add the taco seasoning mix, broth, onion, garlic, and peppers.

Secure the lid. Choose the "Manual" mode and cook for 10 minutes at High pressure. Once cooking is complete, use a natural pressure release; carefully remove the lid.

Divide the meat mixture between four serving bowls. Add the tomato puree, chipotle paste, and black beans; gently stir to combine.

Top with the cheese and serve garnished with fresh cilantro leaves. Enjoy!

63. Country-Style Rump Steak

(Ready in about 1 hour | Servings 6)

Per serving: 355 Calories; 14.2g Fat; 6.5g Carbs; 50.9g Protein; 1.3g Sugars

INGREDIENTS

Sea salt, to taste
1 teaspoon mixed peppercorns, crushed
1/2 teaspoon marjoram
1/2 teaspoon ginger powder

1/4 cup flour
2 tablespoons olive oil
3 pounds rump steak, trimmed and sliced into small pieces
3 garlic cloves, halved

2 carrots, sliced
1 cup vegetable broth
2 ripe tomatoes, pureed
1/2 teaspoon hot sauce

DIRECTIONS

In a shallow dish, combine the salt, black peppercorns, marjoram, ginger powder, and flour. Dredge the beef pieces in the seasoned mixture to coat on all sides.

Press the "Sauté" button to preheat your Instant Pot. Heat the oil and brown beef until no longer pink.

Add the remaining ingredients.

Secure the lid. Choose the "Manual" mode and cook for 60 minutes at High pressure. Once cooking is complete, use a quick pressure release; carefully remove the lid. Bon appétit!

64. Italian-Style Beef Peperonata

(Ready in about 30 minutes + marinating time | Servings 4)

Per serving: 432 Calories; 28g Fat; 21.1g Carbs; 24.5g Protein; 6.3g Sugars

INGREDIENTS

2 tablespoons soy sauce
2 tablespoons tomato paste
1/4 cup rice vinegar
1 tablespoon brown sugar
3 cloves garlic, minced

1 pound blade roast, sliced into 1/2-inch pieces
1 tablespoon canola oil
Salt and ground black pepper, to taste
1 teaspoon cayenne pepper

1 ½ cups broth
1 onion, thinly sliced
4 sweet peppers, cut Julienne
1 serrano pepper, minced
2 tablespoons capers with juices

DIRECTIONS

In a ceramic or glass dish, mix the soy sauce, tomato paste, vinegar, sugar, and garlic. Place the blade roast in the dish, cover with plastic wrap and let it marinate at least 3 hours in the refrigerator.

Press the "Sauté" button to preheat your Instant Pot. Heat the oil and brown the beef for 4 to 5 minutes, brushing occasionally with the marinade. Add the other ingredients. Secure the lid. Choose the "Meat/Stew" mode and cook for 20 minutes at High pressure. Once cooking is complete, use a quick pressure release; carefully remove the lid.

Serve warm.

65. Braised Beef Brisket and Broccoli

(Ready in about 30 minutes | Servings 4)

Per serving: 350 Calories; 24.2g Fat; 13.5g Carbs; 20.9g Protein; 3.6g Sugars

INGREDIENTS

2 tablespoons sesame oil
1 pound beef brisket, thinly sliced against the grain
1/4 cup rice wine
1 cup beef bone broth
1/4 cup tamari sauce
1 tablespoon yellow mustard
1 teaspoon fresh ginger, grated

2 cloves garlic, minced
Pink salt and ground black pepper, to taste
1/2 teaspoon paprika
1 head broccoli, broken into florets
1 tablespoon arrowroot flour
1/2 cup spring onions, sliced

DIRECTIONS

Press the "Sauté" button to preheat your Instant Pot. Heat the sesame oil and brown the beef in batches; cook for about 3 minutes per batch. Add the wine to deglaze the pot. Once your beef is browned, add the beef broth, tamari sauce, mustard, ginger, garlic, salt, pepper, and paprika. Secure the lid. Choose the "Manual" mode and cook for 15 minutes at High pressure. Once cooking is complete, use a quick pressure release; carefully remove the lid.

Add the broccoli and arrowroot flour and press the "Sauté" button again. Cook until the broccoli florets are tender, but still slightly crisp and not mushy, about 4 minutes.

Garnish with spring onions and serve immediately. Bon appétit!

66. Sunday Sesame Beef

(Ready in about 45 minutes | Servings 5)

Per serving: 322 Calories; 17.8g Fat; 3.1g Carbs; 38.1g Protein; 1.6g Sugars

INGREDIENTS

2 tablespoons sesame oil
2 pounds chuck roast, slice into pieces
1/2 cup beef bone broth
1/2 (12-ounce) bottle beer
1 tablespoon mustard

1 tablespoon granulated sugar
Kosher salt and freshly ground black pepper, to taste
1 teaspoon onion powder
1 teaspoon garlic powder

1 teaspoon ginger powder
1/4 teaspoon ground allspice
2 tablespoons sesame seeds, toasted

DIRECTIONS

Press the "Sauté" button to preheat your Instant Pot. Heat the oil and brown the beef in batches; cook for about 3 minutes per batch.

Add the broth, beer, mustard, sugar, salt, black pepper, onion powder, garlic powder, ginger, and ground allspice.

Secure the lid. Choose the "Manual" mode and cook for 40 minutes at High pressure. Once cooking is complete, use a quick pressure release; carefully remove the lid.

Serve garnished with toasted sesame seeds. Enjoy!

67. Tender Pot Roast with Garden Vegetables

(Ready in about 50 minutes | Servings 5)

Per serving: 425 Calories; 19.2g Fat; 15.5g Carbs; 48.8g Protein; 4.8g Sugars

INGREDIENTS

1 tablespoon lard, melted
2 pounds pot roast
Pink salt and ground black pepper, to taste
1/2 teaspoon ground cumin

1 teaspoon onion powder
1 teaspoon garlic powder
2 cups cream of celery soup
2 celery stalks
4 carrots

1 onion, halved
2 tablespoons fresh parsley leaves, roughly chopped

DIRECTIONS

Press the "Sauté" button to preheat your Instant Pot. Melt the lard and cook your pot roast until slightly brown on all sides.

Season with salt, black pepper, cumin, onion powder, and garlic powder. Pour in the cream of celery soup.

Secure the lid. Choose the "Meat/Stew" mode and cook for 35 minutes at High pressure. Once cooking is complete, use a natural pressure release; carefully remove the lid.

After that, stir in the celery, carrots, and onion.

Secure the lid. Choose the "Manual" mode and cook for 8 minutes at High pressure. Once cooking is complete, use a quick pressure release; carefully remove the lid.

Garnish with fresh parsley and serve immediately. Bon appétit!

68. Hearty Ground Beef Frittata

(Ready in about 25 minutes | Servings 2)

Per serving: 368 Calories; 24.1g Fat; 3.7g Carbs; 33.9g Protein; 2.4g Sugars

INGREDIENTS

1 tablespoon olive oil
1/2 pound ground chuck
4 eggs, whisked
A small bunch of green onions, chopped

1 small tomato, chopped
Sea salt and freshly ground black pepper, to your liking
1/2 teaspoon paprika
1/2 teaspoon garlic powder

DIRECTIONS

Press the "Sauté" button to preheat your Instant Pot. Heat the oil and brown the beef for 2 to 3 minutes, stirring continuously.

Lightly spritz a baking pan with cooking oil. Add all ingredients, including the browned beef to the baking pan.

Cover with foil. Add 1 cup of water and a metal trivet to the Instant Pot. Lower the baking pan onto the trivet.

Secure the lid. Choose the "Manual" mode and cook for 6 minutes at High pressure. Once cooking is complete, use a natural pressure release for 10 minutes; carefully remove the lid.

Slice in half and serve. Bon appétit!

69. Corned Beef Brisket with Root Vegetables

(Ready in about 1 hour 25 minutes | Servings 6)

Per serving: 563 Calories; 35.8g Fat; 19.5g Carbs; 39.3g Protein; 6.5g Sugars

INGREDIENTS

2 ½ pounds corned beef brisket
2 cloves peeled garlic
2 sprigs thyme
1 sprig rosemary
2 tablespoons olive oil

1 cup chicken broth
1/4 cup tomato puree
1 medium leek, sliced
1/2 pound rutabaga, peeled and cut into 1-inch chunks

1/2 pound turnips, peeled and cut into 1-inch chunks
2 parsnips, cut into 1-inch chunks
2 bell peppers, halved

DIRECTIONS

Place the beef brisket, garlic, thyme, rosemary, olive oil, chicken broth, and tomato puree in the inner pot.

Secure the lid. Choose the "Manual" mode and cook for 80 minutes at High pressure. Once cooking is complete, use a quick pressure release; carefully remove the lid.

Add the other ingredients. Gently stir to combine.

Secure the lid. Choose the "Manual" mode and cook for 4 minutes at High pressure. Once cooking is complete, use a quick pressure release; carefully remove the lid. Bon appétit!

70. Old-Fashioned Short Ribs

(Ready in about 1 hour 45 minutes | Servings 6)

Per serving: 655 Calories; 50.8g Fat; 3.3g Carbs; 43.7g Protein; 0.6g Sugars

INGREDIENTS

4 pounds beef short ribs, bone-in
Sea salt and ground black pepper, to taste
2 tablespoons olive oil
1 medium leek, sliced
2 cloves garlic, sliced

1 cup water
1 packet of onion soup mix
1 sprig thyme
1 sprig rosemary
1/2 teaspoon celery seeds

DIRECTIONS

Place all ingredients in the inner pot.
Secure the lid. Choose the "Manual" mode and cook for 90 minutes at High pressure. Once cooking is complete, use a natural pressure release; carefully remove the lid.
Afterwards, place the short ribs under the broiler until the outside is crisp or about 10 minutes.
Transfer the ribs to a serving platter and enjoy!

71. Tequila Boom-Boom Ribs

(Ready in about 40 minutes + marinating time | Servings 8)

Per serving: 399 Calories; 29.2g Fat; 13.3g Carbs; 20.7g Protein; 5g Sugars

INGREDIENTS

2 racks chuck short ribs
2 shots tequila
Kosher salt and cracked black pepper, to taste
2 tablespoons honey
1 teaspoon garlic powder
1 teaspoon shallot powder
1 teaspoon marjoram

1 tablespoon Sriracha sauce
1/2 teaspoon paprika
1 cup apple cider
2 tablespoons tomato paste
1 tablespoon stone ground mustard
1 cup beef bone broth

DIRECTIONS

Place all ingredients, except for beef broth, in a ceramic dish. Cover with a foil and let it marinate for 3 hours in your refrigerator.
Place the beef along with its marinade in the inner pot. Pour in the beef bone broth.
Secure the lid. Choose the "Meat/Stew" mode and cook for 35 minutes at High pressure. Once cooking is complete, use a natural pressure release; carefully remove the lid.
Bon appétit!

72. Margarita Glazed Chuck Roast

(Ready in about 1 hour | Servings 6)

Per serving: 348 Calories; 14.9g Fat; 10.3g Carbs; 42.7g Protein; 7.7g Sugars

INGREDIENTS

2 pounds chuck roast
1 cup beef broth
1/4 cup soy sauce
1/4 cup champagne vinegar
Sea salt and ground black pepper, to taste
1/2 teaspoon red pepper flakes

2 cloves garlic, sliced
Margarita Glaze:
1/2 cup tequila
1/4 cup orange juice
1/4 lime juice
2 tablespoons dark brown sugar

DIRECTIONS

Add the chuck roast, beef broth, soy sauce, champagne vinegar, salt, black pepper, red pepper flakes, and garlic to the inner pot.
Secure the lid. Choose the "Manual" mode and cook for 40 minutes at High pressure. Once cooking is complete, use a natural pressure release for 10 minutes; carefully remove the lid.
Meanwhile, whisk all ingredients for the margarita glaze. Now, glaze the ribs and place under the broiler for 5 minutes; then, turn them over and glaze on the other side. Broil an additional 5 minutes.
Cut the chuck roast into slices and serve the remaining glaze on the side as a sauce. Bon appétit!

73. Juicy Beef Round Roast with Potatoes

(Ready in about 50 minutes | Servings 6)

Per serving: 426 Calories; 11.4g Fat; 29.9g Carbs; 48.7g Protein; 2.8g Sugars

INGREDIENTS

2 tablespoons olive oil, divided
2 pounds beef round roast, cut into
bite-sized pieces
1 white onion, chopped

1 garlic clove, sliced
1 bell pepper, sliced
1/4 cup tomato puree
1/4 cup dry red wine

1 cup beef broth
2 pounds whole small potatoes

DIRECTIONS '

Press the "Sauté" button to preheat your Instant Pot. Heat the oil and brown the beef round roast for 3 to 4 minutes, working in batches.
Add the white onion, garlic, pepper, tomato puree, red wine, and broth.
Secure the lid. Choose the "Meat/Stew" mode and cook for 35 minutes at High pressure. Once cooking is complete, use a quick pressure release; carefully remove the lid.
Add the potatoes. Secure the lid. Choose the "Manual" mode and cook for 10 minutes at High pressure. Once cooking is complete, use a quick pressure release; carefully remove the lid.
Serve in individual bowls and enjoy!

74. Traditional Spaghetti Bolognese

(Ready in about 15 minutes | Servings 4)

Per serving: 585 Calories; 25.6g Fat; 47.8g Carbs; 43.8g Protein; 8.5g Sugars

INGREDIENTS

2 tablespoons olive oil
1 onion, chopped
2 cloves garlic, chopped
1 pound ground beef
1/4 cup rose wine

2 carrots, thinly sliced
1 (28-ounce) can crushed tomatoes
1/2 cup beef bone broth
1 teaspoon dried basil
1 teaspoon dried oregano

1/2 teaspoon dried rosemary
Sea salt and ground black pepper, to taste
19 ounces spaghetti
1/2 cup Romano cheese, preferably
freshly grated

DIRECTIONS

Press the "Sauté" button to preheat your Instant Pot.
Once hot, heat the olive oil and cook the onion, garlic and beef until the beef is no longer pink.
Use rose wine to scrape the remaining bits of meat off the bottom of the inner pot.
Add the carrots, tomatoes, beef bone broth, basil, oregano, rosemary, salt, and black pepper. Secure the lid. Choose the "Poultry" mode and High pressure; cook for 5 minutes. Once cooking is complete, use a quick release.
Add the spaghetti and gently stir to combine.
Secure the lid and choose the "Manual" mode. Cook for 4 minutes longer. Afterwards, use a quick release and carefully remove the lid. Bon appétit!

75. Asian-Style Back Ribs

(Ready in about 1 hour | Servings 8)

Per serving: 480 Calories; 14.5g Fat; 10.3g Carbs; 70g Protein; 4.1g Sugars

INGREDIENTS

2 racks back ribs
10 ounces beers
1 cup Asian BBQ sauce
1 onion, chopped
2 garlic cloves, minced
1 red Fresno chili, sliced

2-inch piece fresh ginger, minced
4 tablespoons tamari sauce
2 tablespoons agave nectar
Sea salt and ground black pepper, to taste
2 teaspoons toasted sesame seeds

DIRECTIONS

Place the back ribs, beers, BBQ sauce, onion, garlic, Fresno chili, and ginger in the inner pot.
Secure the lid. Choose the "Manual" mode and cook for 40 minutes at High pressure. Once cooking is complete, use a natural pressure release for 10 minutes; carefully remove the lid.
Add the tamari sauce, agave, salt and pepper and place the beef ribs under the broiler. Broil ribs for 10 minutes or until they are evenly browned. Serve garnished with sesame seeds. Bon appétit!

76. Classic Beef Bourguignon

(Ready in about 55 minutes | Servings 6)

Per serving: 418 Calories; 23.5g Fat; 5.3g Carbs; 44.1g Protein; 1.5g Sugars

INGREDIENTS

2 pounds boneless beef steak, cut into bite-sized pieces
2 tablespoons cornstarch
Coarse sea salt and ground black pepper, to taste
1 teaspoon red pepper flakes
2 tablespoons olive oil

1 shallot, chopped
2 cloves garlic, sliced
8 ounces mushrooms, sliced
1/2 cup Burgundy wine
1 cup beef bone broth

DIRECTIONS

Toss the beef steak with the cornstarch, salt, black pepper, and red pepper flakes.

Press the "Sauté" button to preheat your Instant Pot. Heat the oil until sizzling. Now, cook the beef until well browned.

Add the remaining ingredients; gently stir to combine.

Secure the lid. Choose the "Manual" mode and cook for 40 minutes at High pressure. Once cooking is complete, use a natural pressure release for 10 minutes; carefully remove the lid.

Divide between individual bowls and serve warm with garlic croutons if desired. Enjoy!

77. Easiest Cheeseburgers Ever

(Ready in about 45 minutes | Servings 6)

Per serving: 441 Calories; 25.4g Fat; 2.9g Carbs; 47.5g Protein; 1.7g Sugars

INGREDIENTS

2 pounds ground chuck
1 tablespoon tomato puree
Sea salt and freshly ground black pepper, to taste
1/2 teaspoon cayenne pepper

1/2 onion, finely chopped
2 garlic cloves, minced
6 ounces Monterey-Jack cheese, sliced

DIRECTIONS

Mix the ground chuck, tomato puree, salt, black pepper, cayenne pepper, onion, and garlic until well combined.

Form the meat mixture into patties. Place your patties on squares of aluminum foil and wrap them loosely.

Add 1 cup water and a metal trivet to the Instant Pot; lower the foil packs onto the top of the metal trivet.

Secure the lid. Choose the "Meat/Stew" mode and cook for 35 minutes at High pressure. Once cooking is complete, use a natural pressure release; carefully remove the lid.

Place your patties on a baking sheet and broil for 5 to 6 minutes. Serve on buns topped with cheese. Enjoy!

78. Puerto Rican Pot Roast

(Ready in about 55 minutes | Servings 4)

Per serving: 393 Calories; 17g Fat; 11.6g Carbs; 48.5g Protein; 1.9g Sugars

INGREDIENTS

2 pounds pot roast, cut into bite-sized chunks
1/4 cup all-purpose flour
1 tablespoon butter, melted
1 habanero pepper, minced

2 garlic cloves, chopped
1 teaspoon smoked Spanish paprika
1 teaspoon achiote seasoning
1 tablespoon bouillon granules
1 ½ cups water

1/2 cup shallots, chopped
2 carrots, cut into bite-sized chunks
2 celery ribs, cut into bite-sized chunks
Sea salt and ground black pepper, to taste

DIRECTIONS

Toss the beef with flour.

Press the "Sauté" button to preheat your Instant Pot. Melt the butter and cook the beef chunks for 4 to 5 minutes, stirring frequently.

Add the habanero pepper, garlic, Spanish paprika, achiote seasoning, bouillon granules, and water.

Secure the lid. Choose the "Meat/Stew" mode and cook for 35 minutes at High pressure. Once cooking is complete, use a natural pressure release; carefully remove the lid.

Add the vegetables, salt, and black pepper.

Secure the lid. Choose the "Manual" mode and cook for 7 minutes at High pressure. Once cooking is complete, use a quick pressure release; carefully remove the lid. Serve the beef and vegetables in individual bowls and enjoy!

79. Balkan-Style Moussaka with Potatoes

(Ready in about 40 minutes | Servings 4)

Per serving: 592 Calories; 33.3g Fat; 31.6g Carbs; 42.8g Protein; 4.9g Sugars

INGREDIENTS

1 tablespoon olive oil
1 ½ pounds ground beef
1 pound Russet potatoes, peeled and thinly sliced

1 shallot, thinly sliced
2 garlic cloves, sliced
1 cup cream of celery soup
1 egg

1/2 cup half-and-half
Kosher salt and ground pepper, to taste
1/2 cup Colby cheese, shredded

DIRECTIONS

Press the "Sauté" button to preheat your Instant Pot. Heat the olive oil and cook the ground beef until no longer pink.

Now, add the layer of potatoes; top with the layer of shallots and garlic. Pour in the soup.

Whisk the egg with half-and-half until well combined; season with salt and pepper. Pour the egg mixture over the top of the meat and vegetable layers.

Smooth the sauce on top with a spatula.

Secure the lid. Choose the "Meat/Stew" mode and cook for 35 minutes at High pressure. Once cooking is complete, use a quick pressure release; carefully remove the lid.

Add the shredded cheese and seal the lid again. Let it sit in the residual heat until the cheese melts. Bon appétit!

80. Mediterranean Steak Salad

(Ready in about 40 minutes | Servings 4)

Per serving: 474 Calories; 28.8g Fat; 3.6g Carbs; 50.6g Protein; 1.7g Sugars

INGREDIENTS

1 ½ pounds steak
1/2 cup red wine
Sea salt and ground black pepper, to taste
1/2 teaspoon red pepper flakes

1 cup water
1/4 cup extra-virgin olive oil
2 tablespoons wine vinegar
1 red onion, thinly sliced
2 sweet peppers, cut into strips

1 butterhead lettuce, separate into leaves
1/2 cup feta cheese, crumbled
1/2 cup black olives, pitted and sliced

DIRECTIONS

Add the steak, red wine, salt, black pepper, red pepper, and water to the inner pot.

Secure the lid. Choose the "Manual" mode and cook for 25 minutes at High pressure. Once cooking is complete, use a natural pressure release for 10 minutes; carefully remove the lid.

Thinly slice the steak against the grain and transfer to a salad bowl. Toss with the olive oil and vinegar.

Add the red onion, peppers, and lettuce; toss to combine well. Top with cheese and olives and serve. Bon appétit!

81. Granny's Classic Beef and Gravy

(Ready in about 1 hour 15 minutes | Servings 6)

Per serving: 470 Calories; 8.8g Fat; 38.5g Carbs; 60.5g Protein; 2.6g Sugars

INGREDIENTS

3 pounds top round roast
Sea salt and ground black pepper, to taste
1 teaspoon paprika

1 teaspoon dried rosemary
1 tablespoon lard, melted
1 ½ pounds fingerling potatoes
1 onion, thinly sliced

2 cloves garlic, smashed
1 bell pepper, deseeded and sliced
3 cups beef bone broth
1 ½ tablespoons potato starch

DIRECTIONS

Toss the beef with the salt, black pepper, paprika, and rosemary until well coated on all sides.

Press the "Sauté" button to preheat your Instant Pot and melt the lard. Sear the beef for about 4 minutes per side until it is browned.

Scatter the potatoes, onion, garlic, peppers around the top round roast. Add the beef bone broth.

Secure the lid. Choose the "Manual" mode and cook for 60 minutes at High pressure. Once cooking is complete, use a natural pressure release for 10 minutes; carefully remove the lid.

Transfer the roast and vegetables to a serving platter; shred the roast with 2 forks.

Mix the potato starch with 4 tablespoons of water. Press the "Sauté" button to preheat your Instant Pot again. Once the liquid is boiling, add the slurry and let it cook until the gravy thickens.

Taste and adjust the seasonings. Serve warm.

82. Yoshinoya Beef Bowl

(Ready in about 40 minutes + marinating time | Servings 4)

Per serving: 598 Calories; 15.2g Fat; 54.5g Carbs; 57.6g Protein; 7.9g Sugars

INGREDIENTS

2 pounds beef stew meat, cut into
1-inch cubes
1/4 cup Shoyu sauce
1/4 cup brown sugar
2 cloves garlic, minced
1 tablespoon cider vinegar

2 tablespoons sake
2 tablespoons pickled red ginger
1 teaspoon hot sauce
2 tablespoons cornstarch
1 tablespoon olive oil
1 teaspoon onion powder

2 bay leaves
1 rosemary sprig
Salt and black pepper, to taste
1 cup beef broth
2 eggs, whisked
1 cup steamed rice

DIRECTIONS

In a ceramic bowl, place the meat, Shoyu sauce, brown sugar, garlic, cider vinegar, sake, ginger, and hot sauce. Let it marinate for 2 hours.
Discard the marinade and toss the beef cubes with the cornstarch.
Press the "Sauté" button and heat the oil until sizzling. Brown the beef cubes for 3 to 4 minutes, stirring periodically.
Add the onion powder, bay leaves, rosemary sprig, salt, black pepper, and beef broth.
Secure the lid. Choose the "Meat/Stew" mode and cook for 35 minutes at High pressure. Once cooking is complete, use a quick pressure release; carefully remove the lid.
Slowly stir in the whisked eggs and press the "Sauté" button. Continue to cook until the eggs are done.
Serve over steamed rice.

83. Chunky Beef Chili

(Ready in about 25 minutes | Servings 4)

Per serving: 393 Calories; 17.4g Fat; 23.6g Carbs; 37.4g Protein; 6.9g Sugars

INGREDIENTS

1 tablespoon olive oil
1 pound ground chuck
1/2 cup leeks, chopped
2 cloves garlic, minced
1 teaspoon dried oregano
1 teaspoon dried basil

1/2 teaspoon cumin powder
1 teaspoon ancho chili powder
Kosher salt and ground black pepper,
to taste
1 cup beef stock
1 red chili pepper, minced

2 (15-ounces) cans black beans,
drained and rinsed
1 (14-ounce) can tomatoes, diced
4 tablespoon tomato ketchup

DIRECTIONS

Press the "Sauté" button and heat the oil. Once hot, cook the ground chuck, leeks, and garlic until the meat is no longer pink.
Add the remaining ingredients; gently stir to combine.
Secure the lid. Choose the "Manual" mode and cook for 15 minutes at High pressure. Once cooking is complete, use a quick pressure release; carefully remove the lid.
Serve in individual bowls garnished with green onions if desired. Bon appétit!

84. Homestyle Sloppy Joes

(Ready in about 20 minutes | Servings 4)

Per serving: 475 Calories; 16.6g Fat; 43g Carbs; 37.6g Protein; 9.2g Sugars

INGREDIENTS

1 teaspoon lard
1 pound ground beef
1 onion, chopped
1 teaspoon fresh garlic, minced
1 sweet pepper, chopped
1 serrano pepper, chopped

Salt and ground black pepper, to taste
1/2 teaspoon red pepper flakes
1 tablespoon stone ground mustard
1 teaspoon celery seeds
1/2 teaspoon dried rosemary
1 cup beef stock

1/2 cup tomato puree
2 tablespoons ketchup
1 teaspoon brown sugar
4 soft hamburger buns

DIRECTIONS

Press the "Sauté" button and melt the lard. Once hot, cook the ground beef until it is brown.
Add the onion, garlic, and peppers; continue to cook for 1 to 2 minutes more.
Add the salt, black pepper, red pepper flakes, mustard, celery seeds, rosemary, stock, tomato puree, ketchup, and brown sugar. Mix to combine.
Secure the lid. Choose the "Manual" mode and cook for 5 minutes at High pressure. Once cooking is complete, use a natural pressure release for 10 minutes; carefully remove the lid.
Serve on hamburger buns and enjoy!

85. Beef and Rice Stuffed Peppers

(Ready in about 25 minutes | Servings 3)

Per serving: 331 Calories; 13.5g Fat; 36.9g Carbs; 24.1g Protein; 15.2g Sugars

INGREDIENTS

1/2 cup parboiled rice
1 pound ground beef
1 onion, chopped
2 garlic cloves, minced
1 carrot, grated

Sea salt and ground black pepper, to taste
1 teaspoon cayenne pepper
1/2 teaspoon celery seeds
1/2 teaspoon mustard seeds
1 teaspoon basil

3 large bell peppers, deseeded, cored
and halved
1 cup tomato puree
2 tablespoons ketchup
1 cup cheddar cheese, grated

DIRECTIONS

In a mixing bowl, thoroughly combine the rice, ground beef, onion, garlic, carrot, salt, black pepper, cayenne pepper, celery seeds, mustard seeds, and basil.

Add 1 cup of water and a metal trivet to the bottom. Fill the pepper halves with the rice/meat mixture. Place the peppers in a casserole dish; add the tomato puree and ketchup.

Lower the casserole dish onto the trivet in the Instant Pot.

Secure the lid. Choose the "Manual" mode and cook for 9 minutes at High pressure. Once cooking is complete, use a natural pressure release for 5 minutes; carefully remove the lid.

Afterwards, broil your peppers until the cheese melts approximately 5 minutes. Serve and enjoy!

86. Simple Traditional Bulgogi

(Ready in about 50 minutes + marinating time | Servings 4)

Per serving: 530 Calories; 29.5g Fat; 19g Carbs; 50.6g Protein; 13.6g Sugars

INGREDIENTS

1/4 cup tamari sauce
2 tablespoons Korean rice wine
2 tablespoons agave syrup
Salt and black pepper, to taste

2 pounds rib-eye steak, cut into strips
2 tablespoons sesame oil
1 onion, sliced
2 cloves garlic, minced

1 tablespoon pickled red ginger
1/2 Asian pear, cored and sliced
2 tablespoons sesame seeds, toasted

DIRECTIONS

Mix the tamari sauce, rice, wine, agave syrup, salt, and black pepper in a ceramic bowl; add the beef, cover, and let it marinate for 1 hour.

Press the "Sauté" button and heat the sesame oil. Once hot, brown the beef strips in batches. Add the onion, garlic, pickled ginger, and Asian pear.

Secure the lid. Choose the "Meat/Stew" mode and cook for 35 minutes at High pressure. Once cooking is complete, use a natural pressure release for 10 minutes; carefully remove the lid.

Serve garnished with toasted sesame seeds. Enjoy!

87. Delicious Parmesan Meatballs

Ready in about 40 minutes | Servings 4)

Per serving: 509 Calories; 30.2g Fat; 14.6g Carbs; 43.1g Protein; 4.3g Sugars

INGREDIENTS

2/3 pound ground beef
1/3 pound beef sausage, crumbled
1 shallot, minced
2 cloves garlic, smashed
1 egg, beaten

2 slices bread (soaked in 4 tablespoons
of milk)
1/4 cup parmesan cheese
Kosher salt and ground black pepper,
to taste

1/2 teaspoon cayenne pepper
1 tablespoon canola oil
1 cup tomato puree
1 cup chicken bone broth
1 teaspoon Dijon mustard

DIRECTIONS

In a mixing dish, thoroughly combine the beef, sausage, shallot, garlic, egg, soaked bread, parmesan, salt, black pepper, and cayenne pepper Mix to combine well and shape the mixture into 12 meatballs. Set aside.

Press the "Sauté" button and heat the oil. Once hot, brown the meatballs for 7 to 8 minutes, rolling them around so that they will brown evenly all around.

Mix the tomato puree, broth and mustard in the inner pot. Gently fold in the meatballs.

Secure the lid. Choose the "Meat/Stew" mode and cook for 20 minutes at High pressure. Once cooking is complete, use a natural pressure release for 10 minutes; carefully remove the lid. Bon appétit!

88. Filet Mignon with Wild Mushrooms

Ready in about 30 minutes | Servings 4)

Per serving: 332 Calories; 14.6g Fat; 8.8g Carbs; 41.8g Protein; 1.3g Sugars

INGREDIENTS

1 ½ pounds filet mignon, about 1 ½-inch thick
1/2 teaspoon sea salt
1/2 teaspoon red pepper flakes, crushed
1/2 teaspoon ground black pepper
1/4 cup all-purpose flour

2 tablespoons butter
2 cups wild mushrooms, sliced
1 onion, thinly sliced
2 garlic cloves, sliced
1 cup chicken broth

DIRECTIONS

Toss the filet mignon with salt, red pepper, black pepper, and flour.
Press the "Sauté" button and melt the butter. Once hot, sear the filet mignon for 2 minutes. Turn it over and cook for 2 minutes more on the other side.
Add the remaining ingredients and secure the lid.
Choose the "Meat/Stew" mode and cook for 20 minutes at High pressure. Once cooking is complete, use a quick pressure release; carefully remove the lid.
You can thicken the sauce on the "Sauté" mode if desired. Serve warm.

89. Saturday Afternoon Meatloaf

(Ready in about 35 minutes | Servings 4)

Per serving: 564 Calories; 28.7g Fat; 23.8g Carbs; 51.1g Protein; 10.5g Sugars

INGREDIENTS

1 egg, beaten
1/2 cup milk
1 cup tortilla chips, crushed
1 small-sized onion, finely chopped
1 sweet pepper, finely chopped

2 cloves garlic, minced
Sea salt and ground black pepper, to taste
1/2 teaspoon rosemary
1 pound ground beef

1/2 pound ground pork
1 cup tomato puree
1 teaspoon mustard
2 tablespoons brown sugar
1 tablespoon tamari sauce

DIRECTIONS

Place a steamer rack inside the inner pot; add 1/2 cup of water. Cut 1 sheet of heavy-duty foil and brush with cooking spray.
In mixing dish, combine the egg, milk, tortilla chips, onion, sweet pepper, garlic, salt, black pepper, rosemary, and ground meat.
Shape the meat mixture into a loaf; place the meatloaf in the center of foil. Wrap your meatloaf in foil and lower onto the steamer rack.
Secure the lid. Choose the "Meat/Stew" mode and cook for 20 minutes at High pressure. Once cooking is complete, use a quick pressure release; carefully remove the lid.
Then, transfer your meatloaf to a cutting board. Let it stand for 10 minutes before cutting and serving. Bon appétit!

90. Keto-Friendly Cheeseburger Cups

(Ready in about 30 minutes | Servings 6)

Per serving: 390 Calories; 24.8g Fat; 6g Carbs; 33.8g Protein; 3.9g Sugars

INGREDIENTS

1 ½ pounds ground beef
Sea salt and ground black pepper, to taste
1 teaspoon onion powder

1/2 teaspoon garlic powder
1 tablespoon Italian seasoning blend
1/2 cup tomato paste

1 tablespoon maple syrup
1 teaspoon Dijon mustard
1 cup Cheddar cheese, shredded

DIRECTIONS

Spritz a silicone muffin pan with non-stick cooking oil.
In a large bowl, thoroughly combine the ground beef, salt, black pepper, onion powder, garlic powder, Italian seasoning blend, tomato paste, and Dijon mustard with your hands.
Scrape the beef mixture into the silicone muffin pan.
Place a steamer rack inside the inner pot; add 1/2 cup of water. Lower the muffin pan onto the rack.
Secure the lid. Choose the "Manual" mode and cook for 20 minutes at High pressure. Once cooking is complete, use a quick pressure release; carefully remove the lid.
Top with cheese; allow the cheese to melt and serve warm.

91. Delicious Cheeseburger Quiche

(Ready in about 45 minutes | Servings 4)

Per serving: 465 Calories; 28.2g Fat; 9.4g Carbs; 41.5g Protein; 5.7g Sugars

INGREDIENTS

1 tablespoon olive oil
1 pound ground beef
1 onion, chopped
2 cloves garlic, minced
Sea salt and ground black pepper, to taste

1/2 teaspoon basil
1/2 teaspoon thyme
1/2 teaspoon oregano
4 eggs
1/2 cup milk

2 ounces cream cheese, at room temperature
1 cup cheddar cheese, shredded
1 tomato, sliced

DIRECTIONS

Press the "Sauté" button and heat the olive oil until sizzling. Now, cook the ground beef until no longer pink.

Transfer the browned beef to a lightly greased soufflé dish. Add the onion, garlic, and seasonings.

In a mixing dish, whisk the eggs, milk, and cream cheese. Top with the cheddar cheese. Cover with a foil.

Place the rack and 1 ½ cups of water inside the Instant Pot. Lower the soufflé dish onto the rack.

Secure the lid. Choose the "Manual" mode and cook for 30 minutes at High pressure. Once cooking is complete, use a quick pressure release; carefully remove the lid.

Let it rest for 10 minutes before slicing and serving. Garnish with tomatoes and serve. Enjoy!

92. The Classic French Châteaubriand

(Ready in about 25 minutes | Servings 2)

Per serving: 559 Calories; 33.3g Fat; 19.6g Carbs; 47.1g Protein; 5.3g Sugars

INGREDIENTS

1 pound center-cut beef tenderloin
1 cup cream of onion soup
1 tablespoon butter
1 shallot, sliced

2 cloves garlic, finely minced
1/2 cup red wine
Kosher salt and ground black pepper, to taste
1 tablespoon fresh tarragon

DIRECTIONS

Add the beef and cream of onion soup to a lightly greased inner pot.

Secure the lid. Choose the "Manual" mode and cook for 13 minutes at High pressure. Once cooking is complete, use a quick pressure release; carefully remove the lid.

Press the "Sauté" button to preheat your Instant Pot. Melt the butter and cook the shallots until tender or about 3 minutes.

Then, stir in the garlic; cook an additional 30 seconds or so.

Pour the wine into the inner pot, scraping up all the browned bits on the bottom of the pan. Add the salt, pepper, and tarragon.

Continue boiling the sauce until it reduces by half. Serve the sliced chateaubriand with the wine sauce and enjoy!

93. Double Cheese Burger Dip

(Ready in about 25 minutes | Servings 10)

Per serving: 294 Calories; 14.7g Fat; 1.6g Carbs; 38.9g Protein; 0.8g Sugars

INGREDIENTS

3 pounds ground chuck roast
2 cloves garlic, minced
1 teaspoon shallot powder
1 teaspoon mustard powder
1 teaspoon dried rosemary

3 bay leaves
2 tablespoons Worcestershire sauce
4 cups water
4 ounces cream cheese, room temperature
1/2 cup mozzarella, shredded

DIRECTIONS

Add all ingredients, except for the cheese, to your Instant Pot.

Secure the lid. Choose the "Manual" mode and cook for 20 minutes at High pressure. Once cooking is complete, use a quick pressure release; carefully remove the lid.

Top with the cheese and allow it to stand until the cheese has melted

Serve with assorted vegetables or breadsticks if desired. Bon appétit!

94. Famous Philly Cheesesteaks

(Ready in about 35 minutes | Servings 8)

Per serving: 579 Calories; 30.6g Fat; 27.1g Carbs; 45.9g Protein; 6.1g Sugars

INGREDIENTS

1 tablespoon lard, melted
2 ½ pounds top sirloin steak, sliced into thin strips
2 onions, sliced
2 sweet peppers, deseeded and sliced
1 red chili pepper, minced
Kosher salt and freshly ground pepper, to taste
1 teaspoon paprika

1/2 cup dry red wine
1 cup beef broth
8 Hoagie rolls
1 tablespoon Dijon mustard
8 ounces yellow American cheese, sliced
8 ounces mild Provolone cheese, sliced

DIRECTIONS

Press the "Sauté" button to preheat your Instant Pot. Melt the lard and cook your steak for about 4 minutes.
Add the onions, peppers, salt, black pepper, paprika, wine, and broth.
Secure the lid. Choose the "Manual" mode and cook for 25 minutes at High pressure. Once cooking is complete, use a quick pressure release; carefully remove the lid.
Serve the meat mixture in rolls topped with mustard and cheese. Bon appétit!

95. Perfect New York Strip with Cream Sauce

(Ready in about 30 minutes | Servings 4)

Per serving: 439 Calories; 21.9g Fat; 9.8g Carbs; 50g Protein; 2.3g Sugars

INGREDIENTS

2 tablespoons sesame oil
2 pounds New York strip, sliced into thin strips
Kosher salt and ground black pepper, to taste
1/2 cup dry red wine
1 cup cream of mushroom soup

1 small leek, sliced
2 cloves garlic, sliced
2 carrots, sliced
1 tablespoon tamari sauce
1/2 cup heavy cream

DIRECTIONS

Press the "Sauté" button to preheat your Instant Pot. Heat the sesame oil until sizzling. Once hot, brown the beef strips in batches.
Add wine to deglaze the pan. Stir in the remaining ingredients, except for the heavy cream.
Secure the lid. Choose the "Manual" mode and cook for 20 minutes at High pressure. Once cooking is complete, use a quick pressure release; carefully remove the lid.
Remove the beef from the cooking liquid. Mash the vegetables using a potato masher.
Press the "Sauté" button one more time. Now, bring the liquid to a boil. Heat off and stir in the heavy cream.
Spoon the sauce over the New York strip and serve immediately. Enjoy!

96. Creamed Delmonico Steak

(Ready in about 20 minutes | Servings 4)

Per serving: 572 Calories; 36.9g Fat; 5.8g Carbs; 55.3g Protein; 3.4g Sugars

INGREDIENTS

2 tablespoons butter
1 ½ pounds Delmonico steak, cubed
2 cloves garlic, minced
1 cup beef broth
1 cup double cream

1/4 cup sour cream
1 teaspoon cayenne pepper
Sea salt and ground black pepper, to taste
1/2 cup gorgonzola cheese, shredded

DIRECTIONS

Press the "Sauté" button to preheat your Instant Pot. Melt the butter and brown the beef cubes in batches for about 4 minutes per batch.
Add the garlic, broth, double cream, and sour cream to the inner pot; season with cayenne pepper, salt, and black pepper.
Secure the lid. Choose the "Manual" mode and cook for 10 minutes at High pressure. Once cooking is complete, use a quick pressure release; carefully remove the lid.
Top with gorgonzola cheese and serve. Bon appétit!

97. Asian Braised Beef Shanks

(Ready in about 45 minutes | Servings 4)

Per serving: 316 Calories; 11.4g Fat; 11.6g Carbs; 39.2g Protein; 1.8g Sugars

INGREDIENTS

1 ½ pounds beef shank

1 teaspoon garlic, minced

1 tablespoon sesame oil

1/2 cup rice wine

2 tablespoons soy sauce

1 teaspoon Chinese five spice powder

1 dried red chili, sliced

2 cloves star anise

1 cup instant dashi granules

1 cup water

DIRECTIONS

Add all ingredients to the inner pot.

Secure the lid. Choose the "Manual" mode and cook for 30 minutes at High pressure. Once cooking is complete, use a natural pressure release for 10 minutes; carefully remove the lid.

Slice across the grain and serve over hot cooked rice if desired. Enjoy!

PORK

98. Quick Pork Goulash

(Ready in about 25 minutes | Servings 4)

Per serving: 570 Calories; 37.4g Fat; 22.2g Carbs; 38.2g Protein; 5.1g Sugars

INGREDIENTS

1 tablespoon olive oil
1 pound ground pork
1/2 pound ground turkey
1 onion, chopped
2 cloves garlic, minced
1 bay leaf

1 thyme sprig
1 rosemary sprig
1 teaspoon paprika
Sea salt and ground black pepper, to taste
1 cup beef bone broth

1/2 cup rice wine
2 ripe tomatoes, pureed
1 cup sweet corn kernels
1 cup green peas
1/2 cup Colby cheese, shredded

DIRECTIONS

Press the "Sauté" button to preheat your Instant Pot. Heat the oil and sear the meat until no longer pink, stirring continuously with a spatula. Use a splash of wine to deglaze the pan.

Add the onion and garlic to the meat mixture and cook an additional 3 minutes or until tender and fragrant.

Next, stir in the spices, broth, wine, and tomatoes.

Secure the lid. Choose the "Manual" mode and cook for 10 minutes at High pressure. Once cooking is complete, use a quick pressure release; carefully remove the lid.

Press the "Sauté" button and add the corn and green peas. Cook an additional 3 minutes or until everything is heated through.

Top with cheese and allow it to stand until the cheese has melted. Bon appétit!

99. Old-Fashioned Roast Pork

(Ready in about 1 hour 10 minutes | Servings 6)

Per serving: 545 Calories; 35.4g Fat; 4.2g Carbs; 48.2g Protein; 1.5g Sugars

INGREDIENTS

2 garlic cloves, minced
2 teaspoons stone-ground mustard
Sea salt and ground black pepper, to taste

1 teaspoon freshly grated lemon zest
2 ½ pounds pork butt
1 tablespoon lard, at room temperature

1/2 cup red wine
1 large leek, sliced into long pieces
1 carrot, halved lengthwise

DIRECTIONS

Combine the garlic, mustard, salt, pepper and lemon zest in a mixing bowl. Using your hands, spread the rub evenly onto the pork butt.

Press the "Sauté" button to preheat your Instant Pot. Melt the lard and sear the meat for 3 minutes per side.

Pour a splash of wine into the inner pot, scraping any bits from the bottom with a wooden spoon.

Place a trivet and 1 cup of water in the bottom of the inner pot. Lower the pork butt onto the trivet; scatter the leeks and carrots around.

Secure the lid. Choose the "Manual" mode and cook for 50 minutes at High pressure. Once cooking is complete, use a natural pressure release for 10 minutes; carefully remove the lid.

Transfer the pork butt to a cutting board and let it sit for 5 minutes before carving and serving. Enjoy!

100. Milk-Braised Pork Loin Roast

(Ready in about 45 minutes | Servings 6)

Per serving: 436 Calories; 22.8g Fat; 2.6g Carbs; 52.2g Protein; 2.2g Sugars

INGREDIENTS

2 tablespoons sesame oil
2 ½ pounds pork loin roast, boneless
Sea salt and freshly ground black pepper, to taste

1 teaspoon dried basil
1 teaspoon dried oregano
1/2 teaspoon paprika
1/2 lemon, juiced and zested

1 cup vegetable broth
1 cup milk

DIRECTIONS

Press the "Sauté" button and heat the oil until sizzling; once hot, sear the pork for 4 to 5 minutes or until browned on all sides. Work in batches.

Add the remaining ingredients.

Secure the lid. Choose the "Meat/Stew" mode and cook for 35 minutes at High pressure. Once cooking is complete, use a quick pressure release; carefully remove the lid.

Turn on your broiler. Roast the pork under the broiler for about 3 minutes or until the skin is crisp.

To carve the pork, remove the cracklings and cut the crisp pork skin into strips. Carve the pork roast across the grain into thin slices and serve.

101. Spicy Paprika and Pork Omelet

(Ready in about 25 minutes | Servings 2)

Per serving: 449 Calories; 33.6g Fat; 4.3g Carbs; 32.2g Protein; 1.6g Sugars

INGREDIENTS

1 tablespoon canola oil
1/2 pound ground pork
1 yellow onion, thinly sliced
1 red chili pepper, minced

4 eggs, whisked
1/2 teaspoon garlic powder
1/3 teaspoon cumin powder
1 teaspoon oyster sauce

Kosher salt and ground black pepper, to taste
1/2 teaspoon paprika

DIRECTIONS

Press the "Sauté" button and heat the oil until sizzling; once hot, cook the ground pork until no longer pink, crumbling with a spatula. Add the onion and pepper; cook an additional 2 minutes. Whisk the eggs with the remaining ingredients. Pour the egg mixture over the meat mixture in the inner pot.

Secure the lid. Choose the "Manual" mode and cook for 8 minutes at High pressure. Once cooking is complete, use a natural pressure release for 10 minutes; carefully remove the lid. Bon appétit!

102. Barbecued Pork Spare Ribs

(Ready in about 45 minutes | Servings 4)

Per serving: 500 Calories; 28.6g Fat; 8.9g Carbs; 49.2g Protein; 6.1g Sugars

INGREDIENTS

2 pounds pork spare ribs, cut into 4 equal portions
1 tablespoon sea salt
1/2 teaspoon black pepper
1/2 teaspoon chili flakes

1 teaspoon cayenne pepper
1 teaspoon shallot powder
1 teaspoon garlic powder
1 teaspoon fennel seeds
1 tablespoon sugar

1 cup chicken stock
1 cup tomato ketchup
1/4 cup dark soy sauce

DIRECTIONS

Generously sprinkle the pork spare ribs with all spices and sugar. Add the chicken stock and secure the lid.

Choose the "Meat/Stew" mode and cook for 35 minutes at High pressure. Once cooking is complete, use a quick pressure release; carefully remove the lid.

Transfer the pork ribs to a baking pan. Mix the tomato ketchup and soy sauce; pour the mixture over the pork ribs and roast in the preheated oven at 425 degrees F for 6 to 8 minutes. Bon appétit!

103. Pork Medallions with Asian Flair

(Ready in about 30 minutes | Servings 3)

Per serving: 355 Calories; 10.1g Fat; 13g Carbs; 51g Protein; 7.2g Sugars

INGREDIENTS

1 tablespoon sesame oil
1 ½ pounds pork medallions
1/2 cup tamari sauce
1/2 cup chicken stock
1/4 cup rice vinegar
1/2 teaspoon cayenne pepper
1/2 teaspoon salt

1 tablespoon maple syrup
1 tablespoon Sriracha sauce
2 cloves garlic, minced
6 ounces mushrooms, chopped
1 tablespoon arrowroot powder, dissolved in 2 tablespoons of water

DIRECTIONS

Press the "Sauté" button and heat the oil; once hot, cook the pork medallions for 3 minutes per side.

Add the tamari sauce, chicken stock, vinegar, cayenne pepper, salt, maple syrup, Sriracha, garlic, and mushrooms to the inner pot.

Secure the lid. Choose the "Meat/Stew" mode and cook for 20 minutes at High pressure. Once cooking is complete, use a quick pressure release; carefully remove the lid. Remove the pork from the inner pot.

Add the thickener to the cooking liquid. Press the "Sauté" button again and let it boil until the sauce has reduced slightly and the flavors have concentrated.

Serve over hot steamed rice if desired. Enjoy!

104. Cholula Pork Sandwiches

(Ready in about 40 minutes | Servings 4)

Per serving: 516 Calories; 14.4g Fat; 37.1g Carbs; 56.7g Protein; 15.2g Sugars

INGREDIENTS

1 tablespoon olive oil

2 pounds pork shoulder roast

1/2 cup tomato paste

1/2 cup beef bone broth

1/4 cup balsamic vinegar

1/4 cup brown sugar

1 tablespoon mustard

1 teaspoon Cholula hot sauce

2 cloves garlic, minced

1 teaspoon dried marjoram

4 hamburger buns

DIRECTIONS

Add all ingredients, except for the hamburger buns, to the inner pot.

Secure the lid. Choose the "Meat/Stew" mode and cook for 35 minutes at High pressure. Once cooking is complete, use a quick pressure release; carefully remove the lid.

Remove the pork from the inner pot and shred with two forks. Spoon the pulled pork into the hamburger buns and serve with your favorite toppings. Bon appétit!

105. Pork Chops in White Mushroom Sauce

(Ready in about 30 minutes | Servings 6)

Per serving: 438 Calories; 25.8g Fat; 7.2g Carbs; 42.8g Protein; 2.7g Sugars

INGREDIENTS

2 tablespoons butter

6 pork chops

1 tablespoon Italian seasoning blend

1/2 teaspoon coarse sea salt

1/2 teaspoon cracked black pepper

1 pound white mushrooms, sliced

1 tablespoon fresh coriander, chopped

1 teaspoon dill weed, minced

2 cloves garlic crushed

1/2 cup double cream

1/2 cup cream of onion soup

DIRECTIONS

Press the "Sauté" button and melt the butter. Once hot, sear the pork chops until golden browned, about 4 minutes per side.

Add the remaining ingredients and gently stir to combine.

Secure the lid. Choose the "Meat/Stew" mode and cook for 20 minutes at High pressure. Once cooking is complete, use a quick pressure release; carefully remove the lid.

Serve over mashed potatoes. Bon appétit!

106. Aunt's Pork and Pepper Casserole

(Ready in about 40 minutes | Servings 4)

Per serving: 501 Calories; 26.8g Fat; 10g Carbs; 53.5g Protein; 4.7g Sugars

INGREDIENTS

1 tablespoon lard, melted

2 pounds pork steaks, cut into large pieces

1 onion, thinly

2 cloves garlic, sliced

4 mixed colored peppers, deveined and chopped

1 serrano pepper, deveined and chopped

Sea salt and ground black pepper, to taste

1 tablespoon Cajun seasonings

4 sage leaves

1 teaspoon mustard

2 tablespoons red wine

1 cup chicken broth

1 cup goat cheese, crumbled

DIRECTIONS

Press the "Sauté" button and melt the lard; once hot, sear the pork in batches until golden brown all over.

Add the onions, garlic, and peppers. Season with salt, black pepper, and Cajun seasonings. Add the sage leaves, mustard, wine, and broth.

Secure the lid. Choose the "Manual" mode and cook for 30 minutes at High pressure. Once cooking is complete, use a quick pressure release; carefully remove the lid.

Add the goat cheese on top, seal the lid again, and let it sit in the residual heat until the cheese melts.

Let it rest for 5 to 10 minutes before slicing and serving. Bon appétit!

107. Lemon Rosemary Pork Medallions

(Ready in about 30 minutes | Servings 4)

Per serving: 340 Calories; 12.5g Fat; 1.7g Carbs; 52.2g Protein; 0.4g Sugars

INGREDIENTS

1 tablespoon butter, melted

2 pounds pork medallions

Kosher salt and freshly ground black pepper, to taste

1 teaspoon garlic powder

1 teaspoon shallot powder

1 cup vegetable broth

2 sprigs fresh rosemary

1 lemon, juice and zest

DIRECTIONS

Press the "Sauté" button and melt the butter. Sear the pork medallions until no longer pink.

Add the salt, black pepper, garlic powder, shallot powder, and vegetable broth.

Secure the lid. Choose the "Manual" mode and cook for 20 minutes at High pressure. Once cooking is complete, use a quick pressure release; carefully remove the lid.

Remove the pork medallions to a serving platter. Now, add the fresh rosemary, lemon juice and zest to the cooking liquid. Let it simmer for 2 to 3 minutes.

Spoon the sauce over the pork medallions and serve immediately. Enjoy!

108. Mexican Pork Carnitas

(Ready in about 50 minutes | Servings 4)

Per serving: 555 Calories; 12.4g Fat; 54.3g Carbs; 55.2g Protein; 29.5g Sugars

INGREDIENTS

2 pounds pork butt roast

1 cup Mexican coke

1 cup beef bone broth

1/2 cup tomato ketchup

1/4 cup honey

1 teaspoon liquid smoke

2 tablespoons balsamic vinegar

1 jalapeno, deveined and chopped

1/2 teaspoon cumin powder

1 teaspoon shallot powder

1 teaspoon garlic powder

1/2 teaspoon Mexican oregano

Sea salt and ground black pepper, to taste

4 warm tortillas

DIRECTIONS

Place all ingredients, except for the tortillas, in the inner pot.

Secure the lid. Choose the "Meat/Stew" mode and cook for 35 minutes at High pressure. Once cooking is complete, use a quick pressure release; carefully remove the lid.

Remove the pork from the inner pot and shred with two forks.

Transfer the pork to a baking sheet lightly greased with cooking spray. Pour 1 ladle of the cooking liquid over the pork. Broil for 7 to 10 minutes until the meat becomes crispy on the edges.

Spoon the pulled pork into the warm tortillas and serve with your favorite toppings. Bon appétit!

109. Bavarian-Style Pork and Sauerkraut

(Ready in about 40 minutes | Servings 4)

Per serving: 435 Calories; 27.7g Fat; 6.5g Carbs; 38.2g Protein; 2.5g Sugars

INGREDIENTS

1 tablespoon oil

1 ½ pounds pork shoulder, cubed

4 ounces pork sausage, sliced

Sea salt and, to taste

1/2 teaspoon black peppercorns

14 ounces sauerkraut, drained

1 cup beef broth

1 onion, sliced

2 garlic cloves, minced

2 bay leaves

1/2 teaspoon smoked paprika

1 dried chili pepper, minced

DIRECTIONS

Press the "Sauté" button and heat the oil. Once hot, cook the pork and sausage until they are no longer pink.

Add the remaining ingredients; gently stir to combine.

Secure the lid. Choose the "Meat/Stew" mode and cook for 35 minutes at High pressure. Once cooking is complete, use a quick pressure release; carefully remove the lid. Enjoy!

110. Parmesan Pork Chops

(Ready in about 20 minutes | Servings 4)

Per serving: 475 Calories; 21.7g Fat; 5.8g Carbs; 60.4g Protein; 0.7g Sugars

INGREDIENTS

1 tablespoon lard, at room temperature
4 pork chops, bone-in
Sea salt and freshly ground black pepper, to taste

1/4 cup tomato puree
1 cup chicken bone broth
4 ounces parmesan cheese, preferably freshly grated

DIRECTIONS

Press the "Sauté" button and melt the lard. Sear the pork chops for 3 to 4 minutes per side. Season with salt and pepper.
Place the tomato puree and chicken broth in the inner pot.
Secure the lid. Choose the "Manual" mode and cook for 10 minutes at High pressure. Once cooking is complete, use a natural pressure release; carefully remove the lid.
Top with parmesan cheese and serve warm. Bon appétit!

111. Festive Pork Roast with Gravy

(Ready in about 20 minutes | Servings 4)

Per serving: 388 Calories; 22.1g Fat; 6.8g Carbs; 36.7g Protein; 3.7g Sugars

INGREDIENTS

2 tablespoons olive oil
1 pound Boston-style butt, sliced into four pieces
Coarse sea salt and freshly ground black pepper, to taste
1 shallot, sliced
2 cloves garlic, sliced
1 stalk celery, chopped
1 bell pepper, deveined and sliced

1/2 cup apple juice
1/2 cup chicken broth
1 tablespoon stone ground mustard
1 teaspoon basil
1 teaspoon thyme
2 tablespoons plain flour, mixed with 2 tablespoons of cold water

DIRECTIONS

Press the "Sauté" button and heat the oil. Then, sear the Boston butt until it is golden brown on all sides.
Add the salt, pepper, shallot, garlic, celery, bell pepper, apple juice, chicken broth, mustard, basil, and thyme to the inner pot.
Secure the lid. Choose the "Manual" mode and cook for 15 minutes at High pressure. Once cooking is complete, use a quick pressure release; carefully remove the lid. Remove the meat from the cooking liquid.
Add the slurry and press the "Sauté" button one more time. Let it simmer until your sauce has thickened. Spoon the gravy over the pork and serve. Bon appétit!

112. Venezuelan-Style Arepas with Pork

(Ready in about 40 minutes | Servings 6)

Per serving: 386 Calories; 17.2g Fat; 21.2g Carbs; 34.7g Protein; 5.4g Sugars

INGREDIENTS

1 tablespoon butter
2 pounds boneless pork butt roast
1 cup cream of mushroom soup
2 tablespoons Worcestershire sauce
4 cloves garlic, finely chopped
Sea salt and ground black pepper, to taste

1 teaspoon cayenne pepper
1 teaspoon garlic powder
1 teaspoon onion powder
1/4 teaspoon ground cumin
6 Venezuelan-style arepas (corn cakes)

DIRECTIONS

Place all ingredients, except for the arepas, in the inner pot.
Secure the lid. Choose the "Meat/Stew" mode and cook for 35 minutes at High pressure. Once cooking is complete, use a quick pressure release; carefully remove the lid.
Remove the pork from the inner pot and shred with two forks.
Fill each arepa with the pork mixture and serve with your favorite toppings. Enjoy!

113. Loin Chops with Garlic Mayo

(Ready in about 25 minutes | Servings 4)

Per serving: 444 Calories; 30.5g Fat; 2.1g Carbs; 38.1g Protein; 0.8g Sugars

INGREDIENTS

1 ½ pounds center-cut loin chops
Kosher salt and ground black pepper, to taste
1 teaspoon paprika
1/2 teaspoon mustard powder
1/2 teaspoon celery seeds

1 tablespoon canola oil
1 cup beef bone broth
1/2 cup mayonnaise
2 cloves garlic, crushed

DIRECTIONS

Press the "Sauté" button and heat the oil. Sear the pork until it is golden brown on both sides.
Add the salt, black pepper, mustard powder, celery seeds oil, and broth.
Secure the lid. Choose the "Manual" mode and cook for 10 minutes at High pressure. Once cooking is complete, use a natural pressure release for 10 minutes; carefully remove the lid.
Meanwhile, whisk the mayonnaise with the garlic; serve the warm loin chops with the garlic mayo on the side. Bon appétit!

114. Spicy Peppery Pork Burgers

(Ready in about 20 minutes | Servings 3)

Per serving: 428 Calories; 15.4g Fat; 28.4g Carbs; 44.2g Protein; 6.5g Sugars

INGREDIENTS

1 pound ground pork
1 large sweet pepper, minced
1 chipotle pepper, minced
2 cloves garlic, minced

Sea salt and ground black pepper, to taste
1/2 teaspoon red pepper flakes, crushed
3 burger buns
3 (1-ounce) slices Swiss cheese, sliced

DIRECTIONS

Mix the ground pork, peppers, garlic, salt, black pepper, and red pepper flakes until well combined.
Form the meat mixture into 3 patties. Place your patties on squares of aluminum foil and wrap them loosely.
Add 1 cup water and a metal trivet to the Instant Pot; lower the foil packs onto the top of the metal trivet.
Secure the lid. Choose the "Meat/Stew" mode and cook for 10 minutes at High pressure. Once cooking is complete, use a natural pressure release; carefully remove the lid.
Place your patties on a baking sheet and broil for 5 to 6 minutes. Serve on buns topped with Swiss cheese. Enjoy!

115. Country-Style Pork Meatballs

(Ready in about 20 minutes | Servings 4)

Per serving: 468 Calories; 24g Fat; 19.7g Carbs; 44.8g Protein; 6.2g Sugars

INGREDIENTS

2 tablespoons vegetable oil
Meatballs:
1 ½ pounds ground pork
Kosher salt and ground black pepper, to your liking
1 teaspoon chili flakes
1 teaspoon mustard powder

1 egg
1/2 cup Parmesan, grated
2 bread slices, soaked in 4 tablespoons of milk
Marinara Sauce:
2 tablespoons olive oil
1 onion, chopped

3 cloves garlic, minced
1 tablespoon cayenne pepper
1 teaspoon maple syrup
2 large ripe tomatoes, crushed
1 teaspoon dried parsley flakes
1 cup water

DIRECTIONS

Mix all ingredients for the meatballs until everything is well incorporated. Shape the mixture into small meatballs.
Press the "Sauté" button and heat 2 tablespoons of vegetable oil. Sear your meatballs until golden brown on all sides. Work in batches as needed. Reserve.
Press the "Sauté" button one more time; heat 2 tablespoons of olive oil. Cook the onion and garlic until tender and fragrant.
Now, add the remaining ingredients for the marinara sauce. Gently fold in the meatballs and secure the lid.
Choose the "Poultry" mode and cook for 5 minutes at High pressure. Once cooking is complete, use a quick pressure release; carefully remove the lid. Serve warm.

116. Loin Roast in Cheesy Garlic Sauce

(Ready in about 30 minutes | Servings 4)

Per serving: 491 Calories; 32.9g Fat; 10.9g Carbs; 36.4g Protein; 8.6g Sugars

INGREDIENTS

1 tablespoon lard, at room temperature
1 pound pork loin roast, cut into three pieces

Sauce:
2 garlic cloves, chopped
2 tablespoons maple syrup
1/4 cup rice vinegar
1/2 cup water

1/4 cup dry white wine
2 tablespoons tamari sauce
1 tablespoons flaxseed meal
1 cup cream cheese

DIRECTIONS

Press the "Sauté" button and melt the lard. Once hot, cook the pork loin until no longer pink.
Add the garlic, maple syrup, vinegar, water, wine and tamari sauce.
Secure the lid. Choose the "Manual" mode and cook for 10 minutes at High pressure. Once cooking is complete, use a natural pressure release for 10 minutes; carefully remove the lid. Reserve the meat.
Meanwhile, make the slurry by whisking the flaxseed meal with 2 tablespoons of cold water.
Stir in the slurry and press the "Sauté" button again. Cook the sauce until it has thickened; fold in the cheese and stir until heated through.
Bon appétit!

117. Marinated Roasted Pork Picnic Ham

(Ready in about 30 minutes + marinating time | Servings 5)

Per serving: 427 Calories; 28.1g Fat; 9.5g Carbs; 32.9g Protein; 3.1g Sugars

INGREDIENTS

2 tablespoons olive oil
1/2 teaspoon cayenne pepper
1/3 cup red wine
2/3 cup fresh orange juice

2 cloves garlic, minced
1 tablespoon mustard
2 pounds picnic ham
2 tablespoons parsley, chopped

1 shallot, sliced
2 sweet peppers, julienned

DIRECTIONS

Mix the olive oil, cayenne pepper, red wine, orange juice, garlic, and mustard in a glass bowl. Add the pork and let it marinate for 2 hours.
Transfer the pork along with its marinade to the inner pot. Add the parsley, shallot, and peppers.
Secure the lid. Choose the "Meat/Stew" mode and cook for 20 minutes at High pressure. Once cooking is complete, use a quick pressure release; carefully remove the lid.
Spoon over hot steamed rice. Bon appétit!

118. Pork Masala Curry

(Ready in about 30 minutes | Servings 3)

Per serving: 436 Calories; 19.8g Fat; 18.3g Carbs; 43.7g Protein; 5.2g Sugars

INGREDIENTS

1 pound pork stew meat, cubed
1/3 cup all-purpose flour
1 tablespoon ghee
2 onions, sliced
1 (1-inch) piece ginger
2 cloves garlic, sliced

2 green cardamoms
1/2 teaspoon ground allspice
1 tablespoon garam masala
1 tablespoon cider vinegar
Salt and black pepper, to taste
1 teaspoon curry powder

1 teaspoon coriander seeds
1/2 teaspoon Fenugreek seeds
2 dried chiles de árbol, chopped
1 cup yogurt

DIRECTIONS

Toss the pork stew meat with the flour until well coated.
Press the "Sauté" button and melt the ghee. Once hot, cook the pork for 3 to 4 minutes, stirring frequently to ensure even cooking.
Add the remaining ingredients, except for the yogurt.
Secure the lid. Choose the "Manual" mode and cook for 15 minutes at High pressure. Once cooking is complete, use a natural pressure release for 10 minutes; carefully remove the lid.
Add the yogurt and press the "Sauté" button; let it cook for a few minutes more or until everything is thoroughly heated. Bon appétit!

119. Tender Pork in Ricotta Sauce

(Ready in about 30 minutes | Servings 3)

Per serving: 447 Calories; 30.3g Fat; 3.6g Carbs; 38.1g Protein; 0.6g Sugars

INGREDIENTS

2 tablespoons olive oil

3 pork cutlets

Sea salt and freshly ground black pepper, to taste

1 onion, thinly sliced

2 chicken bouillon cubes

1 cup water

6 ounces Ricotta cheese

DIRECTIONS

Press the "Sauté" button and heat the oil until sizzling. Sear the pork cutlets for 3 minutes per side.

Add the salt, black pepper, onion, chicken bouillon cubes, water to the Instant Pot.

Secure the lid. Choose the "Manual" mode and cook for 10 minutes at High pressure. Once cooking is complete, use a natural pressure release for 10 minutes; carefully remove the lid.

Top with Ricotta cheese; seal the lid and let it stand for 5 to 10 minutes or until thoroughly heated. Bon appétit!

120. Pork Chops with Pineapple Glaze

(Ready in about 35 minutes | Servings 4)

Per serving: 480 Calories; 34.3g Fat; 13.6g Carbs; 30.1g Protein; 11.5g Sugars

INGREDIENTS

1 tablespoon canola oil

1 pound pork tenderloin, slice into 4 pieces

Kosher salt and freshly ground black pepper, to taste

1 shallot, chopped

2 garlic cloves, chopped

1 teaspoon ground ginger

1 thyme sprig

1 rosemary sprig

1/2 cup unsweetened pineapple juice

1/2 cup vegetable broth

4 pineapple rings

DIRECTIONS

Press the "Sauté" button to preheat your Instant Pot. Heat the canola oil.

Season the pork tenderloin on both sides with salt and black pepper. Cook the pork chops with shallot and garlic for 3 minutes or until the pork chops are no longer pink.

Add the ginger, thyme, rosemary, pineapple juice, and vegetable broth.

Secure the lid. Choose the "Manual" mode and cook for 10 minutes at High pressure. Once cooking is complete, use a natural pressure release for 10 minutes; carefully remove the lid.

Preheat the broiler. Place the pork chops on a broil pan. Brush with the pan juices and place one pineapple ring on top of each pork piece. Broil for 5 minutes. Serve warm.

121. Pork and Romano Cheese Meatloaf

(Ready in about 35 minutes | Servings 4)

Per serving: 520 Calories; 36.6g Fat; 18.7g Carbs; 28.4g Protein; 5.7g Sugars

INGREDIENTS

4 ounces bacon, chopped

1 onion, chopped

4 cloves garlic, minced

1 pound ground pork

1 egg, beaten

1 tablespoon fish sauce

1/2 cup breadcrumbs

1/4 cup Romano cheese, grated

1/2 cup tomato sauce

1 tablespoon mustard

1 teaspoon dried basil

1 teaspoon dried sage

1 teaspoon dried oregano

1/2 teaspoon chili flakes

DIRECTIONS

Place a steamer rack inside the inner pot; add 1/2 cup of water. Cut 1 sheet of heavy-duty foil and brush with cooking spray.

In mixing dish, thoroughly combine all ingredients.

Shape the meat mixture into a loaf; place the meatloaf in the center of the foil. Wrap your meatloaf in foil and lower onto the steamer rack.

Secure the lid. Choose the "Meat/Stew" mode and cook for 20 minutes at High pressure. Once cooking is complete, use a quick pressure release; carefully remove the lid. Let it stand for 10 minutes before cutting and serving. Bon appétit!

122. Marsala Pork Ribs

(Ready in about 45 minutes | Servings 4)

Per serving: 386 Calories; 14.9g Fat; 4.9g Carbs; 54.7g Protein; 2.9g Sugars

INGREDIENTS

1 rack country style pork ribs
Coarse sea salt and freshly ground black pepper, to taste
1 teaspoon red pepper flakes

1/2 cup Marsala wine
1/2 cup chicken broth
1 cup BBQ sauce

DIRECTIONS

Place the pork ribs, salt, black pepper, red pepper, wine, and chicken broth in the inner pot.

Choose the "Meat/Stew" mode and cook for 35 minutes at High pressure. Once cooking is complete, use a quick pressure release; carefully remove the lid.

Transfer the pork ribs to a baking pan. Pour the BBQ sauce over the pork ribs and roast in the preheated oven at 425 degrees F for 6 to 8 minutes. Bon appétit!

123. Tender St. Louis-Style Ribs

(Ready in about 45 minutes | Servings 6)

Per serving: 381 Calories; 13.4g Fat; 11.6g Carbs; 48.5g Protein; 6.6g Sugars

INGREDIENTS

1 (3-pounds) rack St. Louis-style pork ribs
1 cup tomato sauce
1/2 cup water
1 tablespoon brown sugar
2 cloves garlic, minced

1 tablespoon oyster sauce
1 tablespoon soy sauce
1 tablespoon paprika
Pink salt and ground black pepper, to taste

DIRECTIONS

Place all ingredients in the inner pot.

Choose the "Meat/Stew" mode and cook for 35 minutes at High pressure. Once cooking is complete, use a quick pressure release; carefully remove the lid.

Turn your broiler to low. Coat the ribs with the pan juices and cook under the broiler for about 2 minutes.

Turn them over, coat with another layer of sauce and cook for 2 to 3 minutes more. Taste, adjust the seasonings and serve. Enjoy!

124. Pork Tenderloin Fajitas

(Ready in about 50 minutes | Servings 4)

Per serving: 618 Calories; 18.8g Fat; 53.8g Carbs; 55.7g Protein; 11.7g Sugars

INGREDIENTS

1 teaspoon paprika
1 tablespoon brown sugar
1 teaspoon dried sage
1/2 teaspoon ground cumin
Coarse sea salt and freshly ground pepper, to taste
2 pounds pork tenderloins, halved crosswise
1 tablespoon grapeseed oil

1/4 cup balsamic vinegar
1/4 cup tomato puree
1/2 cup beef broth
16 small flour tortillas
A bunch of scallions, chopped
1 cup sour cream
1 cup Pico de Gallo

DIRECTIONS

Mix the paprika, sugar, sage, cumin, salt, and black pepper. Rub the spice mixture all over the pork tenderloins.

Press the "Sauté" button to preheat your Instant Pot. Heat the oil and sear the pork until browned, about 4 minutes per side.

Add the balsamic vinegar, tomato puree, and beef broth.

Secure the lid. Choose the "Manual" mode and cook for 40 minutes at High pressure. Once cooking is complete, use a quick pressure release; carefully remove the lid.

Warm the tortillas until soft; serve with the pork mixture, scallions, sour cream, and Pico de Gallo. Enjoy!

125. Smothered Pork Chop

(Ready in about 30 minutes | Servings 3)

Per serving: 472 Calories; 28.8g Fat; 11.1g Carbs; 42.7g Protein; 6.6g Sugars

INGREDIENTS

1 tablespoon ghee, at room temperature
3 pork chops
1 cup beef broth
1 teaspoon garlic powder

1/2 teaspoon onion powder
1 tablespoon paprika
Sea salt and ground black pepper, to taste

1/2 cup double cream
1/2 teaspoon xanthan gum

DIRECTIONS

Press the "Sauté" button and melt the ghee. Once hot, sear the pork chops until golden browned, about 4 minutes per side.

Add the beef broth, garlic powder, onion powder, paprika, salt, and black pepper to the inner pot.

Secure the lid. Choose the "Manual" mode and cook for 10 minutes at High pressure. Once cooking is complete, use a natural pressure release; carefully remove the lid.

Transfer just the pork chops to a serving plate and cover to keep them warm. Press the "Sauté" button again.

Whisk in the cream and xanthan gum. Let it simmer approximately 4 minutes or until the sauce has thickened. Spoon the sauce over the pork chops and enjoy!

126. Pork Liver Pâté

(Ready in about 20 minutes | Servings 6)

Per serving: 177 Calories; 11.7g Fat; 3.1g Carbs; 14.4g Protein; 1.5g Sugars

INGREDIENTS

2 tablespoons butter
1 onion, chopped
2 cloves garlic, minced
1 pound pork livers

1 cup water
2 sprigs thyme
2 sprigs rosemary

Himalayan pink salt and ground black pepper, to taste
1/4 cup brandy
1/2 cup heavy cream

DIRECTIONS

Press the "Sauté" button and melt the butter. Then, sauté the onion and garlic until just tender and aromatic.

Add the pork livers and cook for 3 minutes on both sides or until the juices run clear. Deglaze the pan with a splash of brandy.

Add the water, thyme, rosemary, salt, and ground black pepper.

Secure the lid. Choose the "Manual" mode and cook for 5 minutes at High pressure. Once cooking is complete, use a quick pressure release; carefully remove the lid.

Add the brandy and heavy cream. Press the "Sauté" button and cook for 2 to 3 minutes more.

Transfer to your food processor and blend the mixture to a fine mousse. Bon appétit!

127. Boston Butt with Root Vegetables

(Ready in about 30 minutes | Servings 5)

Per serving: 511 Calories; 38.9g Fat; 11.6g Carbs; 29.7g Protein; 3.6g Sugars

INGREDIENTS

1 ½ pounds Boston butt, cut into small chunks
1 teaspoon garlic powder
1 teaspoon shallot powder
Sea salt and ground black pepper
1 teaspoon dried marjoram

1 teaspoon mustard powder
1 teaspoon smoked paprika
2 tablespoons olive oil
1/2 cup port
1/2 cup roasted vegetable broth
2 large carrots, cut into 1.5-inch chunks

2 large celery stalks, cut into 1.5-inch chunks
1 parsnip, cut into 1.5-inch chunks
2 mild green chilies, roasted, seeded and diced
1 tablespoon arrowroot powder

DIRECTIONS

In a resealable bag, mix the garlic powder, shallot powder, salt, black pepper, marjoram, mustard powder, and paprika.

Add the pork cubes and shake to coat well. Press the "Sauté" button and heat the oil until sizzling.

Cook the Boston butt for 2 to 4 minutes, stirring periodically to ensure even cooking. Add the remaining ingredients, except for the arrowroot powder.

Secure the lid. Choose the "Meat/Stew" mode and cook for 20 minutes at High pressure. Once cooking is complete, use a quick pressure release; carefully remove the lid.

Stir in the arrowroot powder and let it simmer until the sauce thickens. Serve in individual bowls and enjoy!

128. Pork Chile Verde

(Ready in about 40 minutes | Servings 4)

Per serving: 444 Calories; 18.1g Fat; 23.6g Carbs; 46.4g Protein; 8g Sugars

INGREDIENTS

2 pounds pork shoulder, cut into bite-sized pieces
1/4 cup all-purpose flour
Kosher salt and ground black pepper, to your liking
1 tablespoon canola oil
1 onion, chopped

2 cloves garlic, sliced
1 teaspoon Mexican oregano
1/2 teaspoon coriander seeds
1 teaspoon ground cumin
1/2 teaspoon turmeric powder
1 cup beef broth
1 sweet pepper, seeded and sliced

3 fresh chili pepper, seeded and sliced
1 pound fresh tomatillos, husked and sliced into 1/2-inch wedges
1/4 cup fresh cilantro leaves, roughly chopped

DIRECTIONS

Toss the pork pieces with the flour until everything is well coated. Generously season the pork with salt and pepper.

Press the "Sauté" button and heat the oil. Once hot, sear the pork, stirring periodically to ensure even cooking.

Now, add the remaining ingredients, except for the cilantro leaves.

Secure the lid. Choose the "Meat/Stew" mode and cook for 35 minutes at High pressure. Once cooking is complete, use a quick pressure release; carefully remove the lid.

Serve in individual bowls, garnished with fresh cilantro. Enjoy!

129. Spicy Sausage Bake

(Ready in about 20 minutes | Servings 4)

Per serving: 484 Calories; 41.8g Fat; 6.3g Carbs; 21.6g Protein; 4.1g Sugars

INGREDIENTS

2 tablespoons canola oil
1 pound pork sausages, sliced
4 ounces streaky bacon
1 onion, sliced
4 garlic cloves, minced

1 bell pepper, sliced
1 red chili pepper, sliced
1 teaspoon brown sugar
1 teaspoon dried rosemary
1 teaspoon dried basil

Sea salt and freshly ground black pepper, to taste
2 tomatoes, pureed
1 cup chicken stock
1 cup white wine

DIRECTIONS

Press the "Sauté" button and heat the oil. Sear the pork sausage until no longer pink. Add the bacon and cook until it is crisp.

Add a layer of onions and garlic; then, add the peppers. Sprinkle with sugar, rosemary, basil, salt and black pepper.

Add the tomatoes, chicken stock, and wine to the inner pot.

Secure the lid. Choose the "Manual" mode and cook for 10 minutes at High pressure. Once cooking is complete, use a natural pressure release; carefully remove the lid. Bon appétit!

130. Pork and Mushroom Stuffed Peppers

(Ready in about 30 minutes | Servings 4)

Per serving: 499 Calories; 26.4g Fat; 35.6g Carbs; 30.8g Protein; 8.1g Sugars

INGREDIENTS

1 tablespoon olive oil
1 onion, chopped
2 cloves garlic, minced
3/4 pound ground pork
1/2 pound brown mushrooms, sliced

1 1/2 cups cooked rice
Sea salt and white pepper, to taste
1 teaspoon cayenne pepper
1/2 teaspoon celery seeds
1/2 teaspoon ground cumin

4 bell peppers, deveined and halved
1 (15-ounce) can tomatoes, crushed
2 ounces Colby cheese, shredded

DIRECTIONS

Press the "Sauté" button and heat the oil. Cook the onion, garlic, and pork until the onion is translucent and the pork is no longer pink. Add the mushrooms and sauté until fragrant or about 2 minutes.

Add the rice, salt, white pepper, cayenne pepper, celery seeds, and ground cumin.

Add 1 cup of water and a metal trivet to the bottom. Fill the pepper halves with the meat/mushroom mixture. Place the peppers in a casserole dish; stir in the canned tomatoes.

Lower the casserole dish onto the trivet in the Instant Pot.

Secure the lid. Choose the "Manual" mode and cook for 9 minutes at High pressure. Once cooking is complete, use a natural pressure release for 5 minutes; carefully remove the lid.

Top with the cheese and secure the lid again; let it sit in the residual heat until the cheese melts approximately 10 minutes. Serve and enjoy!

131. Pulled Pork and Cream Cheese Frittata

(Ready in about 50 minutes | Servings 3)

Per serving: 533 Calories; 36.6g Fat; 4.4g Carbs; 44.3g Protein; 2.6g Sugars

INGREDIENTS

2 tablespoons butter, at room temperature

1 pound pork shoulder

1 cup chicken broth

Sea salt and ground black pepper, to taste

2 cloves garlic, minced

1 shallot, thinly sliced

6 eggs, beaten

1/2 cup cream cheese

1/2 teaspoon paprika

1/2 teaspoon hot sauce

DIRECTIONS

Press the "Sauté" button to preheat your Instant Pot. Melt the butter and brown the pork for 4 minutes per side.

Add the chicken broth, salt, and black pepper.

Secure the lid. Choose the "Manual" mode and cook for 15 minutes at High pressure. Once cooking is complete, use a natural pressure release for 5 minutes; carefully remove the lid.

Shred the meat with two forks.; add the remaining ingredients and stir to combine well.

Lightly spritz a baking pan with cooking oil. Spoon the meat/egg mixture into the baking pan.

Cover with foil. Add 1 cup of water and a metal trivet to the Instant Pot. Lower the baking pan onto the trivet.

Secure the lid. Choose the "Manual" mode and cook for 15 minutes at High pressure. Once cooking is complete, use a natural pressure release for 10 minutes; carefully remove the lid. Bon appétit!

132. Pork Huevos Rancheros

(Ready in about 35 minutes | Servings 4)

Per serving: 533 Calories; 18.3g Fat; 29.5g Carbs; 62.2g Protein; 8.8g Sugars

INGREDIENTS

1 tablespoon coarse sea salt

1/2 teaspoon ground black pepper

1 teaspoon paprika

1 teaspoon onion powder

1 teaspoon garlic powder

1 teaspoon ancho chili powder

1 tablespoon dark brown sugar

2 pounds Boston butt, cut into bite-sized pieces

1 tablespoon olive oil

1 cup tomato paste

1/2 cup roasted vegetable broth

1 tablespoon fish sauce

4 eggs

2 tablespoons corn salsa

4 warm corn tortillas

DIRECTIONS

In a resealable bag, mix the all spices and sugar. Add the pork chunks and shake to coat well.

Press the "Sauté" button and heat the oil until sizzling. Now, sear and brown the Boston butt on all sides until you have a crispy crust.

Add the tomato paste, broth, and fish sauce.

Secure the lid. Choose the "Manual" mode and cook for 30 minutes at High pressure. Once cooking is complete, use a quick pressure release; carefully remove the lid.

Meanwhile, crack the eggs into a lightly greased pan; fry your eggs until the whites are set.

Stack the tortilla, pork mixture, and corn salsa on a plate. Place the fried egg onto the stack using a spatula. Make four servings and enjoy!

133. Classic Pork Chops and Potatoes

(Ready in about 20 minutes | Servings 4)

Per serving: 484 Calories; 24.3g Fat; 20.2g Carbs; 43.7g Protein; 1.1g Sugars

INGREDIENTS

2 tablespoons lard, at room temperature

4 pork chops

1 cup chicken broth

1 onion, sliced

1 pound potatoes, quartered

Sea salt and ground black pepper, to taste

DIRECTIONS

Press the "Sauté" button and melt the lard. Once hot, brown the pork chops for 3 minutes per side.

Add the remaining ingredients.

Secure the lid. Choose the "Manual" mode and cook for 10 minutes at High pressure. Once cooking is complete, use a natural pressure release; carefully remove the lid.

Serve warm.

134. Easy Pork Mélange with Polenta

(Ready in about 30 minutes | Servings 4)

Per serving: 474 Calories; 22.4g Fat; 16.8g Carbs; 45.9g Protein; 1.5g Sugars

INGREDIENTS

1 tablespoon olive oil
1 pound boneless pork top loin roast, cut into cubes
2 spicy pork sausages, sliced
1 bell pepper, sliced
1 jalapeno pepper, sliced
2 garlic cloves, chopped

1 cup chicken bone broth
Salt and ground black pepper, to taste
1 cup polenta
4 cups water
1 teaspoon salt
1/2 teaspoon paprika

DIRECTIONS

Press the "Sauté" button and heat the oil. Once hot, cook the pork until no longer pink; add the sausage and cook for 2 to 3 minutes more. Add the peppers, garlic, broth, salt, and black pepper.

Secure the lid. Choose the "Manual" mode and cook for 15 minutes at High pressure. Once cooking is complete, use a quick pressure release; carefully remove the lid.

Clean the inner pot. Add the polenta, water and 1 teaspoon of salt and mix to combine.

Secure the lid. Choose the "Manual" mode and cook for 9 minutes at High pressure. Once cooking is complete, use a quick pressure release; carefully remove the lid.

Divide your polenta between serving bowls; top with the pork mélange and paprika. Serve warm.

135. Japanese Ground Pork (Buta Niku No Mushimono)

(Ready in about 15 minutes | Servings 4)

Per serving: 460 Calories; 28.9g Fat; 2.7g Carbs; 42.7g Protein; 0.8g Sugars

INGREDIENTS

1 teaspoon sesame oil
1 pound ground pork
4 fresh shiitake, sliced
1 cup chicken broth
2 tablespoons tamari sauce

2 cloves garlic, minced
2 tablespoons sake
1 teaspoon fresh ginger, grated
Sea salt and ground black pepper, to taste

DIRECTIONS

Press the "Sauté" button and heat the oil. Once hot, cook the ground pork until no longer pink.

Add the fresh shiitake, chicken broth, tamari sauce, garlic, sake, ginger, salt, and black pepper.

Secure the lid. Choose the "Poultry" mode and High pressure; cook for 5 minutes. Once cooking is complete, use a quick release.

Spoon into individual bowls. Enjoy!

136. Ground Pork and Vegetable Casserole

(Ready in about 25 minutes | Servings 4)

Per serving: 462 Calories; 29.9g Fat; 19.1g Carbs; 33.2g Protein; 5.7g Sugars

INGREDIENTS

1 teaspoon olive oil
1 ½ pounds ground pork
2 carrots, sliced
1 parsnip, sliced
1 stalk celery, sliced

2 sweet peppers, sliced
1 onion, sliced
4 cloves garlic, sliced
1 cup whole kernel corn, frozen
1/4 cup Marsala wine

2 fresh tomatoes, pureed
1/2 cup water
Kosher salt and ground black pepper, to taste

DIRECTIONS

Press the "Sauté" button and heat the oil. Once hot, cook the ground pork for 2 to 3 minutes, stirring frequently.

Add a splash of wine to deglaze the pot. Add the remaining ingredients.

Secure the lid. Choose the "Manual" mode and cook for 18 minutes at High pressure. Once cooking is complete, use a quick pressure release; carefully remove the lid.

Taste and adjust the seasonings. Bon appétit!

137. Holiday Orange Glazed Ham

(Ready in about 20 minutes | Servings 6)

Per serving: 415 Calories; 19.5g Fat; 20g Carbs; 37.8g Protein; 9.7g Sugars

INGREDIENTS

3 pounds spiral sliced ham
1/2 cup orange juice
2 tablespoons bourbon
4 tablespoons maple syrup
Sea salt and ground black pepper, to taste

DIRECTIONS

Place 1 cup of water and a metal trivet in the inner pot.

Then, thoroughly combine the orange juice, bourbon, maple syrup, salt and pepper.

Place the ham on foil. Fold up the sides of the foil to make a bowl-like shape. Pour the orange glaze all over the ham; wrap the foil around the ham. Lower the ham onto the trivet.

Secure the lid. Choose the "Manual" mode and cook for 10 minutes at High pressure. Once cooking is complete, use a quick pressure release; carefully remove the lid.

Transfer to a cooling rack before serving. Bon appétit!

FISH & SEAFOOD

138. Easy Tuna Fillets with Onions

(Ready in about 10 minutes | Servings 2)

Per serving: 333 Calories; 7g Fat; 8.7g Carbs; 56.3g Protein; 3.7g Sugars

INGREDIENTS

1 cup water
A few sprigs of tarragon
1 lemon, sliced
1 pound tuna filets

1 tablespoon butter, melted
Sea salt and freshly ground black pepper, to taste
1 large onion, sliced into rings

DIRECTIONS

Put the water, herbs and lemon slices in the inner pot; now, place the steamer rack in the inner pot.
Lower the tuna fillets onto the rack. Add butter, salt, and pepper; top with onion slices.
Secure the lid. Choose the "Steam" mode and cook for 3 minutes at Low pressure. Once cooking is complete, use a quick pressure release; carefully remove the lid. Serve immediately.

139. Haddock Fillets with Steamed Green Beans

(Ready in about 15 minutes | Servings 4)

Per serving: 288 Calories; 13.1g Fat; 9.1g Carbs; 33.7g Protein; 1.9g Sugars

INGREDIENTS

1 lime, cut into wedges
1/2 cup water
4 haddock fillets
1 rosemary sprig
2 thyme sprigs

1 tablespoon fresh parsley
4 teaspoons ghee
Sea salt and ground black pepper, to taste
2 cloves garlic, minced
4 cups green beans

DIRECTIONS

Place the lime wedges and water in the inner pot. Add a steamer rack.
Lower the haddock fillets onto the rack; place the rosemary, thyme, parsley, and ghee on the haddock fillets. Season with salt and pepper.
Secure the lid. Choose the "Steam" mode and cook for 3 minutes at Low pressure. Once cooking is complete, use a quick pressure release; carefully remove the lid. Reserve.
Then, add the garlic and green beans to the inner pot.
Secure the lid. Choose the "Steam" mode and cook for 3 minutes at Low pressure. Once cooking is complete, use a quick pressure release; carefully remove the lid.
Serve the haddock fillets with green beans on the side. Bon appétit!

140. Greek-Style Shrimp with Feta Cheese

(Ready in about 15 minutes | Servings 4)

Per serving: 210 Calories; 8.2g Fat; 9.4g Carbs; 27g Protein; 5.7g Sugars

INGREDIENTS

1 pound frozen shrimp
1 ½ tablespoons extra-virgin olive oil
2 gloves garlic, minced
1 teaspoon basil
1/2 teaspoon dry dill weed
1 teaspoon oregano

1 (26-ounce) canned diced tomatoes
1/2 cup Kalamata olives
2 ounces feta cheese, crumbled
1/2 lemon, sliced
Chopped fresh mint leaves, for garnish

DIRECTIONS

Add the shrimp, olive oil, garlic, basil, dill, oregano, and tomatoes to the inner pot.
Secure the lid. Choose the "Manual" mode and cook for 2 minutes at Low pressure. Once cooking is complete, use a quick pressure release; carefully remove the lid.
Top with Kalamata olives and feta cheese. Serve garnished with lemon and mint leaves. Enjoy!

141. Indian Meen Kulambu

(Ready in about 10 minutes | Servings 4)

Per serving: 313 Calories; 20.8g Fat; 7.9g Carbs; 25.1g Protein; 3.1g Sugars

INGREDIENTS

2 tablespoons butter
6 curry leaves
1 onion, chopped
2 cloves garlic, crushed
1 (1-inch) piece fresh ginger, grated

1 dried Kashmiri chili, minced
1 cup canned tomatoes, crushed
1/2 teaspoon turmeric powder
1 teaspoon ground coriander
1/2 teaspoon ground cumin

Kosher salt and ground black pepper,
to taste
1/2 (14-ounce) can coconut milk
1 pound salmon fillets
1 tablespoon lemon juice

DIRECTIONS

Press the "Sauté" button and melt the butter. Once hot, cook the curry leaves for about 30 seconds.

Stir in the onions, garlic, ginger and Kashmiri chili and cook for 2 minutes more or until they are fragrant.

Add the tomatoes, turmeric, coriander, cumin, salt, and black pepper. Continue to sauté for 30 seconds more.

Add the coconut milk and salmon.

Secure the lid. Choose the "Manual" mode and cook for 2 minutes at Low pressure. Once cooking is complete, use a quick pressure release; carefully remove the lid.

Spoon the fish curry into individual bowls. Drizzle lemon juice over the fish curry and serve. Enjoy!

142. Cod Fish with Potatoes and Goat Cheese

(Ready in about 10 minutes | Servings 4)

Per serving: 390 Calories; 17.6g Fat; 20.8g Carbs; 36.5g Protein; 1.1g Sugars

INGREDIENTS

1 pound baby potatoes
2 tablespoons coconut oil, at room temperature
Sea salt and freshly ground pepper, to taste
1 ½ pounds cod fish fillets
1/2 teaspoon smoked paprika

2 tablespoons fresh Italian parsley, chopped
1/2 teaspoon fresh ginger, grated
2 cloves garlic, minced
1 cup goat cheese, crumbled

DIRECTIONS

Place the potatoes in the bottom of the inner pot. Add 1 cup of water; then, add coconut oil, salt and pepper. Place the rack over the potatoes. Place the cod fish fillets on the rack. Season the fillets with paprika and parsley.

Secure the lid. Choose the "Steam" mode and cook for 3 minutes at Low pressure. Once cooking is complete, use a quick pressure release; carefully remove the lid.

Remove the salmon and the rack from the inner pot. Continue to cook the potatoes until fork tender; add the ginger and garlic and cook for 2 minutes more.

Top with goat cheese and serve. Bon appétit!

143. Three-Cheese Crab Dip

(Ready in about 10 minutes | Servings 10)

Per serving: 183 Calories; 11.1g Fat; 3.3g Carbs; 17.6g Protein; 0.9g Sugars

INGREDIENTS

1 pound lump crab meat
6 ounces Cottage cheese, at room temperature
1/2 cup Romano cheese, shredded
1 cup sour cream
Kosher salt and ground black pepper, to taste

1 teaspoon smoked paprika
1 ½ cups Cheddar cheese, shredded
1/4 cup fresh chives, chopped
2 tablespoons fresh lime juice

DIRECTIONS

Place 1 cup of water and a metal trivet in the inner pot.

Spritz a casserole dish with nonstick cooking spray. Place the crab meat, Cottage cheese, Romano cheese and sour cream in the casserole dish. Season with salt, black pepper, and smoked paprika. Top with the Cheddar cheese. Lower the dish onto the trivet.

Secure the lid. Choose the "Manual" mode and cook for 3 minutes at Low pressure. Once cooking is complete, use a quick pressure release; carefully remove the lid.

Scatter the chopped chives over the top and add a few drizzles of lime juice. Serve warm or at room temperature. Enjoy!

144. Classic Creole Gumbo

(Ready in about 15 minutes | Servings 4)

Per serving: 339 Calories; 8.7g Fat; 18g Carbs; 47.3g Protein; 8.5g Sugars

INGREDIENTS

2 tablespoons butter, melted
1 shallot, diced
1 sweet pepper, sliced
1 jalapeno pepper, sliced
1 pound tuna, cut into 2-inch chunks
1 tablespoon Creole seasoning
2 carrots, sliced
2 celery stalks, diced

2 ripe tomatoes, pureed
1/4 cup ketchup
1 bay leaf
1 cup beef broth
2 tablespoons Worcestershire sauce
1 pound raw shrimp, deveined
1 teaspoon filé powder
Sea salt and freshly ground black pepper, to taste

DIRECTIONS

Press the "Sauté" button and melt the butter. Once hot, cook the shallot and peppers for about 3 minutes until just tender and fragrant. Add the remaining ingredients; gently stir to combine.

Secure the lid. Choose the "Manual" mode and cook for 5 minutes at High pressure. Once cooking is complete, use a quick pressure release; carefully remove the lid. Serve in individual bowls and enjoy!

145. Blue Crabs with Wine and Herbs

(Ready in about 15 minutes | Servings 4)

Per serving: 145 Calories; 4.3g Fat; 2.1g Carbs; 23.7g Protein; 0.9g Sugars

INGREDIENTS

2 pounds frozen blue crab
1/2 cup water
1/2 cup dry white wine
Sea salt and ground black pepper, to taste

2 sprigs rosemary
2 sprigs thyme
1 lemon, cut into wedges

DIRECTIONS

Add the frozen crab legs, water, wine, salt, black pepper, rosemary, and thyme to the inner pot.

Secure the lid. Choose the "Manual" mode and cook for 3 minutes at High pressure. Once cooking is complete, use a quick pressure release; carefully remove the lid.

Serve warm, garnished with fresh lemon wedges. Bon appétit!

146. Sausage and Prawn Boil with Old Bay Sauce

(Ready in about 15 minutes | Servings 4)

Per serving: 441 Calories; 28.6g Fat; 14.5g Carbs; 32.4g Protein; 1.6g Sugars

INGREDIENTS

1/2 pound beef sausage, sliced
4 baby potatoes
1 cup fume (fish stock)
1/4 cup butter
2 cloves garlic, minced

1 teaspoon Old Bay seasoning
1/4 teaspoon Tabasco sauce
Sea salt and white pepper, to taste
1 pound prawns
1 fresh lemon, juiced

DIRECTIONS

Place the sausage and potatoes in the inner pot; cover with the fish stock.

Secure the lid. Choose the "Manual" mode and cook for 5 minutes at High pressure. Once cooking is complete, use a quick pressure release; carefully remove the lid. Reserve. Clean the inner pot.

Press the "Sauté" button and melt the butter. Once hot, sauté the minced garlic until aromatic or about 1 minute. Stir in the Old Bay seasoning, Tabasco, salt, and white pepper. Lastly, stir in the prawns.

Continue to simmer for 1 to 2 minutes or until the shrimp turn pink. Press the "Cancel" button. Add the sausages and potatoes, drizzle lemon juice over the top and serve warm.

147. Braised Sole Fillets with Vegetables

(Ready in about 20 minutes | Servings 4)

Per serving: 218 Calories; 9.8g Fat; 16.6g Carbs; 18.2g Protein; 8.2g Sugars

INGREDIENTS

2 tablespoons coconut oil
1 small shallot, quartered
4 cloves garlic, sliced
1 cup beef stock

1 ripe tomato, puréed
Salt and ground black pepper, to taste
1 pound fennel, quartered
1 pound sole fillets

1 lemon, cut into wedges
2 tablespoons fresh Italian parsley

DIRECTIONS

Press the "Sauté" button and melt the coconut oil. Once hot, sauté the shallot and garlic until tender and aromatic.

Add the beef stock, tomato, salt, pepper, and fennel.

Secure the lid. Choose the "Manual" mode and cook for 10 minutes at High pressure. Once cooking is complete, use a quick pressure release; carefully remove the lid.

Then, remove all the vegetables with a slotted spoon and reserve, keeping them warm.

Add the sole fillets to the inner pot. Secure the lid. Choose the "Steam" mode and cook for 3 minutes at Low pressure. Once cooking is complete, use a quick pressure release; carefully remove the lid.

Garnish the fish fillets with lemon and parsley; serve with the reserved vegetables. Enjoy!

148. Louisiana-Style Seafood Boil

(Ready in about 25 minutes | Servings 4)

Per serving: 492 Calories; 13.1g Fat; 52.1g Carbs; 41.2g Protein; 2.6g Sugars

INGREDIENTS

1 cup jasmine rice
1 tablespoon butter
1 tablespoon olive oil
1/2 pound chicken breasts, cubed
1 pound shrimp
2 sweet peppers, deveined and sliced

1 habanero pepper, deveined and sliced
1 onion, chopped
4 cloves garlic, minced
1 cup chicken bone broth
2 bay leaves
1 teaspoon oregano

1 teaspoon sage
1 teaspoon basil
1 teaspoon paprika
1 tablespoon fish sauce
Sea salt and ground black pepper, to taste
1 tablespoon cornstarch

DIRECTIONS

Combine the rice, butter and 1 ½ cups of water in a pot and bring to a rapid boil. Cover and let it simmer on low for 15 minutes. Fluff with a fork and reserve.

Press the "Sauté" button and heat the oil. Once hot, cook the chicken breasts for 3 to 4 minutes, stirring periodically.

Add the remaining ingredients, except for the cornstarch.

Secure the lid. Choose the "Manual" mode and cook for 3 minutes at Low pressure. Once cooking is complete, use a quick pressure release; carefully remove the lid.

Mix the cornstarch with 2 tablespoons of cold water. Add the cornstarch slurry to the cooking liquid and stir on the "Sauté" mode until the sauce thickens.

Serve over hot jasmine rice. Bon appétit!

149. Southern California Famous Cioppino

(Ready in about 50 minutes | Servings 6)

Per serving: 413 Calories; 19.3g Fat; 16.2g Carbs; 44.8g Protein; 6.8g Sugars

INGREDIENTS

2 tablespoons coconut oil
1 onion, diced
4 garlic cloves, minced
2 celery stalks, diced
2 carrots, diced
1 sweet pepper, diced
2 (14-ounce) cans of tomatoes, crushed

1 cup clam juice
1 teaspoon oyster sauce
1/2 teaspoon dried parsley flakes
1 teaspoon dried rosemary
1 teaspoon dried basil
1 teaspoon paprika
1 bay leaf

Sea salt and freshly ground black pepper, to taste
1 pound halibut steaks, cubed
1/2 pound sea scallops, rinsed and drained
1 pound shrimp, peeled and deveined
1/2 pound crab legs
1/4 cup dry white wine

DIRECTIONS

Press the "Sauté" button to heat the coconut oil. Once hot, sauté the onion, garlic, celery, carrots, and pepper for about 3 minutes or until they are just tender.

Add the canned tomatoes, clam juice, oyster sauce, parsley, rosemary, basil, paprika, bay leaf, salt, and black pepper to the inner pot.

Secure the lid. Choose the "Soup/Broth" mode and cook for 30 minutes at High pressure. Once cooking is complete, use a natural pressure release for 10 minutes; carefully remove the lid.

Add the seafood and wine.

Secure the lid. Choose the "Steam" mode and cook for 3 minutes at Low pressure. Once cooking is complete, use a quick pressure release; carefully remove the lid. Serve in individual bowls and enjoy!

150. Foil-Packet Fish and Vegetables

(Ready in about 15 minutes | Servings 4)

Per serving: 238 Calories; 16.4g Fat; 9.5g Carbs; 13.5g Protein; 6.5g Sugars

INGREDIENTS

12 ounces halibut steaks, cut into four pieces
1 red bell pepper, sliced
1 green bell pepper, sliced
1 onion, sliced
2 garlic cloves, minced
1 cup cherry tomatoes, halved

Sea salt and ground black pepper, to taste
1 teaspoon dried rosemary
1 teaspoon basil
1/2 teaspoon oregano
1/2 teaspoon paprika
4 teaspoon olive oil

DIRECTIONS

Place 1 cup of water and a metal trivet in the bottom of the inner pot.
Place 4 large sheets of heavy-duty foil on a flat surface. Divide the ingredients between sheets of foil. Add a splash of water.
Bring the ends of the foil together; fold in the sides to seal. Place the fish packets on the trivet.
Secure the lid. Choose the "Steam" mode and cook for 10 minutes at Low pressure. Once cooking is complete, use a quick pressure release; carefully remove the lid. Bon appétit!

151. Japanese Seafood Curry

(Ready in about 15 minutes | Servings 4)

Per serving: 390 Calories; 25.5g Fat; 7.1g Carbs; 34.4g Protein; 3.2g Sugars

INGREDIENTS

2 tablespoons butter, softened
1 onion, chopped
2 cloves garlic, minced
1 (1-inch) pieces fresh ginger, ground
1 red chili, deseeded and minced

1 pound pollack, cut into large chunks
1/2 pound shrimps, deveined
2 tablespoons sesame oil
1 tablespoon garam masala
1 teaspoon curry paste

1 (3-inch) kombu (dried kelp)
1 package Japanese curry roux
2 tablespoons Shoyu sauce
2 ripe tomatoes, pureed

DIRECTIONS

Press the "Sauté" button and melt the butter; cook the onion, garlic, ginger, and red chili until just tender and fragrant.
Add the pollack and shrimp and continue to sauté for a couple of minutes more. Add the remaining ingredients.
Secure the lid. Choose the "Manual" mode and cook for 5 minutes at Low pressure. Once cooking is complete, use a quick pressure release; carefully remove the lid.
Serve your curry over hot steamed rice. Enjoy!

152. Spicy Thai Prawns

(Ready in about 10 minutes | Servings 4)

Per serving: 283 Calories; 11.1g Fat; 12.3g Carbs; 32.7g Protein; 7.4g Sugars

INGREDIENTS

2 tablespoons coconut oil
1 small white onion, chopped
2 cloves garlic, minced
1 ½ pounds prawns, deveined
1/2 teaspoon red chili flakes
1 bell pepper, seeded and sliced

1 cup coconut milk
2 tablespoons fish sauce
2 tablespoons lime juice
1 tablespoon sugar
Kosher salt and white pepper, to your liking

1/2 teaspoon cayenne pepper
1 teaspoon fresh ginger, ground
2 tablespoons fresh cilantro, roughly chopped

DIRECTIONS

Press the "Sauté" button and heat the coconut oil; once hot, sauté the onion and garlic until aromatic.
Add the prawns, red chili flakes, bell pepper, coconut milk, fish sauce, lime juice, sugar, salt, white pepper, cayenne pepper, and ginger.
Secure the lid. Choose the "Manual" mode and cook for 3 minutes at Low pressure. Once cooking is complete, use a quick pressure release; carefully remove the lid.
Divide between serving bowls and serve garnished with fresh cilantro. Enjoy!

153. East Indian Haddock Curry

(Ready in about 10 minutes | Servings 4)

Per serving: 315 Calories; 22.4g Fat; 8.4g Carbs; 21.9g Protein; 4.3g Sugars

INGREDIENTS

2 tablespoons peanut oil

1 onion, chopped

2 garlic cloves, minced

1 (1-inch) piece fresh root ginger, peeled and grated

2 long red chilis, deseeded and minced

2 tablespoons tamarind paste

1 teaspoon mustard seeds

1 teaspoon turmeric powder

1 teaspoon ground cumin

Sea salt and freshly ground black pepper

1 can reduced fat coconut milk

1 cup chicken stock

1 pound haddock

DIRECTIONS

Press the "Sauté" button and heat the peanut oil; once hot, sauté the onion, garlic, ginger, and chilis until aromatic.

Add the remaining ingredients and gently stir to combine.

Secure the lid. Choose the "Manual" mode and cook for 4 minutes at Low pressure. Once cooking is complete, use a quick pressure release; carefully remove the lid.

Divide between serving bowls and serve warm. Enjoy!

154. Tuna and Asparagus Casserole

(Ready in about 15 minutes | Servings 4)

Per serving: 494 Calories; 30.3g Fat; 21.1g Carbs; 36.4g Protein; 5.3g Sugars

INGREDIENTS

1 pound tuna fillets

1 pound asparagus, trimmed

2 ripe tomatoes, pureed

Sea salt and ground black pepper, to taste

1 teaspoon paprika

A pinch of fresh thyme

1 tablespoon dry white wine

1 cup Cheddar cheese, grated

DIRECTIONS

Place the tuna fillets in a lightly greased baking dish. Add the asparagus, tomatoes, salt, black pepper, paprika, thyme, and wine.

Place a steamer rack inside the inner pot; add 1/2 cup water. Cut 1 sheet of heavy-duty foil and brush with cooking spray.

Top with the cheese. Cover with foil and lower the baking dish onto the rack.

Secure the lid. Choose the "Manual" mode and cook for 9 minutes at Low pressure. Once cooking is complete, use a quick pressure release; carefully remove the lid.

Place the baking dish on a cooling rack for a couple of minutes before slicing and serving. Bon appétit!

155. Mozzarella and Spinach-Stuffed Salmon

(Ready in about 10 minutes | Servings 3)

Per serving: 374 Calories; 19.9g Fat; 7.7g Carbs; 40.7g Protein; 1.2g Sugars

INGREDIENTS

3 (6-ounce) salmon fillets

Kosher salt and freshly ground black pepper, to taste

1/2 teaspoon cayenne pepper

1/2 teaspoon celery seed, crushed

1/2 teaspoon dried basil

1/2 teaspoon dried marjoram

1/2 cup sour cream

1/2 cup mozzarella, shredded

1 cup frozen spinach, defrosted

2 cloves garlic, minced

1 tablespoon olive oil

1 lemon, cut into wedges

DIRECTIONS

Add 1 cup of water and a steamer rack to the bottom of your Instant Pot.

Sprinkle your salmon with all spices. In a mixing bowl, thoroughly combine sour cream, mozzarella, spinach, and garlic.

Cut a pocket in each fillet to within 1/2-inch of the opposite side. Stuff the pockets with the spinach/cheese mixture. Drizzle with olive oil.

Wrap the salmon fillets in foil and lower onto the rack.

Secure the lid. Choose the "Manual" mode and cook for 4 minutes at Low pressure. Once cooking is complete, use a quick pressure release; carefully remove the lid.

Garnish with lemon wedges and serve warm.

156. Steamed Tilapia with Butter and Spinach

(Ready in about 15 minutes | Servings 4)

Per serving: 265 Calories; 11.9g Fat; 2.7g Carbs; 36.5g Protein; 0.7g Sugars

INGREDIENTS

1 cup chicken broth
2 cloves garlic, sliced
1 pound tilapia, cut into 4 pieces
1 tablepsoon Worcestershire sauce

Salt and ground black pepper, to taste
2 tablepsoons butter, melted
2 cups fresh spinach

DIRECTIONS

Place the chicken broth and garlic in the inner pot. Place the trivet on top.

Place the tilapia fillets on a sheet of foil; add Worcestershire sauce, salt, pepper, and butter. Bring up all sides of the foil to create a packet around your fish.

Secure the lid. Choose the "Steam" mode and cook for 10 minutes at Low pressure. Once cooking is complete, use a quick pressure release; carefully remove the lid.

Add the spinach leaves to the cooking liquid. Press the "Sauté" function and let it simmer for 1 to 2 minutes or until wilted.

Place the fish fillets on top of the wilted spinach, adjust the seasonings, and serve immediately. Bon appétit!

157. Smoked Codfish with Scallions

(Ready in about 10 minutes | Servings 3)

Per serving: 203 Calories; 4.8g Fat; 1.5g Carbs; 36.3g Protein; 0.5g Sugars

INGREDIENTS

1 lemon, sliced
1/2 cup water
3 fillets smoked codfish

3 teaspoons butter
3 tablespoons scallions, chopped
Sea salt and ground black pepper, to taste

DIRECTIONS

Place the lemon and water in the bottom of the Instant Pot. Place the steamer rack on top.

Place the cod fish fillets on the steamer rack. Add the butter, scallions, salt, and black pepper.

Secure the lid. Choose the "Steam" mode and cook for 3 minutes at Low pressure. Once cooking is complete, use a quick pressure release; carefully remove the lid.

Serve warm and enjoy!

158. Teriyaki Fish Steaks

(Ready in about 15 minutes | Servings 4)

Per serving: 325 Calories; 16.1g Fat; 11.5g Carbs; 31.8g Protein; 7.9g Sugars

INGREDIENTS

2 tablespoons butter, melted
4 (6-ounce) salmon steaks
2 cloves garlic, smashed
1 (1-inch) piece fresh ginger, peeled and grated
1/3 cup soy sauce

1/2 cup water
2 tablespoons brown sugar
2 teaspoons wine vinegar
1 tablespoon cornstarch

DIRECTIONS

Press the "Sauté" button and melt the butter. Once hot, cook the salmon steaks for 2 minutes per side.

Add the garlic, ginger, soy sauce, water, sugar, and vinegar.

Secure the lid. Choose the "Manual" mode and cook for 5 minutes at Low pressure. Once cooking is complete, use a quick pressure release; carefully remove the lid. Reserve the fish steaks.

Mix the cornstarch with 2 tablespoons of cold water. Add the slurry to the cooking liquid. Let it simmer until the sauce thickens. Spoon the sauce over the fish steaks. Bon appétit!

159. Traditional Fish Tacos

(Ready in about 13 minutes | Servings 4)

Per serving: 475 Calories; 23.4g Fat; 40g Carbs; 25.2g Protein; 2.9g Sugars

INGREDIENTS

1 lemon, sliced
2 tablespoons olive oil
1 pound haddock fillets
1/2 teaspoon ground cumin
1/2 teaspoon onion powder

1 teaspoon garlic powder
1/2 teaspoon paprika
Sea salt and freshly ground black pepper, to taste
1 teaspoon dried basil

1 tablespoon ancho chili powder
4 (6-inch) flour tortillas
4 tablespoons mayonnaise
4 tablespoons sour cream
2 tablespoons fresh cilantro, chopped

DIRECTIONS

Add 1/2 cup of water, 1/2 of lemon slices, and a steamer rack to the bottom of the inner pot.

Press the "Sauté" button and heat the olive oil until sizzling. Now, sauté the haddock fillets for 1 to 2 minutes per side.

Season the fish fillets with all the spices and lower them onto the rack.

Secure the lid. Choose the "Steam" mode and cook for 3 minutes at Low pressure. Once cooking is complete, use a quick pressure release; carefully remove the lid.

Break the fish fillets into large bite-sized pieces and divide them between the tortillas.

Add the mayonnaise, sour cream and cilantro to each tortilla. Garnish with the remaining lemon slices and enjoy!

160. Halibut Steaks with Mayo Sauce and Wild Rice

(Ready in about 1 hour | Servings 6)

Per serving: 431 Calories; 28.5g Fat; 21.7g Carbs; 21.8g Protein; 1.5g Sugars

INGREDIENTS

1 cup wild rice, rinsed and drained
1 tablespoon butter
1/2 teaspoon salt flakes
1/2 teaspoon red pepper flakes, crushed

1 ½ pounds halibut steaks
2 tablespoons olive oil
Sea salt and ground pepper, to your liking
4 tablespoons cream cheese

4 tablespoons mayonnaise
1 teaspoon stone-ground mustard
2 cloves garlic, minced

DIRECTIONS

In a saucepan, bring 3 cups of water and rice to a boil. Reduce the heat to simmer; cover and let it simmer for 45 to 55 minutes. Add the butter, salt, and red pepper; fluff with a fork. Cover and reserve, keeping your rice warm.

Cut 4 sheets of aluminum foil. Place the halibut steak in each sheet of foil. Add the olive oil, salt, and black pepper to the top of the fish; close each packet and seal the edges.

Add 1 cup of water and a steamer rack to the bottom of your Instant Pot. Lower the packets onto the rack.

Secure the lid. Choose the "Steam" mode and cook for 3 minutes at Low pressure. Once cooking is complete, use a natural pressure release; carefully remove the lid.

Meanwhile, mix the cream cheese, mayonnaise, stone-ground mustard, and garlic until well combined. Serve the steamed fish with the mayo sauce and wild rice on the side. Bon appétit!

161. Shrimp Scampi with Scallions and Carrots

(Ready in about 10 minutes | Servings 4)

Per serving: 267 Calories; 9.4g Fat; 5.1g Carbs; 38.3g Protein; 1.6g Sugars

INGREDIENTS

1 tablespoon olive oil
2 garlic cloves, sliced
1 bunch scallions, chopped
2 carrots, grated
1 ½ pounds shrimp, deveined and rinsed

1/2 cup dry white wine see
1/2 cup cream of celery soup
Sea salt and freshly cracked black pepper, to taste
1 teaspoon cayenne pepper

1/2 teaspoon dried basil
1 teaspoon dried rosemary
1/2 teaspoon dried oregano

DIRECTIONS

Press the "Sauté" button and heat the oil. Once hot, cook the garlic, scallions, and carrots for 2 to 3 minutes or until fragrant; add a splash of wine to deglaze the inner pot.

Add the remaining ingredients.

Secure the lid. Choose the "Manual" mode and cook for 3 minutes at Low pressure. Once cooking is complete, use a quick pressure release; carefully remove the lid.

Divide between serving bowls and enjoy!

162. Sticky Orange Sea Bass

(Ready in about 15 minutes | Servings 4)

Per serving: 217 Calories; 9.4g Fat; 7.8g Carbs; 26.4g Protein; 6.5g Sugars

INGREDIENTS

1 tablespoon safflower oil

1 pound sea bass

Sea salt, to taste

1/4 teaspoon white pepper

2 tablespoons tamari sauce

2 cloves garlic, minced

1/2 teaspoon dried dill weed

1 orange, juiced

1 tablespoon honey

DIRECTIONS

Press the "Sauté" button and heat the oil. Now, cook the sea bass for 1 to 2 minutes per side. Season your fish with salt and pepper.

Add 1 cup of water and a steamer rack to the bottom of your Instant Pot. Lower the fish onto the rack.

Secure the lid. Choose the "Steam" mode and cook for 10 minutes at Low pressure. Once cooking is complete, use a quick pressure release; carefully remove the lid. Reserve.

Add the remaining ingredients to the cooking liquid and stir to combine well. Press the "Sauté" button again and let it simmer until the sauce thickens.

Spoon the sauce over the reserved fish. Bon appétit!

163. Almost-Famous Prawn Dipping Sauces

(Ready in about 10 minutes | Servings 8)

Per serving: 205 Calories; 16.7g Fat; 4.6g Carbs; 9.2g Protein; 2.2g Sugars

INGREDIENTS

2 cups crabmeat, flaked

1 onion, chopped

2 cloves garlic, smashed

1/2 cup cream cheese, softened

1/2 cup mayonnaise

1/2 cup Parmesan cheese, grated

1 ½ tablespoons cornichon, finely chopped

1/4 cup tomato paste

2 or so dashes of Tabasco

1/2 cup fresh breadcrumbs

DIRECTIONS

Place all ingredients, except for the breadcrumbs, in a baking dish. Stir until everything is well incorporated.

Top with breadcrumbs.

Secure the lid. Choose the "Steam" mode and cook for 3 minutes at Low pressure. Once cooking is complete, use a quick pressure release; carefully remove the lid.

Serve with raw vegetable sticks if desired. Bon appétit!

164. Tilapia Fillets with Peppers

(Ready in about 10 minutes | Servings 4)

Per serving: 239 Calories; 7.6g Fat; 8.5g Carbs; 35.6g Protein; 1.3g Sugars

INGREDIENTS

1 lemon, sliced

4 (6-ounce) tilapia fillets, skin on

4 teaspoons olive oil

Sea salt and white pepper, to taste

1 tablespoon fresh parsley, chopped

1 tablespoon fresh tarragon, chopped

1 red onion, sliced into rings

2 sweet peppers, julienned

4 tablespoons dry white wine

DIRECTIONS

Place the lemon slices, 1 cup of water, and a metal trivet in the bottom of the inner pot.

Place 4 large sheets of heavy-duty foil on a flat surface. Divide the ingredients between the sheets of foil.

Bring the ends of the foil together; fold in the sides to seal. Place the fish packets on the trivet.

Secure the lid. Choose the "Steam" mode and cook for 3 minutes at Low pressure. Once cooking is complete, use a quick pressure release; carefully remove the lid. Bon appétit!

165. Extraordinary Greek-Style Fish

(Ready in about 10 minutes | Servings 4)

Per serving: 246 Calories; 9.9g Fat; 7.1g Carbs; 31.6g Protein; 2.5g Sugars

INGREDIENTS

2 tablespoons olive oil
1 ½ pounds cod fillets
1 pound tomatoes, chopped
Sea salt and ground black pepper, to taste
2 sprigs rosemary, chopped

2 sprigs thyme, chopped
1 bay leaf
2 cloves garlic, smashed
1/2 cup Greek olives, pitted and sliced

DIRECTIONS

Place 1 cup of water and a metal trivet in the bottom of the inner pot. Brush the sides and bottom of a casserole dish with olive oil.
Place the cod fillets in the greased casserole dish. Add the tomatoes, salt, pepper, rosemary, thyme, bay leaf, and garlic.
Lower the dish onto the trivet.
Secure the lid. Choose the "Steam" mode and cook for 3 minutes at Low pressure. Once cooking is complete, use a quick pressure release; carefully remove the lid.
Serve garnished with Greek olives and enjoy!

166. French Fish en Papillote

(Ready in about 10 minutes | Servings 4)

Per serving: 285 Calories; 12.5g Fat; 6.9g Carbs; 34.6g Protein; 3.5g Sugars

Ingredients
2 tablespoons olive oil
4 (7-ounces) rainbow trout fillets
1 tablespoon fresh chives, chopped
1 tablespoon fresh parsley, chopped

Sea salt and white pepper, to taste
1/2 pound sugar snap peas, trimmed
2 tomatillos, sliced
2 garlic cloves, minced

DIRECTIONS

Place 1 cup of water and a metal rack in your Instant Pot.
Place all ingredients in a large sheet of foil. Fold up the sides of the foil to make a bowl-like shape. Lower the fish packet onto the rack.
Secure the lid. Choose the "Steam" mode and cook for 3 minutes at Low pressure. Once cooking is complete, use a quick pressure release; carefully remove the lid. Bon appétit!

167. Seafood Quiche with Colby Cheese

(Ready in about 20 minutes | Servings 4)

Per serving: 468 Calories; 26.9g Fat; 4.5g Carbs; 50.4g Protein; 2.4g Sugars

INGREDIENTS

6 eggs
1/2 cup cream cheese
1/2 cup Greek-style yogurt
Himalayan salt and ground black pepper, to taste
1 teaspoon cayenne pepper

1 teaspoon dried basil
1 teaspoon dried oregano
1 pound crab meat, chopped
1/2 pound raw shrimp, chopped
1 cup Colby cheese, shredded

DIRECTIONS

In a mixing bowl, whisk the eggs with the cream cheese and yogurt. Season with salt, black pepper, cayenne pepper, basil, and oregano.
Stir in the seafood; stir to combine and spoon the mixture into a lightly greased baking pan. Lastly, top with the shredded cheese.
Cover with a piece of aluminum foil.
Secure the lid. Choose the "Steam" mode and cook for 10 minutes at Low pressure. Once cooking is complete, use a quick pressure release; carefully remove the lid. Bon appétit!

168. Traditional Spanish Paella

(Ready in about 15 minutes | Servings 5)

Per serving: 435 Calories; 19.6g Fat; 24.8g Carbs; 46g Protein; 2.6g Sugars

INGREDIENTS

2 tablespoons olive oil

2 links (6-ounce) Spanish chorizo sausage, cut into slices

1 yellow onion, chopped

3 cloves garlic, minced

2 sweet peppers, sliced

1 Chiles de Árbol, minced

1 cup Arborio rice, rinsed

1 ½ pounds shrimp, deveined

1 cup chicken broth

1 cup water

1/3 cup white wine

1/2 teaspoon curry paste

Sea salt and white pepper, to taste

1 cup green peas, fresh or thawed

1/4 cup fresh parsley leaves, roughly chopped

DIRECTIONS

Press the "Sauté" button and heat the oil until sizzling. Cook the sausage for 2 minutes, stirring continuously to ensure even cooking.

Stir in the onions and garlic; cook for about a minute longer, stirring frequently.

Add the peppers, rice, shrimp, broth, water, wine, curry paste, salt, and white pepper.

Secure the lid. Choose the "Manual" mode and cook for 3 minutes at High pressure. Once cooking is complete, use a quick pressure release; carefully remove the lid.

Add the green peas and seal the lid one more time; let it sit in the residual heat until warmed through.

Serve garnished with fresh parsley and enjoy!

169. Crabs in Butter-Garlic Sauce

(Ready in about 15 minutes | Servings 5)

Per serving: 285 Calories; 19.8g Fat; 1.2g Carbs; 24.8g Protein; 0.6g Sugars

INGREDIENTS

1 ½ pounds crabs

1 stick butter

2 cloves garlic, minced

1 teaspoon Old Bay seasoning

1 lemon, sliced

DIRECTIONS

Place 1 cup water and a metal trivet in the bottom of your Instant Pot.

Lower the crabs onto the trivet.

Secure the lid. Choose the "Steam" mode and cook for 3 minutes at Low pressure. Once cooking is complete, use a quick pressure release; carefully remove the lid. Reserve.

Press the "Sauté" button and melt butter. Once hot, sauté the garlic and Old Bay seasoning for 2 to 3 minutes or until fragrant and thoroughly heated.

Add the cooked crabs and gently stir to combine. Serve with lemon slices. Bon appétit!

170. Easy Lobster Tails with Butter

(Ready in about 10 minutes | Servings 4)

Per serving: 292 Calories; 14.1g Fat; 4.2g Carbs; 35.1g Protein; 0.1g Sugars

INGREDIENTS

1 ½ pounds lobster tails, halved

1/2 stick butter, at room temperature

Sea salt and freshly ground black pepper, to taste

1/2 teaspoon red pepper flakes

DIRECTIONS

Add a metal trivet, steamer basket, and 1 cup of water in your Instant Pot.

Place the lobster tails, shell side down, in the prepared steamer basket.

Secure the lid. Choose the "Steam" mode and cook for 3 minutes at Low pressure. Once cooking is complete, use a quick pressure release; carefully remove the lid.

Drizzle with butter. Season with salt, black pepper, and red pepper and serve immediately. Enjoy!

171. Steamed Mussels in Scallion Sauce

(Ready in about 10 minutes | Servings 4)

Per serving: 225 Calories; 9.6g Fat; 7.8g Carbs; 20.4g Protein; 0.4g Sugars

INGREDIENTS

1 cup water
1/2 cup cooking wine
2 garlic cloves, sliced

1 ½ pounds frozen mussels, cleaned and debearded
2 tablespoons butter
1 bunch scallion, chopped

DIRECTIONS

Add the water, wine, and garlic to the inner pot. Add a metal rack to the inner pot.

Put the mussels into the steamer basket; lower the steamer basket onto the rack.

Secure the lid. Choose the "Steam" mode and cook for 3 minutes at Low pressure. Once cooking is complete, use a quick pressure release; carefully remove the lid.

Press the "Sauté" button and add butter and scallions; let it cook until the sauce is thoroughly heated and slightly thickened. Press the "Cancel" button and add the mussels. Serve warm. Bon appétit!

172. Spicy and Saucy Red Snapper

(Ready in about 10 minutes | Servings 4)

Per serving: 289 Calories; 15.4g Fat; 13.8g Carbs; 24.5g Protein; 5.5g Sugars

INGREDIENTS

1 tablespoon ghee, at room temperature
1 medium-sized leek, chopped
4 cloves garlic, minced
1 tablespoon capers
2 medium ripe tomatoes, chopped
1 cup chicken broth
1 red chili pepper, seeded and chopped

1 teaspoon basil
1/2 teaspoon oregano
1/2 teaspoon rosemary
3 (6-ounce) red snapper fillets
Coarse sea salt and ground black pepper, to taste
1 teaspoon Fish taco seasoning mix
1 lemon, cut into wedges

DIRECTIONS

Press the "Sauté" button and melt the ghee. Once hot, sauté the leek and garlic until tender.

Add the remaining ingredients, except for the lemon wedges, to the inner pot.

Secure the lid. Choose the "Manual" mode and cook for 4 minutes at High pressure. Once cooking is complete, use a quick pressure release; carefully remove the lid.

Serve in individual bowls, garnished with lemon wedges. Enjoy!

173. Delicious Shrimp Salad

(Ready in about 15 minutes + chilling time | Servings 4)

Per serving: 271 Calories; 15.4g Fat; 10.8g Carbs; 25.7g Protein; 2.9g Sugars

INGREDIENTS

1 pound shrimp, deveined
Kosher salt and white pepper, to taste
1 onion, thinly sliced
1 sweet pepper, thinly sliced
1 jalapeno pepper, deseeded and minced

2 heaping tablespoons fresh parsley, chopped
1 head romaine lettuce, torn into pieces
4 tablespoons extra-virgin olive oil
1 lime, juiced and zested
1 tablespoon Dijon mustard

DIRECTIONS

Add a metal trivet and 1 cup of water to your Instant Pot.

Put the shrimp into the steamer basket. Lower the steamer basket onto the trivet.

Secure the lid. Choose the "Steam" mode and cook for 3 minutes at Low pressure. Once cooking is complete, use a quick pressure release; carefully remove the lid.

Transfer steamed shrimp to a salad bowl; toss your shrimp with the remaining ingredients and serve well chilled. Bon appétit!

174. Crab Salad Sliders

(Ready in about 10 minutes | Servings 4)

Per serving: 413 Calories; 25g Fat; 28.5g Carbs; 18.5g Protein; 2.1g Sugars

INGREDIENTS

10 ounces crabmeat
4 heaping tablespoons fresh chives, chopped
2 garlic cloves, minced
1/2 cup mayonnaise
1/2 teaspoon hot sauce

1 teaspoon Old Bay seasoning
1/2 cup celery stalk, chopped
1 tablespoon fresh lime juice
8 mini slider rolls
2 cups Iceberg lettuce, torn into pieces

DIRECTIONS

Add 1 cup of water, metal trivet, and a steamer basket to your Instant Pot.
Place the crabmeat in the prepared steamer basket.
Secure the lid. Choose the "Steam" mode and cook for 3 minutes at Low pressure. Once cooking is complete, use a quick pressure release; carefully remove the lid.
Add the chives, garlic, mayo, hot sauce, Old Bay seasoning, celery, and lime juice; stir to combine well.
Divide the mixture between slider rolls and garnish with lettuce. Serve and enjoy!

175. Vietnamese-Style Caramel Fish

(Ready in about 10 minutes | Servings 4)

Per serving: 335 Calories; 15g Fat; 10.5g Carbs; 38.5g Protein; 8.7g Sugars

INGREDIENTS

2 tablespoons coconut oil, melted
1/4 cup brown sugar
2 tablespoons fish sauce
2 tablespoons soy sauce
1 (1-inch) ginger root, grated

Juice of 1/2 lime
Sea salt and white pepper, to taste
1 cup chicken broth
4 (7-ounce) sea bass fillets
2 tablespoons fresh chives, chopped

DIRECTIONS

Press the "Sauté" button and heat the coconut oil. Once hot, cook the brown sugar, fish sauce, soy sauce, ginger, lime, salt, white pepper, and broth. Bring to a simmer and press the "Cancel" button.
Add sea bass. Secure the lid. Choose the "Manual" mode and cook for 4 minutes at High pressure. Once cooking is complete, use a quick pressure release; carefully remove the lid.
Remove the sea bass fillets from the cooking liquid. Press the "Sauté" button one more time. Reduce the sauce until it is thick and syrupy.
Spoon the sauce over the reserved sea bass fillets. Garnish with fresh chives. Bon appétit!

176. Traditional Fish and Couscous Biryani

(Ready in about 10 minutes | Servings 4)

Per serving: 505 Calories; 11.2g Fat; 61.1g Carbs; 37.7g Protein; 5.1g Sugars

INGREDIENTS

2 tablespoons butter
1 yellow onion, chopped
2 cups couscous
2 cups water
1 cup vegetable broth
1 cup coconut milk

Sea salt and ground black pepper, to taste
1 teaspoon cayenne pepper
1 teaspoon dried basil
2 ripe tomatoes, pureed
1 ½ pounds halibut, cut into chunks
1 teaspoon coriander

1 teaspoon curry paste
1 teaspoon ancho chili powder
2 bay leaves
4 cardamom pods
1 teaspoon garam masala
2 tablespoons almonds, slivered

DIRECTIONS

Press the "Sauté" button and melt the butter. Once hot, cook the onions until tender and translucent.
Add the remaining ingredients, except for the slivered almonds, to the inner pot; stir to combine.
Secure the lid. Choose the "Manual" mode and cook for 4 minutes at High pressure. Once cooking is complete, use a quick pressure release; carefully remove the lid.
Serve garnished with almonds. Bon appétit!

177. Salmon Salad Croissants

(Ready in about 10 minutes + chilling time | Servings 6)

Per serving: 412 Calories; 2.7g Fat; 26.8g Carbs; 28.8g Protein; 9.8g Sugars

INGREDIENTS

1 ½ pounds salmon fillets

1 red onion, thinly sliced

1/4 cup prepared horseradish, drained

1/4 cup mayonnaise

2 tablespoons sour cream

Salt and white pepper, to taste

1/2 teaspoon red pepper flakes, crushed

1/2 teaspoon dried rosemary, only leaves crushed

1/2 teaspoon dried oregano

1 cup cherry tomatoes, halved

2 cups Iceberg lettuce leaves, torn into pieces

6 croissants, split

DIRECTIONS

Add 1 cup of water and metal trivet to your Instant Pot. Lower the salmon fillets onto the trivet.

Secure the lid. Choose the "Steam" mode and cook for 3 minutes at Low pressure. Once cooking is complete, use a quick pressure release; carefully remove the lid.

Add the remaining ingredients and stir to combine well. Place in your refrigerator until ready to serve.

Serve on croissants and enjoy!

SOUPS

178. Old-Fashioned Ham Bone Soup

(Ready in about 30 minutes | Servings 5)

Per serving: 197 Calories; 10.2g Fat; 9.3g Carbs; 17.7g Protein; 3.7g Sugars

INGREDIENTS

2 tablespoons olive oil
1/2 cup onion, chopped
2 carrots, diced

1 rib celery, diced
1 parsnip, diced
1 ham bone

5 cups chicken stock
Sea salt and ground black pepper, to taste

DIRECTIONS

Press the "Sauté" button and heat the olive oil until sizzling. Then, sauté the onion, carrot, celery, and parsnip until tender.

Add the ham bone, chicken stock, salt, and black pepper to the inner pot.

Secure the lid. Choose the "Manual" mode and cook for 15 minutes at High pressure. Once cooking is complete, use a natural pressure release for 10 minutes; carefully remove the lid.

Remove the ham bone from the inner pot. Chop the meat from the bone; add back into the soup.

Serve in individual bowls and enjoy!

179. Chicken Tortilla Soup

(Ready in about 25 minutes | Servings 4)

Per serving: 428 Calories; 27.2g Fat; 30.7g Carbs; 19.8g Protein; 6.4g Sugars

INGREDIENTS

2 tablespoons olive oil
1/2 cup shallots, chopped
1 sweet pepper, chopped
1 Poblano chili pepper, chopped
1/2 pound chicken thighs, boneless and skinless
2 ripe tomatoes, chopped

1 can (10-ounce) red enchilada sauce
2 teaspoons ground cumin
1 teaspoon ground coriander
1 teaspoon chili powder
Seasoned salt and freshly cracked pepper, to taste
4 cups roasted vegetable broth

1 bay leaf
1 can (15-ounce) black beans, drained and rinsed
4 (6-inch) corn tortillas, cut crosswise into 1/4-inch strips
1 avocado, cut into 1/2-inch dice
1 cup cheddar cheese, shredded

DIRECTIONS

Press the "Sauté" button and heat the olive oil. Once hot, sauté the shallots and peppers until tender and aromatic.

Add the chicken thighs, tomatoes, enchilada sauce, cumin, coriander, chili powder, salt, black pepper, vegetable broth, and bay leaf to the inner pot.

Secure the lid. Choose the "Manual" mode and cook for 8 minutes at High pressure. Once cooking is complete, use a natural pressure release for 10 minutes; carefully remove the lid.

Stir in the canned beans and seal the lid; let it sit in the residual heat until everything is heated through.

Divide your soup between individual bowls and serve garnished with tortilla strips, avocado, and cheddar cheese.

180. Greek-Style Lentil and Tomato Soup

(Ready in about 15 minutes | Servings 4)

Per serving: 305 Calories; 7.4g Fat; 45.9g Carbs; 17g Protein; 8.5g Sugars

INGREDIENTS

2 tablespoons butter
1 red onion, chopped
1/2 cup celery, chopped
1 teaspoon ground cumin

1 teaspoon ground coriander
1 teaspoon garlic powder
1 cup yellow lentils
1 teaspoon dried parsley flakes

2 cups roasted vegetable broth
2 cups tomato puree
2 green onions, sliced

DIRECTIONS

Press the "Sauté" button and melt the butter. Once hot, cook the onion and celery until just tender.

Stir in the remaining ingredients, except for the green onions.

Secure the lid. Choose the "Manual" mode and cook for 8 minutes at High pressure. Once cooking is complete, use a quick pressure release; carefully remove the lid.

Serve warm garnished with green onions. Enjoy!

181. Root Vegetable and Wild Rice Soup

(Ready in about 45 minutes | Servings 5)

Per serving: 240 Calories; 2g Fat; 44.6g Carbs; 12.8g Protein; 5.7g Sugars

INGREDIENTS

3 carrots, chopped

3 stalks celery, chopped

1 turnip, chopped

1 shallot, chopped

1 ½ cups wild rice

10 ounces button mushrooms, sliced

5 cups vegetable broth

1 teaspoon granulated garlic

Sea salt and red pepper, to taste

DIRECTIONS

Place the ingredients in the inner pot; stir to combine.

Secure the lid. Choose the "Soup/Broth" mode and cook for 40 minutes at High pressure. Once cooking is complete, use a quick pressure release; carefully remove the lid.

Serve warm garnished with a few drizzles of olive oil if desired. Bon appétit!

182. Grandma's Noodle Soup

(Ready in about 20 minutes | Servings 6)

Per serving: 362 Calories; 25.4g Fat; 21.6g Carbs; 11.5g Protein; 2.9g Sugars

INGREDIENTS

2 tablespoons olive oil

2 carrots, diced

2 parsnips, diced

1 yellow onion, chopped

2 cloves garlic, minced

6 cups chicken bone broth

1 bay leaf

Salt and freshly ground black pepper

2 pounds chicken thighs drumettes

2 cups wide egg noodles

1/4 cup fresh cilantro, roughly chopped

DIRECTIONS

Press the "Sauté" button and heat the oil. Once hot, cook the carrots, parsnips, and onions until they are just tender.

Add the minced garlic and continue to cook for a minute more.

Add the chicken bone broth, bay leaf, salt, black pepper, and chicken to the inner pot.

Secure the lid. Choose the "Manual" mode and cook for 9 minutes at High pressure. Once cooking is complete, use a quick pressure release; carefully remove the lid.

Shred the cooked chicken and set aside. Stir in noodles and press the "Sauté" button. Cook approximately 5 minutes or until thoroughly heated.

Afterwards, add the chicken back into the soup. Serve garnished with fresh cilantro. Bon appétit!

183. Classic Minestrone Soup

(Ready in about 10 minutes | Servings 4)

Per serving: 413 Calories; 21.1g Fat; 39.5g Carbs; 19.8g Protein; 10.6g Sugars

INGREDIENTS

2 tablespoons canola oil

1 onion, chopped

2 stalks celery, diced

2 carrots, diced

2 cloves garlic, pressed

2 pounds tomatoes, pureed

2 cups chicken broth

1 cup pasta, uncooked

2 teaspoons Italian seasoning

Sea salt and ground black pepper, to taste

1/2 cup fresh corn kernels

2 cups cannellini beans, canned and rinsed

6 ounces Parmesan cheese, grated

DIRECTIONS

Press the "Sauté" button and heat oil until sizzling, Then, sauté the onion, celery, and carrots for 3 to 4 minutes or until tender.

Add the garlic, tomatoes, broth, pasta, Italian seasoning, salt, and black pepper.

Secure the lid. Choose the "Manual" mode and cook for 5 minutes at High pressure. Once cooking is complete, use a quick pressure release; carefully remove the lid.

Lastly, stir in the corn kernels and beans. Seal the lid and let it sit in the residual heat for 5 to 8 minutes. Ladle into individual bowls and serve topped with Parmesan cheese. Bon appétit!

184. Beef Soup with Garden Vegetables

(Ready in about 40 minutes | Servings 5)

Per serving: 244 Calories; 18.6g Fat; 13.1g Carbs; 7g Protein; 6.2g Sugars

INGREDIENTS

2 tablespoons olive oil
1 ½ pounds beef stew meat, cubed
Sea salt and ground black pepper, to taste
1 onion, chopped

2 celery stalks, chopped
2 carrots, chopped
2 cloves garlic, chopped
2 rosemary sprigs
2 thyme sprigs

1/4 cup tamari sauce
2 bay leaves
5 cups beef bone broth
2 ripe tomatoes, pureed
6 ounces green beans, fresh or thawed

DIRECTIONS

Press the "Sauté" button and heat the oil until sizzling. Now, brown the beef meat for 3 to 4 minutes, stirring frequently to ensure even cooking. Add the remaining ingredients, except for the green beans.

Secure the lid. Choose the "Manual" mode and cook for 13 minutes at High pressure. Once cooking is complete, use a natural pressure release for 15; carefully remove the lid.

Add the green beans.

Secure the lid. Choose the "Manual" mode and cook for 2 minutes at High pressure. Once cooking is complete, use a quick pressure release; carefully remove the lid. Bon appétit!

185. Autumn Acorn Squash Soup

(Ready in about 20 minutes | Servings 4)

Per serving: 152 Calories; 3.9g Fat; 27.4g Carbs; 5.1g Protein; 6.6g Sugars

INGREDIENTS

1 tablespoon butter, softened
2 cloves garlic, sliced
1 medium-sized leek, chopped
1 turnip, chopped

1 carrot, chopped
1 ½ pounds acorn squash, chopped
2 cups vegetable broth
2 cups water

1/2 teaspoon ground allspice
1 sprig fresh thyme
Himalayan salt and black pepper, to taste

DIRECTIONS

Press the "Sauté" button and melt the butter. Once hot, cook the garlic and leek until just tender and fragrant.

Add the remaining ingredients to the inner pot.

Secure the lid. Choose the "Manual" mode and cook for 10 minutes at High pressure. Once cooking is complete, use a quick pressure release; carefully remove the lid.

Puree the soup in your blender until smooth and uniform. Serve warm and enjoy!

186. Seafood and Pinot Grigio Soup

(Ready in about 20 minutes | Servings 4)

Per serving: 320 Calories; 8.4g Fat; 27.1g Carbs; 31.6g Protein; 7.7g Sugars

INGREDIENTS

2 slices bacon, chopped
1 medium leek, chopped
1 celery stalk, chopped
2 carrots, chopped
2 parsnips, chopped

1/3 cup Pinot Grigio
3 cups chicken broth
1/3 cup whole milk
1/2 pound frozen corn kernels, thawed
1 serrano pepper, minced

1 teaspoon granulated garlic
Seas salt and ground black pepper, to taste
1 pound shrimp, deveined

DIRECTIONS

Press the "Sauté" button and cook the bacon until it is crisp. Chop the bacon and set aside.

Then, sauté the leeks, celery, carrots, and parsnips in the bacon drippings. Cook for about 4 minutes or until they have softened. Add a splash of wine to deglaze the pot.

Press the "Cancel" button. Stir in the broth, milk, corn, pepper, granulated garlic, salt, and black pepper.

Secure the lid. Choose the "Manual" mode and cook for 2 minutes at High pressure. Once cooking is complete, use a quick pressure release; carefully remove the lid.

Stir in the shrimp and seal the lid again; allow it to stand in the residual heat for 5 to 10 minutes. Garnish with the reserved crumbled bacon. Bon appétit!

187. Simple Clam Chowder

(Ready in about 15 minutes | Servings 4)

Per serving: 349 Calories; 18.4g Fat; 41.1g Carbs; 7.3g Protein; 8.4g Sugars

INGREDIENTS

2 tablespoons butter
1 onion, chopped
1 garlic clove, minced
1 stalk celery, diced
1 carrot, diced

1 cup water
2 cups fish stock
Sea salt and white pepper, to taste
1 pound Russet potatoes, peeled and diced

1 teaspoon cayenne pepper
18 ounces canned clams, chopped with juice
1 cup heavy cream

DIRECTIONS

Press the "Sauté" button and melt the butter; once hot, cook the onion, garlic, celery, and carrot for 3 minutes or until they have softened. Add the water, stock, salt, white pepper, potatoes, and cayenne pepper.

Secure the lid. Choose the "Manual" mode and cook for 2 minutes at High pressure. Once cooking is complete, use a quick pressure release; carefully remove the lid.

Press the "Sauté" button and use the lowest setting. Stir in the clams and heavy cream. Let it simmer for about 5 minutes or until everything is thoroughly heated. Bon appétit!

188. Cod Fish and Tomato Soup

(Ready in about 12 minutes | Servings 4)

Per serving: 232 Calories; 12.4g Fat; 7.3g Carbs; 20.1g Protein; 3.9g Sugars

INGREDIENTS

1/2 stick butter, at room temperature
1 onion, chopped
2 garlic cloves, minced
2 ripe tomatoes, pureed
2 tablespoons tomato paste
1 cup shellfish stock
1/4 cup cooking wine

1 pound cod fish, cut into bite-sized pieces
1/2 teaspoon basil
1/2 teaspoon dried dill weed
1/4 teaspoon dried oregano
1/4 teaspoon hot sauce
1/2 teaspoon paprika
Sea salt and freshly ground black pepper, to taste

DIRECTIONS

Press the "Sauté" button and melt the butter; once hot, cook the onion and garlic for about 2 minutes or until they are just tender. Add the remaining ingredients.

Secure the lid. Choose the "Manual" mode and cook for 5 minutes at High pressure. Once cooking is complete, use a quick pressure release; carefully remove the lid.

Ladle into serving bowls and serve immediately.

189. Rustic Beef Stroganoff Soup

(Ready in about 1 hour | Servings 4)

Per serving: 267 Calories; 9.6g Fat; 11.4g Carbs; 34.2g Protein; 2.2g Sugars

INGREDIENTS

1 pound beef stew meat, cubed
5 cups beef bone broth
1/2 teaspoon dried basil
1/2 teaspoon dried oregano
1/2 teaspoon dried rosemary

1 teaspoon dried sage
1 teaspoon shallot powder
1/2 teaspoon porcini powder
1 teaspoon garlic powder
Sea salt and ground black pepper, to taste

7 ounces button mushrooms, sliced
1/2 cup sour cream
2 tablespoons potato starch, mixed with 4 tablespoons of cold water

DIRECTIONS

In the inner pot, place the stew meat, broth, and spices.

Secure the lid. Choose the "Manual" mode and cook for 50 minutes at High pressure. Once cooking is complete, use a quick pressure release; carefully remove the lid.

Add the mushrooms and sour cream to the inner pot.

Choose the "Soup/Broth" mode. Bring to a boil and add the potato starch slurry. Continue to simmer until the soup thickens.

Ladle into serving bowls and serve immediately. Bon appétit!

190. Spicy Broccoli and Cheese Soup

(Ready in about 10 minutes | Servings 4)

Per serving: 398 Calories; 24.4g Fat; 32.3g Carbs; 17.1g Protein; 10.9g Sugars

INGREDIENTS

4 tablespoons butter
2 cloves garlic, pressed
1 teaspoon shallot powder
4 cups cream of celery soup

1 pound small broccoli florets
Sea salt and ground black pepper, to taste
1/2 teaspoon chili powder

2 cups half and half
2 cups sharp cheddar cheese, freshly grated
2 scallions stalks, chopped

DIRECTIONS

Add the butter, garlic, shallot powder, cream of celery soup, broccoli, salt, black pepper, and chili powder to the inner pot.

Secure the lid. Choose the "Manual" mode and cook for 2 minutes at High pressure. Once cooking is complete, use a quick pressure release; carefully remove the lid.

Stir in the half and half and cheese. Let it simmer until everything is thoroughly heated.

Divide between serving bowls and serve garnished with chopped scallions. Bon appétit!

191. Authentic French Onion Soup

(Ready in about 10 minutes | Servings 4)

Per serving: 325 Calories; 13.9g Fat; 31.7g Carbs; 19.2g Protein; 7.6g Sugars

INGREDIENTS

4 tablespoons butter, melted
1 pound onions, thinly sliced
Kosher salt and ground white pepper, to taste
1/2 teaspoon dried sage

4 cups chicken bone broth
1 loaf French bread, sliced
1 cup mozzarella cheese, shredded

DIRECTIONS

Press the "Sauté" button and melt the butter. Once hot, cook the onions until golden and caramelized.

Add the salt, pepper, sage, and chicken bone broth.

Secure the lid. Choose the "Manual" mode and cook for 2 minutes at High pressure. Once cooking is complete, use a quick pressure release; carefully remove the lid.

Divide the soup between four oven safe bowls; top with the bread and shredded cheese; now, place the bowls under the broiler for about 4 minutes or until the cheese has melted. Bon appétit!

192. Meatball and Noodle Soup

(Ready in about 30 minutes | Servings 4)

Per serving: 487 Calories; 21.9g Fat; 30.1g Carbs; 40.8g Protein; 4.7g Sugars

INGREDIENTS

Meatballs:
1/2 pound ground beef
1/2 pound ground turkey
1/2 cup panko crumbs
1/4 cup Pecorino Romano cheese, grated
1 egg, beaten

2 cloves garlic, crushed
2 tablespoons cilantro, chopped
Sea salt and ground black pepper, to taste
Soup:
1 tablespoon olive oil
1 onion, chopped

1 celery stalk, chopped
2 cloves garlic, minced
2 tomatoes, crushed
4 cups chicken broth
2 bay leaves
6 ounces noodles

DIRECTIONS

In a mixing bowl, thoroughly combine all ingredients for the meatballs.

Form the mixture into 20 meatballs. Press the "Sauté" button and heat the oil. Now, brown the meatballs in batches; reserve.

Heat the olive oil; sauté the onion, celery, and garlic for 3 to 4 minutes or until they are fragrant.

Add the tomatoes, broth, and bay leaves to the inner pot.

Secure the lid. Choose the "Manual" mode and cook for 12 minutes at High pressure. Once cooking is complete, use a quick pressure release; carefully remove the lid.

Next, sit in the noodles and secure the lid again.

Choose the "Manual" mode and cook for 5 minutes at High pressure. Once cooking is complete, use a quick pressure release; carefully remove the lid. Bon appétit!

193. Chipotle Chili Soup

(Ready in about 45 minutes | Servings 4)

Per serving: 343 Calories; 17.5g Fat; 10.9g Carbs; 34.7g Protein; 3.3g Sugars

INGREDIENTS

1 tablespoon canola oil
1 pound ground beef
2 cloves garlic, smashed
1 medium leek, chopped

2 chipotle chilis in adobo sauce, roughly chopped
1 (14 ½ -ounce) can tomatoes, diced
2 cups vegetable broth

16 ounces pinto beans, undrained
1/2 teaspoon cumin powder
1 teaspoon stone-ground mustard
1 teaspoon chili powder

DIRECTIONS

Press the "Sauté" button and heat the oil. Brown the ground beef for 2 to 3 minutes, stirring frequently.

Add the remaining ingredients and stir to combine well.

Secure the lid. Choose the "Bean/Chili" mode and cook for 30 minutes at High pressure. Once cooking is complete, use a natural pressure release for 10 minutes; carefully remove the lid. Bon appétit!

194. Creamed Corn and Chicken Soup

(Ready in about 20 minutes | Servings 6)

Per serving: 313 Calories; 15.5g Fat; 19.4g Carbs; 24.7g Protein; 4.6g Sugars

INGREDIENTS

1 tablespoon olive oil
1 yellow onion, chopped
1 celery stalk, diced
1 carrot, finely diced
1 turnip, diced

6 cups roasted vegetable broth
1 pound chicken breasts, skinless, boneless and diced
1 teaspoon garlic powder
1 teaspoon mustard powder

1 (15-ounce) can creamed corn
4 large eggs, whisked
Kosher salt and ground black pepper, to taste

DIRECTIONS

Press the "Sauté" button and heat the oil. Now, sauté the onion until just tender and translucent.

Add the celery, carrot, turnip, vegetable broth, chicken, garlic powder, and mustard powder.

Secure the lid. Choose the "Manual" mode and cook for 9 minutes at High pressure. Once cooking is complete, use a quick pressure release; carefully remove the lid.

Press the "Sauté" button and use the lowest setting. Stir in the creamed corn and eggs; let it simmer, stirring continuously for about 5 minutes or until everything is thoroughly heated.

Season with salt and pepper to taste and serve warm. Bon appétit!

195. Kidney Bean and Chicken Soup

(Ready in about 20 minutes | Servings 4)

Per serving: 374 Calories; 16.8g Fat; 18.9g Carbs; 36g Protein; 2.8g Sugars

INGREDIENTS

2 tablespoons butter, softened
1 onion, chopped
1 sweet pepper, deseeded and chopped
1 habanero pepper, deseeded and chopped

2 cloves garlic, minced
Sea salt and ground black pepper, to taste
1 teaspoon dried basil
1 teaspoon dried oregano
1 teaspoon cayenne pepper

4 cups vegetable broth
1 pound chicken thighs
2 cans (15-ounce) red kidney beans
1/4 cup fresh cilantro, chopped
1/2 cup tortilla chips

DIRECTIONS

Press the "Sauté" button and melt the butter. Once hot, cook the onion until tender and translucent.

Stir in the peppers and sauté for a few minutes more. Add the minced garlic and continue to sauté for another minute.

Add the spices, vegetable broth, and chicken thighs to the inner pot.

Secure the lid. Choose the "Manual" mode and cook for 13 minutes at High pressure. Once cooking is complete, use a quick pressure release; carefully remove the lid.

Remove the chicken to a cutting board. Add the kidney beans to the inner pot and seal the lid again. Let it sit in the residual heat until thoroughly heated.

Shred the chicken and discard the bones; put it back into the soup. Serve with fresh cilantro and tortilla chips. Enjoy!

196. Sweet Potato Soup with Swiss Chard

(Ready in about 15 minutes | Servings 4)

Per serving: 254 Calories; 9.7g Fat; 36.3g Carbs; 7.1g Protein; 10.9g Sugars

INGREDIENTS

2 tablespoons butter, softened at room temperature

1 white onion, chopped

1 sweet pepper, deveined and chopped

2 cloves garlic, pressed

1 pound sweet potatoes, peeled and diced

2 ripe tomatoes, pureed

2 cups chicken bone broth

2 cups water

Kosher salt and freshly ground black pepper, to taste

1/4 cup peanut butter

2 cups Swiss chard, torn into pieces

DIRECTIONS

Press the "Sauté" button and melt the butter. Once hot, cook the onion, pepper, and garlic until tender and fragrant.

Add the sweet potatoes and continue to sauté for about 3 minutes longer. Now, stir in the tomatoes, broth, water, salt, and black pepper.

Secure the lid. Choose the "Manual" mode and cook for 4 minutes at High pressure. Once cooking is complete, use a quick pressure release; carefully remove the lid.

Stir in the peanut butter and Swiss chard; seal the lid again and let it sit in the residual heat until your greens wilt. Serve warm.

197. Indian Turkey and Basmati Rice Soup

(Ready in about 15 minutes | Servings 4)

Per serving: 254 Calories; 9.7g Fat; 36.3g Carbs; 7.1g Protein; 10.9g Sugars

INGREDIENTS

1 tablespoon sesame oil

1 onion, chopped

1 large thumb-sized pieces fresh ginger, peeled and grated

1 pound turkey breast, boneless and cut into chunks

2 carrots, sliced

1 celery stalk, sliced

5 cups chicken broth

1 teaspoon garlic powder

1 teaspoon cumin seeds

1 teaspoon garam masala

1 teaspoon turmeric powder

1 cup basmati rice, rinsed

1 small handful of fresh coriander, roughly chopped

DIRECTIONS

Press the "Sauté" button and heat the sesame oil until sizzling. Now, sauté the onion and ginger until tender and aromatic.

Add the turkey, carrot, and celery to the inner pot; continue to cook for 3 to 4 minutes more or until the turkey is no longer pink.

Add the chicken broth and spices to the inner pot. Secure the lid. Choose the "Manual" mode and cook for 5 minutes at High pressure. Once cooking is complete, use a quick pressure release; carefully remove the lid.

After that, stir in the basmati rice.

Secure the lid. Choose the "Manual" mode and cook for 4 minutes at High pressure. Once cooking is complete, use a quick pressure release; carefully remove the lid.

Ladle into four serving bowls and serve with fresh coriander. Enjoy!

198. Beef and Barley Soup

(Ready in about 25 minutes | Servings 4)

Per serving: 300 Calories; 5.7g Fat; 52.6g Carbs; 11.6g Protein; 5.9g Sugars

INGREDIENTS

1 tablespoon canola oil

2 shallots, chopped

2 garlic cloves, minced

2 celery stalks, chopped

1 parsnip, chopped

1 cup tomato puree

4 cups beef broth

1 cup pearl barley

2 sprigs thyme

Sea salt and white pepper, to taste

1 teaspoon red pepper flakes, crushed

DIRECTIONS

Press the "Sauté" button and heat the canola oil. Once hot, sauté the shallots, garlic, celery, and parsnip until tender and aromatic.

Add the remaining ingredients and stir to combine.

Secure the lid. Choose the "Soup/Broth" mode and cook for 20 minutes at High pressure. Once cooking is complete, use a quick pressure release; carefully remove the lid.

Serve in individual bowls. Bon appétit!

199. Peppery Ground Pork Soup

(Ready in about 30 minutes | Servings 4)

Per serving: 382 Calories; 26.2g Fat; 10.5g Carbs; 26.3g Protein; 2.4g Sugars

INGREDIENTS

1 pound ground pork
1 teaspoon Italian seasoning
1 teaspoon garlic powder

Sea salt and ground black pepper, to taste
2 sweet peppers, seeded and sliced

1 jalapeno pepper, seeded and minced
2 ripe tomatoes, pureed
4 cups chicken stock

DIRECTIONS

Press the "Sauté" button to preheat your Instant Pot. Then, brown the ground pork until no longer pink or about 3 minutes.

Add the remaining ingredients to the inner pot and stir.

Secure the lid. Choose the "Manual" mode and cook for 10 minutes at High pressure. Once cooking is complete, use a natural pressure release for 10; carefully remove the lid.

Serve warm. Bon appétit!

200. Mediterranean-Style Lima Bean Soup

(Ready in about 25 minutes | Servings 5)

Per serving: 263 Calories; 8.1g Fat; 35.7g Carbs; 15.4g Protein; 10.1g Sugars

INGREDIENTS

2 tablespoons sesame oil
1 pound cremini mushrooms, thinly sliced
1 large-sized eggplant, sliced into rounds
1 red onion, chopped
2 garlic cloves, chopped

2 carrots, sliced
2 sweet potatoes, peeled and diced
1/2 teaspoon red curry paste
1/2 teaspoon cayenne pepper
Sea salt and ground black pepper, to taste
2 sprigs thyme

2 sprigs rosemary
2 medium-sized tomatoes, pureed
5 cups roasted vegetable broth
16 ounces lima beans, soaked overnight
Juice of 1 fresh lemon

DIRECTIONS

Press the "Sauté" button and heat the oil until sizzling. Now, cook the mushrooms, eggplant, onion, and garlic until just tender and fragrant.

Add the carrots, sweet potatoes, curry paste, spices, tomatoes, broth, and lima beans.

Secure the lid. Choose the "Manual" mode and cook for 13 minutes at High pressure. Once cooking is complete, use a quick pressure release; carefully remove the lid.

Divide your soup between individual bowls; add a few drizzles of lemon juice to each serving and enjoy!

201. Rich Lobster Bisque

(Ready in about 15 minutes | Servings 4)

Per serving: 345 Calories; 14.6g Fat; 31.2g Carbs; 22g Protein; 10.4g Sugars

INGREDIENTS

1 pound lump lobster meat
2 tablespoons olive oil
1 yellow onion, chopped
1 celery stalk, diced
1 carrot, diced
2 cloves garlic, minced
1 teaspoon rosemary

1 teaspoon basil
1 teaspoon thyme
1/2 teaspoon turmeric powder
1 tomato, pureed
1/4 cup cooking sherry
3 cups clam juice
1 tablespoon soy sauce

1/2 teaspoon smoked paprika
Sea salt and ground white pepper, to taste
1 teaspoon Tabasco sauce
1 cup heavy cream

DIRECTIONS

In the inner pot of your Instant Pot, place the lobster meat, olive oil, onion, celery, carrot, garlic, rosemary, basil, thyme, turmeric, tomato puree, cooking sherry, and clam juice.

Secure the lid. Choose the "Manual" mode and cook for 4 minutes at High pressure. Once cooking is complete, use a quick pressure release; carefully remove the lid. Set the lobster meat aside and chop into small chunks.

Now, add in the soy sauce, smoked paprika, salt, white pepper, Tabasco sauce, and heavy cream; continue to stir and simmer until it's all blended together and heated through.

Lastly, put the lobster meat back into your bisque. Serve in individual bowls and enjoy!

202. Seafood Chowder with Bacon and Celery

(Ready in about 15 minutes | Servings 4)

Per serving: 264 Calories; 9.4g Fat; 26.2g Carbs; 20.8g Protein; 9.9g Sugars

INGREDIENTS

3 strips bacon, chopped
1 onion, chopped
2 carrots, diced
2 stalks celery, diced
2 cloves garlic, minced

1 tablespoon Creole seasoning
Sea salt and ground black pepper, to taste
3 cups seafood stock
2 ripe tomatoes, pureed

2 tablespoons tomato paste
2 bay leaves
1 pound clams, chopped
1 ½ tablespoons flaxseed meal

DIRECTIONS

Press the "Sauté" button to preheat your Instant Pot. Now, cook the bacon until it is crisp; crumble the bacon and set it aside.

Now, sauté the onion, carrot, celery, and garlic in bacon drippings.

Add the remaining ingredients, except for the chopped clams, to the inner pot.

Secure the lid. Choose the "Manual" mode and cook for 4 minutes at High pressure. Once cooking is complete, use a quick pressure release; carefully remove the lid.

Stir in the chopped clams and flaxseed meal.

Press the "Sauté" button and let it simmer for 2 to 3 minutes longer or until everything is heated through.

Serve in individual bowls topped with the reserved bacon. Bon appétit!

203. Corn and Potato Chowder

(Ready in about 25 minutes | Servings 4)

Per serving: 439 Calories; 20.4g Fat; 56.2g Carbs; 12.8g Protein; 9.3g Sugars

INGREDIENTS

2 tablespoons butter
1 sweet onion, chopped
2 garlic cloves, minced
1 sweet pepper, deveined and sliced
1 jalapeno pepper, deveined and sliced

4 tablespoons all-purpose flour
4 cups vegetable broth
1 pound potatoes, cut into bite-sized pieces
3 cups creamed corn kernels

1 cup double cream
Kosher salt and ground black pepper, to taste
1/2 teaspoon cayenne pepper

DIRECTIONS

Press the "Sauté" button and melt the butter. Once hot, sauté the sweet onions, garlic, and peppers for about 3 minutes or until they are tender and fragrant.

Sprinkle the flour over the vegetables; continue stirring approximately 4 minutes or until your vegetables are coated.

Add the broth and potatoes and gently stir to combine.

Secure the lid. Choose the "Manual" mode and cook for 5 minutes at High pressure. Once cooking is complete, use a quick pressure release; carefully remove the lid.

Press the "Sauté" button and use the lowest setting. Stir in the creamed corn, double cream, salt, black pepper, and cayenne pepper.

Let it simmer, stirring continuously for about 5 minutes or until everything is thoroughly heated. Taste and adjust the seasonings. Bon appétit!

204. Halibut Chowder with Swiss Cheese

(Ready in about 15 minutes | Servings 5)

Per serving: 456 Calories; 20.2g Fat; 15.7g Carbs; 50.2g Protein; 7.7g Sugars

INGREDIENTS

2 tablespoons butter
1 medium-sized leek, sliced
1 carrot, shredded
1 celery stalk, shredded
2 cloves garlic, minced

5 cups chicken bone broth
2 ripe tomatoes, chopped
1 ½ pounds halibut, cut into small cubes
Kosher salt and cracked black pepper, to taste

1 cup milk
1/2 cup double cream
1 cup Swiss cheese, shredded

DIRECTIONS

Press the "Sauté" button and melt the butter. Once hot, sauté the leeks, carrot, celery, and garlic until they are just tender and fragrant.

Then, add the chicken bone broth, tomatoes, halibut, salt, and black pepper.

Secure the lid. Choose the "Manual" mode and cook for 5 minutes at High pressure. Once cooking is complete, use a quick pressure release; carefully remove the lid.

Press the "Sauté" button and use the lowest setting. Stir in the milk and double cream. Allow it to simmer for about 3 minutes or until heated through.

Ladle your chowder into five serving bowls; top with the shredded Swiss cheese and serve immediately.

205. Red Lentil and Spinach Soup

(Ready in about 10 minutes | Servings 5)

Per serving: 295 Calories; 1.9g Fat; 52.7g Carbs; 19.2g Protein; 1.6g Sugars

INGREDIENTS

2 cups red lentils, rinsed
1 onion, chopped
2 cloves garlic, minced
1 teaspoon cumin

1 teaspoon smoked paprika
Sea salt and ground black pepper, to taste
2 carrots, sliced

6 cups water
2 bay leaves
2 cups fresh spinach leaves, torn into small pieces

DIRECTIONS

Place all ingredients, except for the fresh spinach, in the inner pot.
Secure the lid. Choose the "Manual" mode and cook for 3 minutes at High pressure. Once cooking is complete, use a quick pressure release; carefully remove the lid.
Stir in the spinach and seal the lid again; let it sit until the spinach just starts to wilt.
Serve in individual bowls and enjoy!

206. Chicken Soup with Garden Vegetable

(Ready in about 20 minutes | Servings 3)

Per serving: 257 Calories; 13.1g Fat; 13.6g Carbs; 22.5g Protein; 6.1g Sugars

INGREDIENTS

2 tablespoons butter, melted
1/2 pound chicken legs, boneless and skinless
1 onion, diced
1 teaspoon garlic, minced

1 teaspoon ginger, peeled and grated
3 cups chicken stock
1/2 teaspoon dried sage
1/2 teaspoon dried thyme leaves
Sea salt and ground black pepper, to taste

2 tablespoons tamari sauce
2 carrots, diced
2 parsnips, diced
2 cups cauliflower florets

DIRECTIONS

Press the "Sauté" button and melt the butter. Once hot, sauté the chicken until golden brown; reserve.
Cook the onion, garlic, and ginger in pan drippings until just tender and aromatic.
Add the reserved chicken, stock, and spices.
Secure the lid. Choose the "Manual" mode and cook for 13 minutes at High pressure. Once cooking is complete, use a quick pressure release; carefully remove the lid.
Now, add the tamari sauce and vegetables to the inner pot.
Secure the lid. Choose the "Manual" mode and cook for 5 minutes at High pressure. Once cooking is complete, use a quick pressure release; carefully remove the lid. Serve immediately.

207. Farmhouse Vegetable Soup

(Ready in about 15 minutes | Servings 4)

Per serving: 176 Calories; 9.2g Fat; 15.9g Carbs; 9.5g Protein; 6.1g Sugars

INGREDIENTS

2 tablespoons canola oil
1 shallot, chopped
2 garlic cloves, minced
1/2 teaspoon dried oregano
1/2 teaspoon dried basil
1/2 teaspoon dried rosemary
4 ounces frozen carrots, chopped

4 ounces frozen green peas
8 ounces frozen broccoli, chopped
4 ounces frozen green beans
2 ripe tomatoes, pureed
4 cups vegetable broth
Sea salt and ground black pepper, to taste
1/2 teaspoon red pepper flakes

DIRECTIONS

Press the "Sauté" button and heat the oil. Sauté the shallot until softened, approximately 4 minutes. Stir in the garlic and cook for 30 seconds more.
Add the dried herbs, frozen vegetables, tomatoes, vegetable broth, salt, and black pepper.
Secure the lid. Choose the "Manual" mode and cook for 4 minutes at High pressure. Once cooking is complete, use a quick pressure release; carefully remove the lid.
Divide between serving bowls and garnish with red pepper flakes. Bon appétit!

208. Spring Tomato Soup

(Ready in about 30 minutes | Servings 4)

Per serving: 245 Calories; 18g Fat; 15g Carbs; 8.3g Protein; 10.1g Sugars

INGREDIENTS

1 tablespoon olive oil

1 cup green onions, chopped

2 stalks green garlic, chopped

1 celery stalk, diced

2 carrots, diced

2 cups vegetable broth

Sea salt and ground black pepper, to your liking

1/2 teaspoon cayenne pepper

1 teaspoon fresh basil, chopped

1 teaspoon fresh rosemary, chopped

1 (28-ounce) can tomatoes, crushed

1/2 cup double cream

1/2 cup feta cheese, cubed

1 tablespoon olive oil

DIRECTIONS

Press the "Sauté" button and heat 1 tablespoon of olive oil. Sauté the green onions, garlic, celery, and carrots until softened.

Add the vegetable broth, salt, black pepper, cayenne pepper, basil, rosemary, and tomatoes to the inner pot.

Secure the lid. Choose the "Manual" mode and cook for 6 minutes at High pressure. Once cooking is complete, use a natural pressure release for 10 minutes; carefully remove the lid.

Stir in the double cream and seal the lid again; let it sit for 10 minutes more. Ladle into soup bowls; garnish with feta and 1 tablespoon of olive oil. Bon appétit!

209. Soup Hang Wuao

(Ready in about 1 hour 10 minutes | Servings 4)

Per serving: 335 Calories; 9.5g Fat; 37.9g Carbs; 24.3g Protein; 3.8g Sugars

INGREDIENTS

2 pounds oxtails

4 cloves garlic, sliced

2 bay leaves

1 thyme sprig

2 rosemary sprigs

1 tablespoon soy sauce

1 teaspoon cumin powder

1 teaspoon paprika

2 potatoes, peeled and diced

2 carrots, diced

1 parsnip, diced

1 cup vegetable broth

2 bird's eye chilis, pounded in a mortar and pestle

2 star anise

Sea salt and ground black pepper, to taste

DIRECTIONS

Place the oxtails in the inner pot. Cover the oxtails with water. Stir in the garlic, bay leaves, thyme, rosemary, soy sauce, cumin, and paprika.

Secure the lid. Choose the "Manual" mode and cook for 50 minutes at High pressure. Once cooking is complete, use a natural pressure release for 10 minutes; carefully remove the lid.

After that, add the other ingredients to the inner pot.

Secure the lid. Choose the "Manual" mode and cook for 4 minutes at High pressure. Once cooking is complete, use a quick pressure release; carefully remove the lid.

Serve with crusty bread and enjoy!

210. Creamy and Minty Asparagus Soup

(Ready in about 10 minutes | Servings 4)

Per serving: 146 Calories; 6.2g Fat; 14.4g Carbs; 11.3g Protein; 8g Sugars

INGREDIENTS

1 tablespoon butter

1 Asian shallot, chopped

2 garlic cloves, minced

2 pounds asparagus stalks, trimmed and chopped

Kosher salt and ground black pepper, to taste

3 cups chicken broth

1 cup yogurt

2 tablespoons fresh mint leaves, chopped

DIRECTIONS

Press the "Sauté" button and melt the butter. Once hot, cook the Asian shallots and garlic until just tender and fragrant.

Add the asparagus, salt, pepper, and broth.

Secure the lid. Choose the "Manual" mode and cook for 4 minutes at High pressure. Once cooking is complete, use a quick pressure release; carefully remove the lid.

Add the yogurt and blend the soup until it is completely smooth. Taste and season with more salt if desired.

Ladle into individual bowls; then, top each bowl with fresh mint leaves and serve.

211. Zucchini and Quinoa Soup

(Ready in about 10 minutes | Servings 4)

Per serving: 307 Calories; 11.2g Fat; 38.3g Carbs; 15.3g Protein; 3.8g Sugars

INGREDIENTS

2 tablespoons olive oil
1 shallot, diced
1 teaspoon fresh garlic, minced
Sea salt and ground black pepper, to your liking

1 pound zucchini, cut into rounds
1 cup quinoa
4 cups vegetable broth
2 tablespoons fresh parsley leaves

DIRECTIONS

Press the "Sauté" button and heat the oil. Once hot, sweat the shallot for 2 to 3 minutes. Stir in the garlic and continue to cook for another 30 seconds or until aromatic.

Stir in the salt, black pepper, zucchini, quinoa, and vegetable broth.

Secure the lid. Choose the "Manual" mode and cook for 3 minutes at High pressure. Once cooking is complete, use a quick pressure release; carefully remove the lid.

Ladle into soup bowls; serve garnished with fresh parsley leaves. Enjoy!

212. Shrimp and Vegetable Bisque

(Ready in about 15 minutes | Servings 4)

Per serving: 362 Calories; 18.9g Fat; 20.3g Carbs; 29.6g Protein; 7.8g Sugars

INGREDIENTS

2 tablespoons butter
1/2 cup white onion, chopped
1 celery rib, chopped
1 parsnip, chopped

1 carrot, chopped
2 tablespoons all-purpose flour
1/4 cup sherry wine
Sea salt and ground black pepper

1 cup tomato puree
3 cups chicken bone broth
16 ounces shrimp, deveined
1 cup heavy whipping cream

DIRECTIONS

Press the "Sauté" button and melt the butter. Once hot, cook the onion, celery, parsnip, and carrot until softened.

Add the flour and cook for 3 minutes more or until everything is well coated. Pour in sherry wine to deglaze the pot.

Now, add the salt, pepper, tomato puree, and broth.

Secure the lid. Choose the "Manual" mode and cook for 5 minutes at High pressure. Once cooking is complete, use a quick pressure release; carefully remove the lid.

Now, add the shrimp and heavy cream and cook on the "Sauté" function for a further 2 to 3 minutes or until everything is heated through. Bon appétit!

213. Authentic Ukrainian Borscht Soup

(Ready in about 20 minutes | Servings 4)

Per serving: 276 Calories; 9g Fat; 20.3g Carbs; 9.6g Protein; 16.6g Sugars

INGREDIENTS

2 tablespoons safflower oil
1 red onion, chopped
2 cloves garlic, minced
1 pound Yukon potatoes, peeled and diced
2 carrots, chopped
1 small red bell pepper, finely chopped
1/2 pound red bee roots, grated

1 tablespoon cider vinegar
2 tablespoons tomato paste
Sea salt and freshly ground black pepper, to taste
2 bay leaves
1/2 teaspoon ground cumin
4 cups chicken stock

DIRECTIONS

Press the "Sauté" button and heat the oil. Once hot, cook the onion for about 2 minutes or until softened.

Add the garlic, potatoes, carrots, bell pepper, and beets to the inner pot. Add the remaining ingredients to the inner pot and stir until everything is well combined.

Secure the lid. Choose the "Manual" mode and cook for 10 minutes at High pressure. Once cooking is complete, use a natural pressure release; carefully remove the lid.

To serve, add more salt and vinegar if desired. Bon appétit!

214. Chicken Alfredo Ditalini Soup

(Ready in about 25 minutes | Servings 4)

Per serving: 476 Calories; 20.4g Fat; 38.6g Carbs; 34.4g Protein; 6.6g Sugars

INGREDIENTS

2 tablespoons coconut oil, melted
1 pound chicken breast, skinless and
boneless
1 white onion, chopped
2 cloves garlic, pressed

12 serrano pepper, minced
1/4 cup all-purpose flour
4 cups vegetable broth
2 cups cauliflower florets, frozen
2 cups Ditalini pasta

1 cup heavy cream
Sea salt and ground black pepper, to
taste

DIRECTIONS

Press the "Sauté" button and heat the oil. Once hot, brown the chicken for 3 to 4 minutes per side; set aside.
Then, sauté the onion, garlic, and serrano pepper in pan drippings. Add the flour and continue to stir until your veggies are well coated.
Add the vegetable broth, cauliflower, and pasta to the inner pot; put the chicken back into the inner pot.
Secure the lid. Choose the "Manual" mode and cook for 6 minutes at High pressure. Once cooking is complete, use a quick pressure release; carefully remove the lid.
Stir in the cauliflower and Ditalini pasta. Secure the lid. Choose the "Manual" mode and cook for 5 minutes at High pressure. Once cooking is complete, use a quick pressure release; carefully remove the lid.
Shred the cooked chicken and add it back into the soup. Afterwards, add the heavy cream, salt, and black pepper. Seal the lid and let it sit in the residual heat for 5 minutes. Bon appétit!

215. Chunky Hamburger Soup

(Ready in about 30 minutes | Servings 5)

Per serving: 283 Calories; 14.4g Fat; 6g Carbs; 29.4g Protein; 1.9g Sugars

INGREDIENTS

1 tablespoon olive oil
1 pound ground beef
1 leek, diced
2 cloves garlic, sliced
2 tablespoons cooking sherry

4 cups beef broth
1 can condensed tomato soup
1 teaspoon fish sauce
1 teaspoon basil
1/2 teaspoon oregano

2 bay leaves
1/4 teaspoon paprika
Sea salt and ground black pepper, to
taste

DIRECTIONS

Press the "Sauté" button and heat the oil. Once hot, brown the ground beef for 2 to 3 minutes, stirring and crumbling with a wooden spoon.
Stir in the leeks and garlic; continue to sauté an additional 2 minutes, stirring continuously.
Add a splash of cooking sherry to deglaze the pot. Add the other ingredients to the inner pot.
Secure the lid. Choose the "Manual" mode and cook for 10 minutes at High pressure. Once cooking is complete, use a natural pressure release for 10 minutes; carefully remove the lid.
Serve warm with crusty bread, if desired. Bon appétit!

216. Italian Sausage and Cabbage Soup

(Ready in about 20 minutes | Servings 5)

Per serving: 427 Calories; 33.4g Fat; 15.1g Carbs; 17.8g Protein; 5.8g Sugars

INGREDIENTS

2 tablespoons olive oil
1 pound beef sausage, thinly sliced
1 onion, chopped
3 cloves garlic. minced
1 stalk celery, chopped

1 carrot, peeled and chopped
1/4 cup Italian cooking wine
1 (1-pound) head cabbage, shredded
into small pieces
5 cups beef bone broth

1 tablespoon Italia seasoning blend
1 teaspoon cayenne pepper
1 bay leaf
Salt and cracked black pepper, to taste

DIRECTIONS

Press the "Sauté" button and heat the oil. Once hot, cook the beef sausage until no longer pink. Now, stir in the onion and garlic; continue to sauté until they are fragrant.
Add a splash of cooking wine, scraping up any browned bits from the bottom of the inner pot. Add the remaining ingredients.
Secure the lid. Choose the "Manual" mode and cook for 6 minutes at High pressure. Once cooking is complete, use a quick pressure release; carefully remove the lid.
Divide between soup bowls and serve immediately.

217. Old-Fashioned Duck Soup with Millet

(Ready in about 20 minutes | Servings 4)

Per serving: 411 Calories; 25.3g Fat; 21.5g Carbs; 23.3g Protein; 1.1g Sugars

INGREDIENTS

2 tablespoons olive oil

1 pound duck portions with bones

2 garlic cloves, minced

4 cups water

1 tablespoon chicken bouillon granules

1/2 cup millet, rinsed

Salt and freshly cracked black pepper, to taste

1/4 cup fresh scallions, chopped

DIRECTIONS

Press the "Sauté" button and heat the oil. Once hot, brown your duck for 4 to 5 minutes; stir in the garlic and cook an additional 30 seconds or until aromatic.

Add the remaining ingredients.

Secure the lid. Choose the "Manual" mode and cook for 12 minutes at High pressure. Once cooking is complete, use a quick pressure release; carefully remove the lid.

Remove the cooked duck to a cutting board. Shred the meat and discard the bones. Put your duck back into the inner pot. Stir and serve immediately. Bon appétit!

STEWS

218. Beef Stew with Green Peas

(Ready in about 35 minutes | Servings 4)

Per serving: 540 Calories; 29g Fat; 25.5g Carbs; 44.7g Protein; 10.7g Sugars

INGREDIENTS

2 tablespoons olive oil
1 ½ pounds beef stew meat, cut bite-sized pieces
1 red onion, chopped
4 cloves garlic, minced

1 carrot, cut into rounds
1 parsnip, cut into rounds
2 stalks celery, diced
Sea salt and ground black pepper, to taste
1 teaspoon cayenne pepper

4 cups beef bone broth
1/2 cup tomato paste
1 tablespoon fish sauce
2 bay leaves
1 cup frozen green peas

DIRECTIONS

Press the "Sauté" button and heat the oil. Once hot, brown the beef stew meat for 4 to 5 minutes; set aside.

Then, cook the onion in pan drippings until tender and translucent; stir in the garlic and cook an additional 30 seconds or until aromatic.

Add the carrots, parsnip, celery, salt, black pepper, cayenne pepper, beef broth, tomato paste, fish sauce, and bay leaves. Stir in the reserved beef stew meat.

Secure the lid. Choose the "Meat/Stew" mode and cook for 20 minutes at High pressure. Once cooking is complete, use a quick pressure release; carefully remove the lid.

Stir in the green peas, cover, and let it sit in the residual heat until warmed through or 5 to 7 minutes. Serve and enjoy!

219. Northern Italian Beef Stew

(Ready in about 35 minutes | Servings 6)

Per serving: 434 Calories; 16.6g Fat; 29.5g Carbs; 40.7g Protein; 6.1g Sugars

INGREDIENTS

2 pounds beef top round, cut into bite-sized chunks
1/4 cup all-purpose flour
1 tablespoon Italian seasoning
Sea salt and ground black pepper, to taste
1 tablespoon lard, at room temperature

1 onion, chopped
4 cloves garlic, pressed
1/4 cup cooking wine
1/4 cup tomato paste
1 pound sweet potatoes, diced
1/2 pound carrots, sliced into rounds
2 bell peppers, deveined and sliced

1 teaspoon fish sauce
2 bay leaves
4 cups beef broth
2 tablespoons fresh Italian parsley, roughly chopped

DIRECTIONS

Toss the beef chunks with the flour, Italian seasoning, salt, and pepper until well coated.

Press the "Sauté" button and melt the lard; brown the beef chunks on all sides, stirring frequently; reserve.

Then, sauté the onion and garlic for a minute or so; add the wine and stir, scraping up any browned bits from the bottom of the inner pot.

Add the beef back into the inner pot. Stir in the tomato paste, sweet potatoes, carrots, bell peppers, fish sauce, bay leaves, and beef broth.

Secure the lid. Choose the "Meat/Stew" mode and cook for 20 minutes at High pressure. Once cooking is complete, use a natural pressure release for 10 minutes; carefully remove the lid. Serve garnished with Italian parsley.

220. Bosnian Pot Stew (Bosanski Lonac)

(Ready in about 45 minutes | Servings 5)

Per serving: 406 Calories; 13.8g Fat; 23.5g Carbs; 45.7g Protein; 3.3g Sugars

INGREDIENTS

2 tablespoons safflower oil
2 pounds pork loin roast, cut into cubes
2 garlic cloves, chopped
1 onion, chopped
2 carrots, cut into chunks

2 celery ribs, cut into chunks
1 pound potatoes, cut into chunks
Se salt and ground black pepper, to taste
1 teaspoon paprika
2 tomatoes, pureed

2 cups chicken bone broth
1/2 pound green beans, cut into 1-inch pieces
2 tablespoons fresh parsley leaves, roughly chopped

DIRECTIONS

Press the "Sauté" button and heat the oil until sizzling. Once hot, cook the pork until it is no longer pink on all sides.

Add the garlic and onion and cook for a minute or so, stirring frequently.

Stir in the carrots, celery, potatoes, salt, black pepper, paprika, tomatoes, and chicken bone broth.

Secure the lid. Choose the "Meat/Stew" mode and cook for 35 minutes at High pressure. Once cooking is complete, use a quick pressure release; carefully remove the lid.

Add the green beans to the inner pot. Press the "Sauté" button again and let it simmer for a few minutes more. Serve in individual bowls garnished with fresh parsley.

221. Favorite Chickpea Stew

(Ready in about 40 minutes | Servings 4)

Per serving: 520 Calories; 12.8g Fat; 83g Carbs; 22.4g Protein; 14.7g Sugars

INGREDIENTS

2 tablespoons olive oil
1 large-sized leek, chopped
3 cloves garlic, pressed
3 potatoes, diced
2 carrots, diced

1 sweet pepper, seeded and chopped
1 jalapeno pepper, seeded and chopped
1 cup tomato puree
1/2 teaspoon cumin powder

1/2 teaspoon turmeric powder
1 teaspoon mustard seeds
2 cups roasted vegetable broth
1 ½ cups chickpeas, soaked overnight

DIRECTIONS

Press the "Sauté" button and heat the oil until sizzling. Once hot, cook the leeks and garlic for 2 to 3 minutes or until they are just tender. Add the remaining ingredients and stir to combine well.

Secure the lid. Choose the "Meat/Stew" mode and cook for 35 minutes at High pressure. Once cooking is complete, use a quick pressure release; carefully remove the lid.

Serve in individual bowls. Bon appétit!

222. Smoked Sausage and Bean Stew

(Ready in about 40 minutes | Servings 4)

Per serving: 396 Calories; 21.8g Fat; 25.8g Carbs; 6.2g Protein; 14.7g Sugars

INGREDIENTS

1 tablespoon olive oil
10 ounces smoked beef sausage, sliced
2 carrots, chopped
1 onion, chopped
2 garlic cloves, minced

Sea salt and ground black pepper, to taste
1/2 teaspoon fresh rosemary, chopped
1 teaspoon fresh basil, chopped
1 cup canned tomatoes, crushed

1 cup chicken broth
20 ounces pinto beans, soaked overnight
6 ounces kale, torn into pieces

DIRECTIONS

Press the "Sauté" button and heat the oil. Once hot, brown the sausage for 3 to 4 minutes.

Add the remaining ingredients, except for the kale, to the inner pot.

Secure the lid. Choose the "Bean/Chili" mode and cook for 25 minutes at High pressure. Once cooking is complete, use a quick pressure release; carefully remove the lid.

Next, stir in the kale and seal the lid. Let it sit for 5 minutes before serving. Bon appétit!

223. Winter Squash and Chicken Stew with Apples

(Ready in about 35 minutes | Servings 4)

Per serving: 413 Calories; 15.4g Fat; 28.5g Carbs; 40.4g Protein; 10.7g Sugars

INGREDIENTS

2 tablespoons olive oil, divided
2 pounds chicken thighs
1 onion, chopped
2 garlic cloves, minced
1 (1-inch) piece fresh ginger, peeled and minced

Kosher salt and freshly ground black pepper, to taste
1 teaspoon paprika
1 tablespoon fresh sage, chopped
1 pound winter squash, peeled and cubed

2 carrots, trimmed and diced
1 cup apple cider
1 cup chicken stock
2 cups chopped peeled Granny Smith apple

DIRECTIONS

Press the "Sauté" button and heat the oil. Once hot, sear the chicken thighs for about 2 minutes per side; reserve.

Add the onion, garlic, and ginger and sauté them for 2 to 3 minutes or until just tender. Add the salt, pepper, paprika, sage, winter squash, carrots, apple cider, and chicken stock. Add the reserved chicken thighs.

Secure the lid. Choose the "Manual" mode and cook for 10 minutes at High pressure. Once cooking is complete, use a natural pressure release for 10 minutes; carefully remove the lid.

Remove the chicken thighs and shred with two forks; discard the bones. Add the shredded chicken back into the inner pot.

Afterwards, stir in the apples; cover, press the "Sauté" button on Low and let it simmer for 10 to 12 minutes longer or until the apples are tender.

224. Chicken, Shrimp and Sausage Gumbo

(Ready in about 25 minutes | Servings 4)

Per serving: 413 Calories; 15.4g Fat; 28.5g Carbs; 40.4g Protein; 10.7g Sugars

INGREDIENTS

2 tablespoons olive oil
1 onion, diced
1 teaspoon garlic, minced
1/2 pound chicken breasts, boneless, skinless and cubed
1/2 pound smoked chicken sausage, cut into slices

2 sweet peppers, diced
1 jalapeno pepper, minced
1 celery stalk, diced
2 cups chicken bone broth
2 tomatoes, chopped
1 tablespoon Creole seasoning
Sea salt and ground black pepper, to taste

1 teaspoon cayenne pepper
1 tablespoon oyster sauce
1 bay leaf
1 pound shrimp, deveined
1/2 pound okra, frozen
2 stalks green onions, sliced thinly
1 tablespoon fresh lemon juice

DIRECTIONS

Press the "Sauté" button and heat the oil. Sweat the onion and garlic until tender and aromatic or about 3 minutes; reserve.
Then, heat the remaining tablespoon of olive oil and cook the chicken and sausage until no longer pink, about 4 minutes. Make sure to stir periodically to ensure even cooking.
Stir in the peppers, celery, broth, tomatoes, Creole seasoning, salt, black pepper, cayenne pepper, oyster sauce, and bay leaf. Add the reserved onion mixture.
Secure the lid. Choose the "Manual" mode. Cook for 7 minutes at High pressure. Once cooking is complete, use a quick pressure release; carefully remove the lid.
Afterwards, stir in the shrimp and okra.
Secure the lid. Choose the "Manual" mode. Cook for 3 minutes at High pressure. Once cooking is complete, use a natural pressure release; carefully remove the lid.
Divide between individual bowls and garnish with green onions. Drizzle lemon juice over each serving. Bon appétit!

225. Steak and Kidney Bean Chili

(Ready in about 25 minutes | Servings 5)

Per serving: 551 Calories; 12.4g Fat; 58.6g Carbs; 51.4g Protein; 9.2g Sugars

INGREDIENTS

2 pounds beef steak, cut into bite-sized cubes
4 tablespoons all-purpose flour
2 tablespoons vegetable oil
1 onion, chopped
2 cloves garlic, minced
1 jalapeño pepper, seeded and minced

2 cups beef broth
Sea salt and ground black pepper, to taste
1 teaspoon paprika
1 teaspoon celery seeds
1 teaspoon mustard seeds
2 tablespoons ground cumin

1 tablespoon brown sugar
2 cups red kidney beans, soaked overnight and rinsed
1 cup tomato sauce
2 tablespoons cornstarch, mixed with 4 tablespoons of water

DIRECTIONS

Toss the beef steak with the the flour. Press the "Sauté" button and heat the oil until sizzling. Now, cook the beef steak in batches until browned on all side. Reserve.
Then, cook the onion, garlic, and jalapeño until they soften. Scrape the bottom of the pot with a splash of beef broth. Add the beef broth, spices, sugar, beans, and tomato sauce to the inner pot; stir to combine well.
Secure the lid. Choose the "Manual" mode. Cook for 18 minutes at High pressure. Once cooking is complete, use a natural pressure release; carefully remove the lid.
Press the "Sauté" button. Stir in the cornstarch slurry; stir for a few minutes to thicken the cooking liquid. Bon appétit!

226. Marsala Fish Stew

(Ready in about 15 minutes | Servings 5)

Per serving: 487 Calories; 31.5g Fat; 19.9g Carbs; 30.4g Protein; 2.8g Sugars

INGREDIENTS

2 tablespoons canola oil
1 onion, sliced
3 garlic cloves, sliced
1/2 cup Marsala wine
1 ½ cups shellfish stock

1 cup water
1 pound Yukon Gold potatoes, diced
2 ripe tomatoes, pureed
Sea salt and ground black pepper, to taste
2 bay leaves

1 teaspoon smoked paprika
1/2 teaspoon hot sauce
2 pounds halibut, cut into bite-sized pieces
2 tablespoons fresh cilantro, chopped

DIRECTIONS

Press the "Sauté" button and heat the oil. Once hot, cook the onions until softened; stir in the garlic and continue to sauté an additional 30 seconds.
Add the wine to deglaze the bottom of the inner pot, scraping up any browned bits.
Add the shellfish stock, water, potatoes, tomatoes, salt, black pepper, bay leaves, paprika, hot sauce, and halibut to the inner pot.
Secure the lid. Choose the "Manual" mode. Cook for 5 minutes at High pressure. Once cooking is complete, use a quick pressure release; carefully remove the lid. Serve with fresh cilantro and enjoy!

227. Bœuf à la Bourguignonne

(Ready in about 30 minutes | Servings 6)

Per serving: 364 Calories; 14.5g Fat; 5.3g Carbs; 49.4g Protein; 2.4g Sugars

INGREDIENTS

4 thick slices bacon, diced

2 pounds beef round roast, cut into 1-inch cubes

Sea salt and ground black pepper, to taste

1 cup red Burgundy wine

2 onions, thinly sliced

2 carrots, diced

2 celery stalks, diced

4 cloves garlic, minced

2 tablespoons tomato paste

2 thyme sprigs

2 bay leaves

2 cups beef broth

2 tablespoons bouquet garni, chopped

DIRECTIONS

Press the "Sauté" button to preheat your Instant Pot. Cook the bacon until it is golden-brown; reserve.

Add the beef to the inner pot; sear the beef until browned or about 3 minutes per side.

Stir in the other ingredients; stir to combine well.

Secure the lid. Choose the "Meat/Stew" mode. Cook for 20 minutes at High pressure. Once cooking is complete, use a quick pressure release; carefully remove the lid.

Serve in individual bowls topped with the reserved bacon. Bon appétit!

228. Hungarian Beef Goulash

(Ready in about 30 minutes | Servings 5)

Per serving: 311 Calories; 16g Fat; 4.3g Carbs; 38.1g Protein; 2.1g Sugars

INGREDIENTS

2 tablespoons olive oil

2 pounds beef chuck, cut into bite-sized pieces

1/4 cup Hungarian red wine

2 onions, sliced

2 garlic cloves, crushed

1 red chili pepper, minced

Sea salt and freshly ground black pepper, to taste

1 tablespoon Hungarian paprika

1 beef stock cube

2 cups water

2 ripe tomatoes, puréed

2 bay leaves

DIRECTIONS

Press the "Sauté" button and heat the oil. Once hot, cook the beef until no longer pink. Add the red wine and stir with a wooden spoon, scraping up the browned bits on the bottom of the inner pot.

Stir in the remaining ingredients

Secure the lid. Choose the "Meat/Stew" mode. Cook for 20 minutes at High pressure. Once cooking is complete, use a quick pressure release; carefully remove the lid.

Serve in individual bowls and enjoy!

229. Authentic Mexican Pork Chile Verde

(Ready in about 30 minutes | Servings 6)

Per serving: 518 Calories; 26.6g Fat; 10.8g Carbs; 55.9g Protein; 5.3g Sugars

INGREDIENTS

1 pound tomatillos, halved

4 garlic cloves, sliced

2 chili peppers, minced

2 heaping tablespoons cilantro, chopped

2 tablespoons olive oil

3 pounds pork stew meat, cut into 2-inch cubes

1 onion, chopped

1 bell pepper, deveined and sliced

Salt and freshly ground black pepper, to taste

2 cups vegetable broth

DIRECTIONS

Place the tomatillos under a preheated broiler for about 6 minutes. Let cool enough to handle.

Purée the tomatillos with the garlic, chili peppers, and cilantro in your blender; process until everything is finely chopped and mixed.

Press the "Sauté" button and heat the oil. Once hot, cook the pork until no longer pink. Add the onion and cook for a few minutes more or until it is tender and translucent.

Add the remaining ingredients, including tomatillo sauce, to the inner pot.

Secure the lid. Choose the "Meat/Stew" mode. Cook for 20 minutes at High pressure. Once cooking is complete, use a quick pressure release; carefully remove the lid.

Ladle into serving bowls and garnish with tortillas if desired. Bon appétit!

230. Italian Beef Ragù

(Ready in about 20 minutes | Servings 5)

Per serving: 475 Calories; 40.6g Fat; 6.1g Carbs; 20.7g Protein; 2.5g Sugars

INGREDIENTS

2 tablespoons butter, melted
1 medium leek, diced
2 carrots, diced
1 stalk celery, diced

5 ounces bacon, diced
1 pound ground chuck
1/2 cup Italian red wine
1/4 cup tomato puree

2 cups chicken stock
1 tablespoon Italian seasoning blend
1/2 teaspoon kosher salt
1/2 teaspoon black pepper

DIRECTIONS

Press the "Sauté" button and melt the butter. Sauté the leek, carrot, celery and garlic for 2 to 3 minutes.
Add the bacon and ground beef to the inner pot; continue to cook an additional 3 minutes, stirring frequently. Add the remaining ingredients to the inner pot.
Secure the lid. Choose the "Manual" mode and cook for 5 minutes at High pressure. Once cooking is complete, use a quick pressure release; carefully remove the lid.
Serve with hot pasta if desired. Bon appétit!

231. Traditional Brunswick Stew

(Ready in about 20 minutes | Servings 4)

Per serving: 479 Calories; 25.6g Fat; 31.6g Carbs; 31.3g Protein; 7.3g Sugars

INGREDIENTS

2 tablespoons lard, melted
1 onion, diced
2 cloves garlic, minced
1 pound chicken breast, cut into
1-inch cubes

2 cups lima beans, soaked
1 (14 ½-ounce) can tomatoes, diced
2 cups chicken broth
1 tablespoon Worcestershire sauce
1 teaspoon Creole seasoning

Sea salt and ground black pepper, to taste
1 teaspoon hot sauce
1 cup corn kernels

DIRECTIONS

Press the "Sauté" button and melt the lard. Once hot, cook the onion and garlic until just tender and aromatic.
Now, add the chicken and cook an additional 3 minutes, stirring frequently.
Add the lima beans, tomatoes, broth, Worcestershire sauce, Creole seasoning, salt, black pepper, and hot sauce to the inner pot.
Secure the lid. Choose the "Manual" mode and cook for 12 minutes at High pressure. Once cooking is complete, use a natural pressure release; carefully remove the lid.
Stir in the corn kernels and seal the lid. Let it sit in the residual heat until heated through. Enjoy!

232. Bigos (Traditional Polish Stew)

(Ready in about 20 minutes | Servings 5)

Per serving: 417 Calories; 22.4g Fat; 23.6g Carbs; 31.8g Protein; 8.7g Sugars

INGREDIENTS

2 slices smoked bacon, diced
1 pound Kielbasa, sliced
1/2 pound pork stew meat, cubed
1 onion, chopped
4 garlic cloves, sliced
2 carrots, trimmed and diced
1 pound sauerkraut, drained

1 pound fresh cabbage, shredded
1 teaspoon dried thyme
1 teaspoon dried basil
2 bay leaves
1 tablespoon cayenne pepper
1 teaspoon mustard seeds
1 teaspoon caraway seeds, crushed

Sea salt, to taste
1/2 teaspoon black peppercorns
1/2 cup dry red wine
2 ½ cups beef stock
1/2 cup tomato puree

DIRECTIONS

Press the "Sauté" button to preheat your Instant Pot. Now, cook the bacon, Kielbasa, and pork stew meat until the bacon is crisp; reserve.
Add the onion and garlic, and sauté them until they're softened and starting to brown. Add the remaining ingredients to the inner pot, including the reserved meat mixture.
Secure the lid. Choose the "Manual" mode and cook for 15 minutes at High pressure. Once cooking is complete, use a quick pressure release; carefully remove the lid.
Ladle into individual bowls and serve warm.

233. Vegan Pottage Stew

(Ready in about 15 minutes | Servings 4)

Per serving: 315 Calories; 11.1g Fat; 41.6g Carbs; 12.8g Protein; 5.7g Sugars

INGREDIENTS

2 tablespoons olive oil
1 onion, chopped
2 garlic cloves, minced
2 carrots, diced
2 parsnips, diced

1 turnip, diced
4 cups vegetable broth
2 bay leaves
2 thyme sprigs
2 rosemary sprigs

Kosher salt and freshly ground black
pepper, to taste
1/4 cup red wine
1 cup porridge oats

DIRECTIONS

Press the "Sauté" button and heat the olive oil until sizzling. Now, sauté the onion and garlic until just tender and fragrant.

Add the remaining ingredients to the inner pot; stir to combine.

Secure the lid. Choose the "Manual" mode and cook for 10 minutes at High pressure. Once cooking is complete, use a quick pressure release; carefully remove the lid.

Ladle into individual bowls and serve immediately. Bon appétit!

234. Burgoo (Mulligan Stew)

(Ready in about 30 minutes | Servings 8)

Per serving: 522 Calories; 20.4g Fat; 22.2g Carbs; 61.6g Protein; 9.3g Sugars

INGREDIENTS

1 tablespoon lard, melted
2 pounds pork butt roast, cut into
2-inch pieces
2 pounds beef stew meat, cut into
2-inch pieces
2 chicken thighs, boneless

2 bell peppers, chopped
1 red chili pepper, chopped
1 onion, chopped
2 carrots, chopped
4 garlic cloves, chopped
4 cups beef bone broth

1 cup beer
1 (28-ounce) can tomatoes, crushed
Sea salt and ground black pepper, to
taste
1 pound frozen corn kernels
3 tablespoons Worcestershire sauce

DIRECTIONS

Press the "Sauté" button and melt the lard. Once hot, brown the meat in batches. Remove the browned meats to a bowl.

Then, sauté the peppers, onion, carrots for about 3 minutes or until tender and fragrant. Add the garlic and continue to cook for 30 seconds more.

Add the meat back to the Instant Pot. Stir in the remaining ingredients, except for the corn kernels.

Secure the lid. Choose the "Meat/Stew" mode and cook for 20 minutes at High pressure. Once cooking is complete, use a quick pressure release; carefully remove the lid.

Lastly, stir in the corn and continue to cook for a few minutes more on the "Sauté" function. Serve immediately.

235. Irish Bean and Cabbage Stew

(Ready in about 35 minutes | Servings 4)

Per serving: 577 Calories; 3.7g Fat; 85g Carbs; 32.6g Protein; 12.5g Sugars

INGREDIENTS

2 cups white beans, soaked and rinsed
1/2 cup pearled barley
4 cups roasted vegetable broth
1 shallot, chopped
2 carrots, chopped
2 ribs celery, chopped

1 sweet pepper, chopped
1 serrano pepper, chopped
4 cloves garlic, minced
1 pound cabbage, chopped
1/2 pound potatoes, diced
2 bay leaves

1/2 teaspoon mustard seeds
1/2 teaspoon caraway seeds
1 teaspoon cayenne pepper
Sea salt and freshly ground black
pepper, to taste
1 (14 ½-ounce) can tomatoes, diced

DIRECTIONS

Place the white beans, barley, and vegetable broth in the inner pot.

Secure the lid. Choose the "Bean/Chili" mode and cook for 25 minutes at High pressure. Once cooking is complete, use a quick pressure release; carefully remove the lid.

Add the remaining ingredients and stir to combine.

Secure the lid. Choose the "Manual" mode and cook for 5 minutes at High pressure. Once cooking is complete, use a quick pressure release; carefully remove the lid.

Serve in individual bowls and enjoy!

236. Rich and Easy Chicken Purloo

(Ready in about 25 minutes | Servings 8)

Per serving: 407 Calories; 9.4g Fat; 40.9g Carbs; 36.5g Protein; 1.7g Sugars

INGREDIENTS

1 tablespoon olive oil
1 onion, chopped
3 pounds chicken legs, boneless and skinless
2 garlic cloves, minced

5 cups water
2 carrots, diced
2 celery ribs, diced
2 bay leaves
1 teaspoon mustard seeds

1/4 teaspoon marjoram
Seasoned salt and freshly ground black pepper, to taste
1 teaspoon cayenne pepper
2 cups white long-grain rice

DIRECTIONS

Press the "Sauté" button and heat the olive oil. Now, add the onion and chicken legs; cook until the onion is translucent or about 4 minutes. Stir in the minced garlic and continue to cook for a minute more. Add the water.

Secure the lid. Choose the "Manual" mode and cook for 10 minutes at High pressure. Once cooking is complete, use a quick pressure release; carefully remove the lid.

Add the remaining ingredients.

Secure the lid. Choose the "Manual" mode and cook for 5 minutes at High pressure. Once cooking is complete, use a quick pressure release; carefully remove the lid. Serve warm.

237. Creamy Almond and Lentil Vegetable Stew

(Ready in about 20 minutes | Servings 4)

Per serving: 450 Calories; 28.6g Fat; 41.9g Carbs; 12.4g Protein; 10.2g Sugars

INGREDIENTS

1 tablespoon olive oil
1 onion, chopped
1 teaspoon fresh garlic, minced
1 dried chili pepper, crushed
1 pound potatoes, cut into 1-inch pieces
1 pound cauliflower, broken into florets

1 cup green lentils
3 cups tomato juice
3 cups vegetable broth
Seasoned salt and ground black pepper, to taste
1 teaspoon cayenne pepper

1/2 cup almond butter
2 heaping tablespoons cilantro, roughly chopped
1 heaping tablespoon parsley, roughly chopped

DIRECTIONS

Press the "Sauté" button and heat the olive oil. Now, sauté the onion until it is transparent. Add garlic and continue to sauté an additional minute. Stir in the chili pepper, potatoes, cauliflower, lentils, tomato juice, vegetable broth, salt, black pepper, and cayenne pepper.

Secure the lid. Choose the "Manual" mode and cook for 10 minutes at High pressure. Once cooking is complete, use a quick pressure release; carefully remove the lid.

Stir in the almond butter. Press the "Sauté" button and simmer for about 3 minutes on the lowest setting. Garnish with cilantro and parsley. Bon appétit!

238. Zarzuela de Mariscos (Catalan Shellfish Stew)

(Ready in about 30 minutes | Servings 6)

Per serving: 393 Calories; 14.6g Fat; 34g Carbs; 30.8g Protein; 10.5g Sugars

INGREDIENTS

4 tablespoons olive oil
1 onion, chopped
3 cloves garlic, minced
4 ounces prosciutto, diced
1 ½ pounds shrimp
1 ½ pounds clams

1 Chile de Árbol, minced
1/2 cup dry white wine
4 cups clam juice
1 laurel (bay leaf)
Sea salt and ground black pepper, to taste

1 teaspoon guindilla (cayenne pepper)
1 teaspoon rosemary, chopped
1 teaspoon basil, chopped
2 tomatoes, pureed
1 fresh lemon, sliced

DIRECTIONS

Press the "Sauté" button and heat the olive oil. Now, sauté the onion until it is transparent. Add the garlic and continue to sauté an additional 1 minute.

Add the prosciutto and cook an additional 3 minutes. Add the remaining ingredients, except for the lemon.

Secure the lid. Choose the "Manual" mode and cook for 10 minutes at High pressure. Once cooking is complete, use a natural pressure release for 10 minutes; carefully remove the lid.

Serve in individual bowls garnished with lemon slices. Enjoy!

239. Beef and Potato Stew

(Ready in about 30 minutes | Servings 6)

Per serving: 425 Calories; 11.7g Fat; 35.3g Carbs; 44g Protein; 7.5g Sugars

INGREDIENTS

1 tablespoon lard, melted

2 pounds chuck roast, cut into 2-inch cubes

2 onions, chopped

2 cloves garlic, minced

2 tablespoons Hungarian paprika

4 bell peppers, deveined and chopped

1 chili pepper, chopped

1 cup tomato puree

4 potatoes, diced

4 cups beef broth

2 bay leaves

Seasoned salt and ground black pepper, to taste

DIRECTIONS

Press the "Sauté" button and melt the lard. Once hot, cook the beef until no longer pink. Add a splash of broth and stir with a wooden spoon, scraping up the browned bits on the bottom of the inner pot.

Add the onion to the inner pot; continue sautéing an additional 3 minutes. Now, stir in the garlic and cook for 30 seconds more.

Stir in the remaining ingredients

Secure the lid. Choose the "Meat/Stew" mode. Cook for 20 minutes at High pressure. Once cooking is complete, use a quick pressure release; carefully remove the lid.

Discard the bay leaves and serve in individual bowls. Bon appétit!

240. Hungarian Chicken Stew (Paprikás Csirke)

(Ready in about 30 minutes | Servings 6)

Per serving: 304 Calories; 9.4g Fat; 18.6g Carbs; 35.7g Protein; 4.5g Sugars

INGREDIENTS

2 tablespoons lard, at room temperature

2 pounds chicken, cut into pieces

2 onions, chopped

2 cloves garlic, minced

1 cup tomato puree

1 Hungarian pepper, diced

2 tablespoons Hungarian paprika

2 cups chicken stock

Kosher salt and cracked ground black pepper

3 tablespoons all-purpose flour

1 cup full-fat sour cream

DIRECTIONS

Press the "Sauté" button and melt the lard. Once hot, cook the chicken for about 3 minutes or until no longer pink.

Add the onion to the inner pot; continue sautéing an additional 3 minutes. Now, stir in the garlic and cook for 30 seconds more.

Add the tomato puree, Hungarian pepper, paprika, chicken stock, salt, and black pepper to the inner pot.

Secure the lid. Choose the "Manual" mode. Cook for 15 minutes at High pressure. Once cooking is complete, use a quick pressure release; carefully remove the lid. Remove the chicken from the inner pot; shred the chicken and discard the bones.

In a mixing bowl, stir the flour into the sour cream. Add the flour/cream mixture to the cooking liquid, stirring constantly with a wire whisk.

Let it simmer until the sauce is thickened. Return the chicken to your paprikas, stir and press the "Cancel" button. Enjoy!

241. Indian Bean Stew (Rajma)

(Ready in about 30 minutes | Servings 4)

Per serving: 432 Calories; 9.5g Fat; 62.3g Carbs; 26.6g Protein; 4.1g Sugars

INGREDIENTS

2 tablespoons sesame oil

1 onion, sliced

4 cloves garlic, finely chopped

1 (1-inch) piece fresh ginger root, peeled and grated

2 cups red kidney beans, soaked overnight

2 Bhut jolokia peppers, minced

1 teaspoon red curry paste

5 cups vegetable broth

1 teaspoon coriander seeds

1/2 teaspoon cumin seeds

1/4 teaspoon ground cinnamon

Seasoned salt and ground black pepper, to taste

2 tomatoes, pureed

2 tablespoons fresh coriander, chopped

DIRECTIONS

Press the "Sauté" button and heat the oil. Now, sauté the onion until it is transparent. Add the garlic and ginger and continue to sauté an additional 1 minute.

Add the beans, peppers, curry paste, vegetable broth spices, and tomatoes.

Secure the lid. Choose the "Bean/Chili" mode. Cook for 25 minutes at High pressure. Once cooking is complete, use a quick pressure release; carefully remove the lid.

Serve in individual bowls garnished with fresh coriander. Enjoy!

242. Mediterranean Chicken Stew

(Ready in about 35 minutes | Servings 4)

Per serving: 400 Calories; 27.9g Fat; 11.3g Carbs; 24.6g Protein; 5.1g Sugars

INGREDIENTS

2 tablespoons olive oil
1 onion, chopped
1 stalk celery, chopped
2 carrots, chopped
1 teaspoon garlic, minced
4 chicken legs, boneless skinless
1/4 cup dry red wine

2 ripe tomatoes, pureed
2 cups chicken bone broth
2 bay leaves
Sea salt and ground black pepper, to taste
1/2 teaspoon dried basil
1 teaspoon dried oregano
1/2 cup Kalamata olives, pitted and sliced

DIRECTIONS

Press the "Sauté" button and heat the oil. Now, sauté the onion, celery, and carrot for 4 to 5 minutes or until they are tender.
Add the other ingredients, except for the Kalamata olives, and stir to combine.
Secure the lid. Choose the "Manual" mode. Cook for 15 minutes at High pressure. Once cooking is complete, use a natural pressure release for 10 minutes; carefully remove the lid.
Serve warm garnished with Kalamata olives. Bon appétit!

243. Seafood and Vegetable Ragout

(Ready in about 20 minutes | Servings 4)

Per serving: 312 Calories; 11.9g Fat; 15.9g Carbs; 36.6g Protein; 5g Sugars

INGREDIENTS

2 tablespoons olive oil
1 shallot, diced
2 carrots, diced
1 parsnip, diced
1 teaspoon fresh garlic, minced
1/2 cup dry white wine
2 cups fish stock
1 tomato, pureed

1 bay leaf
1 pound shrimp, deveined
1/2 pound scallops
Seasoned salt and freshly ground pepper, to taste
1 tablespoon paprika
2 tablespoons fresh parsley, chopped
1 lime, sliced

DIRECTIONS

Press the "Sauté" button and heat the oil. Now, sauté the shallot, carrot, and parsnip for 4 to 5 minutes or until they are tender.
Stir in the garlic and continue to sauté an additional 30 second or until aromatic.
Stir in the white wine, stock, tomato, bay leaf, shrimp, scallops, salt, black pepper, and paprika.
Secure the lid. Choose the "Manual" mode. Cook for 5 minutes at High pressure. Once cooking is complete, use a natural pressure release for 5 minutes; carefully remove the lid. Serve garnished with fresh parsley and lime slices. Enjoy!

244. Spanish Favorite Olla Podrida

(Ready in about 30 minutes | Servings 6)

Per serving: 418 Calories; 20.1g Fat; 11.6g Carbs; 47.6g Protein; 2.7g Sugars

INGREDIENTS

2 ½ pounds meaty pork ribs in adobo
1/2 pound Spanish chorizo sausage, sliced
1 tablespoon olive oil
2 onions, chopped

2 carrots, sliced
2 garlic cloves, sliced
Salt and black pepper, to taste
1 pound alubias de Ibeas beans, soaked overnight

DIRECTIONS

Place the pork and sausage in the inner pot; cover with water.
Add the other ingredients and stir to combine.
Secure the lid. Choose the "Meat/Stew" mode. Cook for 20 minutes at High pressure. Once cooking is complete, use a quick pressure release; carefully remove the lid.
Serve hot with corn tortilla if desired. Enjoy!

245. Basque Squid Stew

(Ready in about 15 minutes | Servings 4)

Per serving: 277 Calories; 9.3g Fat; 26.5g Carbs; 22.3g Protein; 8.7g Sugars

INGREDIENTS

2 tablespoons olive oil
1 onion, finely diced
2 cloves garlic, minced
1 thyme sprig, chopped
1 rosemary sprig, chopped
1 serrano pepper, deseeded and chopped

2 tomatoes, pureed
1/2 cup clam juice
1 cup chicken stock
1/2 cup cooking sherry
1 pound fresh squid, cleaned and sliced into rings
Sea salt and ground black pepper, to

taste
1 teaspoon cayenne pepper
1 bay leaf
1/4 teaspoon saffron
1 lemon, cut into wedges

DIRECTIONS

Press the "Sauté" button and heat the oil. Now, sauté the onion until tender and translucent.

Now, add the garlic and continue to sauté an additional minute. Add the remaining ingredients, except for the lemon.

Secure the lid. Choose the "Manual" mode. Cook for 10 minutes at High pressure. Once cooking is complete, use a quick pressure release; carefully remove the lid. Serve garnished with lemon wedges. Bon appétit!

246. Winter Slumgullion Stew

(Ready in about 20 minutes | Servings 4)

Per serving: 536 Calories; 15.1g Fat; 66.8g Carbs; 39g Protein; 11.9g Sugars

INGREDIENTS

1 tablespoon canola oil
1 leek, chopped
2 garlic cloves, minced
2 carrots, chopped
1/2 (16-ounce) package macaroni
1/2 pound ground beef

1/2 pound pork sausage, crumbled
1 ½ cups tomato puree
1 ½ cups chicken broth
Seasoned salt and black pepper, to taste
1 (14.5-ounce) can stewed tomatoes
2 cups green beans, cut into thirds

DIRECTIONS

Press the "Sauté" button and heat the oil. Now, sauté the leek, garlic and carrot until they have softened.

Then, add the macaroni, ground beef, sausage, tomato puree, chicken broth, salt, and black pepper to the inner pot.

Secure the lid. Choose the "Manual" mode. Cook for 10 minutes at High pressure. Once cooking is complete, use a quick pressure release; carefully remove the lid.

After that, add the canned tomatoes and green beans; let it simmer on the "Sauté" function for 2 to 3 minutes more or until everything is heated through. Bon appétit!

247. Traditional Lobscouse Stew

(Ready in about 55 minutes | Servings 6)

Per serving: 502 Calories; 14.1g Fat; 20.6g Carbs; 70.2g Protein; 4.4g Sugars

INGREDIENTS

2 tablespoons olive oil
2 ½ pounds beef stew meat, diced
1 onion, chopped
1 teaspoon garlic, chopped
2 carrots, sliced

1 pound potatoes, peeled and diced
1 pound rutabaga, peeled and diced
2 bay leaves
Sea salt and ground black pepper, to taste
4 cups beef bone broth

DIRECTIONS

Press the "Sauté" button and heat the oil. Brown the beef stew meat in batches; reserve.

Now, sauté the onion and garlic until just tender and fragrant.

Stir in the remaining ingredients, including the reserved meat.

Secure the lid. Choose the "Meat/Stew" mode. Cook for 45 minutes at High pressure. Once cooking is complete, use a quick pressure release; carefully remove the lid.

Ladle into serving bowls and enjoy!

248. Lentil and Root Vegetable Hotpot

(Ready in about 15 minutes | Servings 4)

Per serving: 510 Calories; 7.4g Fat; 84.2g Carbs; 31.5g Protein; 10.3g Sugars

INGREDIENTS

1 tablespoon olive oil
1 onion, chopped
3 cloves garlic, minced
1 carrot, chopped
1 stalk celery, chopped

1 parsnip, chopped
2 cups brown lentils
2 tomatoes, pureed
1 sprig thyme, chopped
1 sprig rosemary, chopped

1 teaspoon basil
Kosher salt and ground black pepper, to taste
2 cups vegetable broth
3 cups Swiss chard, torn into pieces

DIRECTIONS

Press the "Sauté" button and heat the oil. Sauté the onion until tender and translucent or about 4 minutes.

Then, stir in the garlic and cook an additional 30 seconds or until fragrant.

Now, stir in the carrot, celery, parsnip, lentils, tomatoes, spices, and broth.

Secure the lid. Choose the "Manual" mode. Cook for 10 minutes at High pressure. Once cooking is complete, use a quick pressure release; carefully remove the lid.

Afterwards, add the Swiss chard to the inner pot. Seal the lid and allow it to wilt completely. Bon appétit!

249. Easy Vegetarian Ratatouille

(Ready in about 25 minutes | Servings 4)

Per serving: 231 Calories; 11.1g Fat; 33.1g Carbs; 5.7g Protein; 11.3g Sugars

INGREDIENTS

1 pound eggplant, cut into rounds
1 tablespoon sea salt
3 tablespoons olive oil
1 red onion, sliced
4 cloves garlic, minced

4 sweet peppers, seeded and chopped
1 red chili pepper, seeded and minced
Sea salt and ground black pepper, to taste
1 teaspoon capers

1/2 teaspoon celery seeds
2 tomatoes, pureed
1 cup roasted vegetable broth
2 tablespoons coriander, chopped

DIRECTIONS

Toss the eggplant with 1 tablespoon of sea salt; allow it to drain in a colander.

Press the "Sauté" button and heat the olive oil. Sauté the onion until tender and translucent, about 4 minutes.

Add the garlic and continue to sauté for 30 seconds more or until fragrant. Add the remaining ingredients to the inner pot, including the drained eggplant.

Secure the lid. Choose the "Manual" mode. Cook for 7 minutes at High pressure. Once cooking is complete, use a quick pressure release; carefully remove the lid.

Press the "Sauté" button and cook on low setting until the ratatouille has thickened or about 7 minutes. Bon appétit!

250. Classic French Pot-Au-Feu

(Ready in about 1 hour 10 minutes | Servings 5)

Per serving: 473 Calories; 25.7g Fat; 12.3g Carbs; 48g Protein; 6.2g Sugars

INGREDIENTS

2 tablespoons olive oil
2 pounds beef pot roast, cut into 2-inch pieces
1 onion, chopped
2 carrots, chopped

3 garlic cloves, pressed
2 tomatoes, pureed
1 cup dry red wine
3 cups beef broth
1/2 teaspoon marjoram

1/2 teaspoon sage
Sea salt and ground black pepper, to taste
1 shallot, sliced
1 pound cremini mushrooms, sliced
1 cup chèvres cheese, crumbled

DIRECTIONS

Press the "Sauté" button and heat the olive oil. Cook the beef in batches and transfer to a bowl.

Then, cook the onion in pan drippings. Stir in the carrots and garlic and continue to cook an additional 3 minutes.

Add the tomatoes, wine, broth, marjoram, sage, salt, and black pepper. Add the browned beef.

Secure the lid. Choose the "Meat/Stew" mode. Cook for 45 minutes at High pressure. Once cooking is complete, use a quick pressure release; carefully remove the lid.

Now, add the shallot and mushrooms; continue to simmer on the "Sauté" function for about 10 minutes or until everything is thoroughly heated.

Transfer your stew to a lightly greased casserole dish; top with the cheese and place under a preheated broiler for 10 minutes or until the cheese melts. Serve warm.

251. Chicken Fricassee with Sherry Wine

(Ready in about 30 minutes | Servings 4)

Per serving: 442 Calories; 25.5g Fat; 22.4g Carbs; 29.7g Protein; 6.5g Sugars

INGREDIENTS

2 tablespoons canola oil
6 chicken wings
1 onion, chopped
2 garlic cloves, minced
Kosher salt and ground black pepper,
to taste

1 teaspoon cayenne pepper
1 teaspoon celery seeds
1/2 teaspoon mustard powder
2 carrots, chopped
2 celery stalks, chopped

3 cups vegetable broth
1/2 cup cooking sherry
2 tablespoons all-purpose flour
1 cup double cream

DIRECTIONS

Press the "Sauté" button and heat 1 tablespoon of olive oil. Now, cook the chicken wings for 2 to 3 minutes per side; set aside. Add a splash of cooking sherry to deglaze the pot.

Then, heat the remaining tablespoon of olive oil; sauté the onion until just tender or about 3 minutes. Stir in the garlic and continue to cook an additional minute, stirring frequently.

Next, add the reserved chicken, salt, black pepper, cayenne pepper, celery seeds, mustard powder, carrots, celery, broth, and sherry to the inner pot.

Secure the lid. Choose the "Poultry" mode. Cook for 15 minutes at High pressure. Once cooking is complete, use a quick pressure release; carefully remove the lid.

Meanwhile, mix the flour with the double cream. Add the flour mixture to the hot cooking liquid; seal the lid and let it sit in the residual heat until thoroughly warmed.

Ladle into individual bowls and serve. Bon appétit!

252. Barley Vegetable Pottage

(Ready in about 25 minutes | Servings 4)

Per serving: 401 Calories; 6.5g Fat; 74.4g Carbs; 14.7g Protein; 5.7g Sugars

INGREDIENTS

1 tablespoon olive oil
1 onion, chopped
2 cloves garlic, minced
1 red chili pepper, minced
2 sweet peppers, seeded and chopped

1 ½ cups pearled barley
2 cups water
4 cups vegetable broth
2 stalks celery, chopped
2 carrots, chopped

2 tomatoes, pureed
1 teaspoon red pepper flakes
Sea salt and ground black pepper, to
taste

DIRECTIONS

Press the "Sauté" button and heat the olive oil. Now, sauté the onion until tender and translucent.

Then, stir in the garlic and peppers and cook an additional 3 minutes. Stir in the pearled barley. Pour in water and broth.

Secure the lid. Choose the "Manual" mode. Cook for 15 minutes at High pressure. Once cooking is complete, use a quick pressure release; carefully remove the lid.

Add the remaining ingredients to the inner pot.

Secure the lid. Choose the "Manual" mode. Cook for 5 minutes at High pressure. Once cooking is complete, use a quick pressure release; carefully remove the lid. Bon appétit!

253. Hyderabadi-Style Lentil Stew

(Ready in about 20 minutes | Servings 4)

Per serving: 492 Calories; 10.1g Fat; 77.5g Carbs; 24g Protein; 9g Sugars

INGREDIENTS

2 tablespoons canola oil
1 teaspoon cumin seeds
1 onion, chopped
1 teaspoon garlic paste

2 cups yellow lentils, soaked for 30
minutes and rinsed
1/2 teaspoon tamarind paste
1/2 teaspoon red chili powder

10 curry leaves
1 cup tomato sauce
Kosher salt and white pepper, to taste

DIRECTIONS

Press the "Sauté" button and heat the oil. Then, sauté the cumin seeds for 1 to 2 minutes, stirring frequently.

Then, add the onion and cook an additional 2 minutes. Stir in the remaining ingredients.

Secure the lid. Choose the "Manual" mode. Cook for 5 minutes at High pressure. Once cooking is complete, use a natural pressure release for 10 minutes; carefully remove the lid.

Ladle into individual bowls and serve immediately. Bon appétit!

254. Authentic Kentucky Burgoo

(Ready in about 1 hour | Servings 8)

Per serving: 503 Calories; 17.6g Fat; 33.7g Carbs; 58g Protein; 7.5g Sugars

INGREDIENTS

2 tablespoons lard, melted
2 onions, chopped
1 pound pork shank, cubed
2 pounds beef shank, cubed
1 pound chicken legs
1/2 cup Kentucky bourbon
4 cups chicken broth

2 cups dry lima beans, soaked
2 cups tomato puree
1 pound potatoes, diced
2 carrots, sliced thickly
2 parsnips, sliced thickly
1 celery rib, sliced thickly
2 sweet peppers, seeded and sliced

1 jalapeno pepper, seeded and minced
1 teaspoon dried sage, crushed
1 teaspoon dried basil, crushed
Salt and freshly ground black pepper,
to taste

DIRECTIONS

Press the "Sauté" button and melt 1 tablespoon of lard. Once hot, sauté the onion until tender and translucent; reserve.

Add the remaining tablespoon of lard; brown the meat in batches until no longer pink or about 4 minutes.

Add a splash of Kentucky bourbon to deglaze the pot. Pour chicken broth into the inner pot.

Secure the lid. Choose the "Meat/Stew" mode. Cook for 45 minutes at High pressure. Once cooking is complete, use a quick pressure release; carefully remove the lid.

Shred chicken meat and discard the bones; add the chicken back to the inner pot. Next, stir in lima beans and tomato puree.

Secure the lid. Choose the "Manual" mode. Cook for 5 minutes at High pressure. Once cooking is complete, use a quick pressure release; carefully remove the lid. Then, stir in the remaining ingredients, including the sautéed onion.

Secure the lid. Choose the "Manual" mode. Cook for 5 minutes at High pressure. Once cooking is complete, use a quick pressure release; carefully remove the lid. Serve with cornbread if desired.

255. Thai Coconut Curry Stew

(Ready in about 50 minutes | Servings 5)

Per serving: 487 Calories; 28.6g Fat; 16.7g Carbs; 45.5g Protein; 7.4g Sugars

INGREDIENTS

2 tablespoons sesame oil
2 pounds beef chuck, cubed
2 onions, thinly sliced
2 cloves garlic, pressed
1 (2-inch) galangal piece, peeled and
sliced
1 Bird's eye chili pepper, seeded and
minced

1/2 cup tomato paste
4 cups chicken bone broth
1/4 cup Thai red curry paste
1 tablespoon soy sauce
1/2 teaspoon ground cloves
1/2 teaspoon cardamom
1/2 teaspoon cumin
1 cinnamon quill

Sea salt and ground white pepper, to
taste
1/2 (13.5-ounce) can full-fat coconut
milk
2 cups cauliflower florets
2 tablespoons fresh cilantro, roughly
chopped

DIRECTIONS

Press the "Sauté" button and heat the sesame oil. When the oil starts to sizzle, cook the meat until browned on all sides.

Add a splash of broth and use a spoon to scrape the brown bits from the bottom of the pot.

Next, stir in the onion, garlic, galangal, chili pepper, tomato paste, broth, curry paste, soy sauce, and spices.

Secure the lid. Choose the "Soup/Broth" mode and cook for 40 minutes at High pressure. Once cooking is complete, use a quick pressure release; carefully remove the lid. After that, add the coconut milk and cauliflower to the inner pot.

Secure the lid. Choose the "Manual" mode and cook for 4 minutes at High pressure. Once cooking is complete, use a quick pressure release; carefully remove the lid. Serve garnished with fresh cilantro. Enjoy!

256. Oyster Stew with Spanish Chorizo

(Ready in about 15 minutes | Servings 4)

Per serving: 393 Calories; 30.8g Fat; 12.9g Carbs; 19.4g Protein; 2.3g Sugars

INGREDIENTS

2 tablespoons olive oil
8 ounces Spanish chorizo sausage,
sliced
1 onion, chopped
1 teaspoon ginger-garlic paste

1/2 teaspoon dried rosemary
1/2 teaspoon smoked paprika
1/2 pound fresh oysters, cleaned
Sea salt and freshly ground black
pepper, to taste

3 cups chicken broth
2 cups kale leaves, washed
1 cup heavy cream

DIRECTIONS

Press the "Sauté" button and heat the sesame oil. When the oil starts to sizzle, cook the sausage until no longer pink.

Add the onion to the inner pot and continue to sauté for a further 3 minutes or until tender and translucent.

Now, stir in the ginger-garlic paste, rosemary, paprika, oysters, salt, pepper, and chicken broth.

Secure the lid. Choose the "Manual" mode and cook for 6 minutes at Low pressure. Once cooking is complete, use a quick pressure release; carefully remove the lid.

Add the kale leaves and heavy cream, seal the lid again, and let it sit in the residual heat until thoroughly warmed. Serve warm and enjoy!

257. Dal Tadka (Indian Lentil Curry Stew)

(Ready in about 20 minutes | Servings 4)

Per serving: 420 Calories; 11.4g Fat; 57.6g Carbs; 24.9g Protein; 6.9g Sugars

INGREDIENTS

Dahl:

2 tablespoons butter

1 brown onion, chopped

4 garlic cloves, minced

1 (1-inch) piece ginger, peeled and grated

1 red chili pepper, deseeded and minced

6 fresh curry leaves

2 tomatoes, chopped

1/2 teaspoon ground cumin

1/4 teaspoon ground cardamom

1 ½ cups dried chana dal, soaked

4 cups vegetable broth

1/2 teaspoon turmeric powder

Kosher salt and ground black pepper, to taste

Tadka (Tempering):

1 tablespoon butter

A pinch of asafetida

1/2 teaspoon cumin seeds

1 teaspoon mustard seeds

1/2 onion, sliced

1 bay leaf

2 dried chili peppers, seeded and cut in half

DIRECTIONS

Press the "Sauté" button and melt 2 tablespoons of butter. Once hot, cook the onion until tender and translucent or about 3 minutes.

Then, stir in the garlic and ginger; continue to cook an additional minute or until they are fragrant.

Add the remaining ingredients for the Dal.

Secure the lid. Choose the "Manual" mode and cook for 10 minutes at High pressure. Once cooking is complete, use a quick pressure release; carefully remove the lid.

Clean the inner pot and press the "Sauté" button again. Melt 1 tablespoon of butter.

Now, add a pinch of asafetida, cumin seeds, mustard seeds, onion and bay leaf; sauté for a minute. Stir in the dried chili peppers and cook for 30 seconds longer.

Pour the hot tadka over the hot dal and serve.

STOCKS & SAUCES

258. Chicken and Vegetable Stock

(Ready in about 1 hour 10 minutes | Servings 9)

Per serving: 79 Calories; 2.9g Fat; 2.6g Carbs; 21.9g Protein; 1.2g Sugars

INGREDIENTS

1 chicken carcass
2 carrots, cut into 2-inch pieces
1 celery rib, cut into 2-inch pieces
1 large onion, quartered
Sea salt, to taste

1 teaspoon mixed peppercorns
1 bay leaf
1 bunch parsley
9 cups cold water

DIRECTIONS

Place all ingredients in the inner pot.

Secure the lid. Choose the "Soup/Broth" mode and cook for 40 minutes at High pressure. Once cooking is complete, use a natural pressure release for 20 minutes; carefully remove the lid.

Remove the bones and vegetables with a slotted spoon. Use immediately or store for later use.

Bon appétit!

259. Chicken and Herb Broth

(Ready in about 2 hours 15 minutes | Servings 10)

Per serving: 69 Calories; 2.3g Fat; 3.6g Carbs; 8.5g Protein; 1g Sugars

INGREDIENTS

Chicken bones from 3 pounds roast chicken
1 parsnip
1 celery
2 tablespoons fresh parsley
1 tablespoon fresh thyme

2 tablespoons fresh coriander
1 teaspoon fresh dill
2 tablespoons cider vinegar
1 teaspoon sea salt
1 teaspoon ground black pepper

DIRECTIONS

Place all ingredients in the inner pot. Add cold water until the pot is 2/3 full.

Secure the lid. Choose the "Soup/Broth" mode and cook for 120 minutes at Low pressure. Once cooking is complete, use a natural pressure release for 10 minutes; carefully remove the lid.

Remove the bones and vegetables using a metal spoon with holes and discard. Pour the liquid through the sieve into the bowl.

Use immediately or store in your refrigerator. Bon appétit!

260. Classic Fish Stock

(Ready in about 55 minutes | Servings 8)

Per serving: 63 Calories; 3.5g Fat; 2.7g Carbs; 4.9g Protein; 1.3g Sugars

INGREDIENTS

2 pounds meaty bones and heads of halibut, washed
2 lemongrass stalks, chopped
2 carrots, chopped
1 parsnip, chopped

1 onion, quartered
2 sprigs rosemary
2 sprigs thyme
2 tablespoons olive oil

DIRECTIONS

Place all ingredients in the inner pot. Add cold water until the pot is 2/3 full.

Secure the lid. Choose the "Soup/Broth" mode and cook for 40 minutes at High pressure. Once cooking is complete, use a natural pressure release for 10 minutes; carefully remove the lid.

Strain the vegetables and fish. Bon appétit!

261. Homemade Shrimp Stock

(Ready in about 55 minutes | Servings 8)

Per serving: 69 Calories; 6.7g Fat; 1.9g Carbs; 0.3g Protein; 0.7g Sugars

INGREDIENTS

Shrimp shells from 3 pounds shrimp
8 cups water
1/2 cup cilantro, chopped
2 celery stalks, diced
4 cloves garlic

1 onion, quartered
1 teaspoon mixed peppercorns
1 tablespoon sea salt
2 bay leaves
4 tablespoons olive oil

DIRECTIONS

Add all ingredients to the inner pot.

Secure the lid. Choose the "Soup/Broth" mode and cook for 30 minutes at High pressure. Once cooking is complete, use a natural pressure release for 10 minutes; carefully remove the lid.

Strain the shrimp shells and vegetables using a colander. Bon appétit!

262. White Chicken Stock

(Ready in about 1 hour | Servings 10)

Per serving: 53 Calories; 1.1g Fat; 5.1g Carbs; 5.7g Protein; 1.5g Sugars

INGREDIENTS

2 pounds chicken white meat
1 white onion, quartered
1 leek, white parts
2 parsnips, sliced thickly
1 celery rib, sliced thickly

2 bay leaves
2 stalks flat-leaf parsley
1/2 teaspoon dried dill weed
1 teaspoon mixed peppercorns

DIRECTIONS

Add all ingredients to the inner pot.

Secure the lid. Choose the "Soup/Broth" mode and cook for 40 minutes at High pressure. Once cooking is complete, use a natural pressure release for 20 minutes; carefully remove the lid.

Discard the vegetables and bones; save the chicken meat for later use. Bon appétit!

263. French Brown Stock

(Ready in about 2 hours 10 minutes | Servings 10)

Per serving: 91 Calories; 4.1g Fat; 3.3g Carbs; 9.9g Protein; 1.5g Sugars

INGREDIENTS

3 pounds meaty pork bones
2 carrots, chopped
1 celery stalk, chopped
2 brown onions, quartered
1 tablespoon olive oil

DIRECTIONS

Add all ingredients to the inner pot of your Instant Pot.

Secure the lid. Choose the "Soup/Broth" mode and cook for 120 minutes at Low pressure. Once cooking is complete, use a natural pressure release for 10 minutes; carefully remove the lid.

Remove the bones and vegetables using a metal spoon with holes and discard. Pour the liquid through the sieve into the bowl.

Use immediately or store in your refrigerator. Bon appétit!

264. Simple Court Bouillon

(Ready in about 45 minutes | Servings 8)

Per serving: 55 Calories; 3.4g Fat; 1.6g Carbs; 0.1g Protein; 0.6g Sugars

INGREDIENTS

1 tablespoon salt

1 teaspoon mixed peppercorns

1 cup white wine

2 onions, sliced

2 celery ribs, sliced

2 carrots, sliced

2 bay leaves

2 sprig fresh rosemary

A bunch of fresh parsley

1 lemon, sliced

2 tablespoons olive oil

DIRECTIONS

Add all ingredients to the inner pot of your Instant Pot. Add cold water until the inner pot is 2/3 full.

Secure the lid. Choose the "Soup/Broth" mode and cook for 30 minutes at High pressure. Once cooking is complete, use a natural pressure release for 10 minutes; carefully remove the lid.

Discard the vegetables. Bon appétit!

265. Beef Bone Broth

(Ready in about 3 hours 5 minutes | Servings 8)

Per serving: 65 Calories; 2.4g Fat; 4.6g Carbs; 6.7g Protein; 1.9g Sugars

INGREDIENTS

3 pounds frozen beef bones

2 onions, halved

2 stalks celery, chopped

2 carrots, chopped

4 cloves garlic, whole

2 bay leaves

2 tablespoons apple cider vinegar

1 teaspoon sea salt

1 teaspoon black pepper

8 cups water

DIRECTIONS

Start by preheating your oven to 390 degrees F. Line a baking pan with aluminum foil.

Place the beef bones, onions, celery, carrots, and garlic on the baking pan. Roast for 40 to 45 minutes.

Transfer the roasted beef bones and vegetables to the inner pot of your Instant Pot. Add the bay leaves, apple cider vinegar, sea salt, pepper, and boiling water to the inner pot.

Secure the lid. Choose the "Manual" mode and cook for 120 minutes at High pressure. Once cooking is complete, use a natural pressure release for 20 minutes; carefully remove the lid.

Remove the beef bones and vegetables and discard. Pour the broth through a strainer. Enjoy!

266. Roasted Vegetable Stock

(Ready in about 1 hour 15 minutes | Servings 10)

Per serving: 56 Calories; 3.4g Fat; 3.2g Carbs; 0.3g Protein; 1.4g Sugars

INGREDIENTS

4 carrots, cut into 2-inch pieces

4 medium celery ribs, cut into 2-inch pieces

2 onions, peeled and quartered

2 sprigs fresh rosemary

2 sprigs fresh thyme

3 tablespoons olive oil

Kosher salt and black peppercorns, to taste

1 cup dry white wine

10 cups water

DIRECTIONS

Start by preheating your oven to 400 degrees F. Grease a large roasting pan with cooking spray

Place the carrots, celery, onions, and herbs in the prepared roasting pan. Roast, tossing halfway through the cooking time, until the vegetables are tender about 35 minutes.

Transfer the vegetables to the inner pot. Add the remaining ingredients.

Secure the lid. Choose the "Soup/Broth" mode and cook for 30 minutes at High pressure. Once cooking is complete, use a natural pressure release for 10 minutes; carefully remove the lid.

Strain the broth through a fine-mesh sieve and discard the solids. Let it cool completely before storing.

267. Home-Style Pork Stock

(Ready in about 55 minutes | Servings 10)

Per serving: 91 Calories; 4.1g Fat; 3.3g Carbs; 9.9g Protein; 1.5g Sugars

INGREDIENTS

2 pounds pork bones
4 celery stalks, cut into large chunks
4 carrots, cut into large chunks

1 onion, quartered
3 garlic cloves, smashed
2 bay leaves

Sea salt and black peppercorns, to taste
10 cups water, divided in half

DIRECTIONS

Preheat your oven to 400 degrees F. Coat a roasting pan with a piece of aluminum foil; brush with a little oil.

Arrange the pork bones and vegetables on the prepared roasting pan. Roast in the preheated oven for 25 to 30 minutes.

Transfer the roasted pork bones and vegetables to the inner pot of your Instant Pot. Now, stir in the bay leaves, salt, black peppercorns, and water.

Secure the lid. Choose the "Manual" mode and cook for 25 minutes at High pressure. Once cooking is complete, use a quick pressure release; carefully remove the lid.

Strain the stock and discard the solids. Keep in your refrigerator or freezer if desired. Enjoy!

268. Vegan Tikka Masala Sauce

(Ready in about 30 minutes | Servings 4)

Per serving: 206 Calories; 17.2g Fat; 12.2g Carbs; 4.1g Protein; 6.1g Sugars

INGREDIENTS

2 teaspoons olive oil
1 onion, chopped
4 cloves garlic, chopped
1 (1-inch) piece fresh ginger, peeled and grated
1 bird's eye chili, minced

1 bell pepper, seeded and chopped
Sea salt and ground black pepper, to taste
1 teaspoon cayenne pepper
1 teaspoon coriander powder
1/2 teaspoon turmeric powder

1 teaspoon Garam Masala
2 ripe tomatoes, pureed
1 cup vegetable broth
1 cup plain coconut yogurt

DIRECTIONS

Press the "Sauté" button to preheat your Instant Pot. Add the oil and sauté the onion for about 3 minutes or until tender and fragrant.

Now, add the garlic, ginger and peppers; continue to sauté an additional minute or until they are aromatic.

Add the spices, tomatoes, and broth.

Secure the lid. Choose the "Manual" mode and cook for 11 minutes at High pressure. Once cooking is complete, use a natural pressure release for 10 minutes; carefully remove the lid.

Afterwards, add the coconut yogurt to the inner pot and stir to combine. Serve with chickpeas or roasted vegetables. Enjoy!

269. Easy Herby Tomato Sauce

(Ready in about 45 minutes | Servings 6)

Per serving: 115 Calories; 7.5g Fat; 12.1g Carbs; 2.6g Protein; 7.9g Sugars

INGREDIENTS

2 (28-ounce) cans tomatoes, crushed
3 tablespoons olive oil
3 cloves garlic, minced
1/2 teaspoon dried rosemary
1/2 teaspoon dried basil

1/2 tablespoon dried oregano
1 onion, quartered
Kosher salt and freshly ground black pepper, to taste
1 teaspoon tamari sauce
2 tablespoons fresh parsley leaves, finely chopped

DIRECTIONS

Reserve 1 cup of the crushed tomatoes.

Press the "Sauté" button and heat olive oil. Once hot, cook the garlic for a minute or so or until it is fragrant but not browned.

Now, stir in the rosemary, basil, and oregano; continue to sauté for 30 seconds more. Stir in the tomatoes, onion, salt, and pepper.

Secure the lid. Choose the "Soup/Broth" mode and cook for 40 minutes at High pressure. Once cooking is complete, use a quick pressure release; carefully remove the lid.

Add the reserved tomatoes, tamari sauce and parsley to your tomato sauce. Bon appétit!

270. Sicilian-Style Meat Sauce

(Ready in about 55 minutes | Servings 10)

Per serving: 378 Calories; 24.5g Fat; 3.2g Carbs; 34.2g Protein; 1.1g Sugars

INGREDIENTS

2 tablespoons olive oil

2 ½ pounds pork butt

1 onion, chopped

4 garlic cloves, pressed

1/4 cup Malvasia wine, or other Sicilian wine

2 fresh tomatoes, pureed

5 ounces tomato paste

2 bay leaves

2 tablespoons fresh cilantro, chopped

1 teaspoon dried basil

1 teaspoon dried rosemary

1/2 teaspoon cayenne pepper

1/2 teaspoon black pepper, freshly cracked

1/2 teaspoon salt

1 cup chicken broth

DIRECTIONS

Press the "Sauté" button and heat the oil. When the oil starts to sizzle, cook the pork until no longer pink.

Add the onion and garlic and continue to cook for a few minutes more or until they are tender and fragrant. Add a splash of wine to deglaze the pot.

Stir in the other ingredients.

Secure the lid. Choose the "Meat/Stew" mode and cook for 35 minutes at High pressure. Once cooking is complete, use a natural pressure release for 15 minutes; carefully remove the lid.

Next, remove the meat from the inner pot; shred the meat, discarding the bones. Return the meat to your sauce and serve over pasta if desired.

271. Homemade Applesauce with Dates

(Ready in about 25 minutes | Servings 8)

Per serving: 97 Calories; 0.3g Fat; 25.7g Carbs; 0.6g Protein; 19.8g Sugars

INGREDIENTS

6 Honeycrisp apples, peeled, cored and chopped

1 cup water

1 tablespoon fresh lemon juice

1/4 teaspoon ground cloves

1/2 teaspoon cinnamon powder

10 dates, pitted and chopped

DIRECTIONS

Add all ingredients to the inner pot; stir to combine.

Secure the lid. Choose the "Manual" mode and cook for 10 minutes at High pressure. Once cooking is complete, use a natural pressure release for 10 minutes; carefully remove the lid.

Mash the apple mixture to the desired consistency. Serve warm or cold.

272. Mixed Berry Sauce

(Ready in about 25 minutes | Servings 12)

Per serving: 117 Calories; 3g Fat; 22.4g Carbs; 1.2g Protein; 17.5g Sugars

INGREDIENTS

2 cups frozen blueberries, thawed

2 cups frozen raspberries, thawed

2 cups frozen strawberries, thawed

1/2 cup granulated sugar

1 teaspoon cornstarch

1 cup water

2 tablespoons orange juice

1/2 cup cream cheese, at room temperature

DIRECTIONS

Add the berries, sugar, and cornstarch, and water to the inner pot; stir to combine.

Secure the lid. Choose the "Manual" mode and cook for 10 minutes at High pressure. Once cooking is complete, use a natural pressure release for 10 minutes; carefully remove the lid.

Stir in the orange juice and cream cheese; stir to combine and serve with waffles or pancakes.

273. Easiest Marinara Sauce Ever

(Ready in about 25 minutes | Servings 8)

Per serving: 86 Calories; 7g Fat; 5.4g Carbs; 1.3g Protein; 3.6g Sugars

INGREDIENTS

4 tablespoons olive oil
4 garlic cloves, minced
4 tablespoons tomato paste
1 (28-ounce) can crushed tomatoes with juice

1 cup water
Sea salt to taste
2 tablespoons fresh basil, minced
1 tablespoon fresh parsley, minced

DIRECTIONS

Press the "Sauté" button and heat olive oil. Once hot, cook the garlic for a minute or so or until it is fragrant but not browned. Now, stir in the remaining ingredients.

Secure the lid. Choose the "Soup/Broth" mode and cook for 40 minutes at High pressure. Once cooking is complete, use a quick pressure release; carefully remove the lid. Bon appétit!

274. Beef Bolognese Pasta Sauce

(Ready in about 20 minutes | Servings 4)

Per serving: 358 Calories; 20.3g Fat; 8.7g Carbs; 34.1g Protein; 4.7g Sugars

INGREDIENTS

2 tablespoons olive oil
1 pound ground beef
1 onion, chopped
1 teaspoon fresh garlic, minced
Sea salt and ground black pepper, to taste

1 teaspoon brown sugar
1/2 teaspoon dried sage
1 teaspoon dried oregano
1 teaspoon dried basil
1/2 teaspoon cayenne pepper, or to taste

2 cups beef broth
2 ripe tomatoes, pureed
2 tablespoons tomato ketchup

DIRECTIONS

Press the "Sauté" button and heat the oil. When the oil starts to sizzle, cook the ground beef until no longer pink; crumble it with a wooden spatula.

Add the onion and garlic and continue to cook for a few minutes more or until they are tender and fragrant. Add a splash of beef broth to deglaze the pot.

Stir in the remaining ingredients; stir to combine well.

Secure the lid. Choose the "Manual" mode and cook for 6 minutes at High pressure. Once cooking is complete, use a natural pressure release for 5 minutes; carefully remove the lid.

Serve over pasta if desired. Bon appétit!

275. 20-Minute Chicken Ragù

(Ready in about 20 minutes | Servings 4)

Per serving: 431 Calories; 18g Fat; 33.7g Carbs; 29.1g Protein; 17.1g Sugars

INGREDIENTS

2 tablespoons olive oil
1 pound ground chicken
1 onion, chopped
2 cloves garlic, minced
1/4 cup dry red wine

1 stalk celery, chopped
1 bell pepper, chopped
1 teaspoon fresh basil, chopped
1 teaspoon fresh rosemary, chopped
1 teaspoon cayenne pepper

Salt and fresh ground pepper to taste
2 cups tomato sauce
1 cup chicken bone broth

DIRECTIONS

Press the "Sauté" button and heat the oil. When the oil starts to sizzle, cook the ground chicken until no longer pink; crumble it with a wooden spatula.

Add the onion and garlic to the browned chicken; let it cook for a minute or so. Add a splash of wine to deglaze the pan.

Stir in the remaining ingredients.

Secure the lid. Choose the "Manual" mode and cook for 6 minutes at High pressure. Once cooking is complete, use a natural pressure release for 10 minutes; carefully remove the lid. Bon appétit!

276. Perfect Cranberry Sauce

(Ready in about 20 minutes | Servings 8)

Per serving: 431 Calories; 18g Fat; 33.7g Carbs; 29.1g Protein; 17.1g Sugars

INGREDIENTS

1 ½ pounds fresh cranberries, rinsed
2 blood oranges, juiced
1 tablespoon blood orange zest
3/4 cup sugar

1/4 cup golden cane syrup
2-3 cloves
1 cinnamon stick
1 teaspoon vanilla extract

DIRECTIONS

Add the cranberries to the inner pot of your Instant Pot.
Add the remaining ingredients to the inner pot; stir to combine well.
Secure the lid. Choose the "Manual" mode and cook for 3 minutes at High pressure. Once cooking is complete, use a natural pressure release for 10 minutes; carefully remove the lid. Bon appétit!
Let it cool. Serve your sauce chilled or at room temperature. Bon appétit!

277. Spanish Chorizo Sauce

(Ready in about 20 minutes | Servings 4)

Per serving: 385 Calories; 24.9g Fat; 20.2g Carbs; 21.1g Protein; 11.1g Sugars

INGREDIENTS

1 tablespoon olive oil
1 pound Chorizo sausage, sliced
1 onion, chopped
1 teaspoon garlic, minced
1 sweet pepper, seeded and finely chopped
1 habanero pepper, seeded and minced
2 tablespoons sugar

1 teaspoon dried basil
1 teaspoon dried rosemary
1 teaspoon red pepper flakes
Sea salt and freshly ground black pepper, to taste
1 (28-ounce) can diced tomatoes, with juice
1 cup chicken broth

DIRECTIONS

Press the "Sauté" button and heat the oil. When the oil starts to sizzle, cook the Chorizo until no longer pink; crumble it with a wooden spatula.
Add the onion, garlic, and peppers and cook for a minute or so. Add a splash of chicken broth to deglaze the pan.
Stir in the remaining ingredients.
Secure the lid. Choose the "Manual" mode and cook for 6 minutes at High pressure. Once cooking is complete, use a natural pressure release for 10 minutes; carefully remove the lid. Bon appétit!

278. Carolina-Style Sticky Barbecue Sauce

(Ready in about 20 minutes | Servings 6)

Per serving: 215 Calories; 4.4g Fat; 37.5g Carbs; 3.4g Protein; 27.3g Sugars

INGREDIENTS

2 tablespoons butter
1 shallot, chopped
2 cloves garlic, minced
2 cups tomato sauce
1/2 cup cider vinegar

2 tablespoons coconut sugar
1/3 cup molasses
2 tablespoons Worcestershire sauce
1 teaspoon yellow mustard
1 teaspoon hot sauce

Kosher salt and ground black pepper
1/2 teaspoon paprika
1 cup vegetable broth

DIRECTIONS

Press the "Sauté" button and melt the butter. Then, sauté the shallot until tender and translucent, about 4 minutes. Add the garlic and cook for a further 30 seconds.
Stir in the remaining ingredients.
Secure the lid. Choose the "Manual" mode and cook for 5 minutes at High pressure. Once cooking is complete, use a natural pressure release for 5 minutes; carefully remove the lid. Bon appétit!

279. Zesty Pear Sauce

(Ready in about 25 minutes | Servings 8)

Per serving: 73 Calories; 0.1g Fat; 19.2g Carbs; 0.3g Protein; 14.4g Sugars

INGREDIENTS

1 ½ pounds cup pears, cored, peeled and chopped
2 teaspoons freshly squeezed lemon juice
1/2 cup sugar

1 teaspoon ground cinnamon
1/2 teaspoon ground cardamom
1 teaspoon vanilla essence

DIRECTIONS

Add all ingredients to the inner pot; stir to combine.

Secure the lid. Choose the "Manual" mode and cook for 10 minutes at High pressure. Once cooking is complete, use a natural pressure release for 10 minutes; carefully remove the lid.

Mash the pear mixture to the desired consistency. Serve at room temperature or cold. Bon appétit!

280. Spinach and Artichoke Dipping Sauce

(Ready in about 15 minutes | Servings 8)

Per serving: 222 Calories; 17.4g Fat; 8.6g Carbs; 9.9g Protein; 2.4g Sugars

INGREDIENTS

2 tablespoons butter
1 onion, chopped
2 cloves garlic, minced
10 ounces artichoke hearts
1 cup chicken broth

Sea salt and freshly ground black pepper, to taste
1 teaspoon red pepper flakes
1 pound fresh or frozen spinach leaves
9 ounces cream cheese
1 cup goat cheese, crumbled

DIRECTIONS

Press the "Sauté" button and melt the butter. Then, sauté the onion and garlic until just tender and fragrant.

Then, add the artichoke hearts, broth, salt, black pepper, and red pepper flakes.

Secure the lid. Choose the "Manual" mode and cook for 5 minutes at High pressure. Once cooking is complete, use a quick pressure release; carefully remove the lid.

Add the spinach and cheese to the inner pot; seal the lid and let it sit in the residual heat until thoroughly warmed. Enjoy!

281. Rich Southwest Cheese and Bacon Sauce

(Ready in about 15 minutes | Servings 10)

Per serving: 135 Calories; 9.5g Fat; 4.5g Carbs; 8.3g Protein; 2.5g Sugars

INGREDIENTS

4 ounces bacon, diced
1 onion, chopped
1 red chili pepper, seeded and minced
2 cloves garlic, pressed
2 ripe tomatoes, chopped
1/2 teaspoon ground cumin

1/2 teaspoon turmeric powder
Kosher salt and ground black pepper, to taste
1 cup vegetable broth
10 ounces Cottage cheese, at room temperature
1 cup Pepper Jack cheese, grated

DIRECTIONS

Press the "Sauté" button to preheat your Instant Pot. Then, cook the bacon for 2 to 3 minutes. Reserve.

Add the onion and pepper to the inner pot and continue to cook until they are fragrant. Stir in the garlic and continue to sauté for 30 seconds more.

Now, add the tomatoes, spices, and broth.

Secure the lid. Choose the "Manual" mode and cook for 5 minutes at High pressure. Once cooking is complete, use a quick pressure release; carefully remove the lid.

Lastly, stir in the cheese. Seal the lid again and let it sit in the residual heat until the cheese melts.

Ladle into a nice serving bowl, top with the reserved bacon, and serve.

282. Mexican-Style Black Bean Sauce

(Ready in about 35 minutes | Servings 8)

Per serving: 181 Calories; 4.4g Fat; 27.3g Carbs; 9.5g Protein; 3.1g Sugars

INGREDIENTS

2 tablespoons olive oil

1 brown onion, chopped

3 garlic cloves, chopped

1 jalapeño pepper, seeded and minced

1 teaspoon dried Mexican oregano

1/2 teaspoon ground cumin

Sea salt and ground black pepper, to taste

1 ½ cups black beans, rinsed, drained

1 ½ cups chicken broth

1/4 cup fresh cilantro, chopped

1/2 cup Pico de Gallo

DIRECTIONS

Press the "Sauté" button and heat the olive oil until sizzling. Once hot, cook the onion for 3 to 4 minutes or until tender and fragrant. After that, stir in the garlic; continue sautéing an additional 30 to 40 seconds.

Add the jalapeño pepper, oregano, cumin, salt, black pepper, beans, and broth to the inner pot.

Secure the lid. Choose the "Bean/Chili" mode and cook for 25 minutes at High pressure. Once cooking is complete, use a quick pressure release; carefully remove the lid.

Then, mash your beans with potato masher or use your blender. Serve garnished with cilantro and Pico de Gallo. Bon appétit!

283. Eggplant Light Sauce with Wine

(Ready in about 10 minutes | Servings 6)

Per serving: 147 Calories; 10.4g Fat; 9.3g Carbs; 5.2g Protein; 4.6g Sugars

INGREDIENTS

2 tablespoons olive oil

1 pound eggplants, sliced

4 garlic cloves, minced

2 tomatoes, chopped

1 cup white wine

1 teaspoon oregano

1/2 teaspoon rosemary

1 teaspoon basil

Sea salt and ground black pepper, to taste

2 tablespoons tahini (sesame butter)

1/2 cup Romano cheese, freshly grated

DIRECTIONS

Press the "Sauté" button and heat the olive oil. Then, cook the eggplant slices until they are charred at the bottom. Work with batches.

Add the garlic, tomatoes, wine, and spices.

Secure the lid. Choose the "Bean/Chili" mode and cook for 3 minutes at High pressure. Once cooking is complete, use a quick pressure release; carefully remove the lid.

Press the "Sauté" button again to thicken the cooking liquid. Add the tahini paste and stir to combine. Top with Romano cheese and serve.

284. Perfect Homemade Salsa

(Ready in about 40 minutes | Servings 8)

Per serving: 83 Calories; 0.4g Fat; 18.8g Carbs; 3.2g Protein; 10.1g Sugars

INGREDIENTS

2 onions, chopped

2 garlic cloves, pressed

2 ripe tomatoes, crushed

12 ounces canned tomato paste

2 sweet peppers, chopped

2 chili peppers, chopped

1/2 cup rice vinegar

2 tablespoons brown sugar

Sea salt and red pepper, to taste

1 teaspoon dried Mexican oregano

DIRECTIONS

Put all ingredients into the inner pot of your Instant Pot.

Secure the lid. Choose the "Manual" mode and cook for 25 minutes at High pressure. Once cooking is complete, use a natural pressure release for 10 minutes; carefully remove the lid.

Allow your salsa to cool completely; store in your refrigerator or freezer. Bon appétit!

285. Salted Caramel Sauce

(Ready in about 20 minutes | Servings 6)

Per serving: 191 Calories; 11.4g Fat; 22.4g Carbs; 0.3g Protein; 22.1g Sugars

INGREDIENTS

1/2 cup water
1 1/3 cups granulated sugar
4 tablespoons butter, cut into small pieces
1/2 cup heavy whipping cream

1/2 teaspoon coarse sea salt
1 teaspoon vanilla
A pinch of cardamom

DIRECTIONS

Press the "Sauté" button to preheat the Instant Pot; now, cook the sugar and water, stirring frequently, until the sugar has dissolved.
Let the mixture boiling until it turns an amber color or about 10 minutes.
Then, whisk in the butter, followed by the remaining ingredients.
Allow your sauce to cool. It will thicken up once it's cooled in your refrigerator. Bon appétit!

286. Raspberry Ginger Coulis

(Ready in about 20 minutes | Servings 6)

Per serving: 134 Calories; 0.2g Fat; 34g Carbs; 0.5g Protein; 30.3g Sugars

INGREDIENTS

1 (12-ounce) bag fresh or frozen raspberries
1 cup brown sugar
1 cup water

1/2 cup fresh orange juice
1 tablespoon fresh ginger root, peeled and finely grated
Zest from 1 organic orange, finely grated

DIRECTIONS

Add all the ingredients to the inner pot of your Instant Pot.
Secure the lid. Choose the "Manual" mode and cook for 3 minutes at High pressure. Once cooking is complete, use a natural pressure release for 10 minutes; carefully remove the lid.
Let it cool. Serve your sauce chilled or at room temperature. Bon appétit!

287. Classic Gravy Sauce

(Ready in about 15 minutes | Servings 6)

Per serving: 89 Calories; 0.2g Fat; 21.9g Carbs; 0.2g Protein; 13.3g Sugars

INGREDIENTS

3 cups pan juices
1/3 cup cornstarch
1/3 cup cold water
Salt and ground black pepper, to taste
1/2 teaspoon cayenne pepper

DIRECTIONS

Press the "Sauté" button to preheat the Instant Pot; then, cook the pan juices for about 3 minutes, bringing it to a boil.
Whisk the cornstarch with cold water until the cornstarch has dissolved; then whisk the cornstarch slurry into the pan juices.
Add the salt, black pepper, and cayenne pepper; continue cooking on the lowest setting until your sauce has reduced slightly and the flavors have concentrated.
Use the "Keep Warm" function to keep your sauce warm until ready to serve.

288. Perfect Hot Sauce

(Ready in about 40 minutes | Servings 10)

Per serving: 39 Calories; 1.2g Fat; 5.8g Carbs; 0.8g Protein; 3.9g Sugars

INGREDIENTS

1 tablespoon butter, melted
1 banana shallot, chopped
1 teaspoon garlic, minced
5 jalapeño peppers, seeded and chopped
5 serrano peppers, seeded and chopped

2 tomatoes, chopped
1 cup white vinegar
1 cup water
2 tablespoons white sugar
Sea salt and ground black pepper, to taste

DIRECTIONS

Press the "Sauté" button and melt the butter. Once hot, cook the shallot for 3 to 4 minute or until it is tender and fragrant.

Now, add the garlic and continue to cook an additional 30 seconds or until aromatic.

Add the remaining ingredients.

Secure the lid. Choose the "Manual" mode and cook for 25 minutes at High pressure. Once cooking is complete, use a natural pressure release for 10 minutes; carefully remove the lid.

Let it cool. Serve your sauce hot or at room temperature. Bon appétit!

PASTA & GRAINS

289. Spaghetti with Arrabbiata Sauce

(Ready in about 40 minutes | Servings 4)

Per serving: 481 Calories; 29.2g Fat; 44.5g Carbs; 15.8g Protein; 11.5g Sugars

INGREDIENTS

Arrabbiata Sauce:
2 tablespoons olive oil
1 (28-ounce) can tomatoes, with juice
4 garlic cloves, minced
1 tablespoon brown sugar
1 teaspoon dried oregano

1 teaspoon dried basil
Sea salt and ground black pepper, to your liking
1/2 teaspoon cayenne pepper
1/3 cup cooking wine

Pasta:
16 ounces spaghetti
2 cups vegetable stock
10 ounces cream cheese
6 ounces Parmesan cheese, grated

DIRECTIONS

Put all ingredients for the sauce in the inner pot. Secure the lid. Choose the "Manual" mode and cook for 10 minutes at High pressure. Once cooking is complete, use a natural pressure release for 10 minutes; carefully remove the lid.
Stir in the spaghetti and vegetable stock.
Secure the lid. Choose the "Manual" mode and cook for 5 minutes at High pressure. Once cooking is complete, use a natural pressure release for 10 minutes; carefully remove the lid.
Divide your pasta between four serving bowls. Top with cheese and serve. Bon appétit!

290. Italian Sausage Lasagna

(Ready in about 50 minutes | Servings 6)

Per serving: 562 Calories; 25.1g Fat; 50.5g Carbs; 35.8g Protein; 11.1g Sugars

INGREDIENTS

1 tablespoon canola oil
3/4 pound Italian sausage, crumbled
1 small onion, chopped
2 garlic cloves, minced
1 fresh bell pepper, seeded and chopped

Sea salt and ground black pepper, to taste
1 teaspoon dried oregano
1 teaspoon dried basil
1/2 teaspoon dried rosemary
1 teaspoon red pepper flakes, crushed

14 ounces cream cheese
1 egg
1/4 cup Romano cheese, grated
2 ½ cups pasta sauce
8 lasagna sheets
1 cup Asiago cheese, shredded

DIRECTIONS

Press the "Sauté" button and heat the oil. Once hot, cook the sausage for 3 to 4 minutes or until it starts to brown; crumble your sausage with a wooden spatula.
Now, stir in the onion, garlic, and bell pepper. Sauté for about 4 minutes or until the vegetables are fragrant. Season with salt, black pepper, oregano, basil, rosemary, and red pepper.
Add 1 ½ cups of water and a metal trivet in the inner pot of your Instant Pot. Spritz a casserole dish with cooking spray.
Then, thoroughly combine the cream cheese with an egg, and Romano cheese.
Place a thin layer of pasta sauce on the bottom of the prepared casserole dish.
Add 4 lasagna sheets and 1/2 the cheese mixture. Top with 1/2 of the meat/vegetable mixture.
Repeat the layers one more time, ending with the marinara sauce. Top with Asiago cheese. Cover with a sheet of aluminum foil.
Secure the lid. Choose the "Manual" mode and cook for 23 minutes at High pressure. Once cooking is complete, use a natural pressure release for 10 minutes; carefully remove the lid.
Let your lasagna rest for 5 to 6 minutes before slicing and serving. Bon appétit!

291. Homemade Spaghetti with Meat Sauce

(Ready in about 20 minutes | Servings 4)

Per serving: 539 Calories; 21.9g Fat; 49.9g Carbs; 35.1g Protein; 6.1g Sugars

INGREDIENTS

2 teaspoons olive oil
1/2 pound ground pork
1/2 pound ground beef chuck
1/2 cup red wine
1 teaspoon cayenne pepper

Kosher salt and ground black pepper, to taste
1 teaspoon garlic powder
1/2 teaspoon shallot powder
1 cup marinara sauce

2 cups water
8 ounces dry spaghetti
1/2 cup Romano cheese, preferably freshly grated

DIRECTIONS

Press the "Sauté" button and heat the oil. Once hot, brown the ground meat for about 5 minutes until no longer pink, stirring and breaking the meat into smaller chunks.
Scrape the bottom of the pot with red wine. Add the cayenne pepper, salt, black pepper, garlic powder, shallot powder, and marinara sauce; stir to combine.
Pour in the water and gently stir to combine. Add the dry spaghetti.
Secure the lid. Choose the "Manual" mode and cook for 8 minutes at High pressure. Once cooking is complete, use a quick pressure release; carefully remove the lid.
Serve warm with Romano cheese. Bon appétit!

292. Creamy Ziti Florentine

(Ready in about 20 minutes | Servings 4)

Per serving: 459 Calories; 8.2g Fat; 74.9g Carbs; 19.8g Protein; 13g Sugars

INGREDIENTS

2 cups vegetable broth
1/2 cup double cream
2 garlic cloves, minced

Sea salt and ground black pepper, to taste
9 ounces dry ziti pasta

1 ½ cups tomato sauce
1 cup Mozzarella cheese, shredded

DIRECTIONS

Add the broth, double cream, garlic, salt, black pepper, ziti pasta, and tomato sauce to the inner pot.

Secure the lid. Choose the "Manual" mode and cook for 8 minutes at High pressure. Once cooking is complete, use a quick pressure release; carefully remove the lid.

Stir in the Mozzarella cheese and seal the lid; let it sit in the residual heat until the cheese melts. The sauce will thicken as it cools. Bon appétit!

293. Spaghetti à la Philly

(Ready in about 20 minutes | Servings 4)

Per serving: 576 Calories; 29.3g Fat; 30.7g Carbs; 46.5g Protein; 7.7g Sugars

INGREDIENTS

1 tablespoon olive oil
1/2 ground turkey
1/2 pound ground beef
1 onion, chopped
2 garlic cloves, minced

1 tablespoon fish sauce
2 tablespoons tomato paste
Kosher salt and cracked black pepper, to taste
1 bay leaf

2 cups vegetable broth
1/2 cup tomato sauce
8 ounces spaghetti
1 ½ cups Swiss cheese, shredded

DIRECTIONS

Press the "Sauté" button and heat the oil. Once hot, brown the ground meat for about 5 minutes until no longer pink, stirring and breaking the meat into smaller chunks.

Add the onion and garlic and cook for a further 2 minutes or until they are fragrant.

Stir in the fish sauce, tomato paste, salt, black pepper, bay leaf, vegetable broth, tomato sauce and spaghetti; do not stir, but make sure the spaghetti is covered.

Secure the lid. Choose the "Manual" mode and cook for 8 minutes at High pressure. Once cooking is complete, use a quick pressure release; carefully remove the lid.

Top with Swiss cheese and gently stir to combine; serve immediately!

294. Mac 'n' Cheese Pot Pie

(Ready in about 20 minutes | Servings 4)

Per serving: 608 Calories; 39.1g Fat; 32.3g Carbs; 31.2g Protein; 3.9g Sugars

INGREDIENTS

2 tablespoons olive oil
1 pound chicken drumsticks, boneless and cut into small cubes
1 shallot, chopped
2 garlic cloves, minced
1 bell pepper, seeded and chopped
1 habanero pepper, seeded and chopped

Kosher salt and ground black pepper, to taste
1 teaspoon cayenne pepper
2 cups chicken bone broth, preferably homemade
2 cups dried elbow pasta
1 cup cream cheese
1 tablespoon flaxseed meal

DIRECTIONS

Press the "Sauté" button and heat the olive oil. Once hot, brown the chicken drumsticks for 3 to 4 minutes, stirring frequently to ensure even cooking.

Add the shallot, garlic, and peppers; continue to cook an additional 3 minute or until they have softened.

Add the salt, black pepper, cayenne pepper, broth, and pasta to the inner pot.

Secure the lid. Choose the "Manual" mode and cook for 6 minutes at High pressure. Once cooking is complete, use a quick pressure release; carefully remove the lid.

Add the cream cheese and flaxseed meal; stir to combine and press the "Sauté" button; let it cook for a few minutes longer or until your sauce has reduced slightly and the flavors have concentrated. Bon appétit!

295. Millet Porridge with Almonds and Raisins

(Ready in about 25 minutes | Servings 5)

Per serving: 372 Calories; 10.1g Fat; 60.6g Carbs; 10.6g Protein; 10.7g Sugars

INGREDIENTS

1 ½ cups millet
3 cups water
1/2 cup golden raisins

1/4 cup almonds, roughly chopped
1 tablespoon orange juice
A pinch of sea salt

DIRECTIONS

Place all ingredients in the inner pot of your Instant Pot and close the lid.
Secure the lid. Choose the "Manual" mode and cook for 12 minutes at High pressure. Once cooking is complete, use a natural pressure release for 10 minutes; carefully remove the lid.
Taste and adjust the seasonings. Bon appétit!

296. The Easiest Oatmeal Ever

(Ready in about 25 minutes | Servings 4)

Per serving: 228 Calories; 4.1g Fat; 60.6g Carbs; 9.6g Protein; 0g Sugars

INGREDIENTS

1 ½ cups steel cut oats
4 ½ cups water

A pinch of kosher salt
A pinch of grated nutmeg

DIRECTIONS

Place all ingredients in the inner pot.
Secure the lid. Choose the "Manual" mode and cook for 3 minutes at High pressure. Once cooking is complete, use a natural pressure release for 20 minutes; carefully remove the lid.
Serve warm with a splash of milk and fruits of choice. Enjoy!

297. Grandmother's Buttermilk Cornbread

(Ready in about 1 hour | Servings 8)

Per serving: 208 Calories; 7.8g Fat; 31.3g Carbs; 3.6g Protein; 7.7g Sugars

INGREDIENTS

1 cup yellow cornmeal
1 cup all-purpose flour
1 tablespoon baking powder
1/2 cup granulated sugar

A pinch of salt
A pinch of grated nutmeg
1 cup buttermilk
1/4 cup safflower oil

DIRECTIONS

Add 1 cup of water and metal rack to the inner pot. Spritz a baking pan with cooking oil.
Thoroughly combine the cornmeal, flour, baking powder, sugar, salt, and grated nutmeg. In another mixing bowl, whisk buttermilk with safflower oil.
Add the wet mixture to the cornmeal mixture. Scrape the mixture into the prepared baking pan. Cover with a sheet of greased aluminum foil.
Lower the pan onto the rack.
Secure the lid. Choose the "Manual" mode and cook for 55 minutes at High pressure. Once cooking is complete, use a quick pressure release; carefully remove the lid.
Place the cornbread on a cooling rack before slicing and serving. Bon appétit!

298. Easy Pearl Barley with Peppers

(Ready in about 30 minutes | Servings 3)

Per serving: 339 Calories; 8.8g Fat; 60.3g Carbs; 7.6g Protein; 5.2g Sugars

INGREDIENTS

1 tablespoon sesame oil

1 yellow onion, chopped

2 garlic cloves, minced

2 bell peppers, seeded and chopped

1 jalapeno pepper, seeded and chopped

1 cups pearl barley, rinsed

2 ½ cups roasted vegetable broth

1/4 cup chives, chopped

DIRECTIONS

Press the "Sauté" button and heat the oil. Once hot, cook the onion until just tender and fragrant or about 3 minutes.

Stir in the garlic and peppers; continue cooking for 2 minutes more or until they are aromatic. Add the barley and vegetable broth to the inner pot.

Secure the lid. Choose the "Multigrain" mode and cook for 20 minutes at High pressure. Once cooking is complete, use a quick pressure release; carefully remove the lid.

Fluff the barley with a fork; garnish with chopped chives and serve with your favorite main dish. Bon appétit!

299. Fast and Easy Quinoa Salad

(Ready in about 15 minutes + chilling time | Servings 3)

Per serving: 406 Calories; 12.8g Fat; 60.5g Carbs; 14.2g Protein; 3g Sugars

INGREDIENTS

1 cup quinoa, rinsed

1 ½ cups water

1 cup boiled chickpeas

2 sweet peppers, seeded and chopped

1 serrano pepper, seeded and chopped

1 onion, thinly sliced

1/4 cup extra-virgin olive oil

2 tablespoons fresh lime juice

Sea salt and ground black pepper, to taste

1/4 teaspoon red pepper flakes

DIRECTIONS

Spritz the inner pot with cooking oil and stir in the rinsed quinoa and water.

Secure the lid. Choose the "Manual" mode and cook for 1 minute at High pressure. Once cooking is complete, use a natural pressure release for 10 minutes; carefully remove the lid.

Fluff the quinoa with a fork and allow it to cool. Toss the cooled quinoa with the remaining ingredients; toss to combine well and serve. Bon appétit!

300. Creamy Moroccan Couscous with Vegetables

(Ready in about 15 minutes | Servings 4)

Per serving: 360 Calories; 6.8g Fat; 64.7g Carbs; 10.6g Protein; 6.6g Sugars

INGREDIENTS

2 tablespoons butter, softened

1 small onion, chopped

1 teaspoon garlic, pressed

1 (1-inch) piece ginger, peeled and grated

2 carrots, trimmed and chopped

1 stalk celery, peeled and chopped

1 ½ cups couscous

3 cups water

1 tablespoon chicken bouillon granules

Sea salt and ground white pepper, to taste

1 teaspoon dried parsley flakes

1 teaspoon cayenne pepper

1/2 teaspoon ground cumin

1/4 teaspoon ground cinnamon

2 Peppadew peppers, chopped

1 cup tomato puree

DIRECTIONS

Press the "Sauté" button and melt the butter. Once hot, cook the onion, garlic, ginger, carrots, and celery until tender or about 4 minutes. Add the other ingredients; stir to combine well.

Secure the lid. Choose the "Manual" mode and cook for 3 minutes at High pressure. Once cooking is complete, use a quick pressure release; carefully remove the lid. Ladle into serving bowls and enjoy!

301. Mom's Creamed Corn

(Ready in about 15 minutes | Servings 3)

Per serving: 279 Calories; 19.3g Fat; 19.8g Carbs; 10g Protein; 5.6g Sugars

INGREDIENTS

2 cups corn kernels
2 tablespoons cold butter, cut into pieces
6 ounces Cottage cheese, at room temperature
1/2 cup double cream

1 cup water
Kosher salt and ground black pepper, to taste
1/2 teaspoon red pepper flakes
1/2 teaspoon dried parsley flakes

DIRECTIONS

Put all ingredients into the inner pot of your Instant Pot; stir to combine.
Secure the lid. Choose the "Manual" mode and cook for 4 minutes at High pressure. Once cooking is complete, use a quick pressure release; carefully remove the lid.
Ladle into serving bowls and enjoy!

302. Kamut and Chicken Bake

(Ready in about 20 minutes | Servings 4)

Per serving: 495 Calories; 19.5g Fat; 43.1g Carbs; 39.4g Protein; 7.1g Sugars

INGREDIENTS

1 cup kamut
1 cup vegetable broth
1 cup tomato puree
Sea salt and freshly ground black pepper, to taste
1 teaspoon basil
1 teaspoon thyme
1 pound chicken, boneless, skinless and chopped

1 shallot, chopped
1 teaspoon fresh garlic, pressed
1 sweet pepper, chopped
1 serrano pepper, chopped
2 tablespoons butter, melted
4 ounces Colby cheese, shredded

DIRECTIONS

Add the kamut to the bottom of a lightly greased inner pot. Now, pour in the broth and tomato puree; add the spices.
Add the chicken, shallot, garlic, and peppers; drizzle melted butter over everything.
Secure the lid. Choose the "Manual" mode and cook for 12 minutes at High pressure. Once cooking is complete, use a quick pressure release; carefully remove the lid.
Top with shredded cheese and seal the lid again. Let it sit in the residual heat until the cheese melts, Enjoy!

303. Mediterranean-Style Wheat Berry Salad

(Ready in about 40 minutes + chilling time | Servings 4)

Per serving: 246 Calories; 16.5g Fat; 23.3g Carbs; 4.4g Protein; 0.4g Sugars

INGREDIENTS

1 cup wheat berries
3 cups water
2 tomatoes, sliced
1 cucumber, sliced
1 red onion, sliced

1/4 cup good olive oil
1/4 cup red wine vinegar
1/2 teaspoon oregano
1 teaspoon basil
1/2 cup Kalamata olives

DIRECTIONS

Add the wheat berries and water to the inner pot.
Secure the lid. Choose the "Manual" mode and cook for 35 minutes at High pressure. Once cooking is complete, use a quick pressure release; carefully remove the lid.
Now, toss the cooked wheat berries with the remaining ingredients. Cover and refrigerate; the longer your salad sits, the more intense the flavor becomes. Enjoy!

304. Autumn Sweet Amaranth Porridge

(Ready in about 15 minutes | Servings 4)

Per serving: 425 Calories; 9.5g Fat; 74.8g Carbs; 14.4g Protein; 25g Sugars

INGREDIENTS

1 ½ cups amaranth
2 cups coconut milk
2 cups water
1 apple, cored and sliced
2 pears, cored and sliced

1/4 teaspoon ground cardamom
1/4 teaspoon ground cloves
1/2 teaspoon ground cinnamon
2 tablespoons honey

DIRECTIONS

Thoroughly combine all ingredients in the inner pot.
Secure the lid. Choose the "Manual" mode and cook for 4 minutes at High pressure. Once cooking is complete, use a quick pressure release; carefully remove the lid.
Ladle into individual bowls and enjoy!

305. Traditional Jowar Ki Kheer

(Ready in about 25 minutes | Servings 3)

Per serving: 485 Calories; 20.4g Fat; 64.2g Carbs; 14.1g Protein; 30.3g Sugars

INGREDIENTS

1 cup dried sorghum
3 cups soy milk
1 tablespoon ghee

1/2 cup brown sugar
1/2 cup cashews, roughly chopped

DIRECTIONS

Place the dries sorghum, milk, ghee, and brown sugar in the inner pot.
Secure the lid. Choose the "Porridge" mode and cook for 20 minutes at High pressure. Once cooking is complete, use a quick pressure release; carefully remove the lid.
Serve in individual bowls garnished with chopped cashews. Enjoy!

306. Creamy Spanish Buckwheat

(Ready in about 15 minutes | Servings 3)

Per serving: 235 Calories; 12g Fat; 21.4g Carbs; 12.1g Protein; 2.3g Sugars

INGREDIENTS

2 teaspoons olive oil
1 shallot, chopped
1 teaspoon garlic, minced
2 bell peppers, chopped
2 Chiles de árbol, chopped

1 ½ cups buckwheat
2 cups chicken broth
1 cup water
1/2 cup Manchego curado, grated

DIRECTIONS

Press the "Sauté" button and heat the oil until sizzling. Then, sauté the shallot until just tender or about 3 minutes.
Then, cook the garlic and peppers an additional 2 to 3 minutes or until they are fragrant.
Add the buckwheat, broth, and water to the inner pot.
Secure the lid. Choose the "Manual" mode and cook for 3 minutes at High pressure. Once cooking is complete, use a quick pressure release; carefully remove the lid.
Serve garnished with cheese. Enjoy!

307. Savory Za'atar Oatmeal with Eggs

(Ready in about 35 minutes | Servings 2)

Per serving: 381 Calories; 17g Fat; 40.9g Carbs; 17.6g Protein; 8.4g Sugars

INGREDIENTS

1/2 cup steel cut oats

1 ½ cups vegetable broth

1 tomato, pureed

Kosher salt and freshly ground black pepper, to taste

2 teaspoons olive oil

1 onion, chopped

2 bell peppers, seeded and sliced

2 eggs, beaten

DIRECTIONS

Place the steel cut oats, vegetable broth, tomato, salt, and black pepper in the inner pot.

Secure the lid. Choose the "Manual" mode and cook for 3 minutes at High pressure. Once cooking is complete, use a natural pressure release for 20 minutes; carefully remove the lid.

Meanwhile, heat the olive oil in a skillet over medium-high heat. Now, sauté the onion and peppers until they have softened or 3 to 4 minutes.

Then, add the beaten eggs and continue to cook until they are no longer liquid. Serve over the warm oatmeal.

308. Spelt Grains with Cremini Mushrooms

(Ready in about 35 minutes | Servings 3)

Per serving: 307 Calories; 10.5g Fat; 47.7g Carbs; 9.6g Protein; 5.9g Sugars

INGREDIENTS

2 tablespoons olive oil

1 leek, chopped

1 teaspoon garlic, minced

1 cup cremini mushrooms, sliced

1 cup spelt grains

2 cups water

Sea salt and white pepper, to taste

1 tablespoon oyster sauce

1 cup spinach leaves

DIRECTIONS

Press the "Sauté" button and heat the oil until sizzling. Then, sauté the leek for 3 to 4 minutes or until tender.

Add the garlic and mushrooms and cook an additional 2 minutes or until they are fragrant. Reserve the sautéed mixture.

Add the spelt grains, water, salt, pepper, and oyster sauce to the inner pot.

Secure the lid. Choose the "Porridge" mode and cook for 30 minutes at High pressure. Once cooking is complete, use a quick pressure release; carefully remove the lid.

Afterwards, stir in the spinach leaves and seal the lid; let it sit until the leaves wilt. Serve topped with the sautéed mushroom mixture. Bon appétit!

309. Quinoa Pilau with Acorn Squash

(Ready in about 10 minutes | Servings 4)

Per serving: 418 Calories; 9g Fat; 72.5g Carbs; 15.4g Protein; 8.4g Sugars

INGREDIENTS

1 pound acorn squash, peeled and sliced

1 tablespoon coconut oil, melted

2 sweet onions, thinly sliced

1 teaspoon fresh ginger, chopped

3 ½ cups vegetable stock

1 ½ cups quinoa, rinsed

6 prunes, chopped

2 tablespoons fresh mint leaves, roughly chopped

DIRECTIONS

Add the acorn squash, coconut oil, sweet onions, ginger, and 1 cup of stock to the inner pot; stir to combine.

Secure the lid. Choose the "Manual" mode and cook for 3 minutes at High pressure. Once cooking is complete, use a quick pressure release; carefully remove the lid.

Add the remaining stock, quinoa, and prunes to the inner pot.

Secure the lid. Choose the "Manual" mode and cook for 1 minute at High pressure. Once cooking is complete, use a quick pressure release; carefully remove the lid.

Serve garnished with fresh mint leaves. Bon appétit!

310. Greek-Style Polenta

(Ready in about 15 minutes | Servings 4)

Per serving: 309 Calories; 23.9g Fat; 14.7g Carbs; 9.4g Protein; 2.7g Sugars

INGREDIENTS

1 cup polenta
4 cups water
A pinch of sea salt
1/2 teaspoon red pepper flakes, crushed
1/2 teaspoon dried parsley flakes

1/2 teaspoon oregano
1 teaspoon dried onion flakes
4 tablespoons butter
8 ounces Feta cheese, crumbled

DIRECTIONS

Add the polenta, water, and salt to the inner pot of your Instant Pot. Press the "Sauté" button and bring the mixture to a simmer. Press the "Cancel" button.

Add the spices to your polenta. Secure the lid. Choose the "Manual" mode and cook for 8 minutes at High pressure. Once cooking is complete, use a quick pressure release; carefully remove the lid.

Stir the butter into the polenta, whisking until it has melted. Add more salt, if needed.

Top with Feta cheese and serve warm.

311. Authentic Hungarian Kukoricaprósza

(Ready in about 1 hour | Servings 5)

Per serving: 475 Calories; 23.9g Fat; 57g Carbs; 10.1g Protein; 24.7g Sugars

INGREDIENTS

1 ½ cups yellow cornmeal
1 ½ cups yogurt
1 ½ cups sour cream
1/4 cup water
1/4 cup safflower oil

1 egg, beaten
1 teaspoon baking soda
1/4 teaspoon salt
10 tablespoons plum jam

DIRECTIONS

Add 1 cup of water and metal rack to the inner pot. Spritz a baking pan with cooking oil.

Thoroughly combine the cornmeal, yogurt, sour cream, water, oil, egg, baking soda, and salt.

Scrape the mixture into the prepared baking pan. Place the piles of plum jam all over the surface.

Cover with a sheet of greased aluminum foil. Lower the pan onto the rack.

Secure the lid. Choose the "Manual" mode and cook for 55 minutes at High pressure. Once cooking is complete, use a quick pressure release; carefully remove the lid.

Place the Kukoricaprósza on a cooling rack before slicing and serving. Bon appétit!

312. Swiss Cheese and Pancetta Pie

(Ready in about 35 minutes | Servings 5)

Per serving: 489 Calories; 32.4g Fat; 22.5g Carbs; 25.8g Protein; 2.8g Sugars

INGREDIENTS

1 refrigerated pie crust
5 eggs
1/2 cup milk
1/2 cup sour cream

Sea salt and ground black pepper, to taste
4 ounces pancetta, chopped
1 cup Swiss cheese, shredded
4 tablespoons scallions, chopped

DIRECTIONS

Press the pie crust into a baking pan, crimping the top edges. In a mixing bowl, combine the eggs, milk, sour cream, salt, and pepper.

Place the pancetta on the pie crust; pour the egg/milk mixture over the top. Top with Swiss cheese.

Add 1 cup of water and a metal trivet to the Instant Pot. Lower the baking pan onto the trivet; cover with a sheet of greased aluminum foil.

Secure the lid. Choose the "Manual" mode and cook for 25 minutes at High pressure. Once cooking is complete, use a quick pressure release; carefully remove the lid.

Garnish with scallions and serve warm.

313. Croissant Bread Pudding with Strawberries

(Ready in about 55 minutes | Servings 4)

Per serving: 430 Calories; 25.5g Fat; 34.7g Carbs; 14.8g Protein; 17.1g Sugars

INGREDIENTS

4 cups croissants, cut into pieces
4 eggs
10 ounces coconut milk
5 ounces condensed milk
1/4 cup sugar
1 teaspoon vanilla

A pinch of salt
1/4 teaspoon ground cloves
1 teaspoon ground cinnamon
1 cup strawberries
2 tablespoon cold butter, cut into pieces.

DIRECTIONS

Add 1 cup of water and a metal trivet to the Instant Pot. Spritz a 7-inch springform pan with butter spray. Throw the croissant pieces into the pan.

In a mixing bowl, thoroughly combine the eggs, milk, sugar, vanilla, salt, cloves, and cinnamon. Pour 1/2 of the mixture over the croissants and let them soak approximately 15 minutes, until they no longer look dry.

Scatter the strawberries on top. Pour the leftover custard on top. Afterwards, top with the butter pieces and lower the pan onto the trivet.

Secure the lid. Choose the "Manual" mode and cook for 25 minutes at High pressure. Once cooking is complete, use a natural pressure release for 10 minutes; carefully remove the lid. Bon appétit!

314. Cream Cheese Grits

(Ready in about 25 minutes | Servings 3)

Per serving: 412 Calories; 25.7g Fat; 36.7g Carbs; 10.4g Protein; 5.1g Sugars

INGREDIENTS

2 cups of water
1 cup stone ground grits
1/2 teaspoon sea salt
1 cup cream cheese, room temperature

1/2 teaspoon paprika
1/4 teaspoon porcini powder
1/2 teaspoon garlic powder
1/2 cup milk

DIRECTIONS

Place the water, grits, and salt in the inner pot of your Instant Pot.

Secure the lid. Choose the "Manual" mode and cook for 10 minutes at High pressure. Once cooking is complete, use a natural pressure release for 10 minutes; carefully remove the lid.

Now, stir the cheese, paprika, porcini powder, garlic powder and milk into warm grits; stir to combine well and serve immediately.

315. Simple Bulgur Pilaf with Shallots

(Ready in about 25 minutes | Servings 2)

Per serving: 199 Calories; 6.9g Fat; 29.2g Carbs; 7.4g Protein; 1.1g Sugars

INGREDIENTS

1 tablespoon butter
2 shallots, chopped
1 teaspoon fresh garlic, minced
1/2 cup bulgur wheat

1 cup vegetable broth
1/4 teaspoon ground black pepper
1/4 teaspoon fine sea salt

DIRECTIONS

Press the "Sauté" button and melt the butter. Now, cook the shallots until just tender and fragrant.

Then, stir in the garlic and continue to sauté an additional minute or so. Add the remaining ingredients to the inner pot.

Secure the lid. Choose the "Manual" mode and cook for 10 minutes at High pressure. Once cooking is complete, use a natural pressure release for 10 minutes; carefully remove the lid.

Fluff the bulgur wheat with a fork and serve immediately. Bon appétit!

316. Old-Fashioned Chicken and Kamut Soup

(Ready in about 20 minutes | Servings 4)

Per serving: 233 Calories; 9.1g Fat; 26.2g Carbs; 6.9g Protein; 1.1g Sugars

INGREDIENTS

1 tablespoon olive oil
1/2 cup chicken thighs, boneless
1 onion, chopped
1/2 cup kamut
1 celery stalk, chopped
1 parsnip, chopped

1 carrot, chopped
Sea salt and freshly ground black pepper, to taste
1 tablespoon Herbes de Provence
3 cups chicken broth
1 cup tomato puree

DIRECTIONS

Press the "Sauté" button and heat the oil; now, cook chicken thighs for 3 to 4 minutes.

Add the onion and continue to sauté until tender and translucent. Add the remaining ingredients and stir to combine.

Secure the lid. Choose the "Manual" mode and cook for 12 minutes at High pressure. Once cooking is complete, use a quick pressure release; carefully remove the lid.

Ladle your soup into individual bowls. Bon appétit!

317. Farro with Mushrooms and Cheese

(Ready in about 35 minutes | Servings 3)

Per serving: 442 Calories; 16.7g Fat; 61.3g Carbs; 17.3g Protein; 9.6g Sugars

INGREDIENTS

2 tablespoons olive oil
1 onion, chopped
1 cup mushrooms, sliced
2 sweet peppers, chopped
2 garlic cloves, minced
1/2 cup white wine

1 cup farro
2 ½ cups vegetable broth
Sea salt and ground black pepper, to taste
1/2 cup Swiss cheese, grated
1 heaping tablespoon fresh parsley, chopped

DIRECTIONS

Press the "Sauté" button and heat the oil; now, cook the onion until tender or 3 to 4 minutes. Stir in the mushrooms and peppers and cook an additional 3 minutes.

Stir in the garlic and continue to sauté for a minute or so.

Add the white wine to deglaze the pan. Now, add the farro, vegetable broth, salt, and black pepper to the inner pot.

Secure the lid. Choose the "Manual" mode and cook for 11 minutes at High pressure. Once cooking is complete, use a natural pressure release for 10 minutes; carefully remove the lid.

Top each serving with cheese and fresh parsley. Bon appétit!

318. Corn on the Cob with Cilantro Butter

(Ready in about 15 minutes | Servings 6)

Per serving: 225 Calories; 13.4g Fat; 26.7g Carbs; 4.8g Protein; 8.9g Sugars

INGREDIENTS

6 large ears corn, husked and halved
6 tablespoons butter, softened
2 heaping tablespoons cilantro, chopped

1 teaspoon paprika
Sea salt and ground black pepper, to taste

DIRECTIONS

Place 1 cup of water and a metal trivet in your Instant Pot. Now, lower the corn onto the trivet.

Secure the lid. Choose the "Manual" mode and cook for 6 minutes at High pressure. Once cooking is complete, use a quick pressure release; carefully remove the lid.

Press the "Sauté" button and melt the butter; add the cilantro, paprika, salt, and black pepper to the melted butter.

Pour the cilantro butter over the steamed corn and enjoy!

319. Family Truffle Popcorn

(Ready in about 15 minutes | Servings 4)

Per serving: 365 Calories; 30.4g Fat; 18.8g Carbs; 5.1g Protein; 0.2g Sugars

INGREDIENTS

1 stick butter
1 cup popcorn kernels
1 tablespoon truffle oil
1/4 cup parmesan cheese, grated
Sea salt, to taste

DIRECTIONS

Press the "Sauté" button and melt the butter. Stir until it begins to simmer.
Stir in the popcorn kernels and cover. When the popping slows down, press the "Cancel" button.
Now, add the truffle oil, parmesan, and sea salt. Toss to combine and serve immediately.

320. Winter Couscous Chicken Soup

(Ready in about 20 minutes | Servings 4)

Per serving: 343 Calories; 7.2g Fat; 44.7g Carbs; 23.3g Protein; 3.6g Sugars

INGREDIENTS

1 tablespoon chicken schmaltz
1/2 pound chicken breasts, cubed
1 onion, chopped
1 carrot, sliced
1 celery rib, sliced
1 parsnip, sliced

1 tablespoon lemongrass, minced
1 teaspoon garlic paste
1/2 teaspoon turmeric powder
1/4 teaspoon mustard powder
4 cups chicken bone broth
1 cup couscous

Sea salt and ground black pepper, to taste
1 tablespoon fresh parsley, chopped
1 tablespoon fresh chives, chopped

DIRECTIONS

Press the "Sauté" button and melt the chicken schmaltz. Once hot, sauté the chicken until golden brown; reserve.
Cook the onion, carrot, celery, and parsnip in pan drippings until just tender and aromatic.
Add the reserved chicken, lemongrass, garlic paste, turmeric, mustard powder, and broth.
Secure the lid. Choose the "Manual" mode and cook for 11 minutes at High pressure. Once cooking is complete, use a quick pressure release; carefully remove the lid.
Now, stir in the couscous; season with salt and pepper.
Secure the lid. Choose the "Manual" mode and cook for 2 minutes at High pressure. Once cooking is complete, use a quick pressure release; carefully remove the lid.
Serve garnished with fresh parsley and chives. Bon appétit!

321. French Toast Casserole with Chocolate

(Ready in about 20 minutes | Servings 4)

Per serving: 419 Calories; 18.3g Fat; 53.4g Carbs; 10.3g Protein; 25.4g Sugars

INGREDIENTS

8 slices of French bread, broken into pieces
2 eggs, whisked
1/2 cup milk
1/2 cup sour cream
4 tablespoons honey

1 teaspoon vanilla paste
1/4 teaspoon nutmeg, preferably freshly grated
1/2 teaspoon ground cardamom
1 teaspoon ground cinnamon
1 cup chocolate chips

DIRECTIONS

Place 1 cup of water and metal rack in your Instant Pot. Now, spritz a round cake pan with cooking oil. Throw the bread pieces in the pan.
In a mixing bowl, thoroughly combine the eggs, milk, sour cream, honey, and spices. Pour the mixture over the bread pieces and press with a wide spatula.
Cover the pan with a sheet of aluminum foil. Lower the pan onto the rack.
Secure the lid. Choose the "Manual" mode and cook for 13 minutes at High pressure. Once cooking is complete, use a quick pressure release; carefully remove the lid.
Sprinkle with chocolate chips and serve. Bon appétit!

322. Teff Porridge with Kale and Goat Cheese

(Ready in about 20 minutes | Servings 4)

Per serving: 419 Calories; 18.3g Fat; 53.4g Carbs; 10.3g Protein; 25.4g Sugars

INGREDIENTS

1 cup teff grains
4 cups water
1/2 teaspoon sea salt
2 tablespoons olive oil

2 cups kale, torn into pieces
1/2 cup goat cheese, crumbled
2 tomatoes, sliced

DIRECTIONS

Place the teff grains, water, salt, and olive oil in the inner pot of your Instant Pot.

Secure the lid. Choose the "Manual" mode and cook for 3 minutes at High pressure. Once cooking is complete, use a quick pressure release; carefully remove the lid.

Add the kale and seal the lid again; let it sot for 5 to 10 minutes. Serve garnished with goat cheese and fresh tomatoes. Bon appétit!

323. Amaranth Pilau with Fried Eggs

(Ready in about 15 minutes | Servings 2)

Per serving: 536 Calories; 28.6g Fat; 46.5g Carbs; 24.5g Protein; 8.8g Sugars

INGREDIENTS

3/4 cup amaranth
2 cups water
1/2 cup milk
Sea salt and freshly cracked black pepper, to taste

1 tablespoon olive oil
2 eggs
1/2 cup cheddar cheese, shredded
2 tablespoons fresh chives, roughly chopped

DIRECTIONS

Place the amaranth, water, and milk in the inner pot of your Instant Pot.

Secure the lid. Choose the "Manual" mode and cook for 4 minutes at High pressure. Once cooking is complete, use a quick pressure release; carefully remove the lid. Season with salt and black pepper.

Meanwhile, heat the oil in a skillet over medium-high heat. Then, fry the egg until crispy on the edges.

Divide the cooked amaranth between serving bowls; top with the fried eggs and cheese. Garnish with fresh chives. Bon appétit!

324. Three-Grain Kedgeree

(Ready in about 30 minutes | Servings 5)

Per serving: 380 Calories; 8.6g Fat; 62.6g Carbs; 15.1g Protein; 2.2g Sugars

INGREDIENTS

1 tablespoon olive oil
1 medium-sized leek, chopped
2 garlic cloves, pressed
1 sweet pepper, deveined and sliced
Sea salt and freshly ground black pepper, to taste

1/2 cup pearl barley
1/2 cup sorghum
1/2 cup congee
5 cups chicken bone broth

DIRECTIONS

Press the "Sauté" button and heat the oil until sizzling. Once hot, sauté the leeks, garlic and peppers for 3 to 4 minutes or until just tender and fragrant.

Add a splash of broth to deglaze the pot. Next, stir in the remaining ingredients.

Secure the lid. Choose the "Multigrain" mode and cook for 20 minutes at High pressure. Once cooking is complete, use a quick pressure release; carefully remove the lid.

Ladle into individual bowls and serve immediately.

325. Indian Korma with Chicken and Bulgur

(Ready in about 30 minutes | Servings 4)

Per serving: 425 Calories; 17.6g Fat; 35.1g Carbs; 33.4g Protein; 5.4g Sugars

INGREDIENTS

1 tablespoon sesame oil

1 pound chicken breasts, boneless and skinless, cut into bite-sized pieces

1 onion, chopped

1 teaspoon fresh garlic, minced

1 (2-inch) galangal piece, peeled and sliced

1 Bird's eye chili pepper, seeded and minced

1 teaspoon ground cumin

1 teaspoon turmeric powder

1 teaspoon garam masala

1 cup bulgur

1 cup coconut milk

2 cups chicken stock

Sea salt and ground black pepper, to taste

1 tablespoon fresh coriander, chopped

DIRECTIONS

Press the "Sauté" button and heat the sesame oil. Now, brown the chicken breast for 3 to 4 minutes; reserve.

Then, add the onion and cook until just tender and fragrant. Stir in the garlic and continue to sauté an additional minute or so.

Stir in the galangal, chili pepper, cumin, turmeric powder, garam masala, bulgur, coconut milk, chicken stock, salt, and black pepper; add the reserved chicken to the inner pot.

Secure the lid. Choose the "Manual" mode and cook for 10 minutes at High pressure. Once cooking is complete, use a natural pressure release for 10 minutes; carefully remove the lid. Serve garnished with fresh coriander and enjoy!

326. Buckwheat Breakfast Bowl

(Ready in about 10 minutes | Servings 3)

Per serving: 398 Calories; 5g Fat; 82.9g Carbs; 11.2g Protein; 36.8g Sugars

INGREDIENTS

1 cup buckwheat grouts

1 cup water

1 cup orange juice

1 cup coconut milk

2 tablespoons agave nectar

1 teaspoon carob powder

1/2 teaspoon ground cardamom

1/2 teaspoon ground cinnamon

A pinch of kosher salt

A pinch of grated nutmeg

1 cup fresh blueberries

DIRECTIONS

Add the buckwheat, water, orange juice, coconut milk, agave nectar, carob powder, and spices to the inner pot.

Secure the lid. Choose the "Manual" mode and cook for 3 minutes at High pressure. Once cooking is complete, use a quick pressure release; carefully remove the lid.

Serve in individual bowls garnished with fresh blueberries. Bon appétit!

RICE

327. Late Summer Rice Salad

(Ready in about 30 minutes | Servings 4)

Per serving: 544 Calories; 23.6g Fat; 77.9g Carbs; 6.5g Protein; 14.1g Sugars

INGREDIENTS

1 ½ cups long-grain white rice, rinsed
1 3/4 cups water
1/2 teaspoon table salt
4 tablespoons extra-virgin olive oil

1 tablespoon orange zest
1/4 cup orange juice, freshly squeezed
1 cup grapes, cut in half
1/4 cup dried cranberries

1/2 cup pecans
2 tablespoons pomegranate arils

DIRECTIONS

Place the rice, water, and salt in the inner pot of your Instant Pot; stir to combine.

Secure the lid. Choose the "Rice" mode and cook for 10 minutes. Once cooking is complete, use a natural pressure release for 15 minutes; carefully remove the lid.

Fluff the rice with a fork and allow it to cool to room temperature.

Add the remaining ingredients to a nice salad bowl; add the chilled rice. Toss to combine and serve chilled or at room temperature. Bon appétit!

328. Chicken Soup with Brown Basmati Rice

(Ready in about 45 minutes | Servings 4)

Per serving: 435 Calories; 13.1g Fat; 51.9g Carbs; 27.8g Protein; 6.6g Sugars

INGREDIENTS

2 tablespoons olive oil
1/2 pound chicken breast, boneless
and cut into small chunks
1 onion, chopped
2 cloves garlic, minced

2 carrots, peeled and diced
1 rib celery, diced
1 parsnip, peeled and diced
1/2 teaspoon dried basil
1/2 teaspoon dried thyme

5 cups chicken broth
1 cup brown basmati rice
Kosher salt and ground black pepper,
to taste
1/2 cup coconut milk

DIRECTIONS

Press the "Sauté" button and heat the oil until sizzling. Then, cook the chicken breast for 3 to 4 minutes or until no longer pink; reserve.

Now, add the onion and garlic and continue sautéing in pan drippings for 2 to 3 minutes more or until they are tender and fragrant.

Add the carrots, celery, parsnip, basil, thyme, broth, rice, salt, and black pepper. Add the chicken breasts back to the inner pot.

Secure the lid. Choose the "Soup/Broth" mode and cook for 20 minutes at High pressure. Once cooking is complete, use a natural pressure release for 15 minutes; carefully remove the lid.

Pour in the coconut milk; seal the lid and let it sit in the residual heat until heated through. Serve in soup bowls and enjoy!

329. Chicken Fillets Rice Bowl

(Ready in about 40 minutes | Servings 4)

Per serving: 418 Calories; 10.5g Fat; 50.1g Carbs; 29.5g Protein; 4.9g Sugars

INGREDIENTS

2 tablespoons olive oil
1 pound chicken fillets, cut into strips
1 onion, chopped
1 teaspoon garlic, minced
1 teaspoon sea salt

1/2 teaspoon black pepper, divided
1/2 teaspoon ground coriander
1/4 teaspoon paprika
1 cup white rice
1 cup water

2 red chili peppers, seeded and
chopped
1 cup green peas, thawed
1/2 cup salsa

DIRECTIONS

Press the "Sauté" button and heat 1 tablespoon of olive oil until sizzling. Then, cook the chicken until no longer pink or about 4 minutes.

Then, heat another tablespoon of olive oil and add the onion and garlic. Cook for 2 to 3 minutes or until fragrant. Now, sauté the garlic until it is aromatic but not browned.

Add the spices, rice, water, and peppers. Add the reserved chicken back to the inner pot.

Secure the lid. Choose the "Rice" mode and cook for 10 minutes. Once cooking is complete, use a natural pressure release for 15 minutes; carefully remove the lid.

Add the green peas and press the "Sauté" button; cook on Less setting until thoroughly heated. Serve with salsa and enjoy!

330. Risotto ai Funghi

(Ready in about 30 minutes | Servings 4)

Per serving: 296 Calories; 19.5g Fat; 21.6g Carbs; 14.9g Protein; 3.3g Sugars

INGREDIENTS

2 tablespoons olive oil
1 onion, chopped
1 teaspoon garlic, minced
2 cups Cremini mushrooms, chopped

1/2 teaspoon basil
1 teaspoon thyme
Sea salt and ground black pepper, to taste

1/3 cup Sauvignon Blanc
1 cup Arborio rice
4 cups vegetable broth
1/2 cup Romano cheese, grated

DIRECTIONS

Press the "Sauté" button and heat the olive oil until sizzling. Then, cook the onion until tender and translucent.

Now, stir in the garlic and mushrooms; cook until they are just tender or about 3 minutes.

Add the basil, thyme, salt, black pepper, Sauvignon Blanc, rice, and vegetable broth.

Secure the lid. Choose the "Manual" mode and cook for 4 minutes at High pressure. Once cooking is complete, use a natural pressure release for 15 minutes; carefully remove the lid.

Divide between individual bowls and serve garnished with Romano cheese. Bon appétit!

331. Wild Rice with Shrimp

(Ready in about 50 minutes | Servings 4)

Per serving: 334 Calories; 8.5g Fat; 36.1g Carbs; 30.9g Protein; 3.1g Sugars

INGREDIENTS

2 tablespoons olive oil
1 leek, chopped
1 teaspoon garlic, minced
2 bell peppers, chopped
1 cup wild rice

1 cup chicken broth
1 rosemary sprig
1 thyme sprig
1 teaspoon kosher salt
1/2 teaspoon ground black pepper

1/2 teaspoon cayenne pepper
1 pound shrimp, deveined
2 tablespoons fresh chives

DIRECTIONS

Press the "Sauté" button and heat the olive oil. Once hot, sauté the leek until just tender or about 3 minutes.

Then, stir in the garlic and peppers. Continue to cook for 3 minutes more or until they are tender and fragrant.

Add the wild rice, broth, and seasonings to the inner pot.

Secure the lid. Choose the "Manual" mode and cook for 30 minutes at High pressure. Once cooking is complete, use a natural pressure release for 10 minutes; carefully remove the lid.

Add the shrimp to the inner pot. Choose the "Manual" mode and cook for 3 minutes at High pressure. Once cooking is complete, use a quick pressure release; carefully remove the lid.

Serve garnished with fresh chives and enjoy!

332. Famous Seafood Jambalaya

(Ready in about 15 minutes | Servings 4)

Per serving: 551 Calories; 14.5g Fat; 54.9g Carbs; 49.2g Protein; 7.2g Sugars

INGREDIENTS

2 tablespoons olive oil
1/2 pound Andouille sausage, sliced
1/2 pound chicken cutlets, cut into 1-inch cubes
1 onion, chopped
2 bell peppers, seeded and chopped

2 stalks celery, chopped
3 cloves garlic, minced
1 tablespoon pimentón de la Vera
2 tablespoons Cajun seasoning
Sea salt and ground black pepper, to taste
1 teaspoon cayenne pepper

2 ripe tomatoes, pureed
1 tablespoon fish sauce
1 cup white rice
2 cups chicken broth
1 pound shrimp, deveined
1 small handful fresh parsley, chopped

DIRECTIONS

Press the "Sauté" button and heat the olive oil. Once hot, sauté the Andouille sausage and chicken cutlets for 4 to 5 minutes until they are brown; reserve.

Now, cook the onion in pan drippings; cook until it is tender and translucent.

Add the remaining ingredients, except for the fresh parsley, to the inner pot.

Secure the lid. Choose the "Manual" mode and cook for 4 minutes at High pressure. Once cooking is complete, use a quick pressure release; carefully remove the lid.

Serve garnished with fresh parsley. Enjoy!

333. Arborio Rice and Broccoli Pottage

(Ready in about 15 minutes | Servings 4)

Per serving: 356 Calories; 11.9g Fat; 53.2g Carbs; 10.1g Protein; 5.2g Sugars

INGREDIENTS

2 tablespoons butter
1 onion, chopped
2 cloves garlic, minced
1 celery stalk, chopped
1 carrot, chopped

1 pound broccoli, broken into florets
1 cup cream of mushroom soup
1 cup plain milk
1 cup Arborio rice

DIRECTIONS

Press the "Sauté" button and melt the butter. Once hot, cook the onion and garlic for 3 to 4 minutes or until just tender and fragrant.
Add the remaining ingredients and gently stir to combine.
Secure the lid. Choose the "Manual" mode and cook for 4 minutes at High pressure. Once cooking is complete, use a quick pressure release; carefully remove the lid.
Serve warm.

334. Mexican-Style Salsa Rice

(Ready in about 35 minutes | Servings 4)

Per serving: 408 Calories; 15.6g Fat; 40.7g Carbs; 25.7g Protein; 3.2g Sugars

INGREDIENTS

1 cup brown rice
1 cup chicken broth
1 cup chunky salsa
1 cup Cotija cheese, shredded

DIRECTIONS

Add the brown rice, chicken broth, salsa, oregano, salt, and black pepper to the inner pot.
Secure the lid. Choose the "Manual" mode and cook for 22 minutes at High pressure. Once cooking is complete, use a natural pressure release for 10 minutes; carefully remove the lid.
Divide between serving bowls and serve with shredded cheese. Enjoy!

335. Arroz Con Leche (Spanish Rice Pudding)

(Ready in about 25 minutes | Servings 4)

Per serving: 324 Calories; 4.4g Fat; 64.6g Carbs; 7.7g Protein; 24.7g Sugars

INGREDIENTS

1 cup white rice
2 cups milk
4 tablespoons honey

1 teaspoon vanilla paste
1/2 teaspoon ground cinnamon
4 (2-inch) strips lemon zest

DIRECTIONS

Place all ingredients in the inner pot.
Secure the lid. Choose the "Manual" mode and cook for 4 minutes at High pressure. Once cooking is complete, use a natural pressure release for 15 minutes; carefully remove the lid.
Fluff the rice with a fork and serve immediately.

336. Wild Rice Chowder

(Ready in about 35 minutes | Servings 4)

Per serving: 320 Calories; 11.1g Fat; 41.6g Carbs; 13.8g Protein; 4.1g Sugars

INGREDIENTS

1 cup wild rice
4 cups chicken bone broth
1 onion, chopped
2 cloves garlic, pressed
1 carrot, chopped
1 parsnip, chopped
2 bay leaves

1 tablespoon Cajun seasoning
Sea salt and cracked black pepper, to taste
2 tablespoons olive oil
2 tablespoons cornstarch
1 egg, whisked
1 handful fresh cilantro, chopped

DIRECTIONS

Add the wild rice, broth, vegetables, spices, and olive oil to the inner pot of your Instant Pot.

Secure the lid. Choose the "Soup/Broth" mode and cook for 30 minutes at High pressure. Once cooking is complete, use a quick pressure release; carefully remove the lid.

Mix the cornstarch with 4 tablespoons of water and the whisked egg. Stir the mixture into the cooking liquid.

Press the "Sauté" button and let it simmer for 3 to 4 minutes or until heated through.

Ladle into individual bowls. Top each serving with fresh cilantro and serve warm. Bon appétit!

337. Japanese-Style Rice Stew

(Ready in about 45 minutes | Servings 4)

Per serving: 354 Calories; 2.1g Fat; 76.2g Carbs; 7.8g Protein; 2.7g Sugars

INGREDIENTS

1 ½ cups brown rice
3 cups water
1 pound potatoes, peeled and diced
2 tomatoes, pureed
1 teaspoon sweet paprika

Kosher salt and ground black pepper, to your liking
1/3 cup rice wine
1 tablespoon Tonkatsu sauce
2 bay leaves
2 tablespoons soy sauce

DIRECTIONS

Add all ingredients, except for the soy sauce, to the inner pot.

Secure the lid. Choose the "Manual" mode and cook for 24 minutes at High pressure. Once cooking is complete, use a natural pressure release for 15 minutes; carefully remove the lid.

Ladle into individual bowls; drizzle soy sauce over each serving and enjoy!

338. Ground Meat and Rice Bowl

(Ready in about 45 minutes | Servings 4)

Per serving: 435 Calories; 15.1g Fat; 43.4g Carbs; 30.1g Protein; 5.7g Sugars

INGREDIENTS

1 tablespoon lard, melted
1/2 pound ground turkey
1/2 pound ground beef
2 garlic cloves, minced
2 tablespoons brown sugar

2 tablespoons Worcestershire sauce
1/2 teaspoon crushed red pepper flakes
Sea salt and ground black pepper, to taste
1 cup brown rice

DIRECTIONS

Press the "Sauté" button and melt the lard. Once hot, cook the ground meat until no longer pink or about 3 to 4 minutes.

Then, stir in the garlic and let it cook an additional minute or until it is aromatic.

Add the remaining ingredients; stir to combine.

Secure the lid. Choose the "Manual" mode and cook for 22 minutes at High pressure. Once cooking is complete, use a natural pressure release for 10 minutes; carefully remove the lid.

339. Red Rice and Shrimp Risotto

(Ready in about 45 minutes | Servings 4)

Per serving: 352 Calories; 18.5g Fat; 22.2g Carbs; 25.4g Protein; 4.3g Sugars

INGREDIENTS

2 tablespoons butter, melted

1 onion, chopped

2 cloves garlic, minced

1/2 cup rice wine

1 ½ cups red rice

2 tablespoons Shoyu sauce

4 cups shellfish stock

1/2 pound shrimp, deveined

Sea salt and ground black pepper, to taste

4 tablespoons goat cheese, crumbled

DIRECTIONS

Press the "Sauté" button and melt the butter. Once hot, cook the onion and garlic for 2 to 3 minutes or until they are just tender.

Add a splash of rice wine; deglaze the bottom of the inner pot with a wooden spoon. Now, stir in the red rice, wine, Shoyu sauce, and shellfish stock to the inner pot.

Secure the lid. Choose the "Multigrain" mode and cook for 20 minutes at High pressure. Once cooking is complete, use a natural pressure release for 10 minutes; carefully remove the lid.

Next, stir in the shrimp, salt, and black pepper.

Secure the lid. Choose the "Manual" mode and cook for 4 minutes at High pressure. Once cooking is complete, use a quick pressure release; carefully remove the lid. Serve garnished with goat cheese and enjoy!

340. Authentic Paella Valenciana

(Ready in about 25 minutes | Servings 4)

Per serving: 389 Calories; 7.8g Fat; 48.1g Carbs; 31.2g Protein; 2.7g Sugars

INGREDIENTS

2 tablespoons ghee, at room temperature

2 cloves garlic, pressed

1 red bell pepper, cut in strips

1 cup basmati rice

1 pound tiger prawns, deveined

Sea salt and ground black pepper, to taste

1 bay leaf

1 teaspoon paprika

1/4 teaspoon saffron threads

1 tablespoon capers, drained

2 cups chicken broth

1 cup green peas, thawed

DIRECTIONS

Press the "Sauté" button and melt the ghee. Once hot, cook the garlic and pepper for about 2 minutes or until just tender and fragrant.

Add the basmati rice, tiger prawns, salt, black pepper, bay leaf, paprika, saffron, capers, and chicken broth to the inner pot.

Secure the lid. Choose the "Manual" mode and cook for 4 minutes at High pressure. Once cooking is complete, use a natural pressure release for 10 minutes; carefully remove the lid.

Add the green peas to the inner pot; press the "Sauté" button one more time and let it simmer until heated through. Enjoy!

341. Spicy Jasmine Rice with Peppers

(Ready in about 25 minutes | Servings 4)

Per serving: 309 Calories; 4.5g Fat; 59.8g Carbs; 6.4g Protein; 3.8g Sugars

INGREDIENTS

2 teaspoons olive oil

1 onion, chopped

2 cups sweet peppers, chopped

1 jalapeno pepper, minced

1 teaspoon garlic powder

1/2 teaspoon ground bay leaf

1/2 teaspoon dried sage, crushed

1 ½ cups jasmine rice, rinsed

1 ½ cups water

1/2 teaspoon sea salt

DIRECTIONS

Press the "Sauté" button and heat the olive oil. Once hot, cook the onion and peppers until just tender and fragrant.

Now, add the remaining ingredients and stir to combine well.

Secure the lid. Choose the "Manual" mode and cook for 4 minutes at High pressure. Once cooking is complete, use a natural pressure release for 15 minutes; carefully remove the lid.

Serve in individual bowls and enjoy!

342. Asian Congee with Pao Cai

(Ready in about 35 minutes | Servings 3)

Per serving: 326 Calories; 22.5g Fat; 26.8g Carbs; 16.4g Protein; 4.1g Sugars

INGREDIENTS

1 cup sushi rice, rinsed
6 cups roasted vegetable broth
1 teaspoon fresh ginger, grated
Kosher salt and ground black pepper, to taste

2 tablespoons soy sauce
2 tablespoons chili oil
1 cup pao cai

DIRECTIONS

Place the rice, vegetable broth, ginger, and salt in the inner pot of the Instant Pot.

Secure the lid. Choose the "Multigrain" mode and cook for 20 minutes at High pressure. Once cooking is complete, use a natural pressure release for 10 minutes; carefully remove the lid.

Your congee will thicken as it cools. Stir in the black pepper, soy sauce, and chili oil. Serve garnished with pao cai and enjoy!

343. Rice, Yellow Lentil and Kale Porridge

(Ready in about 50 minutes | Servings 3)

Per serving: 380 Calories; 4.7g Fat; 70.8g Carbs; 15.4g Protein; 2.2g Sugars

INGREDIENTS

1 cup brown jasmine rice
9 cups water
1 teaspoon sea salt
2 cups kale, torn into pieces

1/2 cup yellow lentils
Salt and ground black pepper, to taste
2 tablespoons pepitas, toasted

DIRECTIONS

Place the rice, water, and salt in the inner pot.

Secure the lid. Choose the "Manual" mode and cook for 25 minutes at High pressure. Once cooking is complete, use a natural pressure release for 20 minutes; carefully remove the lid.

Add the kale, lentils, salt, and black pepper to the inner pot.

Secure the lid. Choose the "Manual" mode and cook for 2 minutes at High pressure. Once cooking is complete, use a quick pressure release; carefully remove the lid.

Serve in individual bowls garnished with toasted pepitas.

344. Traditional Greek Rizogalo

(Ready in about 30 minutes | Servings 4)

Per serving: 550 Calories; 14.7g Fat; 91.6g Carbs; 12.6g Protein; 31.5g Sugars

INGREDIENTS

2 tablespoons butter
1 ½ cups white rice
4 cups milk
2 ounces sugar

1 (3-inch strip) of lemon rind
1 teaspoon vanilla extract
1 teaspoon ground cinnamon
4 tablespoons honey

DIRECTIONS

Place the butter, rice, milk, sugar, lemon rind, and vanilla extract in the inner pot.

Secure the lid. Choose the "Rice" mode and cook for 10 minutes at Low pressure. Once cooking is complete, use a natural pressure release for 15 minutes; carefully remove the lid.

Ladle your rizogalo into four serving bowls; top with cinnamon and honey and serve at room temperature.

345. Pulao Rice Pakistani Style

(Ready in about 30 minutes | Servings 4)

Per serving: 392 Calories; 7.3g Fat; 72.2g Carbs; 9.2g Protein; 0.9g Sugars

INGREDIENTS

2 tablespoons ghee
1 shallot, chopped
2 garlic cloves, minced
1 ½ cups basmati rice, rinsed

2 cups vegetable broth
Sea salt and white pepper, to taste
1 teaspoon coriander seeds
2 black cardamoms

2 green cardamoms
2 tez patta (bay leaf)
1 teaspoon turmeric powder
1 cup sweet corn kernels, thawed

DIRECTIONS

Press the "Sauté" button and melt the ghee. Once hot, cook the shallot for 4 minutes or until just tender and fragrant. Stir in the garlic and cook an additional minute or until aromatic.
Now, add the basmati rice, broth, and spices.
Secure the lid. Choose the "Manual" mode and cook for 4 minutes at High pressure. Once cooking is complete, use a natural pressure release for 15 minutes; carefully remove the lid.
Add the sweet corn kernels and seal the lid again. Let it sit in the residual heat until thoroughly heated. Enjoy!

346. Kinoko Gohan (Japanese Mushroom Rice)

(Ready in about 30 minutes | Servings 4)

Per serving: 463 Calories; 15.3g Fat; 63.5g Carbs; 9.8g Protein; 1.5g Sugars

INGREDIENTS

4 tablespoons shoyu
2 cups maitake mushrooms, sliced
2 cups shiitake mushrooms, sliced
1/4 cup mirin
1/4 cup sake

2 cups water
1 piece dried kombu
4 tablespoons sesame oil
1 shallot, chopped
1 teaspoon garlic, minced

1 ½ cups Kokuho Rose rice
2 cups chicken stock
Kosher salt and ground black pepper, to taste

DIRECTIONS

Press the "Sauté" button to preheat your Instant Pot. Put the shoyu, mushrooms, mirin, sake, water, and dried kombu.
Bring to a simmer on the lowest setting; allow it to cook for 5 to 6 minutes. Discard the kombu and save for another use.
Add the other ingredients to the inner pot.
Secure the lid. Choose the "Manual" mode and cook for 6 minutes at High pressure. Once cooking is complete, use a natural pressure release for 15 minutes; carefully remove the lid. Serve in individual bowls and enjoy!

347. Chicken, Broccoli and Rice Casserole

(Ready in about 30 minutes | Servings 4)

Per serving: 563 Calories; 21.2g Fat; 56.5g Carbs; 36.5g Protein; 6.7g Sugars

INGREDIENTS

3 tablespoons butter, melted
1 chicken breast, skinless
1 shallot, sliced
1 teaspoon garlic, minced
1 pound broccoli florets
1 cup white rice

1 cup tomato puree
2 cups chicken broth
1 teaspoon paprika
1 teaspoon Italian seasoning blend
Kosher salt and freshly ground pepper, to taste
5 ounces cheddar cheese, shredded

DIRECTIONS

Press the "Sauté" button and melt 1 tablespoon of butter. Once hot, cook the chicken breast until it is golden brown on both sides.
Shred the chicken with two forks. Add it back to the inner pot. Add the shallots, garlic, broccoli, rice, tomato puree, and chicken broth; stir in the remaining butter.
Season with the paprika, Italian seasonings, salt, and black pepper.
Secure the lid. Choose the "Rice" mode and cook for 10 minutes at Low pressure. Once cooking is complete, use a natural pressure release for 10 minutes; carefully remove the lid.
Top with cheese. Seal the lid again and let it sit in the residual heat until the cheese melts. Serve immediately.

348. Vegan Rice and Beans

(Ready in about 40 minutes | Servings 4)

Per serving: 354 Calories; 1.9g Fat; 70.5g Carbs; 15.1g Protein; 5.2g Sugars

INGREDIENTS

1 cup brown rice
1 cup kidney beans
1 cup marinara sauce
2 tablespoons fresh parsley, chopped

2 tablespoons fresh scallions, chopped
1 tablespoon fresh basil, chopped
2 green garlic stalks, chopped
2 ½ cups vegetable broth

DIRECTIONS

Add all ingredients to the inner pot of your Instant Pot.

Secure the lid. Choose the "Manual" mode and cook for 25 minutes at High pressure. Once cooking is complete, use a natural pressure release for 15 minutes; carefully remove the lid.

Ladle into individual bowls and serve warm. Enjoy!

349. Two-Cheese Risotto with Vegetables

(Ready in about 25 minutes | Servings 4)

Per serving: 444 Calories; 14.3g Fat; 48.7g Carbs; 27.2g Protein; 4.3g Sugars

INGREDIENTS

1 cup white rice, rinsed
1 onion, chopped
1 cup carrots, chopped
1 cup celery ribs, chopped
Sea salt and ground black pepper, to taste

1/2 teaspoon dried dill weed
2 cups roasted vegetable broth
1/2 cup Swiss cheese, shredded
1/2 cup Manchego cheese, shredded

DIRECTIONS

Add the rice, onion, carrots, celery, salt, black pepper, dill, and vegetable broth to the inner pot.

Secure the lid. Choose the "Manual" mode and cook for 5 minutes at High pressure. Once cooking is complete, use a natural pressure release for 15 minutes; carefully remove the lid.

After that, stir in the cheese; stir well to combine and seal the lid. Let it sit in the residual heat until the cheese melts. Bon appétit!

350. Authentic Indian Jeera Rice

(Ready in about 30 minutes | Servings 4)

Per serving: 346 Calories; 10.3g Fat; 57.1g Carbs; 6.2g Protein; 1.2g Sugars

INGREDIENTS

1 ½ cups rice basmati rice, rinsed
1 cup water
1 cup cream of celery soup
1 green chili deveined and chopped

Sea salt and ground black pepper, to taste
1 bay leaf
1 teaspoon Jeera (cumin seeds)
2 tablespoons sesame oil

DIRECTIONS

Place all ingredients in the inner pot. Stir until everything is well combined.

Secure the lid. Choose the "Rice" mode and cook for 10 minutes at Low pressure. Once cooking is complete, use a natural pressure release for 15 minutes; carefully remove the lid.

Serve with Indian main dishes of choice. Enjoy!

351. One Pot Enchilada Rice

(Ready in about 35 minutes | Servings 4)

Per serving: 559 Calories; 15.3g Fat; 83.4g Carbs; 24.1g Protein; 6.5g Sugars

INGREDIENTS

1 tablespoon canola oil
1 onion, chopped
2 garlic cloves, minced
1 sweet pepper, seeded and chopped
1 habanero pepper, seeded and minced
1 cup vegetable broth

1 cup long grain rice, rinsed
1 cup pinto beans, boiled
1 cup sweet corn, frozen and thawed
1/2 teaspoon cumin powder
1/3 teaspoon Mexican oregano
Sea salt and ground black pepper, to taste

1 cup enchilada sauce
1 cup Mexican blend cheese, shredded
A small handful of cilantro, roughly chopped

DIRECTIONS

Press the "Sauté" button to preheat your Instant Pot and add the oil. Once hot, cook the onion, garlic, and peppers until they are just tender and fragrant.
Next, add the vegetable broth followed by rice, beans, corn, cumin powder, oregano, salt, black pepper, and enchilada sauce; do not stir.
Secure the lid. Choose the "Manual" mode and cook for 5 minutes at High pressure. Once cooking is complete, use a natural pressure release for 15 minutes; carefully remove the lid.
After that, stir in Mexican blend cheese and seal the lid again. Let it sit in the residual heat for 5 to 10 minutes until the cheese melts.
Serve with fresh cilantro and enjoy!

352. Exotic Peanut Rice

(Ready in about 30 minutes | Servings 4)

Per serving: 473 Calories; 19.5g Fat; 63g Carbs; 14.6g Protein; 8.9g Sugars

INGREDIENTS

1 cup white rice
2 tablespoons peanut oil
1 Vidalia onion, chopped
2 cloves garlic, minced
1 teaspoon cayenne pepper

Sea salt and ground black pepper, to taste
1 tomato, pureed
1 ½ cups vegetable broth
1 bay leaf

1/2 cup frozen petite peas, thawed
1/2 cup peanuts, dry roasted and roughly chopped

DIRECTIONS

Add the white rice, peanut oil, Vidalia onion, garlic, cayenne pepper, salt, black pepper, tomato, vegetable broth, and bay leaf to the inner pot.
Secure the lid. Choose the "Manual" mode and cook for 5 minutes at High pressure. Once cooking is complete, use a natural pressure release for 20 minutes; carefully remove the lid.
Now, stir in the thawed petite peas and seal the lid. Let it sit in the residual heat until everything is heated through.
Serve with roasted peanuts and enjoy!

353. Hot and Spicy Pork Pilaf

(Ready in about 30 minutes | Servings 4)

Per serving: 425 Calories; 19.1g Fat; 44.7g Carbs; 33.3g Protein; 4.3g Sugars

INGREDIENTS

1/2 pound pork sausage, sliced
1/2 pound ground beef
1 medium-sized leek, chopped
2 garlic cloves, minced
1 celery stalk, chopped

2 carrots, chopped
1 parsnip, chopped
2 sweet peppers, chopped
1 poblano pepper, chopped
1 tablespoon Old Bay seasoning

1 teaspoon dried parsley
1 tablespoon fish sauce
1 ½ cups Arborio rice, rinsed
1 ½ cup beef broth

DIRECTIONS

Press the "Sauté" button to preheat your Instant Pot. Once hot, cook the pork sausage and ground beef until they have browned.
Add the leek, garlic, celery, carrots, parsnip, peppers, seasoning, and fish sauce to the inner pot. Continue to cook until the vegetables have softened.
Stir in the rice and beef broth; stir to combine well.
Secure the lid. Choose the "Rice" mode and cook for 10 minutes at Low pressure. Once cooking is complete, use a natural pressure release for 15 minutes; carefully remove the lid. Fluff your rice with a fork before serving. Bon appétit!

354. Southwestern Rice with Chicken and Beans

(Ready in about 40 minutes | Servings 4)

Per serving: 388 Calories; 4.9g Fat; 53.6g Carbs; 31.6g Protein; 1.8g Sugars

INGREDIENTS

1 cup brown rice
1 cup navy beans, drained and rinsed
1 cup chicken stock
1/2 cup salsa
2 garlic cloves, minced
1 sweet pepper, chopped

1/2 teaspoon cumin
1/2 teaspoon salt
1/2 teaspoon black peppercorns
2 bay leaves
1 pound chicken cutlets

DIRECTIONS

Place all ingredients in the inner pot. Stir until everything is well combined.

Secure the lid. Choose the "Bean/Chili" mode and cook for 25 minutes at High pressure. Once cooking is complete, use a natural pressure release for 10 minutes; carefully remove the lid.

Ladle into individual bowls and serve warm. Enjoy!

355. Easy Afghani Pulao

(Ready in about 50 minutes | Servings 3)

Per serving: 291 Calories; 5.9g Fat; 55.2g Carbs; 8.3g Protein; 14.1g Sugars

INGREDIENTS

1 tablespoon coconut oil
2 carrots, grated
1/2 cup raisins, soaked
4 tablespoons granulated sugar
1 cup wild rice

1 ½ cups water
A pinch of salt
A pinch of saffron
1/4 teaspoon cardamom powder

DIRECTIONS

Press the "Sauté" button to preheat your Instant Pot. Once hot, melt the coconut oil. Now, cook the grated carrots for 2 to 3 minutes or until they are tender.

Add the other ingredients to the inner pot.

Secure the lid. Choose the "Manual" mode and cook for 30 minutes at High pressure. Once cooking is complete, use a natural pressure release for 15 minutes; carefully remove the lid. Serve warm.

356. Spanish Arroz Rojo

(Ready in about 45 minutes | Servings 4)

Per serving: 375 Calories; 5.8g Fat; 72.3g Carbs; 8.3g Protein; 6.1g Sugars

INGREDIENTS

1 tablespoon olive oil
1 onion, chopped
1 teaspoon garlic paste
1 teaspoon ginger, grated
2 sweet peppers, deveined and sliced
1 red chili pepper, minced

1 ½ cups red rice
1 ½ cups water
1 cube tomato-chicken bouillon
1/2 cup tomato sauce
1 tablespoon taco seasoning
Sea salt, to taste

DIRECTIONS

Press the "Sauté" button and heat the oil until sizzling. Now, sauté the onion until just tender or about 3 minutes.

Add the remaining ingredients and stir to combine.

Secure the lid. Choose the "Manual" mode and cook for 30 minutes at High pressure. Once cooking is complete, use a natural pressure release for 10 minutes; carefully remove the lid.

Taste, adjust the seasonings and serve with salsa on the side. Enjoy!

357. Authentic Indian Khichri

(Ready in about 30 minutes | Servings 3)

Per serving: 530 Calories; 8.8g Fat; 92.3g Carbs; 20.2g Protein; 1.3g Sugars

INGREDIENTS

2 tablespoons butter
1 teaspoon cumin seeds
2 bay leaves
1 shallot, sliced

1 cup basmati rice
1 cup moong dal lentils
1/2 teaspoon ground turmeric
Sea salt and ground black pepper, to taste

DIRECTIONS

Press the "Sauté" button and melt the butter. Once hot, sauté the cumin seeds and bay leaf until they are fragrant.
Now, add the shallot and continue to sauté an additional 3 minute or until it is just tender.
Add the remaining ingredients; stir to combine.
Secure the lid. Choose the "Manual" mode and cook for 4 minutes at High pressure. Once cooking is complete, use a natural pressure release for 15 minutes; carefully remove the lid. Serve warm.

358. Wild Rice and Chicken Casserole

(Ready in about 50 minutes | Servings 4)

Per serving: 489 Calories; 20.1g Fat; 42.5g Carbs; 36.3g Protein; 5.2g Sugars

INGREDIENTS

2 tablespoons butter
2 cups chicken breasts, cut into chunks
1 onion, chopped
2 celery ribs, chopped

1 teaspoon garlic, minced
1 cup wild rice
1 cup cream of celery soup
1 cup tomato sauce

Sea salt and ground black pepper, to taste
1 cup sour cream
2 cup goat cheese, crumbled

DIRECTIONS

Press the "Sauté" button and melt the butter. Once hot, cook the chicken until it is no longer pink; reserve.
Now, sauté the onion in the pan drippings until tender. Then, add the celery and garlic; continue to sauté an additional minute or so.
Add the wild rice, cream of celery soup, tomato sauce, salt, and black pepper to the inner pot. Stir in the reserved chicken.
Secure the lid. Choose the "Manual" mode and cook for 30 minutes at High pressure. Once cooking is complete, use a natural pressure release for 15 minutes; carefully remove the lid.
Mix the sour cream with goat cheese; place the cheese mixture over your casserole. Let it sit, covered, for 10 minutes before serving. Bon appétit!

359. Easy Vegan Tomato Pilau

(Ready in about 30 minutes | Servings 4)

Per serving: 473 Calories; 4.9g Fat; 98.5g Carbs; 15.1g Protein; 26.2g Sugars

INGREDIENTS

1 tablespoon olive oil
1 onion, chopped
1 teaspoon garlic, chopped
1 ½ cups long grain white rice
2 cups water
2 carrots, thinly sliced
1 green zucchini, cut into thick sliced

2 (12-ounce) cans tomato paste
1 teaspoon Italian seasoning blend
Sea salt and ground black pepper, to your liking
1 bay leaf
4 cups spinach
2 teaspoons fresh lime juice

DIRECTIONS

Press the "Sauté" button and heat the oil. Once hot, cook the onion and garlic for 2 to 3 minutes or until just tender and aromatic.
Stir in the rice, water, carrots, zucchini, tomato paste, Italian seasoning blend, salt, black pepper, and bay leaf.
Secure the lid. Choose the "Rice" mode and cook for 10 minutes at Low pressure. Once cooking is complete, use a natural pressure release for 15 minutes; carefully remove the lid.
Add the spinach and press the "Sauté" button. Let it simmer on the lowest setting until wilts. Drizzle lime juice over each portion and serve. Bon appétit!

360. Perfect Sushi Rice

(Ready in about 30 minutes | Servings 4)

Per serving: 291 Calories; 1.9g Fat; 60.7g Carbs; 5.1g Protein; 3.5g Sugars

INGREDIENTS

1 ½ cups sushi rice, rinsed
1 ½ cups water
1/4 cup rice vinegar

1 tablespoon brown sugar
1/2 teaspoon salt
2 tablespoons soy sauce

DIRECTIONS

Place the sushi rice and water in the inner pot of your Instant Pot.

Secure the lid. Choose the "Rice" mode and cook for 10 minutes at Low pressure. Once cooking is complete, use a natural pressure release for 15 minutes; carefully remove the lid.

Meanwhile, whisk the rice vinegar, sugar, salt and soy sauce in a mixing dish; microwave the sauce for 1 minute.

Pour the sauce over the sushi rice; stir to combine. Assemble your sushi rolls and enjoy!

361. Beef and Rice Stew

(Ready in about 30 minutes | Servings 4)

Per serving: 291 Calories; 1.9g Fat; 60.7g Carbs; 5.1g Protein; 3.5g Sugars

INGREDIENTS

2 tablespoons lard, at room temperature
1 pound beef stew meat, cut into bite-sized chunks
4 cups beef bone broth
1 onion, chopped
2 garlic cloves, minced
2 sweet peppers, deveined and chopped
1 red chili pepper, chopped

1 teaspoon dried basil
1 teaspoon dried oregano
1 teaspoon dried rosemary
Sea salt and ground black pepper, to taste
1 bay leaf
2 tablespoons cornstarch, dissolved in 1/4 cup cold water
1 cup brown rice

DIRECTIONS

Press the "Sauté" button and melt the lard. When the lard starts to sizzle, add the beef stew meat and cook until browned on all sides; reserve.

Add a splash of beef broth to the inner pot; use a spoon to scrape the brown bits from the bottom of the pan.

Then, sauté the onion, garlic, and peppers for about 3 minutes or until they are just tender.

Add the other ingredients and stir to combine.

Secure the lid. Choose the "Soup/Broth" mode and cook for 20 minutes at High pressure. Once cooking is complete, use a quick pressure release; carefully remove the lid.

Mix the cornstarch with cold water in a small bowl; stir the slurry into the stew and cook on the "Sauté" function until the cooking liquid has thickened.

Serve warm and enjoy!

362. Risotto with Smoked Salmon

(Ready in about 20 minutes | Servings 4)

Per serving: 340 Calories; 18.6g Fat; 20.6g Carbs; 30.2g Protein; 3.3g Sugars

INGREDIENTS

1 tablespoon butter
1 onion, chopped
2 cloves garlic, minced
1 cup white rice

1 cup vegetable broth
1/2 cup milk
1 pound smoked salmon steak
4 ounces green beans

Sea salt and ground black pepper, to season

DIRECTIONS

Press the "Sauté" button and melt the butter. When the butter starts to sizzle, add the onion; sauté the onion until just tender and fragrant. Now, stir in the garlic and continue to sauté an additional minute or until fragrant.

Add the rice, broth, milk, salmon, and green beans; season with salt and black pepper.

Secure the lid. Choose the "Manual" mode and cook for 4 minutes at High pressure. Once cooking is complete, use a natural pressure release for 10 minutes; carefully remove the lid. Bon appétit!

BEANS, LEGUMES & LENTILS

363. Best-Ever Beans with Turkey Sausage

(Ready in about 45 minutes | Servings 4)

Per serving: 469 Calories; 13.6g Fat; 57.6g Carbs; 28.8g Protein; 4.9g Sugars

INGREDIENTS

2 tablespoons canola oil
6 ounces turkey sausage sliced
1 onion, chopped
2 cloves garlic, minced
1 bell pepper, sliced

1 ½ cups dry pinto beans
2 bay leaves
1 teaspoon dried sage
Sea salt and ground black pepper, to taste

1 teaspoon cayenne pepper
4 cups chicken broth
1 tomato, crushed

DIRECTIONS

Press the "Sauté" button and heat the oil. Sauté the sausage until it becomes slightly crispy.

Now, add the onion, garlic, and pepper; continue to cook until they are tender. Add the remaining ingredients to the inner pot.

Secure the lid. Choose the "Bean/Chili" mode and cook for 30 minutes at High pressure. Once cooking is complete, use a natural pressure release for 10 minutes; carefully remove the lid.

Press the "Sauté" button and let it simmer until the cooking liquid has thickened. Serve with your favorite toppings. Bon appétit!

364. Rich Kidney Bean Soup

(Ready in about 25 minutes | Servings 4)

Per serving: 534 Calories; 15.2g Fat; 72.5g Carbs; 31.4g Protein; 5.9g Sugars

INGREDIENTS

6 ounces bacon, cut into small pieces
1 leek, chopped
2 garlic cloves, sliced
1 parsnip, coarsely chopped
1 carrot, coarsely chopped
Sea salt and freshly cracked black pepper, to taste

2 canned chipotle chilis in adobo, chopped
1 teaspoon basil
1/2 teaspoon rosemary
2 cups dried red kidney beans, soaked and rinsed
4 cups chicken broth
A small handful cilantro leaves, roughly chopped

DIRECTIONS

Press the "Sauté" button to preheat your Instant Pot. Now, cook the bacon until crisp; reserve.

Add the leek and garlic; continue to sauté an additional 3 minute or until they are fragrant.

Stir in the other ingredients, except for the fresh cilantro.

Secure the lid. Choose the "Manual" mode and cook for 8 minutes at High pressure. Once cooking is complete, use a natural pressure release for 10 minutes; carefully remove the lid.

Afterwards, purée your soup using a food processor or an immersion blender. Serve garnished with fresh cilantro and the reserved bacon. Bon appétit!

365. Easy Spicy Hummus

(Ready in about 1 hour | Servings 6)

Per serving: 266 Calories; 12.2g Fat; 29.5g Carbs; 11.8g Protein; 1.2g Sugars

INGREDIENTS

1 ½ cups dry chickpeas, rinsed
1 ½ teaspoons sea salt
1 teaspoon baking soda
2 tablespoons fresh lemon juice
2 garlic cloves

1/4 cup olive oil
1 teaspoon cayenne pepper
4 dashes hot pepper sauce
2 tablespoons tahini (sesame butter)

DIRECTIONS

Add the dry chickpeas to the inner pot; pour in 6 cups of water. Add the sea salt and baking soda.

Secure the lid. Choose the "Manual" mode and cook for 35 minutes at High pressure. Once cooking is complete, use a natural pressure release for 20 minutes; carefully remove the lid. Reserve the cooking liquid.

Transfer the warm, drained chickpeas to your food processor; add the remaining ingredients. While the food processor is running, pour in the cooking liquid to achieve the desired consistency.

To serve, drizzle olive oil on top of the hummus if desired. Bon appétit!

366. Du Puy Lentils with Brown Rice

(Ready in about 35 minutes | Servings 8)

Per serving: 285 Calories; 2.9g Fat; 53.5g Carbs; 12.2g Protein; 1.9g Sugars

INGREDIENTS

1 ½ cups brown rice, rinsed
1 ½ cups du Puy lentils
2 cups cream of celery soup
1 cup water

1 cup shallots, chopped
1 teaspoon garlic, chopped
1 teaspoon cayenne pepper
1 teaspoon fennel seeds

Kosher salt and black pepper, to season
1 bay leaf
1 tablespoon balsamic vinegar

DIRECTIONS

Place all ingredient, except for the vinegar, in the inner pot of your Instant Pot.
Secure the lid. Choose the "Manual" mode and cook for 15 minutes at High pressure. Once cooking is complete, use a natural pressure release for 15 minutes; carefully remove the lid.
Afterward, stir in the vinegar and serve immediately. Enjoy!

367. Black Eyed Peas with Pancetta

(Ready in about 50 minutes | Servings 6)

Per serving: 308 Calories; 3.7g Fat; 46.3g Carbs; 24.1g Protein; 6.1g Sugars

INGREDIENTS

8 ounces pancetta
2 cups black eyed peas, rinsed
2 cups cream of celery soup
3 cups water

Sea salt and ground black pepper, to taste
1 teaspoon paprika
1 tablespoon fresh parsley, chopped

DIRECTIONS

Press the "Sauté" button to preheat your Instant Pot; now, cook the pancetta until browned and reserve.
Add the black eyed peas, cream of celery soup, water, salt, pepper, and paprika to the inner pot.
Secure the lid. Choose the "Bean/Chili" mode and cook for 30 minutes at High pressure. Once cooking is complete, use a natural pressure release for 15 minutes; carefully remove the lid.
Ladle into serving bowls and garnish with fresh parsley and the reserved pancetta. Bon appétit!

368. Indian Masala Matar

(Ready in about 20 minutes | Servings 4)

Per serving: 239 Calories; 9.1g Fat; 29.2g Carbs; 12.6g Protein; 14.9g Sugars

INGREDIENTS

1 tablespoon ghee, melted
1/2 teaspoon cumin seeds
1 yellow onion, chopped
2 cups green peas
2 tomatoes, pureed
1/2 teaspoon garam masala
1 tablespoon coriander

1/2 teaspoon chili powder
Sea salt and ground black pepper, to taste
4 curry leaves
3 cups vegetable broth
1 tablespoon chickpea flour
1 cup yogurt

DIRECTIONS

Press the "Sauté" button and melt the ghee. Once hot, cook the cumin seeds for about 1 minute or until fragrant.
Add the onion and continue sautéing an additional 3 minutes.
Now, stir in the green peas, tomatoes, garam masala, coriander, chili powder, salt, black pepper, curry leaves, and broth.
Secure the lid. Choose the "Manual" mode and cook for 12 minutes at High pressure. Once cooking is complete, use a quick pressure release; carefully remove the lid.
Now, stir in the chickpea flour and let it simmer on the "Sauté" button until the cooking liquid has thickened. Serve in soup bowls with yogurt on the side. Bon appétit!

369. Classic Minestrone Soup

(Ready in about 35 minutes | Servings 4)

Per serving: 414 Calories; 7.6g Fat; 73.4g Carbs; 15.6g Protein; 5.7g Sugars

INGREDIENTS

2 tablespoons olive oil

1 onion, chopped

1 teaspoon garlic, minced

2 carrots, sliced

2 celery stalks, diced

1 cup yellow squash, diced

1 cup dried Great Northern beans

4 medium-sized potatoes, peeled and diced

6 cups water

2 tomatoes, pureed

1 tablespoon Italian seasoning blend

Sea salt and ground black pepper, to taste

2 cups Swiss chard, torn into pieces

DIRECTIONS

Press the "Sauté" button and heat the olive oil until sizzling. Then, sauté the onion and garlic until just tender and fragrant.

Now, add the remaining ingredients, except for the Swiss chard.

Secure the lid. Choose the "Bean/Chili" mode and cook for 30 minutes at High pressure. Once cooking is complete, use a quick pressure release; carefully remove the lid.

Stir in the Swiss chard. Seal the lid and let it sit in the residual heat until it wilts. Serve warm.

370. Favorite Refried Beans

(Ready in about 1 hour 5 minutes | Servings 4)

Per serving: 472 Calories; 16.6g Fat; 49.1g Carbs; 32.3g Protein; 4.4g Sugars

INGREDIENTS

1 tablespoon olive oil

1 onion, chopped

2 cloves garlic, pressed

1 chili pepper, seeded and chopped

6 cups roasted vegetable broth

1 ½ cups white kidney beans, rinsed

2 bay leaves

Kosher salt and ground black pepper, to taste

1 teaspoon ground cumin

1 cup Colby cheese, shredded

DIRECTIONS

Press the "Sauté" button and heat the olive oil until sizzling. Then, sauté the onion for about 3 minutes or until tender.

Now, stir in the garlic and chili pepper; continue to cook for 1 minute more or until fragrant. Add a splash of broth to deglaze the pan.

Add the remaining broth, beans, bay leaves, salt, black pepper, and cumin to the inner pot of your Instant Pot.

Secure the lid. Choose the "Bean/Chili" mode and cook for 40 minutes at High pressure. Once cooking is complete, use a natural pressure release for 20 minutes; carefully remove the lid. Reserve 1 cup of the cooking liquid.

Then, puree the beans with an immersion blender until they reach your desired consistency. Sprinkle with the shredded Colby cheese and serve warm.

371. Rainbow Lentil Salad

(Ready in about 30 minutes | Servings 4)

Per serving: 492 Calories; 14.9g Fat; 68.6g Carbs; 25.6g Protein; 6.1g Sugars

INGREDIENTS

2 cups green lentils, rinsed

4 cups water

1/2 cup scallions, chopped

1 red bell pepper, seeded and sliced

1 green bell pepper, seeded and sliced

1 carrot, julienned

1 cucumber, sliced

1 cup grape tomatoes, halved

1/4 cup extra-virgin olive oil

1 fresh lemon, juiced

1/2 teaspoon red pepper flakes

Sea salt and ground white pepper, to taste

DIRECTIONS

Add the lentils and water to the inner pot.

Secure the lid. Choose the "Manual" mode and cook for 8 minutes at High pressure. Once cooking is complete, use a natural pressure release for 15 minutes; carefully remove the lid.

In a salad bowl, combine the lentils with the remaining ingredients. Toss to combine well. Serve well chilled. Bon appétit!

372. Brown Lentil Curry

(Ready in about 30 minutes | Servings 3)

Per serving: 319 Calories; 5.6g Fat; 52.1g Carbs; 7.5g Protein; 6.1g Sugars

INGREDIENTS

1 tablespoon sesame oil
1 onion, chopped
1 tablespoon fresh ginger, peeled and grated
2 garlic cloves, minced

1 teaspoon coconut sugar
Sea salt and white pepper, to taste
1/2 teaspoon ground turmeric
4 curry leaves
1 cups brown lentils, rinsed

1 teaspoon cayenne pepper
12 ounces canned coconut milk
2 tablespoons freshly squeezed lime juice

DIRECTIONS

Press the "Sauté" button and heat the sesame oil. Once hot, cook the onion until tender and translucent.
Now, add the ginger and garlic and continue to sauté an additional minute or so.
Stir in the coconut sugar, salt, white pepper, ground turmeric, curry leaves, brown lentils, and cayenne pepper. Pour in 2 cups of water.
Secure the lid. Choose the "Manual" mode and cook for 14 minutes at High pressure. Once cooking is complete, use a natural pressure release for 10 minutes; carefully remove the lid.
Now, pour in the coconut milk and press the "Sauté" button. Let it simmer on the lowest setting until thoroughly warmed.
Taste and adjust the seasoning. Serve with a few drizzles of lime juice. Enjoy!

373. Indian Chote Rajma

(Ready in about 35 minutes | Servings 3)

Per serving: 304 Calories; 5.6g Fat; 50.1g Carbs; 16.5g Protein; 4.6g Sugars

INGREDIENTS

1 tablespoon butter, at room temperature
1 teaspoon cumin seeds
1 onion, chopped
2 cloves garlic, pressed
1 ghost jolokia chili pepper, chopped

1 teaspoon red pepper flakes, crushed
1 teaspoon coriander
2 ripe tomatoes, pureed
1 cup dried adzuki beans
Kosher salt and ground black pepper, to taste

1 teaspoon garam masala
4 cups vegetable broth, preferably homemade
1 bay leaf
1-inch cinnamon stick
1 green cardamom

DIRECTIONS

Press the "Sauté" button and melt the butter. Once hot, cook the cumin seeds for 30 seconds to 1 minute or until the seeds begin to sizzle.
Now, stir in the onion, garlic, and chili pepper; continue to sauté an additional 3 minutes or until they have softened.
Stir in the remaining ingredients.
Secure the lid. Choose the "Bean/Chili" mode and cook for 25 minutes at High pressure. Once cooking is complete, use a quick pressure release; carefully remove the lid.
Serve with hot steamed rice if desired. Enjoy!

374. Chickpea Hot Pot

(Ready in about 55 minutes | Servings 4)

Per serving: 453 Calories; 11.9g Fat; 68.2g Carbs; 21.5g Protein; 14.1g Sugars

INGREDIENTS

1 tablespoon olive oil
1 large yellow onion, chopped
2 cups chickpeas
4 cups water
2 cups tomato sauce

1 teaspoon salt
1 teaspoon baking soda
1 rosemary sprig
1 thyme sprig
1 teaspoon mixed peppercorns

2 bay leaves
1/2 whole capsicum, deseeded and chopped
Sea salt, to taste

DIRECTIONS

Press the "Sauté" button and heat the olive oil; now, sauté the onion until tender and translucent. Then, add the remaining ingredients and stir to combine.
Secure the lid. Choose the "Bean/Chili" mode and cook for 40 minutes at High pressure. Once cooking is complete, use a natural pressure release for 10 minutes; carefully remove the lid.
Ladle into serving bowls and garnish with fresh chives if desired. Bon appétit!

375. Sorakkai Sambar (Indian Lentil Stew)

(Ready in about 35 minutes | Servings 3)

Per serving: 248 Calories; 7.9g Fat; 36.8g Carbs; 6.9g Protein; 13.4g Sugars

INGREDIENTS

1 cup Pigeon pea lentils
2 teaspoons sesame oil
1 yellow onion, chopped
6 curry leaves
1 Indian ghost jolokia chili pepper, chopped
1 tablespoon tamarind

1 teaspoon Urad Dal
1 tablespoon sambar powder
1 teaspoon turmeric powder
Sea salt and ground black pepper, to taste
1 teaspoon cayenne pepper
1 cup tomato sauce

DIRECTIONS

Add the lentils and 4 cups of water to the inner pot.

Secure the lid. Choose the "Manual" mode and cook for 10 minutes at High pressure. Once cooking is complete, use a natural pressure release for 10 minutes; carefully remove the lid.

Meanwhile, heat a saucepan over medium-high heat. Cook the onion for about 3 minutes or until translucent. Now, add the curry leaves and chili pepper to the skillet. Let it cook for a further minute or until they are aromatic.

Add the other ingredients, cover, and reduce the heat to medium-low; let it simmer for about 13 minutes or until everything is thoroughly cooked.

Transfer the onion/tomato mixture to the inner pot of your Instant Pot. Stir to combine and serve immediately. Bon appétit!

376. Spicy Heirloom Beans

(Ready in about 45 minutes | Servings 3)

Per serving: 525 Calories; 1.3g Fat; 95.2g Carbs; 36.3g Protein; 5.2g Sugars

INGREDIENTS

4 cups water
1 pound heirloom beans
1 tablespoon Italian Seasoning blend
1 bell pepper, seeded and chopped

1 jalapeño pepper, seeded and chopped
1 teaspoon liquid smoke
1 teaspoon onion powder
1 teaspoon granulated garlic

DIRECTIONS

Add all ingredients to the inner pot of your Instant Pot.

Secure the lid. Choose the "Bean/Chili" mode and cook for 30 minutes at High pressure. Once cooking is complete, use a natural pressure release for 10 minutes; carefully remove the lid.

Ladle into serving bowls and garnish with fresh scallions if desired. Bon appétit!

377. Green Pea Soup with Herbs

(Ready in about 20 minutes | Servings 4)

Per serving: 178 Calories; 6g Fat; 24.6g Carbs; 4.9g Protein; 9.7g Sugars

INGREDIENTS

2 teaspoons avocado oil
1 shallot, chopped
2 garlic cloves, minced
1 cups cream of mushroom soup
2 cup water

1 cup tomato sauce
1/2 teaspoon dried tarragon
1/2 teaspoon dried dill
Kosher salt and freshly ground black pepper, to taste
1 (10-oz) bag frozen green peas

DIRECTIONS

Press the "Sauté" button and heat the oil. Once hot, cook the shallot until tender and translucent; add the garlic to the inner pot and continue sautéing an additional 30 seconds.

Now, stir in the remaining ingredients.

Secure the lid. Choose the "Manual" mode and cook for 12 minutes at High pressure. Once cooking is complete, use a quick pressure release; carefully remove the lid.

Ladle into soup bowls. Bon appétit!

378. Lima Bean Hot Pot with Bacon

(Ready in about 20 minutes | Servings 4)

Per serving: 493 Calories; 27.7g Fat; 45.6g Carbs; 17.9g Protein; 11.7g Sugars

INGREDIENTS

8 ounces bacon
1 yellow onion, chopped
2 garlic cloves, pressed
1 pound dry lima beans
3 cups chicken broth

3 cups water
1 cup tomato sauce
1 bay leaf
1 sprig rosemary
1 sprig thyme

DIRECTIONS

Press the "Sauté" button to preheat your Instant Pot. Cook the bacon until crisp; crumble with a fork and reserve.
Add the onion and garlic and continue to cook them in pan drippings until tender and fragrant.
Now, stir in the remaining ingredients.
Secure the lid. Choose the "Manual" mode and cook for 12 minutes at High pressure. Once cooking is complete, use a quick pressure release; carefully remove the lid.
Discard the bay leaf and garnish with the reserved bacon; serve warm. Bon appétit!

379. Japanese Black Soybeans (Kuromame)

(Ready in about 30 minutes | Servings 4)

Per serving: 302 Calories; 1.5g Fat; 61.2g Carbs; 12.5g Protein; 26.4g Sugars

INGREDIENTS

1/2 pound black soybeans, rinsed
4 cups water
1 cup sugar

1 tablespoon soy sauce
A pinch of kosher salt
3-inch square of kombu

DIRECTIONS

Add all ingredients to the inner pot of your Instant Pot.
Secure the lid. Choose the "Manual" mode and cook for 15 minutes at High pressure. Once cooking is complete, use a natural pressure release for 10 minutes; carefully remove the lid.
Let the beans soak in the sauce for 24 hours. The black soybeans should be soft and glossy. Cover and refrigerate. Enjoy!

380. Sugar Snap Peas with Chicken and Peanuts

(Ready in about 50 minutes | Servings 4)

Per serving: 387 Calories; 19.8g Fat; 18.7g Carbs; 33.3g Protein; 3.4g Sugars

INGREDIENTS

1 pound chicken breast, cut into small chunks
2 tablespoons arrowroot powder
1 tablespoon teriyaki sauce
2 cloves garlic, minced
1/2 teaspoon cayenne pepper
2 teaspoons sesame oil, toasted

2 cups chicken broth
2 cups sugar snap peas
2 carrots, sliced
1 small onion, chopped
1/4 cup peanuts, dry-roasted and roughly chopped

DIRECTIONS

Combine the chicken breasts, arrowroot powder, teriyaki sauce, garlic, and cayenne pepper in a mixing bowl.
Press the "Sauté" button. Preheat the oil and cook the seasoned chicken for 5 to 6 minutes or until no longer pink.
Pour in a splash of the broth, scraping the pot to loosen the browned bits. Stir in the remaining broth, sugar snap peas, carrots, and onions.
Secure the lid. Choose the "Slow Cook" button and "More" mode; cook for 30 minutes. When time is up, carefully remove the lid.
Garnish with the dry-roasted peanuts and serve warm. Enjoy!

381. Spicy Boiled Peanuts

(Ready in about 1 hour 5 minutes | Servings 10)

Per serving: 235 Calories; 18.8g Fat; 10.7g Carbs; 9.3g Protein; 2.7g Sugars

INGREDIENTS

2 pounds raw peanuts in the shell
1/2 cup salt
2 tablespoons Creole seasoning

1 tablespoon garlic powder
1 tablespoon cayenne pepper
2 jalapenos, sliced

DIRECTIONS

Add all ingredients to the inner pot of your Instant Pot. Pour in enough water to cover the peanuts.
Use a steamer to gently press down your peanuts.
Secure the lid. Choose the "Manual" mode and cook for 45 minutes at High pressure. Once cooking is complete, use a natural pressure release for 15 minutes; carefully remove the lid.
Place in a container with a bunch of the liquid; refrigerate for 3 hours. Bon appétit!

382. Mediterranean Spicy Bean Salad

(Ready in about 35 minutes | Servings 4)

Per serving: 572 Calories; 19.8g Fat; 70.8g Carbs; 30.9g Protein; 4.7g Sugars

INGREDIENTS

1 pound cannellini beans, rinsed
1 cup fresh tomatoes, sliced
1 cucumber, sliced
1 onion, thinly sliced
1 teaspoon garlic, minced
1/2 cup Kalamata olives, pitted and halved
2 sweet peppers, seeded and diced

1 pepperoncini, seeded and diced
1/2 cup Halloumi cheese, crumbled
6 basil leaves, roughly chopped
1/4 cup extra virgin olive oil
3 tablespoons balsamic vinegar, or more to taste
Sea salt and freshly cracked black pepper, to taste

DIRECTIONS

Add the cannellini beans to the inner pot of your Instant Pot. Pour in 8 cups of water.
Secure the lid. Choose the "Bean/Chili" mode and cook for 30 minutes at High pressure. Once cooking is complete, use a quick pressure release; carefully remove the lid.
Transfer your beans to a salad bowl. Add the remaining ingredients and toss to combine well.
Serve well chilled.

383. Green Bean and Lentil Stew

(Ready in about 20 minutes | Servings 3)

Per serving: 306 Calories; 11.5g Fat; 39.3g Carbs; 12.3g Protein; 15.7g Sugars

INGREDIENTS

2 tablespoons peanut oil
1 cup scallions, chopped onion
2 cloves garlic, minced
2 bell peppers, chopped
2 carrots, chopped

1 celery rib, chopped
1 teaspoon oregano
1 teaspoon basil
1/2 teaspoon red pepper flakes, crushed
1 cup green lentils

3 cups vegetable broth
1 cup tomato sauce
1 cup green beans, trimmed
Sea salt and ground black pepper, to season

DIRECTIONS

Press the "Sauté" button and heat the oil until sizzling; once hot, cook the scallions, garlic, bell peppers, carrots, and celery until they have softened.
Add the spices, lentils, broth, and tomato sauce; gently stir to combine.
Secure the lid. Choose the "Manual" mode and cook for 8 minutes at High pressure. Once cooking is complete, use a natural pressure release for 5 minutes; carefully remove the lid.
Afterwards, add the green beans, salt, and black pepper to the inner pot; gently stir to combine.
Secure the lid. Choose the "Manual" mode and cook for 3 minutes at High pressure. Once cooking is complete, use a quick pressure release; carefully remove the lid. Serve warm.

384. Winter Ham and Split Pea Soup

(Ready in about 35 minutes | Servings 3)

Per serving: 403 Calories; 17.8g Fat; 26.7g Carbs; 36.7g Protein; 13g Sugars

INGREDIENTS

2 tablespoons butter
1 leek, diced
1 celery stalk, diced
1 carrot, diced
1 turnip, diced

1 jalapeno pepper, seeded and minced
4 ounces ham, diced
1 ½ cups split peas, rinsed
3 cups chicken stock, veggie stock, water, or a mixture

1/2 teaspoon dried thyme
1/2 teaspoon garlic powder
Kosher salt and ground black pepper, to taste

DIRECTIONS

Press the "Sauté" button and melt the butter. Once hot, sauté the leek, celery, carrot, turnip, and jalapeno until they have softened. Add the remaining ingredients to the inner pot.

Secure the lid. Choose the "Manual" mode and cook for 15 minutes at High pressure. Once cooking is complete, use a natural pressure release for 15 minutes; carefully remove the lid.

Taste and adjust seasonings. Serve warm.

385. Vegetarian Lebanese Mujadara

(Ready in about 35 minutes | Servings 4)

Per serving: 403 Calories; 17.8g Fat; 26.7g Carbs; 36.7g Protein; 13g Sugars

INGREDIENTS

2 tablespoons grapeseed oil
1 large onion, thinly sliced
3 cloves garlic, rough chopped
1 teaspoon cumin
1 cinnamon stick
1 teaspoon turmeric powder
1/2 teaspoon ground ginger
Kosher salt and red pepper, to season

1/2 cup red cooking wine
1 cup brown lentils, sorted and rinsed
3 cups water
2 tablespoons fresh parsley
2 tablespoons fresh lemon juice
1 cup basmati rice, rinsed
4 cups mustard greens

DIRECTIONS

Press the "Sauté" button and heat the oil until sizzling. Once hot, cook the onion and garlic until just tender and fragrant.

Stir in the remaining ingredients, except for the mustard greens. Give it a good stir.

Secure the lid. Choose the "Manual" mode and cook for 10 minutes at High pressure. Once cooking is complete, use a natural pressure release for 10 minutes; carefully remove the lid.

Add the mustard greens to the inner pot. Seal the lid and let it sit in the residual heat for 10 minutes. Serve warm.

386. Old-Fashioned Beans with Turkey Drumsticks

(Ready in about 40 minutes | Servings 4)

Per serving: 422 Calories; 22.3g Fat; 16.3g Carbs; 39.7g Protein; 2.6g Sugars

INGREDIENTS

2 tablespoons grapeseed oil
1 onion, chopped
1 teaspoon garlic, minced
2 sweet peppers, seeded and chopped
1 poblano pepper, seeded and minced
12 ounces dry kidney bean, rinsed

1 smoked turkey drumsticks
2 bay leaves
1 teaspoon dried oregano
1 teaspoon dried basil
Sea salt and ground black pepper, to taste
4 cups chicken broth low sodium

DIRECTIONS

Press the "Sauté" button and heat the oil until sizzling. Once hot, cook the onion for 3 to 4 minutes or until tender.

Now, stir in garlic and peppers; continue to cook until tender and aromatic. Str in the remaining ingredients.

Secure the lid. Choose the "Bean/Chili" mode and cook for 25 minutes at High pressure. Once cooking is complete, use a natural pressure release for 10 minutes; carefully remove the lid. Bon appétit!

387. Anasazi Beans with Smoked Bacon

(Ready in about 40 minutes | Servings 4)

Per serving: 477 Calories; 44.1g Fat; 15.1g Carbs; 6.5g Protein; 5.3g Sugars

INGREDIENTS

6 ounces smoked bacon, chopped
16 ounces Anasazi beans, rinsed
4 cloves garlic, pressed
3 cups vegetable broth
1 cup tomato puree
1 cup water

2 bay leaves
1 teaspoon dried sage
1 teaspoon dried oregano
1 onion, chopped
Kosher salt and ground black pepper, to taste

DIRECTIONS

Press the "Sauté" button to preheat the Instant Pot. Cook the bacon for 2 to 3 minutes or until it is crisp.
Place the other ingredients in the inner pot of your Instant Pot.
Secure the lid. Choose the "Bean/Chili" mode and cook for 25 minutes at High pressure. Once cooking is complete, use a natural pressure release for 10 minutes; carefully remove the lid.
Ladle into soup bowls and serve garnished with the reserved bacon. Serve with salsa if desired. Bon appétit!

388. Black Bean Tacos

(Ready in about 35 minutes | Servings 4)

Per serving: 487 Calories; 11.5g Fat; 75.5g Carbs; 23.8g Protein; 8.1g Sugars

INGREDIENTS

2 tablespoons sesame oil
1 onion, chopped
1 teaspoon garlic, minced
1 sweet pepper, seeded and sliced

1 jalapeno pepper, seeded and minced
1 teaspoon ground cumin
1/2 teaspoon ground coriander
16 ounces black beans, rinsed

4 (8-inches), whole wheat tortillas, warmed
1 cup cherry tomatoes, halved
1/2 cup sour cream

DIRECTIONS

Press the "Sauté" button and heat the oil. Now, cook the onion, garlic, and peppers until tender and fragrant.
Add the ground cumin, coriander, and beans to the inner pot.
Secure the lid. Choose the "Manual" mode and cook for 20 minutes at High pressure. Once cooking is complete, use a natural pressure release for 10 minutes; carefully remove the lid.
Serve the bean mixture in the tortillas; garnish with the cherry tomatoes and sour cream. Enjoy!

389. Tuscan Bean Soup with Parmigiano-Reggiano

(Ready in about 50 minutes | Servings 4)

Per serving: 453 Calories; 11.6g Fat; 65.3g Carbs; 24.5g Protein; 6.1g Sugars

INGREDIENTS

2 tablespoons grapeseed oil
1 onion, chopped
2 garlic cloves, minced
1 carrot, chopped
1 celery rib, sliced
2 cups water
2 cups cream of mushroom soup

2 potatoes, peeled and grated
2 bay leaves
1/2 teaspoon marjoram
Sea salt and ground black pepper, to taste
10 ounces dry white kidney beans, rinsed
2 cups fresh spinach, torn into pieces
4 tablespoons Parmigiano Reggiano cheese, grated

DIRECTIONS

Press the "Sauté" button and heat the oil. Now, cook the onion, garlic, carrot, and celery until they have softened.
Now, add the water, cream of mushrooms soup, potatoes, spices, and beans to the inner pot.
Secure the lid. Choose the "Bean/Chili" mode and cook for 30 minutes at High pressure. Once cooking is complete, use a natural pressure release for 15 minutes; carefully remove the lid.
Mash the soup with a potato masher or use an immersion blender. Add the spinach and press the "Sauté" button again. Let it simmer on the lowest setting until the leaves wilt.
Ladle the soup into four serving bowls. Top each serving with 1 tablespoon of the Parmigiano Reggiano cheese. Bon appétit!

390. Garbanzo Bean and Cream Cheese Dip

(Ready in about 55 minutes | Servings 10)

Per serving: 206 Calories; 8.8g Fat; 22.7g Carbs; 10.3g Protein; 1.7g Sugars

INGREDIENTS

12 ounces garbanzo beans, rinsed
6 cups of water
1/2 cup cream cheese
1 teaspoon hot sauce

1/2 teaspoon dried thyme
1/2 teaspoon cumin
1 teaspoon garlic powder
1 teaspoon onion powder

2 tablespoons lime juice
2 tablespoons tahini (sesame butter)
2 tablespoons cilantro, chopped

DIRECTIONS

Add the garbanzo beans and water to the inner pot.

Secure the lid. Choose the "Bean/Chili" mode and cook for 40 minutes at High pressure. Once cooking is complete, use a natural pressure release for 10 minutes; carefully remove the lid. Reserve the cooking liquid.

Transfer the boiled garbanzo beans to your blender or food processor; add the other ingredients and blend until smooth and creamy. Add the reserved liquid as needed for desired consistency.

Place in your refrigerator until ready to use. Enjoy!

391. Restaurant-Style Vegetarian Chili

(Ready in about 40 minutes | Servings 4)

Per serving: 448 Calories; 12.5g Fat; 65.7g Carbs; 23g Protein; 11.4g Sugars

INGREDIENTS

2 tablespoons olive oil
1 onion, chopped
2 cloves garlic, minced
2 sweet peppers, chopped
1 red chili pepper, chopped
1 carrot, chopped
1 celery stalk, chopped

Sea salt and ground black pepper, to taste
1 teaspoon red pepper
1 teaspoon ground cumin
1 teaspoon Mexican oregano
1 (28-ounce) can tomatoes, diced with their juices

10 ounces dried navy beans
2 cups vegetable broth
1 bay leaf
1 thyme sprig
1/2 cup sour cream

DIRECTIONS

Press the "Sauté" button and heat the oil. Now, cook the onion until it is softened. Stir in the garlic and peppers; continue sautéing an additional 2 minutes or until fragrant.

Add the carrot, celery, salt, black pepper, red pepper, cumin, oregano, tomatoes, beans, broth, bay leaf, and thyme sprig to the inner pot.

Secure the lid. Choose the "Bean/Chili" mode and cook for 25 minutes at High pressure. Once cooking is complete, use a natural pressure release for 10 minutes; carefully remove the lid.

Serve with a dollop of sour cream. Enjoy!

392. Fasolakia (Greek Green Beans)

(Ready in about 15 minutes | Servings 4)

Per serving: 237 Calories; 17.5g Fat; 13.7g Carbs; 9.9g Protein; 4.9g Sugars

INGREDIENTS

2 tablespoons olive oil
4 garlic cloves, chopped
1 ½ pounds fresh green beans
2 vine-ripened tomatoes, pureed

Sea salt and freshly ground black pepper, to season
1 cup bone broth, preferably home-made
1 teaspoon paprika

1/2 teaspoon dried oregano
1/2 teaspoon dried basil
1/2 dried dill
6 ounces Feta cheese, crumbled

DIRECTIONS

Press the "Sauté" button and heat the oil. Now, sauté the garlic until it is fragrant but not browned.

Add the other ingredients, except for the feta cheese, to the inner pot; and stir to combine.

Secure the lid. Choose the "Manual" mode and cook for 5 minutes at High pressure. Once cooking is complete, use a quick pressure release; carefully remove the lid.

Ladle into individual bowls and serve with Feta cheese on the side. Enjoy!

393. Refreshing Wax Bean Salad

(Ready in about 10 minutes + chilling time | Servings 4)

Per serving: 196 Calories; 15.4g Fat; 13.5g Carbs; 3.8g Protein; 3.2g Sugars

INGREDIENTS

14 ounces yellow wax beans, trimmed and halved crosswise
1 red onion, sliced
2 bell peppers, deveined and sliced
1/4 cup extra-virgin olive oil
1 tablespoon fresh lemon juice
1 tablespoon balsamic vinegar

1 tablespoon peanut butter
1 teaspoon Dijon mustard
1/2 teaspoon garlic powder
Salt and white pepper, to taste
1/4 teaspoon red pepper flakes
2 tablespoons fresh Italian parsley, roughly chopped

DIRECTIONS

Place 1 cup of water and a steamer basket in the inner pan of your Instant Pot. Place the wax beans in the steamer basket.
Secure the lid. Choose the "Manual" mode and cook for 3 minutes at High pressure. Once cooking is complete, use a quick pressure release; carefully remove the lid.
Toss the chilled wax beans with the other ingredients; toss to combine well. Serve well chilled.

394. Classic Lima Beans with Ham

(Ready in about 45 minutes | Servings 4)

Per serving: 450 Calories; 3.1g Fat; 74.8g Carbs; 33.3g Protein; 10.6g Sugars

INGREDIENTS

1 pound dry baby lima beans, rinsed
8 ounces cooked ham, chopped
1 onion, chopped
2 cloves garlic, minced
4 cups beef bone broth

1 thyme sprig
1 rosemary sprig
1 teaspoon dried parsley flakes
Sea salt and freshly ground black pepper, to taste
2 bay leaves

DIRECTIONS

Place all ingredients in the inner pot of your Instant Pot.
Secure the lid. Choose the "Bean/Chili" mode and cook for 25 minutes at High pressure. Once cooking is complete, use a natural pressure release for 10 minutes; carefully remove the lid.
Ladle into individual bowls and enjoy!

395. Herby Pea Dipping Sauce

(Ready in about 45 minutes | Servings 8)

Per serving: 42 Calories; 0.1g Fat; 7.8g Carbs; 2.7g Protein; 2.9g Sugars

INGREDIENTS

14 ounces frozen peas
2 cups water
1/4 cup basil leaves, roughly chopped
2 tablespoons fresh parsley, chopped
1 tablespoon fresh cilantro, chopped

2 tablespoons fresh chives, chopped
1 fresh lemon, zested and juiced
1 teaspoon cayenne pepper
1/2 teaspoon hot sauce
Kosher salt and freshly ground black pepper, to taste

DIRECTIONS

Add the frozen peas and water to the inner pot of your Instant Pot.
Secure the lid. Choose the "Manual" mode and cook for 10 minutes at High pressure. Once cooking is complete, use a natural pressure release for 15 minutes; carefully remove the lid.
Transfer the boiled green peas to a bowl of your food processor; add the remaining ingredients and process until creamy and smooth, gradually adding the cooking liquid.
Serve with pita bread, tortilla chips or bread sticks if desired. Bon appétit!

396. Grandam's Scarlet Runner with Smoked Turkey

(Ready in about 45 minutes | Servings 8)

Per serving: 42 Calories; 0.1g Fat; 7.8g Carbs; 2.7g Protein; 2.9g Sugars

INGREDIENTS

2 tablespoons olive oil
1 onion, chopped
2 garlic cloves, minced
1 bell pepper, sliced
1 pound Scarlet Runner beans
10 ounces smoked turkey, boneless and shredded

2 tablespoons sherry wine
2 cups turkey broth
2 bay leaves
1 sprig thyme
1 sprig rosemary
Kosher salt and ground black pepper, to taste

DIRECTIONS

Press the "Sauté" button and heat the oil. Now, sauté the onion until tender and translucent. Then, stir in the garlic and bell pepper and continue to sauté until they are aromatic but not browned.

Add the other ingredients to the inner pot; stir to combine well.

Secure the lid. Choose the "Bean/Chili" mode and cook for 25 minutes at High pressure. Once cooking is complete, use a natural pressure release for 10 minutes; carefully remove the lid.

Taste, adjust the seasonings and serve warm. Bon appétit!

397. Rustic Lahsooni Moong Dal

(Ready in about 20 minutes | Servings 4)

Per serving: 235 Calories; 6.3g Fat; 33.8g Carbs; 12.3g Protein; 2.2g Sugars

INGREDIENTS

Moong Dal:
1 cup moong dal, soaked 2 hours and drained
4 cups water
1 teaspoon curry paste
Kosher salt and red pepper, to taste
1 teaspoon Garam masala

Tarka:
2 tablespoons butter
1/2 teaspoon cumin seeds
3 garlic cloves, pressed
1 white onion, chopped
1 bird eye chili, sliced

DIRECTIONS

Add the moong dal, water, curry paste, salt, pepper, and Garam masala to the inner pot.

Secure the lid. Choose the "Manual" mode and cook for 2 minutes at High pressure. Once cooking is complete, use a natural pressure release for 10 minutes; carefully remove the lid.

Melt the butter in a nonstick skillet over medium-high heat. Then, sauté the cumin seeds for 30 seconds or until fragrant.

After that, sauté the garlic, onion, and chili pepper for 4 to 5 minutes or until they have softened. Stir the contents of the skillet into the warm dal.

Bon appétit!

VEGETABLES

398. Easy Steamed Vegetables

(Ready in about 10 minutes | Servings 3)

Per serving: 147 Calories; 13.7g Fat; 5.8g Carbs; 1.3g Protein; 2.1g Sugars

INGREDIENTS

1/2 pound cauliflower florets
2 carrots, sliced
1 celery rib, sliced
3 tablespoons olive oil

2 cloves garlic, minced
1/2 teaspoon cayenne pepper
Sea salt and freshly ground black pepper, to taste
1 tablespoon fresh cilantro, chopped

DIRECTIONS

Add 1 cup water and a steamer basket to the inner pot of your Instant Pot. Place the vegetables in the steamer basket.
Secure the lid. Choose the "Steam" mode and cook for 3 minutes at High pressure. Once cooking is complete, use a quick pressure release; carefully remove the lid; reserve the steamed vegetables.
Press the "Sauté" button and heat the oil. Now, sauté the garlic until tender. Add the steamed vegetables back to the inner pot.
Season generously with cayenne pepper, salt, and black pepper. Garnish with fresh cilantro and serve.

399. Mom's Mixed Vegetables

(Ready in about 10 minutes | Servings 4)

Per serving: 329 Calories; 7.3g Fat; 60g Carbs; 9.8g Protein; 8.5g Sugars

INGREDIENTS

2 tablespoons butter, at room temperature
2 cloves garlic, minced
2 carrots, cut into 1-inch pieces
2 parsnips, cut into 1-inch pieces

1/2 pound broccoli florets
4 medium waxy potatoes, peeled and cubed
1/2 pound acorn squash
2 cups roasted vegetable broth

DIRECTIONS

Press the "Sauté" button and melt the butter. Once hot, sauté the garlic until aromatic but not browned.
Stir in the remaining ingredients.
Secure the lid. Choose the "Manual" mode and cook for 4 minutes at High pressure. Once cooking is complete, use a quick pressure release; carefully remove the lid.
Add some extra butter if desired and serve warm. Bon appétit!

400. Garden Vegetable Soup

(Ready in about 15 minutes | Servings 4)

Per serving: 227 Calories; 11.9g Fat; 12.3g Carbs; 17.8g Protein; 6.2g Sugars

INGREDIENTS

2 tablespoons olive oil
1 shallot, chopped
Kosher salt and ground black pepper, to taste
2 cups cabbage, shredded
2 carrots, thinly sliced
2 celery stalks, thinly sliced

1 medium zucchini, chopped
1 (15-ounce) can tomatoes, diced with their juice
3 cups vegetable broth
1 teaspoon cayenne pepper
1 teaspoon dried sage
1 teaspoon dried parsley flakes

DIRECTIONS

Press the "Sauté" button and heat the oil. Now, sauté the shallot until tender and translucent.
Add the remaining ingredients; stir to combine well.
Secure the lid. Choose the "Manual" mode and cook for 10 minutes at High pressure. Once cooking is complete, use a quick pressure release; carefully remove the lid.
Ladle into soup bowls and serve with garlic croutons if desired. Bon appétit!

401. Colorful Vegetarian Medley

(Ready in about 15 minutes | Servings 4)

Per serving: 330 Calories; 27.3g Fat; 16.8g Carbs; 8.2g Protein; 7.7g Sugars

INGREDIENTS

1 pound cauliflower florets
1/2 pound carrot
1/2 pound broccoli florets
2 tablespoons olive oil

1 teaspoon garlic, minced
1 cup cream cheese
Fresh juice of 1/2 lemon
1/2 teaspoon oregano

1/2 teaspoon dried basil
Sea salt and ground black pepper, to taste

DIRECTIONS

Add 1 cup of water and a steamer basket to the inner pot. Place the cauliflower, carrots, and broccoli in the steamer basket.

Secure the lid. Choose the "Steam" mode and cook for 2 minutes at High pressure. Once cooking is complete, use a quick pressure release; carefully remove the lid; reserve the steamed vegetables.

Press the "Sauté" button and heat the olive oil until sizzling. Then, cook the garlic until just tender and fragrant.

Add the remaining ingredients and press the "Cancel" button. Add the reserved vegetables to the inner pot. Stir to combine and serve warm. Bon appétit!

402. Root Vegetable Soup

(Ready in about 25 minutes | Servings 4)

Per serving: 149 Calories; 5.4g Fat; 18.8g Carbs; 7.3g Protein; 6.6g Sugars

INGREDIENTS

2 teaspoons olive oil
1 onion, diced
1 garlic clove, minced
4 cups chicken broth
1 teaspoon Italian seasoning mix

Sea salt and ground black pepper, to taste
2 carrots, chopped
1 parsnip, chopped
2 celery ribs, chopped

1 green bell pepper, chopped
1 ½ cups fresh green beans, cut in thirds

DIRECTIONS

Press the "Sauté" button and heat the olive oil until sizzling. Then, cook the onion until tender and fragrant. Stir in the garlic and continue to sauté an additional 2 minutes.

Add a splash of chicken broth to scrape the bottom to remove any left behind bits. Add the seasonings, carrots, parsnip, celery, and bell pepper.

Secure the lid. Choose the "Manual" mode and cook for 10 minutes at High pressure. Once cooking is complete, use a natural pressure release for 10 minutes; carefully remove the lid.

Stir in the green beans and press the "Sauté" button again. Let it cook on the lowest setting until thoroughly warmed. Enjoy!

403. Cauliflower Salad with Mozzarella Cheese

(Ready in about 10 minutes + chilling time | Servings 3)

Per serving: 188 Calories; 8.4g Fat; 14.8g Carbs; 16.3g Protein; 6.2g Sugars

INGREDIENTS

1 pound cauliflower florets
2 bell peppers, thinly sliced
1 red onion, thinly sliced
1/2 cup fresh flat-leaf parsley, coarsely chopped
1/4 cup green olives, pitted and coarsely chopped

1/4 cup extra-virgin olive oil
2 tablespoons fresh lime juice
1 teaspoon hot mustard
Sea salt and ground black pepper, to taste
4 ounces mozzarella cheese, crumbled

DIRECTIONS

Add 1 cup of water and steamer basket to the inner pot. Place the cauliflower in the steamer basket.

Secure the lid. Choose the "Steam" mode and cook for 2 minutes at High pressure. Once cooking is complete, use a quick pressure release; carefully remove the lid.

Toss the cooked cauliflower with peppers, onion, parsley, and olives. In a small bowl, prepare the salad dressing by mixing the olive oil, lime juice, mustard, salt, and black pepper.

Dress your salad and serve garnished with the crumbled mozzarella cheese. Bon appétit!

404. Steamed Artichokes with Mayo Dip

(Ready in about 20 minutes | Servings 3)

Per serving: 331 Calories; 27.7g Fat; 18.8g Carbs; 5.8g Protein; 2.3g Sugars

INGREDIENTS

1 cup water
1 bay leaf
1 lemon wedge
3 medium artichokes, trimmed

Sea salt, to taste
1/2 cup mayonnaise
1 teaspoon garlic, pressed
2 tablespoons fresh parsley, minced

DIRECTIONS

Place water and bay leaf in the inner pot. Rub the lemon wedge all over the outside of the prepared artichokes. Season them with salt.
Place the artichokes in the steamer basket; lower the steamer basket into the inner pot.
Secure the lid. Choose the "Manual" mode and cook for 11 minutes at High pressure. Once cooking is complete, use a quick pressure release; carefully remove the lid.
Meanwhile, mix the mayonnaise with the garlic and parsley. Serve the artichokes with the mayo dip on the side. Bon appétit!

405. Italian-Style Caprese Asparagus

(Ready in about 20 minutes | Servings 4)

Per serving: 351 Calories; 23.8g Fat; 26.1g Carbs; 12.1g Protein; 22.3g Sugars

INGREDIENTS

1 ½ pounds asparagus, trimmed
2 tablespoons balsamic vinegar
1/4 cup honey
1/4 teaspoon dried dill
1/4 cup extra-virgin olive oil

Sea salt and freshly ground black pepper, to taste
2 tomatoes, sliced
1 cup Gorgonzola cheese, crumbled
2 tablespoons fresh chives, chopped

DIRECTIONS

Add 1 cup of water and a steamer basket to the inner pot. Place the asparagus in the steamer basket.
Secure the lid. Choose the "Steam" mode and cook for 3 minutes at High pressure. Once cooking is complete, use a quick pressure release; carefully remove the lid.
In the meantime, make the balsamic glaze. Heat a small pan over a moderate flame. Simmer the balsamic vinegar, honey and dried dill for about 15 minutes or until it is reduced by half.
Transfer the cooked asparagus to a serving bowl. Add the oil, salt, pepper, and tomatoes. Drizzle with the balsamic glaze; garnish with cheese and chives and serve immediately.

406. Indian Beet Thoran

(Ready in about 20 minutes | Servings 2)

Per serving: 184 Calories; 7.2g Fat; 27.1g Carbs; 4.8g Protein; 17.8g Sugars

INGREDIENTS

1 pound small beets
1 tablespoon olive oil
1/2 cup shallots, chopped
2 garlic cloves, minced

1 chili pepper, chopped
10 curry leaves
1/2 teaspoon turmeric powder
Sea salt and ground black pepper, to taste

DIRECTIONS

Add 1 cup of water and a steamer basket to the inner pot. Place the beets in the steamer basket.
Secure the lid. Choose the "Steam" mode and cook for 15 minutes at High pressure. Once cooking is complete, use a quick pressure release; carefully remove the lid.
Once your beets are cool enough to touch, transfer them to a cutting board; peel and chop them into small pieces.
Press the "Sauté" button and heat the olive oil until sizzling. Then, cook the shallots, garlic, chili pepper, and curry leaves for about 4 minutes, or until they have softened.
Add the turmeric, salt, and black pepper; add the cooked beets to the inner pot and press the "Cancel" button. Serve warm.

407. Creamed Broccoli Salad with Seeds

(Ready in about 10 minutes | Servings 3)

Per serving: 407 Calories; 33.8g Fat; 20.1g Carbs; 11.3g Protein; 5.2g Sugars

INGREDIENTS

1 pound broccoli florets
Sea salt and ground black pepper, to taste
1/2 cup scallions, chopped
1/4 cup raisins
1/4 cup sunflower seeds, to toasted

1/4 cup sesame seeds, toasted
1 tablespoon balsamic vinegar
1 tablespoon fresh lemon juice
1/2 cup mayonnaise
1/2 cup sour cream

DIRECTIONS

Add 1 cup of water and steamer basket to the inner pot. Place the broccoli florets in the steamer basket.
Secure the lid. Choose the "Manual" mode and cook for 1 minute at High pressure. Once cooking is complete, use a quick pressure release; carefully remove the lid.
Transfer the chilled broccoli florets to a nice salad bowl. Add the salt, black pepper, scallions, raisins, and seeds to the salad bowl.
Next, stir in the balsamic vinegar, lemon juice, mayo, and sour cream. Bon appétit!

408. Brussels Sprouts with Smoked Turkey

(Ready in about 15 minutes | Servings 4)

Per serving: 212 Calories; 10.1g Fat; 18.1g Carbs; 16.1g Protein; 5.3g Sugars

INGREDIENTS

1 ½ pounds Brussels sprouts, cut into halves
2 tablespoons sesame oil
1 teaspoon garlic, minced
1 shallot, chopped

8 ounces smoked turkey, boneless and shredded
Kosher salt and freshly cracked black pepper, to taste
1 teaspoon red pepper flakes

DIRECTIONS

Add 1 cup of water and a steamer basket to the inner pot. Place the Brussels sprouts in the steamer basket.
Secure the lid. Choose the "Steam" mode and cook for 3 minutes at High pressure. Once cooking is complete, use a quick pressure release; carefully remove the lid.
Drain the water out of the inner pot.
Press the "Sauté" button and heat the oil until sizzling. Then, cook the garlic and shallot for 2 minutes or until tender and aromatic.
Add the smoked turkey and cook an additional 2 minutes. Add the Brussels sprouts, salt, and black pepper, and stir for a few minutes more or until everything is heated through.
Serve garnished with red pepper flakes. Bon appétit!

409. Classic Cabbage with Herbs

(Ready in about 15 minutes | Servings 4)

Per serving: 185 Calories; 13.8g Fat; 15.5g Carbs; 2.5g Protein; 8.2g Sugars

INGREDIENTS

4 tablespoons olive oil
1 (1 ½-pound) head of cabbage, cut into wedges
2 carrots, chopped
1 bell pepper, chopped
1 ½ cups roasted vegetable broth

1 teaspoon cayenne pepper
Sea salt and ground black pepper, to taste
1 bay leaf
2 sprigs thyme
2 sprigs rosemary

DIRECTIONS

Add all ingredients to the inner pot of your Instant Pot. Stir to combine.
Secure the lid. Choose the "Manual" mode and cook for 6 minutes at High pressure. Once cooking is complete, use a quick pressure release; carefully remove the lid.
Ladle into individual bowls and serve warm. Bon appétit!

410. Cheesy Cabbage Casserole

(Ready in about 30 minutes | Servings 4)

Per serving: 463 Calories; 35.5g Fat; 22.2g Carbs; 17.5g Protein; 5.6g Sugars

INGREDIENTS

4 tablespoons olive oil
1 pound green cabbage, shredded
1 onion, thinly sliced
2 garlic cloves, sliced

2 sweet peppers, thinly sliced
1 serrano pepper, chopped
Sea salt and ground black pepper, to taste

1 teaspoon paprika
1 cup cream of mushroom soup
8 ounces Colby cheese, shredded

DIRECTIONS

Grease a casserole dish with 1 tablespoon of olive oil. Add the cabbage, onion, garlic, and peppers to the casserole dish.
Drizzle with remaining oil and season with salt, black pepper, and paprika. Next, pour in the mushroom soup.
Top with the shredded cheese and cover with a piece of aluminum foil.
Add 1 cup of water and a metal trivet to the inner pot. Lower the casserole dish onto the trivet.
Secure the lid. Choose the "Manual" mode and cook for 25 minutes at High pressure. Once cooking is complete, use a quick pressure release; carefully remove the lid. Serve warm.

411. Autumn Soup with Kale

(Ready in about 20 minutes | Servings 4)

Per serving: 245 Calories; 4.5g Fat; 41g Carbs; 12.5g Protein; 10.9g Sugars

INGREDIENTS

2 teaspoons butter, at room temperature
1 onion, chopped
2 garlic cloves, minced
5 cups chicken broth

1 teaspoon dried basil
1 teaspoon dried oregano
Kosher salt and ground black pepper, to taste
2 medium potatoes, chopped

2 carrots, chopped
1 cup turnip, chopped
2 cups tomato puree
2 cups kale, torn into pieces

DIRECTIONS

Press the "Sauté" button and melt the butter. Once hot, cook the onion until tender and translucent.
Then, add the garlic and continue to sauté an additional 30 seconds, stirring continuously. Add a splash of chicken broth to deglaze the pan.
Now, stir in the basil, oregano, salt, black pepper, potatoes, carrots, turnip, and tomato puree; stir to combine.
Secure the lid. Choose the "Manual" mode and cook for 5 minutes at High pressure. Once cooking is complete, use a natural pressure release for 10 minutes; carefully remove the lid.
Stir in the kale and seal the lid; let it sit in the residual heat until thoroughly warmed. Adjust the seasonings to taste and serve immediately.

412. Slow-Cooker Turkey Noodle Soup

(Ready in about 3 hours 15 minutes | Servings 4)

Per serving: 436 Calories; 7.8g Fat; 58.2g Carbs; 30.5g Protein; 7.9g Sugars

INGREDIENTS

1 pound turkey thighs, boneless and chopped
5 cups vegetable broth
1 shallot finely diced
2 carrots, diced

1 parsnip, sliced
1 celery stalk, sliced
Kosher salt and ground black pepper, to taste
1 teaspoon dried parsley flakes

1 teaspoon dried basil
1/2 teaspoon dried sage
1/2 teaspoon granulated garlic
2 cups wheat noodles

DIRECTIONS

Place all ingredients, except for the noodles, in the inner pot.
Secure the lid. Choose the "Slow Cook" mode and cook for 3 hours at High pressure. Once cooking is complete, use a quick pressure release; carefully remove the lid.
Now, stir in the noodles. Secure the lid. Choose the "Manual" mode and cook for 10 minutes at High pressure. Once cooking is complete, use a quick pressure release; carefully remove the lid.
Serve warm and enjoy!

413. Easy Vegan Posole

(Ready in about 1 hour | Servings 4)

Per serving: 233 Calories; 3.3g Fat; 45.8g Carbs; 5.8g Protein; 8.7g Sugars

INGREDIENTS

2 dried pasilla chili peppers, seeded and minced
1 teaspoon cumin seeds
1 teaspoon garlic, sliced
Kosher salt and ground black pepper, to taste
1 onion, chopped
1/2 pound dried hominy, soaked overnight and rinsed

4 cups water
2 Roma tomatoes, chopped
1 tablespoon bouillon granules
2 bay leaves
1 cup radishes, sliced

DIRECTIONS

Put the chilis in a bowl with hot water; let them soak for 15 minutes until soft. Transfer the chilis to your food processor; add the cumin seeds, garlic, salt, and black pepper.

Add 1 cup of water to the food processor and puree the mixture until well blended. Transfer the mixture to your Instant Pot.

Add the onion, hominy, water, tomatoes, bouillon granules, and bay leaves to the inner pot.

Secure the lid. Choose the "Soup/Broth" mode and cook for 40 minutes at High pressure. Once cooking is complete, use a quick pressure release; carefully remove the lid.

Serve warm, garnished with fresh radishes. Bon appétit!

414. Loaded Potato Soup

(Ready in about 20 minutes | Servings 4)

Per serving: 477 Calories; 24.4g Fat; 39.8g Carbs; 25.5g Protein; 5.7g Sugars

INGREDIENTS

2 tablespoons butter
1 shallot, chopped
2 cloves garlic, minced
4 cups chicken broth

1 ½ pounds russet potatoes, peeled and chopped
Kosher salt and ground black pepper, to taste
1 teaspoon cayenne pepper

1/2 teaspoon dried basil
1/2 teaspoon dried oregano
1 cup milk
2 cups Swiss cheese, shredded

DIRECTIONS

Press the "Sauté" button and melt the butter. Once hot, cook the shallot for 3 to 4 minutes or until tender.

Now, stir in the garlic and continue to cook for 30 seconds more, stirring frequently.

Add the broth, potatoes, salt, black pepper, cayenne pepper, basil, and oregano to the inner pot; stir well to combine.

Secure the lid. Choose the "Manual" mode and cook for 10 minutes at High pressure. Once cooking is complete, use a quick pressure release; carefully remove the lid.

Press the "Sauté" button and pour in the milk. Let it simmer approximately 4 minutes. Add in the Swiss cheese and stir until it has melted. Bon appétit!

415. Pisto (Traditional Spanish Stew)

(Ready in about 20 minutes | Servings 4)

Per serving: 178 Calories; 10.7g Fat; 18.2g Carbs; 5.9g Protein; 6g Sugars

INGREDIENTS

2 tablespoons olive oil
1 onion, diced
4 cloves garlic, sliced
1/4 cup Spanish wine

2 cups cream of mushrooms soup
2 bell pepper, diced
1 Guajillo chili pepper, minced
1 pound zucchini, cut into 1-inch cubes

1 can (14-ounce) tomatoes with juice
Se salt and cracked black pepper, or to taste

DIRECTIONS

Press the "Sauté" button and heat the olive oil. Now, cook the onion until just tender and translucent.

Then, stir in the garlic; continue to cook until fragrant. Add a splash of wine to deglaze the pan.

Stir in the remaining ingredients; stir to combine well.

Secure the lid. Choose the "Manual" mode and cook for 10 minutes at High pressure. Once cooking is complete, use a quick pressure release; carefully remove the lid. Serve immediately.

416. Hearty French Ratatouille

(Ready in about 40 minutes | Servings 4)

Per serving: 268 Calories; 15.7g Fat; 26.7g Carbs; 8.4g Protein; 8.1g Sugars

INGREDIENTS

1 pound eggplant, sliced
1 tablespoon sea salt
1 pound zucchini, sliced
3 sweet peppers, seeded and sliced
2 onions, sliced

4 cloves garlic, pressed
1 pound tomatoes, pureed
1 cup vegetable broth
Sea salt and ground red pepper, to taste

1 teaspoon oregano
1 teaspoon basil
1 teaspoon rosemary
4 tablespoons extra-virgin olive oil
4 tablespoons Pinot Noir

DIRECTIONS

Toss the eggplant with 1 teaspoon of salt in a colander. Let it sit for 30 minutes; then squeeze out the excess liquid. Transfer the eggplant to the inner pot of your Instant Pot.
Add the other ingredients to the inner pot
Secure the lid. Choose the "Manual" mode and cook for 6 minutes at High pressure. Once cooking is complete, use a quick pressure release; carefully remove the lid.
Season to taste with salt and pepper and serve warm. Enjoy!

417. South Indian Vegetable Curry

(Ready in about 20 minutes | Servings 4)

Per serving: 355 Calories; 16.7g Fat; 47.7g Carbs; 8.4g Protein; 5.8g Sugars

INGREDIENTS

1 tablespoon grapeseed oil
1 onion, chopped
1 teaspoon ginger-garlic paste
1 teaspoon ground cumin
1 tablespoon ground coriander
1 teaspoon ground turmeric

Sea salt and freshly ground black pepper, to taste
1 cinnamon stick
2 tablespoons tomato paste
1 cup vegetable broth
4 medium-sized sweet potatoes, diced

1 cup tomatoes juice
1 cup coconut milk
4 cups kale, torn into pieces
2 tablespoons fresh cilantro, chopped

DIRECTIONS

Press the "Sauté" button and heat the oil until sizzling. Now, sauté the onion until just tender and fragrant.
Now, stir in the ginger-garlic paste, spices, tomato paste, vegetable broth, sweet potatoes, and tomato juice.
Secure the lid. Choose the "Manual" mode and cook for 6 minutes at High pressure. Once cooking is complete, use a quick pressure release; carefully remove the lid.
After that, add the coconut milk and kale. Press the "Sauté" button and let it simmer for 5 to 6 minutes or until thoroughly heated.
Ladle into soup bowls and serve garnished with fresh cilantro. Enjoy!

418. Classic Spanish Sofrito Sauce

(Ready in about 20 minutes | Servings 6)

Per serving: 178 Calories; 12.4g Fat; 16.7g Carbs; 3.4g Protein; 7.1g Sugars

INGREDIENTS

5 tablespoons extra-virgin olive oil
2 onions, chopped
4 cloves garlic, minced
2 sweet peppers, chopped

10 tomatoes, pureed
1/2 bunch parsley leaves, roughly chopped
2 teaspoons paprika

DIRECTIONS

Press the "Sauté" button and heat 2 tablespoons of olive oil until sizzling. Now, sauté the onion until just tender and fragrant.
Add the garlic and peppers and continue to sauté an additional minute or until fragrant. Add the other ingredients.
Secure the lid. Choose the "Manual" mode and cook for 4 minutes at High pressure. Once cooking is complete, use a natural pressure release for 10 minutes; carefully remove the lid.
Let your sofrito cool completely and store in the refrigerator for a week. Enjoy!

419. Sweet Potato Casserole with Marshmallows

(Ready in about 30 minutes | Servings 6)

Per serving: 580 Calories; 28.9g Fat; 77g Carbs; 6.4g Protein; 47.1g Sugars

INGREDIENTS

6 medium-sized sweet potatoes, peeled and cut into 1-inch pieces
1 cup water
3/4 cup granulated sugar
7 tablespoons butter softened
1 teaspoon vanilla paste

2/3 cup milk
1 egg, whisked
Topping:
3/4 cup brown sugar
1/2 cup all-purpose flour
1/4 teaspoon cinnamon, or to taste

1/8 teaspoon salt
1/2 cup chopped pecans
4 tablespoons butter, at room temperature
1 cup mini marshmallows

DIRECTIONS

Add the sweet potatoes and water to the Instant Pot.

Secure the lid. Choose the "Manual" mode and cook for 8 minutes at High pressure. Once cooking is complete, use a quick pressure release; carefully remove the lid.

Drain the potatoes and transfer them to a mixing bowl. Now, add the granulated sugar, butter, vanilla, milk, and egg to the bowl.

Mash the potatoes using a potato masher or your food processor. Scrape the mashed potatoes into a lightly greased baking dish.

Mix all ingredients for the topping; top your casserole with the pecan/marshmallow mixture. Place a metal trivet and 1 cup of water in the inner pot. Lower the baking dish onto the trivet; make a foil sling if needed.

Secure the lid. Choose the "Manual" mode and cook for 15 minutes at High pressure. Once cooking is complete, use a quick pressure release; carefully remove the lid. Bon appétit!

420. Classic Festive Potato Salad

(Ready in about 20 minutes + chilling time | Servings 6)

Per serving: 448 Calories; 21.5g Fat; 55.4g Carbs; 9.7g Protein; 11.8g Sugars

INGREDIENTS

3 pounds small Yukon Gold potatoes
1 cup mayonnaise
1/2 cup pickle relish
1 tablespoon yellow mustard

1/2 teaspoon cayenne pepper
3 boiled eggs, peeled and chopped
2 celery ribs, diced
1 yellow onion, sliced

1 garlic clove, minced
1 teaspoon fresh rosemary, chopped
Sea salt and ground black pepper, to taste

DIRECTIONS

Place a metal trivet and 1 cup of water in the inner pot of your Instant Pot. Place the Yukon Gold potatoes in a steamer basket. Lower the steamer basket onto the trivet.

Secure the lid. Choose the "Manual" mode and cook for 12 minutes at High pressure. Once cooking is complete, use a quick pressure release; carefully remove the lid.

Peel and slice the potatoes; place them in a large bowl and toss with the other ingredients. Gently stir to combine. Serve well chilled and enjoy!

421. Creamed Yellow Bean Salad

(Ready in about 15 minutes | Servings 4)

Per serving: 232 Calories; 9g Fat; 33.3g Carbs; 8g Protein; 3.7g Sugars

INGREDIENTS

2 tablespoons olive oil
2 tablespoons freshly squeezed lemon juice
1/2 cup coconut milk
1 ½ pounds yellow beans

2 sweet peppers, seeded and sliced
1 red chili pepper, seeded and minced
1 cup scallions, chopped
2 stalks green garlic, sliced
2 tablespoons fresh cilantro, roughly

chopped
Coarse sea salt, to taste
1 cup smoked tofu cubes

DIRECTIONS

Mix the olive oil, lemon juice, and coconut milk in your blender or food processor. Reserve.

Place 1 cup of water and a steamer basket in the inner pot of your Instant Pot. Place the yellow beans in the steamer basket.

Secure the lid. Choose the "Manual" mode and cook for 3 minutes at High pressure. Once cooking is complete, use a quick pressure release; carefully remove the lid.

Toss the chilled yellow beans with the other ingredients, including the reserved dressing; toss to combine well. Serve well chilled and enjoy!

422. Vegetarian Khoreshe Karafs (Persian Celery Stew)

(Ready in about 40 minutes | Servings 4)

Per serving: 293 Calories; 8g Fat; 45.3g Carbs; 8.9g Protein; 4.1g Sugars

INGREDIENTS

2 tablespoons unsalted butter
2 garlic cloves, minced
1 onion, chopped
Sea salt and ground black pepper, to taste
1 teaspoon cayenne pepper
1/2 teaspoon mustard seeds

1 pound celery stalks, diced
2 tablespoons fresh mint, finely chopped
2 tablespoons fresh cilantro, roughly chopped
3 cups vegetable broth
1 Persian lime, prick a few holes
2 cups basmati rice, steamed

DIRECTIONS

Press the "Sauté" button and melt the butter. Once hot, cook the garlic and onions for about 3 minutes or until tender and fragrant. Stir in the spices, celery, herbs, broth, and Persian lime.

Secure the lid. Choose the "Manual" mode and cook for 18 minutes at High pressure. Once cooking is complete, use a natural pressure release for 15 minutes; carefully remove the lid.

Taste for seasoning and add more salt as needed.

Serve with hot basmati rice and enjoy!

423. Collard Greens with Smoked Bacon

(Ready in about 10 minutes | Servings 4)

Per serving: 304 Calories; 19.3g Fat; 19.8g Carbs; 17.8g Protein; 2.9g Sugars

INGREDIENTS

6 smoked bacon slices, chopped
1 onion, chopped
4 garlic cloves, chopped
2 cups chicken broth
2 ½ pounds fresh collard greens

1/4 cup dry white wine
1 teaspoon paprika
1 bay leaf
Kosher salt and ground black pepper, to taste

DIRECTIONS

Press the "Sauté" button to preheat your Instant Pot. Then, cook the bacon until crisp and set aside.

Add the remaining ingredients to the inner pot and stir to combine.

Secure the lid. Choose the "Manual" mode and cook for 5 minutes at High pressure. Once cooking is complete, use a quick pressure release; carefully remove the lid.

Serve garnished with the reserved bacon. Bon appétit!

424. Mediterranean-Style Eggplant Medley

(Ready in about 15 minutes | Servings 4)

Per serving: 342 Calories; 10.4g Fat; 53.4g Carbs; 13.8g Protein; 17.4g Sugars

INGREDIENTS

2 pounds eggplant, cut into cubes
2 tablespoons sea salt
2 tablespoons olive oil
1 red onion, chopped
2 bell peppers, deseeded and diced

4 garlic cloves, sliced
1 teaspoon oregano
1 teaspoon basil
1/2 teaspoon ground turmeric
1/2 teaspoon sea salt

1/2 teaspoon ground black pepper
1 teaspoon paprika
2 vine-ripened tomatoes, pureed
16 ounces chickpeas, boiled and rinsed

DIRECTIONS

Toss the eggplant with 2 tablespoons of sea salt in a colander. Let it sit for 30 minutes; then squeeze out the excess liquid.

Press the "Sauté" button and heat the olive oil. Now, cook the onion until tender and translucent; add the reserved eggplant, peppers and garlic and continue to cook an additional 2 minutes or until they are fragrant.

Add the remaining ingredients to the inner pot. Stir to combine well.

Secure the lid. Choose the "Manual" mode and cook for 3 minutes at High pressure. Once cooking is complete, use a quick pressure release; carefully remove the lid. Ladle into individual bowls and serve immediately.

425. Asian Glazed Bok Choy

(Ready in about 15 minutes | Servings 4)

Per serving: 92 Calories; 5.4g Fat; 8.1g Carbs; 3.8g Protein; 5.1g Sugars

INGREDIENTS

2 teaspoons sesame oil

2 cloves garlic, pressed

1 ½ pounds Bok choy

1 cup water

2 tablespoons rice wine vinegar

4 tablespoons soy sauce

DIRECTIONS

Press the "Sauté" button and heat the oil. Now, cook the garlic for 1 minute or until it is fragrant but not browned.

Add the Bok choy and water to the inner pot.

Secure the lid. Choose the "Manual" mode and cook for 5 minutes at High pressure. Once cooking is complete, use a quick pressure release; carefully remove the lid.

Meanwhile, in a mixing bowl, whisk the rice vinegar and soy sauce. Drizzle this sauce over the Bok choy and serve immediately.

426. Buttery Candied Baby Carrots

(Ready in about 15 minutes | Servings 4)

Per serving: 165 Calories; 8.8g Fat; 21.5g Carbs; 1.8g Protein; 15.5g Sugars

INGREDIENTS

1 ½ pounds baby carrots

3 tablespoons butter

2 tablespoons molasses

1/2 teaspoon kosher salt

1/4 teaspoon white pepper

1/2 teaspoon cayenne pepper

DIRECTIONS

Add water and a steamer basket to the inner pot of your Instant Pot. Place the carrots in the steamer basket.

Secure the lid. Choose the "Steam" mode and cook for 3 minutes at High pressure. Once cooking is complete, use a quick pressure release; carefully remove the lid.

Discard the water and press the "Sauté" button. Once hot, melt the butter. Stir in the cooked carrots, molasses, salt, white pepper, and cayenne pepper. Sauté approximately 2 minutes, stirring frequently. Serve warm.

427. Vegetable Bowl with Tahini Sauce

(Ready in about 10 minutes | Servings 4)

Per serving: 506 Calories; 32g Fat; 48.5g Carbs; 11.2g Protein; 4.3g Sugars

INGREDIENTS

4 carrots, sliced

4 medium potatoes, diced

1 pound cauliflower florets

2 tablespoons olive oil

1/2 teaspoon sea salt

1 cup vegetable broth

1/3 cup tahini

1/4 cup olive oil

1/3 cup water

1 clove garlic, pressed

2 tablespoons fresh lime juice

1 tablespoon fresh parsley, finely chopped

DIRECTIONS

Place the vegetables, olive oil, salt, and vegetable broth in the inner pot of your Instant Pot.

Secure the lid. Choose the "Manual" mode and cook for 4 minutes at High pressure. Once cooking is complete, use a quick pressure release; carefully remove the lid.

Meanwhile, make the tahini sauce by mixing the remaining ingredients. Serve the warm vegetables with the tahini sauce on the side. Bon appétit!

428. Escarole and Meatball Soup (Italian Wedding Soup)

(Ready in about 25 minutes | Servings 4)

Per serving: 485 Calories; 30.2g Fat; 29.2g Carbs; 25.4g Protein; 8.4g Sugars

INGREDIENTS

4 cups chicken broth
1 onion, chopped
2 carrots, chopped
1 teaspoon Italian seasoning mix

18 ounces Italian-style meatballs, frozen
2 tablespoons tomato paste
2 bay leaves

1 cup tubettini pasta
3 cups escarole, chopped

DIRECTIONS

Add the broth, onion, carrots, Italian seasoning mix, meatballs, tomato paste, and bay leaves to the inner pot of your Instant Pot.
Secure the lid. Choose the "Manual" mode and cook for 15 minutes at High pressure. Once cooking is complete, use a quick pressure release; carefully remove the lid.
Next, sit in the tubettini pasta and escarole.
Secure the lid. Choose the "Manual" mode and cook for 5 minutes at High pressure. Once cooking is complete, use a quick pressure release; carefully remove the lid. Bon appétit!

429. Italian Zucchini Bake

(Ready in about 20 minutes | Servings 4)

Per serving: 617 Calories; 45.2g Fat; 29.2g Carbs; 18.4g Protein; 6.7g Sugars

INGREDIENTS

1 tablespoon canola oil
1 pound ground chuck
1/4 pound Italian sausage, crumbled
1 onion, chopped
2 garlic cloves, minced

1/2 cup parmesan cheese, grated
1 cup cream cheese
Sea salt and ground black pepper, to taste
1 teaspoon cayenne pepper

1 teaspoon Italian seasoning blend
1 cup tomato puree
1 pound zucchini, cut into long slices

DIRECTIONS

Press the "Sauté" button and heat the oil. Then, cook the ground chuck, sausage, and onion for 3 to 4 minutes; stir in the garlic and cook an additional minute.
In a mixing bowl, thoroughly combine the cheese and seasonings.
Place a layer of the zucchini strips on the bottom of a lightly greased baking pan. Spoon 1/3 of the meat mixture onto the zucchini layer.
Place 1/2 of the cheese mixture and tomato puree on the meat layer.
Repeat the layers, ending with a cheese layer. Add 1 cup of water and a metal rack to the inner pot. Lower the baking pan onto the rack.
Secure the lid. Choose the "Manual" mode and cook for 6 minutes at High pressure. Once cooking is complete, use a quick pressure release; carefully remove the lid. Bon appétit!

430. Kohlsuppe (Traditional German Cabbage Soup)

(Ready in about 20 minutes | Servings 4)

Per serving: 472 Calories; 34g Fat; 20.5g Carbs; 21.4g Protein; 8.9g Sugars

INGREDIENTS

2 teaspoons chicken schmaltz
1 pound smoked sausage, sliced
1 onion, chopped
2 garlic cloves, minced
2 carrots, chopped

1 celery stalk, chopped
2 fresh tomatoes, chopped
4 cups chicken broth
1/2 teaspoon basil
1/2 teaspoon dried thyme

1/2 teaspoon dried oregano
1 teaspoon paprika
1 pound cabbage, cored and shredded
Salt and ground black pepper, to taste

DIRECTIONS

Press the "Sauté" button and melt the chicken schmaltz. Then, cook the sausage and onion for about 3 minutes. Now, stir in the garlic and continue to sauté for 30 seconds more, stirring frequently.
Add the remaining ingredients; stir to combine.
Secure the lid. Choose the "Manual" mode and cook for 10 minutes at High pressure. Once cooking is complete, use a quick pressure release; carefully remove the lid.
Serve in individual bowls. Bon appétit!

431. Classic French Carrot Salad

(Ready in about 10 minutes + chilling time | Servings 4)

Per serving: 141 Calories; 7.3g Fat; 18.9g Carbs; 1.4g Protein; 9.9g Sugars

INGREDIENTS

1 ½ pounds carrots, sliced to 2-inch chunks
1/2 teaspoon Himalayan salt
1 tablespoon Dijon mustard
1 tablespoon lime juice
2 tablespoons olive oil

1 teaspoon honey
1/4 teaspoon ground white pepper, to taste
1/4 teaspoon red pepper flakes
2 scallions, finely sliced

DIRECTIONS

Add 1 cup of water and a steamer basket to the inner pot of your Instant Pot.

Place the carrots in the steamer basket.

Secure the lid. Choose the "Steam" mode and cook for 3 minutes at High pressure. Once cooking is complete, use a quick pressure release; carefully remove the lid.

Toss your carrots with the remaining ingredients and serve chilled. Enjoy!

432. Braised Endive with Italian Salami

(Ready in about 15 minutes | Servings 4)

Per serving: 393 Calories; 26.2g Fat; 21.3g Carbs; 20.4g Protein; 5.6g Sugars

INGREDIENTS

2 tablespoons extra-virgin olive oil
8 ounces Italian dry salami, cut into 1/2-inch chunks
1 shallot, sliced
2 garlic cloves, minced
2 pounds endive, coarsely chopped
2 tomatoes, chopped

1 tablespoon Italian seasoning mix
1 teaspoon cayenne pepper
Sea salt and freshly ground pepper, to taste
1 cup chicken broth
4 tablespoons Romano cheese, preferably freshly grated

DIRECTIONS

Press the "Sauté" button and heat the olive oil until sizzling. Now, cook the Italian salami for 3 minutes; add the shallot and garlic and cook an additional 2 minutes or until they have softened.

Add the endive, tomatoes, spices, and broth to the inner pot.

Secure the lid. Choose the "Manual" mode and cook for 2 minutes at High pressure. Once cooking is complete, use a quick pressure release; carefully remove the lid.

Divide between serving bowls and serve garnished with the grated Romano cheese. Bon appétit!

433. Spicy and Creamy Green Soup

(Ready in about 15 minutes | Servings 4)

Per serving: 218 Calories; 10.4g Fat; 19.3g Carbs; 15.4g Protein; 8g Sugars

INGREDIENTS

2 teaspoons sesame oil
2 cloves garlic, minced
1 shallot, finely chopped
1 piri piri pepper, minced
1/2 teaspoon ground cumin

1 pound broccoli florets
5 cups vegetable broth, preferably homemade
Sea salt and ground black pepper, to taste

1 teaspoon cayenne pepper
12 ounces spinach
1 cup coconut milk
1/2 cup coconut cream

DIRECTIONS

Press the "Sauté" button and heat the oil until sizzling. Now, cook the garlic, shallot, pepper, and cumin until they are just softened and aromatic.

Then, stir in the broccoli, broth, salt, black pepper, and cayenne pepper.

Secure the lid. Choose the "Manual" mode and cook for 5 minutes at High pressure. Once cooking is complete, use a quick pressure release; carefully remove the lid.

Afterwards, stir in the spinach, coconut milk, and cream. Seal the lid again and let it sit in the residual heat until the spinach wilts.

Now, puree the soup with an immersion blender and serve warm. Bon appétit!

434. North-Indian Authentic Bhindi Masala

(Ready in about 15 minutes | Servings 3)

Per serving: 253 Calories; 16.8g Fat; 24.9g Carbs; 5.4g Protein; 9.5g Sugars

INGREDIENTS

2 tablespoons coconut oil, at room temperature
1 yellow onion, sliced
1 teaspoon ginger garlic paste
1 pound okra, cut into small pieces
1 cup tomato puree
1/2 teaspoon jeera (cumin seeds)

1/2 teaspoon ground turmeric
1 teaspoon Gram masala
1 teaspoon amchur (mango powder)
1 teaspoon Sriracha sauce
Himalayan salt, to taste

DIRECTIONS

Press the "Sauté" button and heat the oil until sizzling. Now, cook the onion until it is tender and translucent.
Stir in the ginger-garlic paste and continue to cook for 30 to 40 seconds. Stir the remaining ingredients into the inner pot.
Secure the lid. Choose the "Manual" mode and cook for 4 minutes at High pressure. Once cooking is complete, use a quick pressure release; carefully remove the lid.
Serve warm.

435. Milagu Rasam (Indian Black Pepper and Tomato Soup)

(Ready in about 15 minutes | Servings 4)

Per serving: 92 Calories; 7.8g Fat; 6.7g Carbs; 1.4g Protein; 2.8g Sugars

INGREDIENTS

1 tablespoon cumin seeds
1 tablespoon whole black pepper
2 cloves garlic
2 dry red chili pepper
2 tablespoons coconut oil
1/2 teaspoon mustard seeds

2 medium tomatoes, diced
6 curry leaves
1/2 teaspoon turmeric
1 small ball of tamarind
Himalayan salt, to taste
4 cups water

DIRECTIONS

Grind the cumin seeds, whole black pepper, garlic, and red chili pepper to a coarse paste.
Press the "Sauté" button and heat the oil until sizzling. Now, cook the mustard seeds for a minute or so. Once they splutter, add chopped tomatoes and curry leaves. Cook for 3 to 4 minutes more.
Add the ground paste, turmeric powder, and freshly squeezed tamarind juice; add salt and the water and stir to combine.
Secure the lid. Choose the "Manual" mode and cook for 4 minutes at High pressure. Once cooking is complete, use a quick pressure release; carefully remove the lid. Serve hot and enjoy!

436. Autumn Pumpkin Pie Oatmeal

(Ready in about 25 minutes | Servings 4)

Per serving: 92 Calories; 7.8g Fat; 6.7g Carbs; 1.4g Protein; 2.8g Sugars

INGREDIENTS

1 ½ cups steel cut oats
3 cups water
1/2 cup pumpkin puree
1 tablespoon pumpkin pie spice
A pinch of salt

A pinch of grated nutmeg
4 tablespoons honey
1 teaspoon ground cinnamon
1 teaspoon vanilla essence

DIRECTIONS

Add all ingredients to the inner pot of your Instant Pot.
Secure the lid. Choose the "Manual" mode and cook for 4 minutes at High pressure. Once cooking is complete, use a natural pressure release for 15 minutes; carefully remove the lid
Ladle the oatmeal into serving bowls and serve immediately. Enjoy!

437. Scandinavian-Style Rutabaga Salad

(Ready in about 15 minutes | Servings 4)

Per serving: 222 Calories; 13.9g Fat; 24.4g Carbs; 2.3g Protein; 15.6g Sugars

INGREDIENTS

1 pound rutabaga, peeled and cut into 1/4-inch chunks
1/2 pound cabbage, shredded
1 Granny Smith apple, cored and diced
1/4 cup almonds, slivered

1/4 cup olive oil
2 tablespoons fresh lemon juice
1 teaspoon Dijon mustard
1 tablespoon agave syrup

DIRECTIONS

Add 1 cup of water and a steamer basket to the inner pot of your Instant Pot. Now, place the rutabaga in the steamer basket.

Secure the lid. Choose the "Manual" mode and cook for 6 minutes at High pressure. Once cooking is complete, use a quick pressure release; carefully remove the lid.

Toss the rutabaga chunks with the cabbage, apple, and almonds. Mix the remaining ingredients to prepare the salad dressing.

Dress your salad and serve chilled. Enjoy!

SIDE DISHES

438. Aromatic Butter Mushrooms

(Ready in about 20 minutes | Servings 3)

Per serving: 147 Calories; 12.2g Fat; 8.7g Carbs; 3.5g Protein; 3.6g Sugars

INGREDIENTS

3 tablespoons butter
1 pound white mushrooms
2 garlic cloves, minced
1 thyme sprig, chopped

1 rosemary sprig, chopped
1 teaspoon cayenne pepper
Sea salt and ground black pepper, to taste

DIRECTIONS

Press the "Sauté" button and melt the butter. Once hot, cook your mushrooms for about 4 minutes, stirring occasionally to ensure even cooking.
Add the garlic and spices; toss to coat.
Secure the lid. Choose the "Manual" mode and cook for 12 minutes at High pressure. Once cooking is complete, use a natural pressure release for 5 minutes; carefully remove the lid. Serve warm.

439. Brussels Sprouts with Cranberries

(Ready in about 10 minutes | Servings 4)

Per serving: 174 Calories; 7.7g Fat; 22.3g Carbs; 7.2g Protein; 9.1g Sugars

INGREDIENTS

2 tablespoons sesame oil
4 cloves garlic, sliced
1 ½ pounds Brussels sprouts, halved
1 cup vegetable broth

6 tablespoons dried cranberries
1/4 cup balsamic vinegar
1/4 teaspoon dried dill weed
Kosher salt and freshly ground black pepper, to taste

DIRECTIONS

Press the "Sauté" button and heat the oil; then, sauté the garlic until just tender and fragrant.
Stir in the Brussels sprouts and continue to sauté an additional 2 to 3 minutes.
Add the remaining ingredients to the inner pot.
Secure the lid. Choose the "Manual" mode and cook for 2 minutes at High pressure. Once cooking is complete, use a quick pressure release; carefully remove the lid. Bon appétit!

440. Mashed Sweet Potatoes with Scallions

(Ready in about 15 minutes | Servings 6)

Per serving: 179 Calories; 4.9g Fat; 31.3g Carbs; 2.8g Protein; 6.4g Sugars

INGREDIENTS

2 pounds sweet potatoes, peeled and diced
1 cup water
1 teaspoon sea salt
A bunch of scallions, finely sliced
2 tablespoons fresh parsley leaves, roughly chopped

1 garlic clove, pressed
1/4 cup sour cream
2 tablespoons butter
A pinch of grated nutmeg
1/2 teaspoon cayenne pepper

DIRECTIONS

Add the sweet potatoes and water to the Instant Pot.
Secure the lid. Choose the "Manual" mode and cook for 8 minutes at High pressure. Once cooking is complete, use a quick pressure release; carefully remove the lid.
Drain the potatoes. Mash the potatoes using a potato masher or your food processor.
Now, add the remaining ingredients and stir well to combine. Enjoy!

441. Baked Potatoes with Salsa and Cheese

(Ready in about 30 minutes | Servings 6)

Per serving: 228 Calories; 5.9g Fat; 39.1g Carbs; 6g Protein; 3g Sugars

INGREDIENTS

6 medium potatoes, peeled
1/2 cup cream cheese
6 tablespoons salsa

DIRECTIONS

Place 1 cup of water and a metal trivet in the inner pot of your Instant Pot. Pierce your potatoes with a fork; place them on the trivet.
Secure the lid. Choose the "Steam" mode and cook for 15 minutes at High pressure. Once cooking is complete, use a natural pressure release for 10 minutes; carefully remove the lid.
Top the warm potatoes with the cream cheese and salsa and serve immediately. Bon appétit!

442. Asparagus with Sesame Seeds

(Ready in about 10 minutes | Servings 2)

Per serving: 156 Calories; 11.9g Fat; 9.7g Carbs; 6.6g Protein; 4.3g Sugars

INGREDIENTS

1 pound fresh asparagus, trimmed
1 tablespoon sesame oil
2 tablespoons sesame seeds, toasted
1 teaspoon garlic powder
Kosher salt and red pepper, to taste

DIRECTIONS

Add 1 cup of water and a steamer basket to the inner pot. Place the asparagus in the steamer basket.
Secure the lid. Choose the "Steam" mode and cook for 3 minutes at High pressure. Once cooking is complete, use a quick pressure release; carefully remove the lid.
Toss the warm asparagus with the other ingredients. Enjoy!

443. Corn on the Cob with Sriracha Aioli

(Ready in about 10 minutes | Servings 5)

Per serving: 207 Calories; 10.2g Fat; 29.5g Carbs; 4.6g Protein; 0g Sugars

INGREDIENTS

5 ears corn on the cob, husked
Sriracha Aioli:
1/2 cup mayonnaise

1 tablespoon lemon juice
2 tablespoons Sriracha
1/4 teaspoon sea salt

DIRECTIONS

Add 1 cup of water and a metal trivet to the inner pot of your Instant Pot. Place your corn on the trivet.
Secure the lid. Choose the "Manual" mode and cook for 2 minutes at High pressure. Once cooking is complete, use a quick pressure release; carefully remove the lid.
Then, whisk the mayonnaise, lemon juice, Sriracha, and salt until well combined. Serve the warm corn on the cob with the Sriracha aioli on the side. Bon appétit!

444. Creamy Couscous Florentine

(Ready in about 10 minutes | Servings 4)

Per serving: 563 Calories; 9.2g Fat; 98g Carbs; 19.6g Protein; 7.3g Sugars

INGREDIENTS

1 tablespoon olive oil
2 bell peppers, diced
1 pound couscous
2 cups vegetable broth
1 cucumber, diced
2 tomatoes, sliced

2 tablespoons fresh mint, roughly chopped
A bunch of scallions, sliced
1/4 cup yogurt
2 tablespoons sesame butter (tahini)
1 tablespoon honey

DIRECTIONS

Press the "Sauté" button and heat the oil; then, sauté the peppers until tender and aromatic. Stir in the couscous and vegetable broth.
Secure the lid. Choose the "Manual" mode and cook for 2 minutes at High pressure. Once cooking is complete, use a quick pressure release; carefully remove the lid.
Then, stir in the remaining ingredients; stir to combine well and enjoy!

445. Eggplant with Mediterranean Dressing

(Ready in about 10 minutes | Servings 4)

Per serving: 198 Calories; 18.2g Fat; 8.2g Carbs; 1.6g Protein; 5g Sugars

INGREDIENTS

1 pound eggplant, sliced
1 tablespoon sea salt
2 tablespoons olive oil
1/4 cup Greek yogurt
1/4 cup mayonnaise

1 teaspoon balsamic vinegar
1 garlic clove, minced
2 tablespoons olives, pitted and minced
1 tablespoon fresh coriander, chopped

DIRECTIONS

Toss the eggplant with sea salt in a colander. Let it sit for 30 minutes; then squeeze out the excess liquid.
Press the "Sauté" button and heat the olive oil. Now, cook the eggplant until lightly charred. Add 1 cup of water to the inner pot.
Secure the lid. Choose the "Manual" mode and cook for 2 minutes at High pressure. Once cooking is complete, use a quick pressure release; carefully remove the lid.
Meanwhile, whisk the remaining ingredients until well combined. Drizzle this dressing over the eggplant and serve at once. Bon appétit!

446. Potatoes Au Gratin

(Ready in about 20 minutes | Servings 4)

Per serving: 440 Calories; 16.2g Fat; 58g Carbs; 16.5g Protein; 3.9g Sugars

INGREDIENTS

6 medium potatoes, peeled and thinly sliced
1 cup vegetable broth
1 shallot, chopped
2 garlic cloves, sliced
1/2 teaspoon dried basil

Sea salt and ground black pepper, to taste
1/2 teaspoon paprika
1/2 cup heavy cream
1 cup Romano cheese, preferably freshly grated

DIRECTIONS

Arrange the sliced potatoes on the bottom of a lightly greased inner pot. Add the vegetable broth, shallot, garlic, basil, salt, black pepper and paprika to the inner pot.
Secure the lid. Choose the "Manual" mode and cook for 4 minutes at High pressure. Once cooking is complete, use a quick pressure release; carefully remove the lid.
Preheat your oven to broil. Transfer the potatoes to an oven-safe dish. Top with the heavy cream and Romano cheese.
Broil until the cheese is bubbling and golden brown. Let it sit on a cooling rack for 5 minutes before slicing and serving. Enjoy!

447. Broccoli with Italian-Style Mayonnaise

(Ready in about 10 minutes | Servings 4)

Per serving: 227 Calories; 21.2g Fat; 6.4g Carbs; 4.5g Protein; 1.4g Sugars

INGREDIENTS

1 pound broccoli florets
3 garlic cloves, smashed
Kosher salt and ground black pepper, to taste

1/2 cup mayonnaise
1 tablespoon Italian seasoning mix

DIRECTIONS

Add 1 cup of water and steamer basket to the inner pot. Place the broccoli florets in the steamer basket.
Secure the lid. Choose the "Manual" mode and cook for 1 minute at High pressure. Once cooking is complete, use a quick pressure release; carefully remove the lid.
Sprinkle the garlic, salt, and black pepper over the cooked broccoli florets.
Mix the mayonnaise with the Italian seasoning mix; serve your broccoli with the Italian mayo on the side. Bon appétit!

448. Black Eyed Peas with Bacon

(Ready in about 40 minutes | Servings 3)

Per serving: 416 Calories; 13.1g Fat; 49.5g Carbs; 27.2g Protein; 6.4g Sugars

INGREDIENTS

3 strips bacon, cut into 1/2-inch pieces
1/2 pound dry black eyed peas
3 cups chicken stock
1/2 teaspoon cayenne pepper
1/4 teaspoon dried dill

1/4 teaspoon dried oregano
1/4 teaspoon dried sage
Kosher salt and freshly ground black pepper, to taste
2 cups spinach, torn into pieces

DIRECTIONS

Press the "Sauté" button to preheat your Instant Pot. Now, cook the bacon until it is crisp; reserve.
Add the black eyed peas, chicken stock, and all the slices to the inner pot.
Secure the lid. Choose the "Manual" mode and cook for 18 minutes at High pressure. Once cooking is complete, use a natural pressure release for 10 minutes; carefully remove the lid.
Lastly, stir in the spinach leaves; seal the lid and let it sit in the residual heat for 5 to 10 minutes.
Ladle into serving bowls and garnish with the reserved bacon. Bon appétit!

449. Vegan Baked Beans

(Ready in about 1 hour 10 minutes | Servings 6)

Per serving: 594 Calories; 5.6g Fat; 114g Carbs; 26.2g Protein; 51.4g Sugars

INGREDIENTS

1 ½ pounds pinto beans, rinsed and drained
8 cups water
2 tablespoons olive oil
2 onions, chopped
5 cloves garlic, minced

1 cup molasses
1 cup ketchup
1 teaspoon salt
2 tablespoons soy sauce
1 tablespoon Cholula hot sauce

DIRECTIONS

Place the beans and water in your Instant Pot.
Secure the lid. Choose the "Bean/Chili" mode and cook for 40 minutes at High pressure. Once cooking is complete, use a natural pressure release for 10 minutes; carefully remove the lid. Set aside.
Press the "Sauté" button and heat the oil until sizzling. Now, cook the onion and garlic until tender and fragrant. Add the reserved beans back to the inner pot. Stir in the remaining ingredients.
Secure the lid. Choose the "Manual" mode and cook for 10 minutes at High pressure. Once cooking is complete, use a quick pressure release. Bon appétit!

450. Kale with Garlic and Lemon

(Ready in about 10 minutes | Servings 4)

Per serving: 89 Calories; 4.4g Fat; 10.4g Carbs; 5g Protein; 2.5g Sugars

INGREDIENTS

1 tablespoon olive oil

3 cloves garlic, slivered

1 pound kale, cleaned and trimmed

1 cup water

Kosher salt and ground black pepper, to taste

1/4 teaspoon cayenne pepper

Fresh juice squeezed from 1/2 a lemon

DIRECTIONS

Press the "Sauté" button and heat the oil until sizzling. Now, cook the garlic until just tender and aromatic.

Add the chopped kale and water to the inner pot. Sprinkle with salt, black pepper, and cayenne pepper.

Secure the lid. Choose the "Manual" mode and cook for 4 minutes at High pressure. Once cooking is complete, use a quick pressure release.

Scoop the kale out of the inner pot with a slotted spoon, leaving as much cooking liquid behind as possible. Drizzle fresh lemon juice over the kale and serve. Bon appétit!

451. Warm Cabbage Slaw

(Ready in about 10 minutes | Servings 4)

Per serving: 136 Calories; 8.4g Fat; 14.5g Carbs; 2.8g Protein; 7.6g Sugars

INGREDIENTS

2 tablespoons olive oil

3 cloves garlic, minced

1/2 cup green onions, sliced

1 pound purple cabbage, shredded

2 carrots, cut into sticks

Kosher salt and ground black pepper, to taste

2 tablespoons soy sauce

DIRECTIONS

Press the "Sauté" button and add the oil. Once hot, cook the garlic and green onions until softened.

Add the cabbage, carrots, salt, and black pepper.

Secure the lid. Choose the "Manual" mode and cook for 4 minutes at High pressure. Once cooking is complete, use a quick pressure release.

Lastly, add the soy sauce to the cabbage mixture and stir to combine well. Place in a serving bowl and serve immediately.

452. Boiled Potatoes with Ranch Dressing

(Ready in about 20 minutes | Servings 4)

Per serving: 379 Calories; 9.4g Fat; 66.7g Carbs; 8.5g Protein; 2.9g Sugars

INGREDIENTS

4 large Yukon gold potatoes

1/2 cup sour cream

4 tablespoons reduced-fat mayonnaise

1 teaspoon fresh parsley, chopped

1 teaspoon fresh chives, chopped

1 garlic clove, minced

Sea salt and ground black pepper, to taste

DIRECTIONS

Add 1 ½ cups of water and a steamer basket to the inner pot. Now, place the potatoes in the steamer basket.

Secure the lid. Choose the "Steam" mode and cook for 10 minutes at High pressure. Once cooking is complete, use a quick pressure release; carefully remove the lid.

Meanwhile, in a mixing bowl, whisk together the sour cream and mayonnaise. Stir in the fresh herbs, garlic, salt, and black pepper.

Drain your potatoes, peel and slice them; toss your potatoes with ranch dressing. Bon appétit!

453. Italian Bucatini Puttanesca

(Ready in about 25 minutes | Servings 4)

Per serving: 374 Calories; 7.1g Fat; 72.7g Carbs; 7.3g Protein; 1.8g Sugars

INGREDIENTS

1 tablespoon olive oil
2 garlic cloves, pressed
1/2 cup black olives, pitted, and thinly sliced
2 tablespoons capers, soaked and rinsed
2 vine-ripened tomatoes, pureed

1 tablespoon Italian seasoning blend
Coarse salt, to taste
3/4 pound bucatini pasta
1 cup water

DIRECTIONS

Press the "Sauté" button and add the oil. Once hot, cook the garlic until aromatic. Add the black olives, capers, tomatoes, Italian seasoning blend, and salt.

Bring to a boil and turn the Instant Pot to the lowest setting; let the sauce simmer for 10 to 13 minutes. Stir in the bucatini pasta and water.

Secure the lid. Choose the "Manual" mode and cook for 8 minutes at High pressure. Once cooking is complete, use a quick pressure release.

Serve warm and enjoy!

454. Quick Chili Rice

(Ready in about 45 minutes | Servings 4)

Per serving: 358 Calories; 10.7g Fat; 57g Carbs; 10.6g Protein; 7.8g Sugars

INGREDIENTS

2 tablespoons canola oil
2 shallots, finely chopped
1 red chili pepper, seeded and minced
1 sweet pepper, seeded and finely chopped
2 tablespoons garlic, minced
1 cup tomato puree

1 cup brown rice
10 ounces black beans
2 ½ cups chicken stock
Sea salt and ground black pepper, to taste
2 tablespoons fresh chives, chopped

DIRECTIONS

Press the "Sauté" button and heat the oil until sizzling. Now, cook the shallots, peppers, and garlic until tender and fragrant.

Add the tomato puree, rice, beans, stock, salt, and black pepper to the inner pot.

Secure the lid. Choose the "Manual" mode and cook for 25 minutes at High pressure. Once cooking is complete, use a natural pressure release for 15 minutes; carefully remove the lid.

Ladle into individual bowls and serve with fresh chives. Enjoy!

455. Authentic Tex-Mex Rice

(Ready in about 30 minutes | Servings 5)

Per serving: 316 Calories; 7.7g Fat; 51g Carbs; 8.9g Protein; 1.3g Sugars

INGREDIENTS

2 tablespoons canola oil
2 garlic cloves, minced
1 medium-sized leek, chopped
1 bell pepper, seeded and finely chopped
2 fresh serrano peppers, seeded and finely chopped
4 cups vegetable stock
2 tablespoons fresh parsley leaves, chopped

1/2 tablespoon cumin seeds
1 teaspoon mustard seeds
1 ½ cups white rice
1 teaspoon salt
1/2 teaspoon cayenne pepper
1/2 teaspoon freshly ground black pepper

DIRECTIONS

Press the "Sauté" button and heat the oil. Once hot, cook the garlic, leek, and peppers until tender and aromatic.

Add the remaining ingredients and stir to combine.

Secure the lid. Choose the "Rice" mode and cook for 10 minutes. Once cooking is complete, use a natural pressure release for 15 minutes; carefully remove the lid.

Serve in individual bowls and enjoy!

456. Colorful Kamut Bowl

(Ready in about 20 minutes | Servings 5)

Per serving: 295 Calories; 12g Fat; 42g Carbs; 8.6g Protein; 5.3g Sugars

INGREDIENTS

1 ½ cups dried kamut
3 cups water
2 cups baby spinach
1 large carrot, cut into sticks
1 celery rib, sliced

1 shallot, finely chopped
4 tablespoons olive oil
Salt and freshly ground black pepper, to taste
2 tablespoons fresh lime juice

DIRECTIONS

Add the kamut and water to the inner pot.
Secure the lid. Choose the "Manual" mode and cook for 9 minutes at High pressure. Once cooking is complete, use a quick pressure release.
Add the vegetables, olive oil, salt, and black pepper.
Secure the lid. Choose the "Manual" mode and cook for 3 minutes at High pressure. Once cooking is complete, use a quick pressure release.
Drizzle fresh lime juice over each serving and enjoy!

457. Buttery Cauliflower Rice

(Ready in about 10 minutes | Servings 3)

Per serving: 127 Calories; 8.3g Fat; 11.7g Carbs; 4.5g Protein; 4.4g Sugars

INGREDIENTS

1 ½ pounds cauliflower
Sea salt, to taste
1/2 teaspoon white pepper

2 tablespoons butter
2 tablespoons fresh parsley, roughly chopped

DIRECTIONS

Add the cauliflower florets and 1 cup of water to the inner pot.
Secure the lid. Choose the "Manual" mode and cook for 2 minutes at High pressure. Once cooking is complete, use a quick pressure release.
Stir the salt, pepper, and butter into warm cauliflower rice.
Serve garnished with fresh parsley and enjoy!

458. French Balsamic Peppers

(Ready in about 10 minutes | Servings 2)

Per serving: 178 Calories; 13.7g Fat; 13.7g Carbs; 2.3g Protein; 8.4g Sugars

INGREDIENTS

2 tablespoons olive oil
4 bell peppers, seeded and sliced
Sea salt and ground black pepper, to taste

1/2 cup court bouillon
1/2 cup water
2 tablespoons balsamic vinegar

DIRECTIONS

Press the "Sauté" button and heat the oil. Once hot, cook the peppers until just tender and fragrant.
Add the salt and black pepper. Pour in the bouillon and water.
Secure the lid. Choose the "Manual" mode and cook for 3 minutes at High pressure. Once cooking is complete, use a quick pressure release.
Drizzle balsamic vinegar over your peppers and serve immediately.

459. Tamatar Wangun (Indian Kashmiri Eggplant)

(Ready in about 40 minutes | Servings 4)

Per serving: 105 Calories; 6.7g Fat; 11.2g Carbs; 2.1g Protein; 6.6g Sugars

INGREDIENTS

1 pound eggplant, sliced
1 tablespoon sea salt
1 tablespoon sesame oil
1 teaspoon cumin seeds
2 shallots, chopped

1 tablespoon butter
1 cup water
1 Kashmiri chili pepper, chopped
2 tomatoes, pureed
4 curry leaves

DIRECTIONS

Toss the eggplant with sea salt in a colander. Let it sit for 30 minutes; then squeeze out the excess liquid.
Press the "Sauté" button and heat the sesame oil; now sauté the cumin seeds for 30 seconds or until aromatic. Then, cook the shallots for 2 to 3 minutes more or until they have softened.
Then, melt the butter. Now, cook the eggplant until lightly charred. Add the water, chili pepper, tomatoes, and curry leaves to the inner pot.
Secure the lid. Choose the "Manual" mode and cook for 2 minutes at High pressure. Once cooking is complete, use a quick pressure release; carefully remove the lid.
Serve in individual bowls and enjoy!

460. Thayir Saadam (Indian Yogurt Rice)

(Ready in about 25 minutes | Servings 5)

Per serving: 323 Calories; 11.7g Fat; 49.2g Carbs; 4.5g Protein; 1.2g Sugars

INGREDIENTS

4 tablespoons grapeseed oil
1 teaspoon fennel seeds
8 curry leaves
1 ½ cups basmati rice, rinsed
1 chili pepper, minced

1 teaspoon fresh ginger, peeled and grated
1 cinnamon stick
Himalayan salt and ground black pepper, to taste
1 cup full-fat yogurt
2 tablespoons fresh dhania (coriander), chopped

DIRECTIONS

Press the "Sauté" button and heat the oil; now sauté the fennel seeds and curry leaves for 30 seconds or until aromatic.
Now, stir in the basmati rice, chili pepper, ginger, cinnamon, salt, and black pepper. Pour in 2 cups of water.
Secure the lid. Choose the "Manual" mode and cook for 4 minutes at High pressure. Once cooking is complete, use a natural pressure release for 15 minutes; carefully remove the lid.
Fluff your rice with a fork and stir in the yogurt. Stir until everything is well combined. Serve garnished with fresh dhania and enjoy!

461. Easy Parmesan Fettuccine

(Ready in about 20 minutes | Servings 6)

Per serving: 348 Calories; 9.6g Fat; 57.2g Carbs; 12.5g Protein; 0.3g Sugars

INGREDIENTS

1 pound fettuccine
4 cups water
4 tablespoons butter, cubed

Sea salt and ground black pepper, to season
4 tablespoons Parmesan cheese, grated

DIRECTIONS

Place the fettuccine and water in the inner pot of your Instant Pot.
Secure the lid. Choose the "Manual" mode and cook for 4 minutes at High pressure. Once cooking is complete, use a natural pressure release for 10 minutes; carefully remove the lid.
Toss the boiled fettuccine with the butter, salt, black pepper, and parmesan cheese; serve immediately. Bon appétit!

462. Garlicky Green Beans

(Ready in about 10 minutes | Servings 4)

Per serving: 117 Calories; 7.2g Fat; 12.6g Carbs; 3.3g Protein; 5.6g Sugars

INGREDIENTS

2 tablespoons olive oil
2 garlic cloves, minced
1 ½ pounds green beans, trimmed

Salt and freshly ground black pepper, to taste
1 teaspoon cayenne pepper
2 tablespoons fresh chives, chopped

DIRECTIONS

Press the "Sauté" button and heat the oil until sizzling. Now, sauté the garlic until tender but not browned.
Add the green beans, salt, black pepper, and cayenne pepper to the inner pot. Pour in 1 cup of water.
Secure the lid. Choose the "Manual" mode and cook for 3 minutes at High pressure. Once cooking is complete, use a quick pressure release; carefully remove the lid.
Garnish with fresh chives and serve warm.

463. Punjabi Bean Curry

(Ready in about 35 minutes | Servings 5)

Per serving: 406 Calories; 6.2g Fat; 66g Carbs; 24.5g Protein; 1.1g Sugars

INGREDIENTS

1 pound red kidney beans
8 cups water
2 tablespoons canola oil
1 onion, finely sliced
1 teaspoon ginger garlic paste
1/4 teaspoon red curry paste
2 small-sized potatoes, peeled and diced

1 green chili pepper, finely chopped
Sea salt and freshly ground black pepper, to taste
1/2 teaspoon turmeric powder
1/2 teaspoon avocado powder
2 tomatoes, pureed
1 tablespoon fenugreek, chopped

DIRECTIONS

Add the red kidney beans and water to the inner pot of your Instant Pot.
Secure the lid. Choose the "Bean/Chili" mode and cook for 25 minutes at High pressure. Once cooking is complete, use a quick pressure release; carefully remove the lid. Drain and reserve.
Press the "Sauté" button and heat the oil until sizzling. Now, sauté the onion until tender and translucent.
Add the remaining ingredients. Gently stir to combine.
Secure the lid. Choose the "Manual" mode and cook for 4 minutes at High pressure. Once cooking is complete, use a quick pressure release; carefully remove the lid.
Stir the reserved beans into the potato mixture and serve warm. Bon appétit!

464. Masala Sweet Corn

(Ready in about 10 minutes | Servings 4)

Per serving: 124 Calories; 6.7g Fat; 16.1g Carbs; 2.8g Protein; 3.1g Sugars

INGREDIENTS

2 cups sweet corn kernels, frozen
2 tablespoons ghee
1/2 teaspoon turmeric powder

Himalayan salt and ground black pepper, to taste
1/2 teaspoon red chili powder
1/2 teaspoon chaat masala powder

DIRECTIONS

Place all ingredients in the inner pot of your Instant Pot.
Secure the lid. Choose the "Manual" mode and cook for 4 minutes at High pressure. Once cooking is complete, use a quick pressure release; carefully remove the lid.
Serve immediately.

465. Okra in Tomato Sauce

(Ready in about 25 minutes | Servings 5)

Per serving: 162 Calories; 4.5g Fat; 27.8g Carbs; 7.8g Protein; 8.7g Sugars

INGREDIENTS

1 tablespoon olive oil
2 shallots, chopped
1 cup tomato puree
4 tablespoons tomato ketchup

2 pounds okra
1 cup chicken stock
1 teaspoon garlic powder
1 teaspoon turmeric powder

1 teaspoon porcini powder
1 teaspoon fish sauce
Sea salt and ground black pepper, to taste

DIRECTIONS

Press the "Sauté" button and heat the oil until sizzling. Now, sauté the shallot until tender and fragrant.

Add in the remaining ingredients and gently stir to combine well.

Secure the lid. Choose the "Manual" mode and cook for 5 minutes at High pressure. Once cooking is complete, use a natural pressure release for 15 minutes; carefully remove the lid.

Divide between serving bowls and serve warm. Bon appétit!

466. Authentic Cauliflower Kurma

(Ready in about 30 minutes | Servings 4)

Per serving: 216 Calories; 11.2g Fat; 28.1g Carbs; 6g Protein; 14.3g Sugars

INGREDIENTS

2 cups cauliflower florets
2 tablespoons grapeseed oil
1 teaspoon cumin seeds
1 teaspoon fennel seeds
1 dried red chili pepper, minced
1 onion, chopped

1 cup tomato puree
Kosher salt and ground black pepper, to taste
1 teaspoon turmeric powder
1 cup fresh coconut, shredded
2 cups water

Tempering:
1 tablespoon peanut oil
1 teaspoon cumin seeds
4 curry leaves

DIRECTIONS

Add 1 cup of water and a steamer basket to the inner pot of your Instant Pot. Place the cauliflower florets in the steamer basket.

Secure the lid. Choose the "Steam" mode and cook for 3 minutes at High pressure. Once cooking is complete, use a quick pressure release; carefully remove the lid. Drain and reserve.

Press the "Sauté" button and heat the grapeseed oil until sizzling. Now, sauté the cumin seeds and fennel seeds for 30 seconds.

Stir in the chili pepper and onion and continue to sauté an additional 2 to 3 minutes. Add the tomato puree and let it cook on the lowest setting for 3 minutes longer. Add the salt, black pepper, turmeric, coconut, and water.

Secure the lid. Choose the "Manual" mode and cook for 5 minutes at High pressure. Once cooking is complete, use a natural pressure release for 10 minutes; carefully remove the lid. Stir in the steamed cauliflower florets.

Meanwhile, heat the peanut oil in a cast-iron skillet over medium heat. Cook the cumin seeds and curry leaves until they are fragrant. Stir the tempering into the cauliflower mixture and serve warm.

467. Roasted Herbed Baby Potatoes

(Ready in about 15 minutes | Servings 4)

Per serving: 198 Calories; 7.1g Fat; 30.3g Carbs; 4.1g Protein; 1.3g Sugars

INGREDIENTS

1 ½ pounds baby potatoes, scrubbed
2 garlic cloves, smashed
1/2 cup roasted vegetable broth
1/2 cup water

2 tablespoons olive oil
1/2 teaspoon paprika
1 teaspoon oregano
1 teaspoon basil

1 teaspoon rosemary
1/2 teaspoon sage
Sea salt and ground black pepper, to taste

DIRECTIONS

Pierce the baby potatoes with a fork; place them in the inner pot along with the garlic, broth, and water.

Secure the lid. Choose the "Manual" mode and cook for 10 minutes at High pressure. Once cooking is complete, use a quick pressure release; carefully remove the lid. Drain and reserve.

Press the "Sauté" button and heat the olive oil until sizzling. Now, sauté the seasonings for 30 seconds, stirring frequently. Throw the reserved potatoes into the inner pot.

Cook until they are browned and crisp on all sides. Serve warm.

468. Italian Caponata with Butternut Squash

(Ready in about 15 minutes | Servings 4)

Per serving: 194 Calories; 15.1g Fat; 13.5g Carbs; 3.4g Protein; 5.3g Sugars

INGREDIENTS

4 tablespoons olive oil
1 onion, diced
2 garlic cloves, minced
Sea salt and ground black pepper
1 cup butternut squash, cut into 1/2-inch chunks

4 bell peppers, cut into 1/2-inch chunks
1 cup vine-ripened tomatoes, pureed
1 tablespoon Italian seasoning mix
4 tablespoons Parmigiano-Reggiano cheese, grated

DIRECTIONS

Press the "Sauté" button and heat the olive oil until sizzling. Now, sauté the onion until tender and translucent.

Stir in the garlic and continue to sauté an additional 30 seconds, stirring frequently.

Stir in the salt, black pepper, butternut squash, peppers, tomatoes, and Italian seasoning mix.

Secure the lid. Choose the "Manual" mode and cook for 4 minutes at High pressure. Once cooking is complete, use a quick pressure release; carefully remove the lid.

Afterwards, scatter the grated cheese over the caponata and serve warm. Bon appétit!

469. Spicy Red Lentils

(Ready in about 10 minutes | Servings 4)

Per serving: 242 Calories; 1g Fat; 47.5g Carbs; 15.1g Protein; 9.3g Sugars

INGREDIENTS

1 cup red lentils
2 cups water
1 sweet pepper, seeded and chopped
1 habanero pepper, seeded and chopped

1 medium-sized leek, sliced
1 teaspoon garlic, pressed
Kosher salt and ground black pepper, to taste
1/4 cup fresh cilantro, roughly chopped

DIRECTIONS

Add all ingredients, except for the fresh cilantro, to the inner pot of your Instant Pot.

Secure the lid. Choose the "Manual" mode and cook for 2 minutes at High pressure. Once cooking is complete, use a quick pressure release; carefully remove the lid.

Spoon the lentil mixture into a nice serving bowl. Serve garnished with fresh cilantro and enjoy!

470. Maple-Orange Glazed Root Vegetables

(Ready in about 20 minutes | Servings 5)

Per serving: 131 Calories; 4.9g Fat; 20.8g Carbs; 2.4g Protein; 13.4g Sugars

INGREDIENTS

1 pound carrots
1/2 pound yellow beets
1/2 pound red beets
2 tablespoons cold butter

2 tablespoons orange juice
1 teaspoon orange peel, finely shredded
1 tablespoon maple syrup
Kosher salt and ground black pepper, to taste

DIRECTIONS

Place 1 cup of water and a steamer basket in your Instant Pot. Place the carrots and beets in the steamer basket.

Secure the lid. Choose the "Steam" mode and cook for 10 minutes at High pressure. Once cooking is complete, use a quick pressure release; carefully remove the lid.

Peel the carrots and beets and reserve; slice them into bite-sized pieces.

Press the "Sauté" button and choose the lowest setting. Cut in butter and add the remaining ingredients.

Drain the carrots and beets and add them back to the inner pot; let them cook until your vegetables are nicely coated with the glaze or about 5 minutes. Bon appétit!

471. Roasted Cauliflower with Tahini Sauce

(Ready in about 15 minutes | Servings 4)

Per serving: 185 Calories; 14.2g Fat; 12.8g Carbs; 5.4g Protein; 3.7g Sugars

INGREDIENTS

1 pound cauliflower florets
1 tablespoon olive oil
1/3 cup tahini
2 tablespoons freshly squeezed lemon juice

2 cloves garlic, grated
1 teaspoon agave syrup
Kosher salt and freshly ground black pepper, to taste
2 tablespoons fresh parsley, chopped

DIRECTIONS

Place 1 cup of water and a steamer basket in your Instant Pot. Place the cauliflower florets in the steamer basket.

Secure the lid. Choose the "Steam" mode and cook for 3 minutes at High pressure. Once cooking is complete, use a quick pressure release; carefully remove the lid.

Press the "Sauté" button and heat the oil. Roast the cauliflower florets for 2 to 3 minutes, stirring periodically to ensure even cooking.

Whisk the tahini, lemon juice, garlic agave syrup, salt, and black pepper until everything is well incorporated. Drizzle the tahini sauce over the roasted cauliflower and garnish with fresh parsley. Enjoy!

472. The Best Sweet Potatoes Ever

(Ready in about 30 minutes | Servings 5)

Per serving: 196 Calories; 9.3g Fat; 26.7g Carbs; 2.1g Protein; 8.7g Sugars

INGREDIENTS

5 medium sweet potatoes, scrubbed
1 cup water
1/2 stick butter

DIRECTIONS

Place 1 cup of water and a steamer basket in your Instant Pot. Place the sweet potatoes in the steamer basket.

Secure the lid. Choose the "Manual" mode and cook for 15 minutes at High pressure. Once cooking is complete, use a natural pressure release for 10 minutes; carefully remove the lid.

Garnish with butter and serve. Bon appétit!

473. Easy and Healthy Vegetable Mash

(Ready in about 10 minutes | Servings 4)

Per serving: 134 Calories; 6.3g Fat; 19.8g Carbs; 2g Protein; 6.9g Sugars

INGREDIENTS

1/2 pound carrots, quartered
1/2 pound parsnip, quartered
1/2 pound pumpkin, cut into small pieces
2 tablespoons butter

2 cloves garlic, crushed
1/2 teaspoon basil
1/2 teaspoon thyme
1/2 teaspoon rosemary

DIRECTIONS

Add the carrots, parsnips, and pumpkin to the inner pot of your Instant Pot. Pour in 1 cup of water.

Secure the lid. Choose the "Manual" mode and cook for 6 minutes at High pressure. Once cooking is complete, use a quick pressure release; carefully remove the lid.

Drain your vegetables and mash them with a potato masher.

Press the "Sauté" button and melt the butter; the, sauté the aromatics for 1 minute or so. Add the vegetable mash and stir to combine well. Transfer to a nice serving bowls and garnish with some extra herbs if desired. Bon appétit!

474. Smoked Sausage Stuffed Mushrooms

(Ready in about 15 minutes | Servings 5)

Per serving: 254 Calories; 20.3g Fat; 7.2g Carbs; 11.5g Protein; 2.7g Sugars

INGREDIENTS

20 button mushrooms, stems removed
1/2 pound smoked pork sausage, crumbled
1 shallot, finely chopped
2 cloves garlic, minced
4 ounces cream cheese, softened

1/2 cup seasoned breadcrumbs
1/2 cup cheddar cheese, shredded
1/2 cup vegetable broth
2 tablespoons fresh parsley leaves, roughly chopped

DIRECTIONS

Clean your mushrooms and set them aside.

Press the "Sauté" button to preheat your Instant Pot. Then, brown the sausage until it is fully cooked.

Stir in the shallot and garlic; cook for a further 4 minutes, or until they have softened. Scoop this mixture out of the inner pot into a mixing bowl. Stir in the cream cheese, breadcrumbs, and cheddar cheese.

Now, add a splash of the vegetable broth to deglaze the pan. Press the "Cancel" button.

Next, fill the mushroom caps with the stuffing mixture. Arrange the mushrooms in the bottom of the inner pot.

Secure the lid. Choose the "Manual" mode and cook for 5 minutes at High pressure. Once cooking is complete, use a quick pressure release; carefully remove the lid.

Sprinkle fresh parsley leaves on top before serving and enjoy!

475. Millet with Roasted Tomatoes

(Ready in about 45 minutes | Servings 6)

Per serving: 162 Calories; 3.8g Fat; 27.2g Carbs; 4.5g Protein; 2.7g Sugars

INGREDIENTS

1 pound small-sized tomatoes, halved
1 tablespoon olive oil
Sea salt and ground black pepper, to taste

1 cup millet
2 cups water

DIRECTIONS

Preheat your oven to 350 degrees F. Place your tomatoes in a roasting pan. Drizzle olive oil over them; season with salt and pepper. Roast for about 35 minutes or until the tomatoes are soft.

Meanwhile, combine the millet with water in the inner pot of your Instant Pot.

Secure the lid. Choose the "Manual" mode and cook for 9 minutes at High pressure. Once cooking is complete, use a natural pressure release for 10 minutes; carefully remove the lid.

Add the roasted tomatoes to the warm millet and serve immediately.

476. Chickpea and Avocado Bowl

(Ready in about 1 hour | Servings 6)

Per serving: 190 Calories; 7g Fat; 26.2g Carbs; 8g Protein; 5.1g Sugars

INGREDIENTS

1 cup chickpeas, rinsed
1 teaspoon sea salt
1 teaspoon baking soda
1 avocado, peeled, pitted, and sliced
1/2 cup scallions, sliced
1 cup cherry tomatoes, halved

1 bell pepper, sliced
1/4 cup olive oil
2 tablespoons fresh lemon juice
1/4 teaspoon curry powder
Sea salt and ground black pepper, to taste

DIRECTIONS

Add the dry chickpeas to the inner pot; pour in 6 cups of water. Add the sea salt and baking soda.

Secure the lid. Choose the "Manual" mode and cook for 35 minutes at High pressure. Once cooking is complete, use a natural pressure release for 20 minutes; carefully remove the lid.

Drain and transfer to a nice serving bowl. Toss the cooked chickpeas with the other ingredients; toss to combine well. Bon appétit!

477. Parmesan Brussels Sprouts

(Ready in about 15 minutes | Servings 6)

Per serving: 184 Calories; 15.8g Fat; 10.1g Carbs; 3.9g Protein; 2.5g Sugars

INGREDIENTS

1 ½ pounds Brussels sprouts, trimmed and halved
1 stick butter
1/2 teaspoon basil
1 teaspoon rosemary

1 teaspoon garlic, minced
1 teaspoon shallot powder
Sea salt and red pepper, to taste

DIRECTIONS

Place 1 cup of water and a steamer basket in the inner pot of your Instant Pot. Place the Brussels sprouts in the steamer basket.

Secure the lid. Choose the "Steam" mode and cook for 3 minutes at High pressure. Once cooking is complete, use a quick pressure release; carefully remove the lid.

Press the "Sauté" button and melt the butter; once hot, cook the basil, rosemary, and garlic for 40 seconds or until aromatic.

Add in the Brussels sprouts, shallot powder, salt, and pepper. Press the "Cancel" button. Scatter the grated parmesan cheese over the Brussels sprouts and serve immediately. Bon appétit!

EGGS & DAIRY

478. Easiest Hard-Boiled Eggs Ever

(Ready in about 15 minutes | Servings 3)

Per serving: 106 Calories; 6.9g Fat; 0.6g Carbs; 9.2g Protein; 0.3g Sugars

INGREDIENTS

5 eggs
1/2 teaspoon salt
1/4 teaspoon red pepper flakes, crushed
2 tablespoons fresh chives, chopped

DIRECTIONS

Place 1 cup of water and a steamer rack in the inner pot. Arrange the eggs on the rack.
Secure the lid. Choose the "Manual" mode and cook for 5 minutes at High pressure. Once cooking is complete, use a quick pressure release; carefully remove the lid.
Transfer the eggs to icy-cold water. Now, let them sit in the water bath a few minutes until cool.
Peel your eggs and season with salt and red pepper. Serve garnished with freshly chopped chives. Enjoy!

479. Cheesy Hash Brown Egg Bake

(Ready in about 30 minutes | Servings 3)

Per serving: 475 Calories; 38g Fat; 17.6g Carbs; 13.6g Protein; 2.9g Sugars

INGREDIENTS

3 ounces bacon, chopped
1 onion, chopped
1 cup frozen hash browns
5 eggs
1/4 cup milk

1/3 cup Swiss cheese, shredded
1 teaspoon garlic powder
1/4 teaspoon turmeric powder
Kosher salt and ground black pepper, to taste

DIRECTIONS

Place 1 cup of water and a metal trivet in the inner pot.
Press the "Sauté" button and cook the bacon until it is crisp and browned. Add in the onions and cook for 3 to 4 minutes, stirring occasionally.
Stir in the frozen hash browns and cook until slightly thawed. Grease an oven-proof dish with cooking oil.
In a mixing bowl, whisk the eggs, milk, shredded cheese, garlic powder, turmeric powder, salt and black pepper; now add the bacon/onion mixture to the egg mixture.
Spoon the egg mixture into the prepared dish. Lower the dish onto the trivet.
Secure the lid. Choose the "Manual" mode and cook for 20 minutes at High pressure. Once cooking is complete, use a quick pressure release; carefully remove the lid. Bon appétit!

480. Mini Egg Frittatas with Cheese

(Ready in about 10 minutes | Servings 3)

Per serving: 277 Calories; 22.3g Fat; 4.7g Carbs; 14.6g Protein; 3.4g Sugars

INGREDIENTS

6 eggs
1/4 cup milk
1/2 teaspoon cayenne pepper
Sea salt and ground black pepper, to taste
1/2 cup cream cheese

DIRECTIONS

Place 1 cup of water and a metal trivet in the inner pot.
Mix all ingredients until everything is well incorporated. Pour the egg mixture into silicone molds.
Lower the molds onto the prepared trivet.
Secure the lid. Choose the "Manual" mode and cook for 5 minutes at High pressure. Once cooking is complete, use a quick pressure release; carefully remove the lid. Bon appétit!

481. Cocktail Party Deviled Eggs

(Ready in about 10 minutes | Servings 6)

Per serving: 93 Calories; 6.5g Fat; 1.6g Carbs; 6.7g Protein; 0.8g Sugars

INGREDIENTS

6 eggs
1/4 cup Cottage cheese, crumbled
1 tablespoon butter, softened

2 tablespoons fresh parsley, minced
1 teaspoon paprika
Sea salt and ground black pepper, to taste

DIRECTIONS

Place 1 cup of water and a steamer rack in the inner pot. Arrange the eggs on the rack.

Secure the lid. Choose the "Manual" mode and cook for 5 minutes at High pressure. Once cooking is complete, use a quick pressure release; carefully remove the lid.

Peel the eggs and slice them into halves.

In a mixing bowl, thoroughly combine the Cottage cheese, butter, parsley, paprika, sea salt, and black pepper. Stir in the egg yolks. Stir to combine well.

Use a piping bag to fill the egg white halves. Place on a nice serving platter and enjoy!

482. Dilled Stuffed Eggs

(Ready in about 10 minutes | Servings 5)

Per serving: 209 Calories; 16.6g Fat; 1.6g Carbs; 12g Protein; 0.9g Sugars

INGREDIENTS

10 eggs
1/2 teaspoon coarse sea salt
1/4 teaspoon black pepper, to taste
1/2 teaspoon turmeric powder

2 teaspoons balsamic vinegar
2 tablespoons Greek-style yogurt
4 tablespoons mayonnaise
1 teaspoon fresh dill, chopped

DIRECTIONS

Place 1 cup of water and a steamer rack in the inner pot. Arrange the eggs on the rack.

Secure the lid. Choose the "Manual" mode and cook for 5 minutes at High pressure. Once cooking is complete, use a quick pressure release; carefully remove the lid.

Peel the eggs and slice them into halves.

In a mixing bowl, thoroughly combine the sea salt, black pepper, turmeric powder, vinegar, yogurt, and mayonnaise. Stir in the egg yolks.

Use a piping bag to fill the egg white halves. Garnish with fresh dill. Bon appétit!

483. Easy Homemade Yogurt

(Ready in about 9 hours | Servings 12)

Per serving: 99 Calories; 5.6g Fat; 7.7g Carbs; 5.2g Protein; 8.2g Sugars

INGREDIENTS

2 quarts milk
2 tablespoons prepared yogurt with cultures
A pinch of salt

DIRECTIONS

Pour the milk into the inner pot. Press the "Yogurt" button; adjust the temperature until the screen reads "Boil".

Let it sit for 5 minutes and then remove the inner pot. Allow the milk to cool to about 115 degrees F. Whisk in the prepared yogurt with the cultures; add a pinch of salt.

Add the inner pot back to the Instant Pot.

Secure the lid. Choose the "Yogurt" mode and adjust until the screen reads 8:00. Once the cycle is complete, remove the lid.

Transfer the prepared yogurt to your refrigerator until ready to use. Bon appétit!

484. Mexican-Style Omelet with Chanterelles

(Ready in about 30 minutes | Servings 4)

Per serving: 333 Calories; 26.6g Fat; 8.6g Carbs; 16.2g Protein; 3.9g Sugars

INGREDIENTS

1 tablespoon olive oil
1 medium onion, chopped
2 cloves garlic, minced
1 cup Mexica cheese blend, crumbled
1 cup Chanterelle mushrooms, chopped

1 bell pepper, sliced
1 Poblano pepper, seeded and minced
5 eggs
4 ounces cream cheese
Sea salt and ground black pepper, to taste

DIRECTIONS

Add 1 cup of water and a metal rack to the inner pot of your Instant Pot. Spray a souffle dish and set aside.
Mix all ingredients until well combined. Scrape the mixture into the prepared dish. Lower the souffle dish onto the rack.
Secure the lid. Choose the "Manual" mode and cook for 11 minutes at High pressure. Once cooking is complete, use a natural pressure release for 15 minutes; carefully remove the lid.
Serve with salsa if desired. Enjoy!

485. Authentic Spanish Tortilla

(Ready in about 30 minutes | Servings 4)

Per serving: 398 Calories; 26.7g Fat; 22.6g Carbs; 18.2g Protein; 4.3g Sugars

INGREDIENTS

8 eggs
8 ounces hash browns
1 ½ tablespoons olive oil
1 onion, sliced
Sea salt and ground black pepper, or to taste

1 teaspoon taco seasoning mix
1 teaspoon fresh garlic, minced
1/3 cup milk
4 ounces Manchego cheese, grated

DIRECTIONS

Add 1 cup of water and a metal rack to the inner pot of your Instant Pot. Spritz a souffle dish with nonstick cooking oil.
In a mixing bowl, thoroughly combine all ingredients, except for the Manchego cheese; mix until everything is well incorporated. Scrape the mixture into the prepared souffle dish.
Secure the lid. Choose the "Manual" mode and cook for 17 minutes at High pressure. Once cooking is complete, use a natural pressure release for 10 minutes; carefully remove the lid.
Top with Manchego cheese and seal the lid again. Let it sit in the residual heat until the cheese melts. Enjoy!

486. Mini Pancakes with Raisins

(Ready in about 25 minutes | Servings 4)

Per serving: 276 Calories; 6.7g Fat; 47.3g Carbs; 8.5g Protein; 18g Sugars

INGREDIENTS

1 cup all-purpose flour
2 teaspoons baking powder
1 teaspoon salt
1/4 cup milk

2 eggs, whisked
2 tablespoons maple syrup
1/2 cup raisins
2 tablespoons almonds, chopped

DIRECTIONS

Add 1 cup of water and a metal trivet to the inner pot.
Mix all ingredients until everything is well combined. Pour the batter into a muffin tin that is previously greased with cooking spray. Lower the muffin tin onto the trivet.
Secure the lid. Choose the "Manual" mode and cook for 8 minutes at High pressure. Once cooking is complete, use a natural pressure release for 10 minutes; carefully remove the lid. Bon appétit!

487. Egg Muffins with Ham and Cheese

(Ready in about 15 minutes | Servings 4)

Per serving: 369 Calories; 23.7g Fat; 6.5g Carbs; 31.3g Protein; 1.5g Sugars

INGREDIENTS

8 eggs
1/4 teaspoon ground black pepper, or more to taste
1 teaspoon paprika
Sea salt, to taste
1 cup green peppers, seeded and chopped
8 ounces ham, chopped

1/2 cup sour cream
1/2 cup Swiss cheese, shredded
2 tablespoons parsley, chopped
2 tablespoons cilantro, chopped
2 tablespoons scallions, chopped

DIRECTIONS

Mix all ingredients until everything is well combined.

Add 1 cup of water and a metal rack to the inner pot of your Instant Pot.

Spoon the prepared mixture into silicone molds. Lower the molds onto the prepared trivet.

Secure the lid. Choose the "Manual" mode and cook for 6 minutes at High pressure. Once cooking is complete, use a quick pressure release; carefully remove the lid. Bon appétit!

488. Home-Style Fresh Cream Cheese

(Ready in about 20 minutes + chilling time | Servings 10)

Per serving: 124 Calories; 7.2g Fat; 12.1g Carbs; 3.3g Protein; 11.9g Sugars

INGREDIENTS

3 ½ cups whole milk
1 cup double cream

1 teaspoon kosher salt
2 tablespoons lemon juice

DIRECTIONS

Place the milk, double cream, and salt in the inner pot of your Instant Pot and stir to combine well.

Secure the lid. Choose the "Manual" mode and cook for 5 minutes at Low pressure. Once cooking is complete, use a natural pressure release for 10 minutes; carefully remove the lid.

Add the lemon juice and stir the mixture one more time.

Line a strainer with cheesecloth and pour the mixture into the cheesecloth. Allow the curds to continue to drain in the strainer for about 1 hour. Discard the whey.

Pat your cheese into a ball and remove from the cheesecloth. This cheese will last about a week in your refrigerator. Bon appétit!

489. Delicious Mac and Cheese

(Ready in about 15 minutes | Servings 6)

Per serving: 518 Calories; 25.9g Fat; 46.2g Carbs; 24.3g Protein; 2.6g Sugars

INGREDIENTS

12 ounces elbow macaroni
2 tablespoons butter
1/2 teaspoon celery seeds
Kosher salt, to taste

3 cups water
4 ounces milk
2 ½ cups cheddar cheese, shredded
1 cup Parmesan cheese, shredded

DIRECTIONS

Throw the elbow macaroni, butter, celery seeds, salt, and water into the inner pot.

Secure the lid. Choose the "Manual" mode and cook for 5 minutes at High pressure. Once cooking is complete, use a quick pressure release; carefully remove the lid.

Next, stir in the milk and half of the cheeses. Stir until the cheeses has melted; add the second half of the cheeses and stir to combine well. The sauce will thicken as it cools. Bon appétit!

490. Mom's Cheese Dip

(Ready in about 15 minutes | Servings 10)

Per serving: 148 Calories; 11.3g Fat; 5.2g Carbs; 6.7g Protein; 2.4g Sugars

INGREDIENTS

1/2 stick butter
1/2 teaspoon onion powder
1/2 teaspoon garlic powder
1/4 teaspoon dried dill weed

Sea salt and ground black pepper, to taste
2 tablespoons tapioca starch
1 ½ cups whole milk
1 ½ cups Swiss cheese, grated

DIRECTIONS

Press the "Sauté" button and melt the butter. Now, add the onion powder, garlic powder, dill, salt, and black pepper. Stir in the tapioca starch and stir to combine well.

Gradually pour in the milk, stirring continuously to avoid clumps. Bring to a boil and press the "Cancel" button.

Add in the Swiss cheese and stir until the cheese has melted. Serve warm with breadsticks or veggie sticks. Bon appétit!

491. Italian Frittata with Mushrooms and Spinach

(Ready in about 15 minutes | Servings 4)

Per serving: 335 Calories; 26.5g Fat; 6.5g Carbs; 18.7g Protein; 2.6g Sugars

INGREDIENTS

6 eggs
1/4 cup double cream
1 cup Asiago cheese, shredded
Sea salt and freshly ground black pepper, to taste
1 teaspoon cayenne pepper
2 tablespoons olive oil

1 yellow onion, finely chopped
2 cloves garlic, minced
6 ounces Italian brown mushrooms, sliced
4 cups spinach, torn into pieces
1 tablespoon Italian seasoning mix

DIRECTIONS

In a mixing bowl, thoroughly combine the eggs, double cream, Asiago cheese, salt, black pepper, and cayenne pepper.

Grease a baking dish with olive oil. Add the remaining ingredients; stir in the egg mixture. Spoon the mixture into the prepared baking dish.

Place 1 cup of water and a metal trivet in the inner pot. Lower the baking dish onto the prepared trivet.

Secure the lid. Choose the "Manual" mode and cook for 5 minutes at High pressure. Once cooking is complete, use a quick pressure release; carefully remove the lid. Bon appétit!

492. Keto Cauliflower Mac n' Cheese

(Ready in about 15 minutes | Servings 4)

Per serving: 387 Calories; 31.2g Fat; 10.2g Carbs; 18.2g Protein; 3.8g Sugars

INGREDIENTS

1 pound cauliflower florets
1 cup heavy cream
4 ounces Ricotta cheese
1 ½ cups Cheddar cheese, shredded
Sea salt and ground white pepper, to taste

1/2 teaspoon garlic powder
1/2 teaspoon shallot powder
1/2 teaspoon celery seeds
1/2 teaspoon red pepper flakes
1/4 cup Parmesan cheese

DIRECTIONS

Place 1 cup of water and a steamer basket in the inner pot of your Instant Pot. Throw the cauliflower florets into the steamer basket.

Secure the lid. Choose the "Manual" mode and cook for 2 minutes at High pressure. Once cooking is complete, use a quick pressure release; carefully remove the lid. Drain and reserve.

Press the "Sauté" button and use the lowest setting. Now, cook the heavy cream, Ricotta cheese, Cheddar cheese, and spices; let it simmer until the cheeses has melted.

Add in the cauliflower and gently stir to combine. Scatter the Parmesan cheese over the cauliflower and cheese and serve warm. Bon appétit!

493. Spanish Dip de Queso

(Ready in about 10 minutes | Servings 10)

Per serving: 146 Calories; 11.2g Fat; 5.1g Carbs; 6.6g Protein; 3.3g Sugars

INGREDIENTS

3 tablespoons butter
3 tablespoons all-purpose flour
1 cup whole milk

8 ounces Monterey Jack, shredded
Kosher salt, to taste
1/2 teaspoon hot sauce

DIRECTIONS

Press the "Sauté" button and melt the butter. Now, add the flour and stir to combine well.

Gradually pour in the milk, stirring continuously to avoid clumps. Bring to a boil and press the "Cancel" button.

Add in the Monterey Jack cheese and stir until cheese has melted; add the salt and hot sauce. Serve warm with tortilla chips if desired. Bon appétit!

SNACKS & APPETIZERS

494. Kid-Friendly Pizza Dip

(Ready in about 25 minutes | Servings 10)

Per serving: 158 Calories; 11.8g Fat; 6.9g Carbs; 5.7g Protein; 3.9g Sugars

INGREDIENTS

10 ounces cream cheese
1 cup tomato sauce
1/2 cup mozzarella cheese, shredded
1/2 cup green olives, pitted and sliced

1/2 teaspoon oregano
1/2 teaspoon basil
1/2 teaspoon garlic salt
1/2 cup Romano cheese, shredded

DIRECTIONS

Add 1 ½ cups of water and metal trivet to the inner pot. Spritz a souffle dish with cooking spray.
Place the cream cheese on the bottom of the souffle dish. Add the tomato sauce and mozzarella cheese. Scatter sliced olives over the top.
Add the oregano, basil, and garlic salt. Top with Romano cheese. Lower the dish onto the prepared trivet.
Secure the lid. Choose the "Manual" mode and cook for 18 minutes at High pressure. Once cooking is complete, use a quick pressure release; carefully remove the lid.
Serve with chips or breadsticks if desired. Enjoy!

495. Spicy Beer Little Smokies

(Ready in about 10 minutes | Servings 12)

Per serving: 209 Calories; 16.1g Fat; 11.5g Carbs; 7g Protein; 6.2g Sugars

INGREDIENTS

16 ounces little smokies
1/2 cup roasted vegetable broth
1/2 cup light beer
14 ounces grape jelly

2 tablespoons white vinegar
1/3 cup chili sauce
1/3 brown sugar
1 jalapeno, minced

DIRECTIONS

Place all ingredients in the inner pot of your Instant Pot.
Secure the lid. Choose the "Manual" mode and cook for 2 minutes at High pressure. Once cooking is complete, use a quick pressure release; carefully remove the lid.
Serve hot or keep on warm in your Instant Pot until ready to serve.

496. Nacho Bean Dip

(Ready in about 35 minutes | Servings 10)

Per serving: 146 Calories; 4.8g Fat; 17.3g Carbs; 8.1g Protein; 2.5g Sugars

INGREDIENTS

1 tablespoon olive oil
1 onion, chopped
2 cloves garlic, minced
1 red chili pepper, finely chopped
1 cup pinto beans, rinsed
1/2 cup chunky salsa
2 cups vegetable broth

1 teaspoon ground cumin
Kosher salt and ground black pepper, to taste
1 ounce package taco seasoning mix
1 cup Cheddar cheese, shredded
1 cup queso fresco cheese, crumbled
2 tablespoons fresh cilantro, chopped

DIRECTIONS

Press the "Sauté" button and heat the olive oil until sizzling. Once hot, cook the onion for 3 to 4 minutes or until tender and fragrant.
After that, stir in the garlic and chili pepper; continue sautéing an additional 30 to 40 seconds.
Stir in the beans, salsa, broth, cumin, salt, black pepper, and taco seasoning mix.
Secure the lid. Choose the "Bean/Chili" mode and cook for 25 minutes at High pressure. Once cooking is complete, use a quick pressure release; carefully remove the lid.
Then, mash your beans with a potato masher or use your blender. Return to the Instant Pot and press the "Sauté" button; stir in the cheese and let it melt on the lowest setting. Serve garnished with cilantro and enjoy!

497. Zingy Cilantro Lime Wings

(Ready in about 30 minutes | Servings 4)

Per serving: 108 Calories; 4.3g Fat; 3.3g Carbs; 13.9g Protein; 0.9g Sugars

INGREDIENTS

2 teaspoons butter
8 chicken wings
3 cloves garlic, minced
1 teaspoon cayenne pepper
1/2 teaspoon smoked paprika

Sea salt and ground black pepper, to taste
1/2 cup chicken broth
1 lime, freshly squeezed
1/4 cup fresh cilantro, chopped

DIRECTIONS

Press the "Sauté" button and heat the olive oil until sizzling. Once hot, brown the chicken wings for 2 to 3 minutes per side.
Add in the remaining ingredients and toss to coat well.
Secure the lid. Choose the "Manual" mode and cook for 10 minutes at High pressure. Once cooking is complete, use a natural pressure release for 10 minutes; carefully remove the lid.
Broil the chicken wings for about 5 minutes or until they are golden brown. Bon appétit!

498. Easy Cocktail Meatballs

(Ready in about 20 minutes | Servings 8)

Per serving: 199 Calories; 9.1g Fat; 17.2g Carbs; 12.9g Protein; 11.4g Sugars

INGREDIENTS

1/2 pound ground chicken
1/2 pound ground turkey
1 egg
1 cup tortilla chips, crumbled
1 onion, finely chopped

2 garlic cloves, minced
1/2 teaspoon basil
Sea salt and ground black pepper, to taste
1 tablespoon olive oil
16 ounces grape jelly

DIRECTIONS

In a mixing bowl, thoroughly combine all ingredients, except for the olive oil and grape jelly. Shape the mixture into 24 meatballs.
Press the "Sauté" button and heat the olive oil. Once hot, brown meatballs for 3 to 4 minutes.
Add the grape jelly to the inner pot.
Secure the lid. Choose the "Manual" mode and cook for 6 minutes at High pressure. Once cooking is complete, use a natural pressure release for 5 minutes; carefully remove the lid.
Serve with cocktail sticks and enjoy!

499. Sinfully Delicious Cinnamon Popcorn

(Ready in about 10 minutes | Servings 4)

Per serving: 295 Calories; 11.5g Fat; 42.2g Carbs; 6.3g Protein; 6.6g Sugars

INGREDIENTS

2 tablespoons coconut oil
1/2 cup popcorn kernels

1/4 cup icing sugar
1/2 tablespoon ground cinnamon

DIRECTIONS

Press the "Sauté" button and melt the coconut oil. Stir until it begins to simmer.
Stir in the popcorn kernels and cover. When the popping slows down, press the "Cancel" button.
Toss the freshly popped corn with icing sugar and cinnamon. Toss to evenly coat the popcorn and serve immediately.

500. Old-Fashioned Short Ribs

(Ready in about 1 hour 45 minutes | Servings 8)

Per serving: 372 Calories; 27.6g Fat; 4.9g Carbs; 25.7g Protein; 3.4g Sugars

INGREDIENTS

1 tablespoon lard
3 pounds short ribs
Sea salt and ground black pepper, to season
1/2 cup port wine
1 teaspoon cayenne pepper
2 tablespoons molasses

2 tablespoons rice vinegar
4 cloves of garlic
2 rosemary sprigs
2 thyme sprigs
1 cup beef bone broth

DIRECTIONS

Press the "Sauté" button and melt the lard. Once hot, cook the short ribs for 4 to 5 minutes, turning them periodically to ensure even cooking.
Add the other ingredients.
Secure the lid. Choose the "Manual" mode and cook for 90 minutes at High pressure. Once cooking is complete, use a natural pressure release; carefully remove the lid.
Afterwards, place the short ribs under the broiler until the outside is crisp or about 10 minutes. Transfer the ribs to a platter and serve immediately.

501. Chinese Sticky Baby Carrots

(Ready in about 10 minutes | Servings 6)

Per serving: 110 Calories; 4.5g Fat; 17.2g Carbs; 2.3g Protein; 8.1g Sugars

INGREDIENTS

2 pounds baby carrots, trimmed and scrubbed
1/2 cup orange juice
1/2 cup water
2 tablespoons raisins
2 tablespoons soy sauce
2 tablespoons Shaoxing wine

1 teaspoon garlic powder
1/2 teaspoon shallot powder
1 teaspoon mustard powder
1/4 teaspoon cumin seeds
2 teaspoons butter, at room temperature
2 tablespoons sesame seeds, toasted

DIRECTIONS

Place all ingredients, except for the sesame seeds, in the inner pot of your Instant Pot.
Secure the lid. Choose the "Manual" mode and cook for 2 minutes at High pressure. Once cooking is complete, use a quick pressure release; carefully remove the lid.
Serve in a nice bowl, sprinkle the sesame seeds over the top and enjoy!

502. Artichokes with Greek Dipping Sauce

(Ready in about 20 minutes | Servings 4)

Per serving: 177 Calories; 10.9g Fat; 17.6g Carbs; 5.8g Protein; 2.1g Sugars

INGREDIENTS

4 artichokes
4 tablespoons mayonnaise
2 tablespoons Greek yogurt
1 tablespoon Dijon mustard
1/2 teaspoon tzatziki spice mix

DIRECTIONS

Place 1 cup of water and a steamer basket in the inner pot of your Instant Pot.
Place the artichokes in the steamer basket.
Secure the lid. Choose the "Manual" mode and cook for 11 minutes at High pressure. Once cooking is complete, use a quick pressure release; carefully remove the lid.
Meanwhile, whisk the remaining ingredients to prepare the sauce. Serve the artichokes with the Greek sauce on the side. Bon appétit!

503. Herbed Butter Mushrooms

(Ready in about 10 minutes | Servings 5)

Per serving: 88 Calories; 5.5g Fat; 7.6g Carbs; 5.2g Protein; 3.6g Sugars

INGREDIENTS

20 ounces button mushrooms, brushed clean
2 cloves garlic, minced
1 teaspoon onion powder
1 teaspoon dried basil
1/2 teaspoon dried oregano
1/2 teaspoon dried rosemary

1 teaspoon smoked paprika
Coarse sea salt and ground black pepper, to taste
1 cup vegetable broth
2 tablespoons butter
2 tablespoons tomato paste

DIRECTIONS

Place the mushrooms, garlic, spices, and broth in the inner pot.

Secure the lid. Choose the "Manual" mode and cook for 4 minutes at High pressure. Once cooking is complete, use a quick pressure release; carefully remove the lid.

Now, stir in the butter and tomato paste. Serve with cocktail sticks or toothpicks. Enjoy!

504. Candied Nuts with Sultanas

(Ready in about 25 minutes | Servings 12)

Per serving: 149 Calories; 9.5g Fat; 14.6g Carbs; 2.8g Protein; 9.1g Sugars

INGREDIENTS

1 cup pecans halves
1 cup almonds
1 cup canned chickpeas
2 tablespoons sunflower seeds
2 tablespoons pumpkin seeds
2 tablespoons butter

1/2 cup maple syrup
1/4 teaspoon grated nutmeg
1/4 teaspoon ground ginger
1/4 teaspoon kosher salt
1 cup Sultanas

DIRECTIONS

Place all ingredients, except for the Sultanas, in the inner pot of your Instant Pot. Stir to combine well.

Press the "Sauté" button and cook until the butter has melted and the nuts are well coated.

Secure the lid. Choose the "Manual" mode and cook for 10 minutes at High pressure. Once cooking is complete, use a quick pressure release; carefully remove the lid.

Bake on a roasting pan at 370 degrees F for about 8 minutes. Add the Sultanas and stir to combine. Bon appétit!

505. Authentic Greek Fava Dip

(Ready in about 50 minutes | Servings 10)

Per serving: 178 Calories; 2.5g Fat; 29.4g Carbs; 11g Protein; 1.7g Sugars

INGREDIENTS

1 tablespoon olive oil
1 red onion, finely chopped
1 teaspoon garlic, minced
Sea salt and ground black pepper, to taste
1 pound fava beans, rinsed

1 teaspoon basil
1 teaspoon oregano
Juice of 1/2 lemon
1/2 cup Kalamata olives, pitted
1 tablespoon fresh mint leaves, roughly chopped

DIRECTIONS

Press the "Sauté" button and heat the oil. Once hot, cook the onion until tender and translucent.

Now, stir in the garlic and let it cook for 30 seconds more, stirring frequently. Then, add the salt, pepper, fava beans, basil, and oregano. Add enough water to fully submerge the beans.

Secure the lid. Choose the "Bean/Chili" mode and cook for 40 minutes at High pressure. Once cooking is complete, use a natural pressure release for 5 minutes; carefully remove the lid.

Add the lemon juice and puree the mixture with an immersion blender, Transfer to a nice serving bowl and serve garnished with Kalamata olives and mint leaves. Enjoy!

506. Buffalo Chicken Dip

(Ready in about 25 minutes | Servings 12)

Per serving: 219 Calories; 17g Fat; 2.6g Carbs; 14g Protein; 1.7g Sugars

INGREDIENTS

1 pound chicken breasts, chopped
10 ounces hot sauce
4 tablespoons butter
1 cup cream cheese, softened

Salt to taste
2 cups cheddar cheese, shredded
2 tablespoons fresh parsley, chopped
2 tablespoons fresh chives, chopped

DIRECTIONS

Add the chicken breasts to the inner pot of your Instant Pot; add in the hot sauce and butter.
Secure the lid. Choose the "Manual" mode and cook for 8 minutes at High pressure. Once cooking is complete, use a quick pressure release; carefully remove the lid.
Stir in the cream cheese and salt. Spoon chicken dip into a baking dish; top with the cheddar cheese and bake at 395 degrees F for about 8 minutes or until cheese is bubbling.
Scatter fresh parsley and chives over the top and serve warm.

507. Garlic Butter Shrimp

(Ready in about 10 minutes | Servings 8)

Per serving: 142 Calories; 6.2g Fat; 4.5g Carbs; 17.4g Protein; 3.3g Sugars

INGREDIENTS

1 ½ pounds shrimp, deveined
1/2 stick butter
1/4 cup soy sauce

2 garlic cloves, minced
Sea salt and ground black pepper, to taste
2 tablespoons fresh scallions, chopped

DIRECTIONS

Throw all ingredients, except for the scallions, into the inner pot of your Instant Pot.
Secure the lid. Choose the "Manual" mode and cook for 4 minutes at High pressure. Once cooking is complete, use a quick pressure release; carefully remove the lid.
Transfer your shrimp to a nice serving bowl. The sauce will thicken as it cools. Garnish with fresh scallions and serve with toothpicks.

508. Asian-Style Lettuce Wraps

(Ready in about 20 minutes | Servings 4)

Per serving: 179 Calories; 9.3g Fat; 9.7g Carbs; 13.7g Protein; 5.4g Sugars

INGREDIENTS

1/2 pound chicken breasts
2 teaspoons sesame oil
1 small onion, finely diced
2 garlic cloves, minced
1 teaspoon ginger, minced

Kosher salt and ground black pepper, to taste
2 tablespoons hoisin sauce
2 tablespoons soy sauce
2 tablespoons rice vinegar
1 small head butter lettuce, leaves separated

DIRECTIONS

Add the chicken breasts and 1 cup of water to the inner pot of your Instant Pot.
Secure the lid. Choose the "Manual" mode and cook for 8 minutes at High pressure. Once cooking is complete, use a quick pressure release; carefully remove the lid. Shred your chicken with two forks.
Press the "Sauté" button and heat the oil. Once hot, cook the onion and garlic for 3 to 4 minutes or until they are softened.
Now, add the chicken and cook for 2 to 3 minutes more. Add the ginger, salt, black pepper, hoisin sauce, soy sauce, and rice vinegar; let it cook for a few minutes more.
Spoon the chicken mixture into the lettuce leaves, wrap them and serve immediately. Bon appétit!

509. Taco Mini Stuffed Peppers

(Ready in about 20 minutes | Servings 5)

Per serving: 234 Calories; 15.7g Fat; 11.9g Carbs; 13.3g Protein; 5.7g Sugars

INGREDIENTS

4 ounces bacon, chopped
1 small onion, chopped
1 garlic clove, minced
6 ounces Mexican cheese blend, crumbled

1 teaspoon Worcestershire sauce
1 teaspoon Taco seasoning mix
10 mini sweet bell peppers, seeds and membranes removed
2 tablespoons fresh cilantro, finely chopped

DIRECTIONS

Press the "Sauté" button to preheat your Instant Pot. Now, cook the bacon until it is crisp; crumble with a spatula and reserve.

Now, cook the onion and garlic in pan drippings until just tender and fragrant. Add the cheese, Worcestershire sauce, and Taco seasoning mix. Stir in the reserved bacon.

Evenly divide the bacon/cheese mixture among the peppers.

Place a metal trivet and 1 cup of water in your Instant Pot. Arrange the stuffed peppers onto the trivet.

Secure the lid. Choose the "Manual" mode and cook for 5 minutes at High pressure. Once cooking is complete, use a natural pressure release for 5 minutes; carefully remove the lid.

Serve on a platter garnished with fresh cilantro. Enjoy!

510. Polenta Bites with Cheese and Herbs

(Ready in about 20 minutes | Servings 8)

Per serving: 181 Calories; 8.2g Fat; 22.6g Carbs; 4.1g Protein; 2.7g Sugars

INGREDIENTS

1 cup cornmeal
3 cups water
1 cup milk
1 teaspoon kosher salt
1 tablespoon butter
1/2 cup cream cheese
2 tablespoons cilantro, finely chopped

2 tablespoons chives, finely chopped
1 tablespoon thyme
1 teaspoon rosemary
1 teaspoon basil
1/2 cup bread crumbs
2 tablespoons olive oil

DIRECTIONS

Add the polenta, water, milk. and salt to the inner pot of your Instant Pot. Press the "Sauté" button and bring the mixture to a simmer. Press the "Cancel" button.

Secure the lid. Choose the "Manual" mode and cook for 8 minutes at High pressure. Once cooking is complete, use a quick pressure release; carefully remove the lid.

Grease a baking pan with butter. Add the cream cheese and herbs to your polenta.

Scoop the hot polenta into the prepared baking pan and refrigerate until firm. Cut into small squares. Spread the breadcrumbs on a large plate; coat each side of the polenta squares with breadcrumbs.

Heat the olive oil in a nonstick pan over medium heat; cook the polenta squares approximately 3 minutes per side or until golden brown. Bon appétit!

DESSERTS & DRINKS

511. Cranberry-Maple Rice Pudding

(Ready in about 20 minutes | Servings 4)

Per serving: 403 Calories; 6.6g Fat; 75.6g Carbs; 9.8g Protein; 31.9g Sugars

INGREDIENTS

1 cup white rice
1 ½ cups water
A pinch of salt
2 cups milk

1/3 cup maple syrup
2 eggs, beaten
1 teaspoon vanilla extract
1/4 teaspoon cardamom

A pinch of grated nutmeg
1/2 cup dried cranberries

DIRECTIONS

Place the rice, water, and salt in the inner pot of your Instant Pot.

Secure the lid. Choose the "Manual" mode and cook for 3 minutes at High pressure. Once cooking is complete, use a natural pressure release for 10 minutes; carefully remove the lid.

Add in the milk, maple syrup, eggs, vanilla extract, cardamom, and nutmeg; stir to combine well.

Press the "Sauté" button and cook, stirring frequently, until your pudding starts to boil. Press the "Cancel" button. Stir in the dried cranberries.

Pudding will thicken as it cools. Bon appétit!

512. Vegan Coconut Mini Cheesecakes

(Ready in about 45 minutes | Servings 4)

Per serving: 439 Calories; 39.2g Fat; 18.1g Carbs; 11.2g Protein; 8.5g Sugars

INGREDIENTS

1/2 cup almonds
1/2 cup sunflower kernels
6 dates, chopped
16 ounces coconut milk
3/4 cup coconut yogurt

DIRECTIONS

Spritz four ramekins with nonstick cooking spray.

Process the almonds, sunflower kernels, and dates in your blender until it turns into a sticky mixture.

Press the crust mixture into the prepared ramekins.

Thoroughly combine the coconut milk and yogurt in a mixing bowl. Pour this mixture into the ramekins and cover them with a piece of foil.

Place a metal trivet and 1 cup of water in your Instant Pot. Lower the ramekins onto the trivet.

Secure the lid. Choose the "Manual" mode and cook for 25 minutes at High pressure. Once cooking is complete, use a natural pressure release for 15 minutes; carefully remove the lid. Bon appétit!

513. Old-Fashioned Apple Cake

(Ready in about 1 hour 25 minutes | Servings 8)

Per serving: 304 Calories; 11.8g Fat; 49.7g Carbs; 2.6g Protein; 30.2g Sugars

INGREDIENTS

4 apples, peeled, cored and chopped
1/2 teaspoon ground cloves
1/2 teaspoon ground cardamom
1 teaspoon ground cinnamon

3 tablespoons sugar
1 1/3 cups flour
1 teaspoon baking powder
A pinch of salt

1 stick butter, melted
1/2 cup honey
2 tablespoons orange juice
1/2 teaspoon vanilla paste

DIRECTIONS

Grease and flour a cake pan and set it aside. Toss the apples with the ground cloves, cardamom. cinnamon and sugar.

In a mixing bowl, thoroughly combine the flour, baking powder and salt.

In another mixing bowl, mix the butter, honey, orange juice, and vanilla paste. Stir the wet ingredients into the dry ones; spoon 1/2 of the batter into the prepared cake pan.

Spread half of the apples on top of the batter. Pour in the remaining batter covering the apple chunks. Spread the remaining apples on top. Cover the cake pan with a paper towel.

Add 1 cup of water and a metal rack to your Instant Pot. Lower the cake pan onto the rack.

Secure the lid. Choose the "Manual" mode and cook for 55 minutes at High pressure. Once cooking is complete, use a natural pressure release for 10 minutes; carefully remove the lid.

Transfer the cake to a cooling rack and allow it to sit for about 15 minutes before slicing and serving.

514. Country-Style Apples

(Ready in about 10 minutes | Servings 4)

Per serving: 128 Calories; 0.3g Fat; 34.3g Carbs; 0.5g Protein; 27.5g Sugars

INGREDIENTS

4 apples
1 teaspoon ground cinnamon
1/2 teaspoon ground cloves
2 tablespoons honey

DIRECTIONS

Add all ingredients to the inner pot. Now, pour in 1/3 cup of water.
Secure the lid. Choose the "Manual" mode and cook for 2 minutes at High pressure. Once cooking is complete, use a quick pressure release; carefully remove the lid.
Serve in individual bowls. Bon appétit!

515. Peach and Raisin Crisp

(Ready in about 25 minutes | Servings 6)

Per serving: 329 Calories; 10g Fat; 56g Carbs; 6.9g Protein; 31g Sugars

INGREDIENTS

6 peaches, pitted and chopped
1/2 teaspoon ground cardamom
1 teaspoon ground cinnamon
1 teaspoon vanilla extract
1/3 cup orange juice
2 tablespoons honey
4 tablespoons raisins

4 tablespoons butter
1 cup rolled oats
4 tablespoons all-purpose flour
1/3 cup brown sugar
A pinch of grated nutmeg
A pinch of salt

DIRECTIONS

Place the peaches on the bottom of the inner pot. Sprinkle with cardamom, cinnamon and vanilla. Top with the orange juice, honey, and raisins.
In a mixing bowl, whisk together the butter, oats, flour, brown sugar, nutmeg, and salt. Drop by a spoonful on top of the peaches.
Secure the lid. Choose the "Manual" mode and cook for 8 minutes at High pressure. Once cooking is complete, use a natural pressure release for 10 minutes; carefully remove the lid. Bon appétit!

516. Mixed Berry Jam

(Ready in about 25 minutes | Servings 10)

Per serving: 143 Calories; 0.3g Fat; 36.1g Carbs; 0.7g Protein; 30.5g Sugars

INGREDIENTS

2 ½ pounds fresh mixed berries
1 ¼ cups granulated sugar

2 tablespoons fresh lemon juice
3 tablespoons cornstarch

DIRECTIONS

Add the fresh mixed berries, sugar, and lemon juice to the inner pot.
Secure the lid. Choose the "Manual" mode and cook for 2 minutes at High pressure. Once cooking is complete, use a natural pressure release for 15 minutes; carefully remove the lid.
Whisk the cornstarch with 3 tablespoons of water until well combined. Stir in the cornstarch slurry.
Press the "Sauté" button and bring the mixture to a rolling boil. Let it boil for about 5 minutes, stirring continuously, until your jam has thickened. Bon appétit!

517. Delicious **Dulce de Leche**

(Ready in about 35 minutes | Servings 2)

Per serving: 360 Calories; 8.4g Fat; 66.1g Carbs; 7g Protein; 57g Sugars

INGREDIENTS

1 can (14-ounce) sweetened condensed milk

DIRECTIONS

Place a trivet and steamer basket in the inner pot. Place the can of milk in the steamer basket.
Add water until the can is covered.
Secure the lid. Choose the "Manual" mode and cook for 20 minutes at High pressure. Once cooking is complete, use a natural pressure release for 10 minutes; carefully remove the lid.
Don't open the can until it is completely cooled. Bon appétit!

518. Light Carrot Souffle

(Ready in about 1 hour | Servings 6)

Per serving: 344 Calories; 24.1g Fat; 26.1g Carbs; 6.8g Protein; 17.1g Sugars

INGREDIENTS

1 ½ pounds carrots, trimmed and cut into chunks
3/4 cup sugar
1 teaspoon baking powder
1 teaspoon vanilla paste
1/4 teaspoon ground cardamom

1/2 teaspoon ground cinnamon
3 tablespoons flour
3 eggs
1/3 cup cream cheese room temperature
1 stick butter, softened

DIRECTIONS

Place 1 cup of water and a steamer basket in the bottom of your Instant Pot. Place the carrots in the steamer basket.
Secure the lid. Choose the "Steam" mode and cook for 10 minutes at High pressure. Once cooking is complete, use a quick pressure release; carefully remove the lid.
Process the mashed carrots, sugar, baking powder, vanilla, cardamom, cinnamon, and flour in your food processor until creamy, uniform, and smooth.
Add the eggs one at a time and mix to combine well. Stir in the cream cheese and butter; mix to combine well.
Spritz a baking pan with cooking spray; spoon the carrot mixture into the baking dish.
Add 1 cup of water and metal trivet to the bottom of the inner pot; cover with a paper towel.
Secure the lid. Choose the "Manual" mode and cook for 35 minutes at High pressure. Once cooking is complete, use a natural pressure release for 10 minutes; carefully remove the lid. Bon appétit!

519. Sunday Banana Bread

(Ready in about 50 minutes | Servings 8)

Per serving: 320 Calories; 17.1g Fat; 37.1g Carbs; 5.4g Protein; 13.1g Sugars

INGREDIENTS

1 stick butter, melted
2 eggs
1 teaspoon vanilla extract
3/4 cup sugar

1 teaspoon baking soda
2 bananas, mashed
1 ½ cups all-purpose flour
1/2 cup coconut flaked

DIRECTIONS

Mix all ingredients in a bowl until everything is well incorporated.
Add 1 cup of water and metal trivet to the bottom of the inner pot. Spritz a baking pan with nonstick cooking oil.
Scrape the batter into the prepared pan. Lower the pan onto the trivet.
Secure the lid. Choose the "Manual" mode and cook for 45 minutes at High pressure. Once cooking is complete, use a quick pressure release; carefully remove the lid.
Allow the banana bread to cool slightly before slicing and serving. Enjoy!

520. Easy Cheesecake with Almonds

(Ready in about 45 minutes | Servings 8)

Per serving: 388 Calories; 28.8g Fat; 25.9g Carbs; 8.4g Protein; 19.9g Sugars

INGREDIENTS

1 cup cookies, crushed
3 tablespoons coconut oil, melted
18 ounces cream cheese
1 cup granulated sugar
2 eggs

1/3 cup sour cream
1/4 teaspoon grated nutmeg
1/2 teaspoon pure vanilla extract
1/2 cup almonds, slivered

DIRECTIONS

Place a metal trivet and 1 cup of water in your Instant Pot. Spritz a baking pan with nonstick cooking spray.

Next, mix the cookies and coconut oil into a sticky crust. Press the crust into the prepared baking pan.

Thoroughly combine the cream cheese, sugar, eggs, sour cream, nutmeg, and vanilla extract in a mixing bowl. Pour this mixture over the crust and cover it with a piece of foil.

Lower the baking pan onto the trivet.

Secure the lid. Choose the "Manual" mode and cook for 25 minutes at High pressure. Once cooking is complete, use a natural pressure release for 15 minutes; carefully remove the lid.

Top with slivered almonds and serve well chilled. Bon appétit!

521. Fresh Blueberry Butter

(Ready in about 25 minutes | Servings 10)

Per serving: 230 Calories; 0.3g Fat; 59g Carbs; 0.7g Protein; 53.6g Sugars

INGREDIENTS

2 pounds fresh blueberries
1 pound granulated sugar
1/2 teaspoon vanilla extract

1 tablespoon freshly grated lemon zest
1/4 cup fresh lemon juice

DIRECTIONS

Place the blueberries, sugar, and vanilla in the inner pot of your Instant Pot.

Secure the lid. Choose the "Manual" mode and cook for 2 minutes at High pressure. Once cooking is complete, use a natural pressure release for 15 minutes; carefully remove the lid.

Stir in the lemon zest and juice. Puree in a food processor; then, strain and push the mixture through a sieve before storing. Enjoy!

522. Valentine's Day Pots de Crème

(Ready in about 25 minutes | Servings 6)

Per serving: 351 Calories; 19.3g Fat; 39.3g Carbs; 5.5g Protein; 32.1g Sugars

INGREDIENTS

2 cups double cream
1/2 cup whole milk
4 egg yolks
1/3 cup sugar

1 teaspoon instant coffee
A pinch of pink salt
9 ounces chocolate chips

DIRECTIONS

Place a metal trivet and 1 cup of water in your Instant Pot.

In a saucepan, bring the cream and milk to a simmer.

Then, thoroughly combine the egg yolks, sugar, instant coffee, and salt. Slowly and gradually whisk in the hot cream mixture.

Whisk in the chocolate chips and blend again. Pour the mixture into mason jars. Lower the jars onto the trivet.

Secure the lid. Choose the "Manual" mode and cook for 6 minutes at High pressure. Once cooking is complete, use a natural pressure release for 10 minutes; carefully remove the lid.

Serve well chilled and enjoy!

523. Lemon Butter Cake

(Ready in about 35 minutes | Servings 6)

Per serving: 369 Calories; 21.1g Fat; 40g Carbs; 7.3g Protein; 28.9g Sugars

INGREDIENTS

1 cup butter cookies, crumbled

3 tablespoons butter, melted

1 egg

2 egg yolks

1/2 cup lemon juice

1 (14-ounce) can sweetened condensed milk

3 tablespoons honey

1/2 cup heavy cream

1/4 cup sugar

DIRECTIONS

Place a metal trivet and 1 cup of water in your Instant Pot. Spritz a baking pan with nonstick cooking spray.

Next, mix the cookies and butter until well combined. Press the crust into the prepared baking pan.

Then, thoroughly combine the eggs, lemon juice, condensed milk, and honey with a hand mixer.

Pour this mixture on top of the prepared crust. Lower the baking pan onto the trivet and cover with a piece of foil.

Secure the lid. Choose the "Manual" mode and cook for 15 minutes at High pressure. Once cooking is complete, use a natural pressure release for 15 minutes; carefully remove the lid.

Afterwards, whip the heavy cream with sugar until the cream becomes stiff. Frost your cake and serve well chilled. Bon appétit!

524. Spring Berry Compote

(Ready in about 30 minutes | Servings 4)

Per serving: 224 Calories; 0.8g Fat; 56.3g Carbs; 2.1g Protein; 46.5g Sugars

INGREDIENTS

1 pound blueberries

1/2 pound blackberries

1/2 pound strawberries

1/2 cup brown sugar

1 tablespoon orange juice

1/4 teaspoon ground cloves

1 vanilla bean

DIRECTIONS

Place your berries in the inner pot. Add the sugar and let sit for 15 minutes. Add in the orange juice, ground cloves, and vanilla bean.

Secure the lid. Choose the "Manual" mode and cook for 2 minutes at High pressure. Once cooking is complete, use a natural pressure release for 10 minutes; carefully remove the lid.

As your compote cools, it will thicken. Bon appétit!

525. Home-Style Mexican Horchata

(Ready in about 20 minutes | Servings 8)

Per serving: 107 Calories; 2.4g Fat; 17.5g Carbs; 4.6g Protein; 17.7g Sugars

INGREDIENTS

20 ounces rice milk, unsweetened

8 ounces almond milk, unsweetened

5 tablespoons agave syrup

1 cinnamon stick

1 vanilla bean

DIRECTIONS

Combine all ingredients in the inner pot of your Instant Pot.

Secure the lid. Choose the "Manual" mode and cook for 5 minutes at High pressure. Once cooking is complete, use a natural pressure release for 10 minutes; carefully remove the lid.

Serve garnished with a few sprinkles of ground cinnamon if desired. Enjoy!

526. Authentic Agua de Jamaica

(Ready in about 20 minutes | Servings 4)

Per serving: 118 Calories; 0.2g Fat; 29.8g Carbs; 0.2g Protein; 28.5g Sugars

INGREDIENTS

4 cups water
1/2 cup dried hibiscus flowers
1/2 cup brown sugar
1/2 teaspoon fresh ginger, peeled and minced
2 tablespoons lime juice

DIRECTIONS

Combine all ingredients, except for the lime juice, in the inner pot of your Instant Pot.
Secure the lid. Choose the "Manual" mode and cook for 5 minutes at High pressure. Once cooking is complete, use a natural pressure release for 10 minutes; carefully remove the lid.
Stir in the lime juice and serve well chilled.

527. Molten Chocolate Cakes

(Ready in about 30 minutes | Servings 4)

Per serving: 671 Calories; 27.4g Fat; 95g Carbs; 10.6g Protein; 53.5g Sugars

INGREDIENTS

1/2 stick butter
1 cup sugar
2 eggs
3 tablespoons coconut milk
1 teaspoon vanilla

1 ½ cups self-rising flour
2 tablespoons cocoa powder
1 tablespoon carob powder
4 ounces bittersweet chocolate
4 ounces semisweet chocolate

DIRECTIONS

Place a metal trivet and 1 cup of water in your Instant Pot. Butter custard cups and set aside.
Then, beat the butter and sugar until creamy. Fold in the eggs, one at a time, and mix until everything is well combined.
Add the milk and vanilla and mix again. Then, stir in the flour, cocoa powder, and carob powder. Fold in the chocolate and stir to combine. Divide the mixture between the prepared custard cups.
Lower the cups onto the trivet.
Secure the lid. Choose the "Steam" mode and cook for 15 minutes at High pressure. Once cooking is complete, use a natural pressure release for 10 minutes; carefully remove the lid. Enjoy!

528. Spanish Arroz Con Leche

(Ready in about 25 minutes | Servings 4)

Per serving: 370 Calories; 4.4g Fat; 72.4g Carbs; 7.6g Protein; 32.2g Sugars

INGREDIENTS

1 cup white pearl rice
1 cup water
A pinch of salt
2 ¼ cups milk
1/2 cup sugar

1/4 teaspoon grated nutmeg
1 teaspoon vanilla extract
1 teaspoon cinnamon
Peel of 1/2 lemon

DIRECTIONS

Place the rice, water, and salt in the inner pot of your Instant Pot.
Secure the lid. Choose the "Rice" mode and cook for 10 minutes at Low pressure. Once cooking is complete, use a natural pressure release for 10 minutes; carefully remove the lid.
Add in the milk, sugar, nutmeg, vanilla, cinnamon, and lemon peel; stir to combine well.
Press the "Sauté" button and cook, stirring continuously, until your pudding starts to boil. Press the "Cancel" button. Enjoy!

529. Granny's Monkey Bread with Walnuts

(Ready in about 40 minutes | Servings 6)

Per serving: 355 Calories; 15.8g Fat; 46.9g Carbs; 7.2g Protein; 12.7g Sugars

INGREDIENTS

12 frozen egg dinner rolls, thawed
1/4 cup brown sugar
1 teaspoon ground cinnamon
1/4 cup walnuts, ground

1/4 cup coconut oil, melted
1/3 cup powdered sugar
1 tablespoon coconut milk

DIRECTIONS

Place 1 cup of water and a metal trivet in the inner pot of your Instant Pot. Spray a Bundt pan with cooking spray and set aside.
Cut each dinner roll in half.
In a mixing bowl, thoroughly combine the brown sugar, cinnamon, and walnuts. In another bowl, place the melted coconut oil. Dip the rolls halves in the coconut oil and roll them in the brown sugar mixture.
Arrange the rolls in the prepared Bundt pan. Cover the pan with a piece of aluminum foil; allow it to rise overnight at room temperature.
On the next day, lower the pan onto the trivet.
Secure the lid. Choose the "Manual" mode and cook for 25 minutes at High pressure. Once cooking is complete, use a natural pressure release for 10 minutes; carefully remove the lid.
After that, invert the bread onto a serving plate.
In a mixing bowl, whisk the powdered sugar and coconut milk until smooth. Drizzle the glaze over the top and sides of your cake. Bon appétit!

530. Cinnamon Pull-Apart Coffee Cake

(Ready in about 40 minutes | Servings 10)

Per serving: 512 Calories; 24.1g Fat; 69.4g Carbs; 5.9g Protein; 21.3g Sugars

INGREDIENTS

2 (16.3-ounce) cans refrigerated biscuits
3/4 cup granulated sugar
1 tablespoon ground cinnamon
1/4 teaspoon nutmeg, preferably freshly grated

1/2 cup raisins, if desired
3/4 cup butter, melted
1/2 cup firmly packed brown sugar

DIRECTIONS

Place 1 cup of water and a metal trivet in the inner pot of your Instant Pot. Lightly grease 12-cup fluted tube pan with cooking spray.
In a food bag, mix the granulated sugar, cinnamon, and nutmeg.
Separate the dough into biscuits and cut each into quarters. Place them in the food bag and shake to coat on all sides. Place them in the prepared pan, adding raisins among the biscuit pieces.
In a small mixing bowl, whisk the melted butter with brown sugar; pour the butter mixture over the biscuit pieces.
Secure the lid. Choose the "Manual" mode and cook for 25 minutes at High pressure. Bake until no longer doughy in the center.
Once cooking is complete, use a natural pressure release for 10 minutes; carefully remove the lid.
Turn upside down onto serving plate and serve warm. Bon appétit!

531. Autumn Compote with Honeyed Greek Yogurt

(Ready in about 20 minutes | Servings 4)

Per serving: 304 Calories; 0.3g Fat; 75.4g Carbs; 5.1g Protein; 69.2g Sugars

INGREDIENTS

1 cup rhubarb
1 cup plums
1 cup apples
1 cup pears

1 teaspoon ground ginger
1 vanilla bean
1 cinnamon stick
1/2 cup caster sugar

1 cup Greek yoghurt
4 tablespoons honey

DIRECTIONS

Place the fruits, ginger, vanilla, cinnamon, and caster sugar in the inner pot of your Instant Pot.
Secure the lid. Choose the "Manual" mode and cook for 2 minutes at High pressure. Once cooking is complete, use a natural pressure release for 10 minutes; carefully remove the lid.
Meanwhile, whisk the yogurt with honey.
Serve your compote in individual bowls with a dollop of honeyed Greek yogurt. Enjoy!

532. Polynesian Hazelnut Pinch Me Cake

(Ready in about 35 minutes | Servings 8)

Per serving: 444 Calories; 28.9g Fat; 42.4g Carbs; 5.9g Protein; 18.3g Sugars

INGREDIENTS

1 cup granulated sugar

4 tablespoons hazelnuts, ground

10 refrigerated biscuits

1 stick butter, melted

4 ounces cream cheese, at room temperature

1/4 cup powdered sugar

2 tablespoons apple juice

1 teaspoon vanilla extract

DIRECTIONS

Place 1 cup of water and a metal trivet in the inner pot of your Instant Pot. Lightly grease 10-inch fluted tube pan with cooking spray. In a shallow bowl, mix the 1 cup of granulated sugar and ground hazelnuts.

Cut each biscuit in half. Dip your biscuits into the melted butter; then, roll them in the hazelnut/sugar mixture. Arrange them in the fluted tube pan.

Secure the lid. Choose the "Manual" mode and cook for 25 minutes at High pressure. Once cooking is complete, use a natural pressure release for 5 minutes; carefully remove the lid.

In the meantime, whip the cream cheese with the powdered sugar, apple juice, and vanilla extract. Drizzle over the hot cake and serve.

533. Chocolate Pudding Cake with Apricots

(Ready in about 55 minutes | Servings 10)

Per serving: 408 Calories; 13.9g Fat; 64.2g Carbs; 8.2g Protein; 39.7g Sugars

INGREDIENTS

4 ounces instant pudding mix

3 cups milk

1 package vanilla cake mix

1/2 cup peanut butter

1 ½ cups chocolate chips

1/2 cup dried apricots, chopped

DIRECTIONS

In a mixing bowl, thoroughly combine the pudding mix and milk. Por the mixture into a lightly greased inner pot.

Prepare the cake mix according to the manufacturer's instructions, gradually adding in the peanut butter. Pour the batter over the pudding.

Secure the lid. Choose the "Manual" mode and cook for 30 minutes at High pressure. Once cooking is complete, use a natural pressure release for 10 minutes; carefully remove the lid.

Sprinkle the chocolate chips and dried apricots on top. Seal the lid and let it stand for 10 to 15 minutes until the chocolate melts. Enjoy!

534. Decadent Caramel Croissant Pudding

(Ready in about 40 minutes | Servings 6)

Per serving: 414 Calories; 22.3g Fat; 39.4g Carbs; 10.2g Protein; 24.1g Sugars

INGREDIENTS

6 stale croissants, cut into chunks

1 cup granulated sugar

4 tablespoons water

1 cup milk

1 cup heavy cream

3 tablespoons rum

1/4 teaspoon ground cinnamon

3 eggs, whisked

DIRECTIONS

Place 1 cup of water and a metal trivet in the inner pot of your Instant Pot. Place the croissants in the lightly greased casserole dish.

Press the "Sauté" button and use the lowest setting. Then, place the granulated sugar and water and let it cook until the mixture turns a deep amber color.

Now, add the milk and heavy cream, and cook until heated through. Stir in the rum, cinnamon, and eggs; stir to combine.

Secure the lid. Choose the "Manual" mode and cook for 25 minutes at High pressure. Once cooking is complete, use a natural pressure release for 10 minutes; carefully remove the lid. Bon appétit!

535. Chai Spiced White Hot Chocolate

(Ready in about 10 minutes | Servings 5)

Per serving: 278 Calories; 15.5g Fat; 27.3g Carbs; 9.7g Protein; 25.7g Sugars

INGREDIENTS

4 cups whole milk
1/3 cup almond butter
4 tablespoons honey
2 tablespoons Masala Chai Syrup

1 teaspoon vanilla extract
A pinch of sea salt
A pinch of grated nutmeg
2 tablespoons gelatin

DIRECTIONS

Add the milk, almond butter, honey, Masala Chai Syrup, vanilla extract, sea salt, and grated nutmeg to the inner to of your Instant Pot.
Secure the lid. Choose the "Manual" mode and cook for 6 minutes at Low pressure. Once cooking is complete, use a quick pressure release; carefully remove the lid.
Add the gelatin and mix with an immersion blender until your hot chocolate is frothy and smooth. Enjoy!

536. Greek Stewed Dried Fruits (Hosafi)

(Ready in about 20 minutes | Servings 8)

Per serving: 215 Calories; 0.4g Fat; 55.4g Carbs; 1.8g Protein; 35.8g Sugars

INGREDIENTS

1/2 cup dried figs
1 cup dried apricots
1/2 cup sultana raisins
1 cup prunes, pitted
1 cup almonds
1 cup sugar

1 cinnamon stick
1 vanilla bean
1/2 teaspoon whole cloves
1/2 teaspoon whole star anise
2 cups water
2 tablespoons Greek honey

DIRECTIONS

Place all ingredients in the inner pot of your Instant Pot.
Secure the lid. Choose the "Manual" mode and cook for 2 minutes at High pressure. Once cooking is complete, use a natural pressure release for 10 minutes; carefully remove the lid.
Serve with Greek yogurt or ice cream, if desired.

537. Hot Spiced Apple Cider

(Ready in about 55 minutes | Servings 6)

Per serving: 173 Calories; 0.4g Fat; 39.5g Carbs; 0.6g Protein; 32.6g Sugars

INGREDIENTS

6 apples, cored and diced
3/4 cup brown sugar
2 cinnamon sticks
1 vanilla bean

1 teaspoon whole cloves
1 small naval orange
4 tablespoons rum
4 cups water

DIRECTIONS

Place the ingredients in the inner pot of your Instant Pot.
Secure the lid. Choose the "Manual" mode and cook for 50 minutes at High pressure. Once cooking is complete, use a quick pressure release; carefully remove the lid.
Mash the apples with a fork or a potato masher. Pour the mixture over a mesh strainer and serve hot. Bon appétit!

538. Hungarian Aranygaluska Cake

(Ready in about 35 minutes | Servings 8)

Per serving: 485 Calories; 23.4g Fat; 64.9g Carbs; 6.8g Protein; 36.9g Sugars

INGREDIENTS

1 cup granulated sugar

4 ounces walnuts, ground

1 tablespoon grated lemon peel

4 tablespoons butter, at room temperature

1 tablespoon fresh lemon juice

16 ounces refrigerated buttermilk biscuits

2 tablespoons cream cheese, at room temperature

1/2 cup powdered sugar

1 teaspoon vanilla extract

DIRECTIONS

Place 1 cup of water and a metal trivet in the inner pot of your Instant Pot. Lightly grease a loaf pan with shortening of choice.

In a shallow bowl mix the granulated sugar, walnuts, and lemon peel. Mix the melted butter and lemon juice in another shallow bowl.

Cut each biscuit in half. Dip your biscuits into the butter mixture; then, roll them in the walnut/sugar mixture.

Arrange them in the loaf pan.

Secure the lid. Choose the "Manual" mode and cook for 25 minutes at High pressure. Once cooking is complete, use a natural pressure release for 5 minutes; carefully remove the lid.

In the meantime, whip the cream cheese with the powdered sugar, and vanilla extract. Drizzle over the hot cake and serve.

539. Perfect Holiday Cupcakes

(Ready in about 40 minutes | Servings 4)

Per serving: 497 Calories; 17.8g Fat; 77g Carbs; 9.8g Protein; 48.5g Sugars

INGREDIENTS

1 cup cake flour

1 ½ teaspoons baking powder

A pinch of salt

1/4 teaspoon ground cardamom

1/4 teaspoon ground cinnamon

1 teaspoon vanilla extract

1 egg

1/2 cup honey

1/4 almond milk

4 ounces cream cheese

1/3 cup powdered sugar

1 cup heavy cream, cold

DIRECTIONS

In a mixing bowl, thoroughly combine the flour, baking powder, salt, cardamom, cinnamon, and vanilla.

Then, gradually add in the egg, honey, and milk. Mix to combine well. Now, spoon the batter into silicone cupcake liners and cover them with foil.

Place 1 cup of water and a metal trivet in your Instant Pot. Lower your cupcakes onto the trivet.

Secure the lid. Choose the "Manual" mode and cook for 25 minutes at High pressure. Once cooking is complete, use a natural pressure release for 10 minutes; carefully remove the lid.

While the cupcakes are cooking, prepare the frosting by mixing the remaining ingredients. Frost your cupcakes and enjoy!

540. Giant German Pancake

(Ready in about 40 minutes | Servings 4)

Per serving: 399 Calories; 19.8g Fat; 42.3g Carbs; 13.1g Protein; 17.5g Sugars

INGREDIENTS

4 tablespoons butter, melted

5 eggs

1 ¼ cups milk

1 cup all-purpose flour

1/4 teaspoon kosher salt

1/2 teaspoon cinnamon powder

1/2 teaspoon vanilla extract

1 cup canned blueberries with syrup

DIRECTIONS

Place 1 cup of water and a metal trivet in your Instant Pot. Line the bottom of a springform pan with parchment paper; grease the bottom and sides of the pan with melted butter.

Mix the eggs, milk, flour, salt, cinnamon, and vanilla until everything is well combined. Now, spoon the batter into the prepared pan. Lower the pan onto the trivet.

Secure the lid. Choose the "Manual" mode and cook for 30 minutes at High pressure. Once cooking is complete, use a quick pressure release; carefully remove the lid.

Serve garnished with fresh blueberries and enjoy!

541. Hot Mulled Apple Cider

(Ready in about 1 hour 35 minutes | Servings 8)

Per serving: 124 Calories; 0.8g Fat; 28.7g Carbs; 0.3g Protein; 24.1g Sugars

INGREDIENTS

8 cups apple cider
1 (1-inch piece) fresh ginger, peeled and sliced
2 cinnamon sticks
2 vanilla beans

1 teaspoon whole cloves
1 teaspoon allspice berries
1 orange, sliced into thin rounds
1/2 cups brandy

DIRECTIONS

Place all ingredients, except for the brandy, in the inner pot of your Instant Pot.
Secure the lid. Choose the "Slow Cook" mode and cook for 1 hour 30 minutes at the lowest temperature.
Strain the cider mixture and stir in the brandy. Serve immediately.

542. Vegan Butternut Squash Pudding

(Ready in about 20 minutes | Servings 6)

Per serving: 315 Calories; 8.8g Fat; 60.5g Carbs; 2.3g Protein; 42.1g Sugars

INGREDIENTS

2 pounds butternut squash, peeled, seeded, and diced
1 cup coconut cream
1/2 cup maple syrup

A pinch of kosher salt
1 teaspoon pumpkin pie spice mix
6 tablespoons almond milk

DIRECTIONS

Add 1 cup of water and a metal rack to the bottom of the inner pot. Place your squash in a steamer basket; lower the basket onto the rack.
Secure the lid. Choose the "Steam" mode and cook for 10 minutes at High pressure. Once cooking is complete, use a quick pressure release; carefully remove the lid.
Stir the remaining ingredients into the cooked squash; combine all ingredients with a potato masher.
Let it cook on the "Sauté" function until everything is thoroughly heated or about 4 minutes. Serve immediately.

543. Dutch Cinnamon Pear Pie

(Ready in about 35 minutes | Servings 8)

Per serving: 497 Calories; 28.6g Fat; 56.5g Carbs; 4.9g Protein; 30.4g Sugars

INGREDIENTS

2 cans (12-ounce) refrigerated cinnamon rolls
1/4 cup all-purpose flour
1/4 cup packed brown sugar
1/2 teaspoon cinnamon

2 tablespoons butter
1/3 cup pecans, chopped
5 pears, cored and sliced

DIRECTIONS

Separate the dough into 8 rolls. Press and flatten the rolls into a lightly greased pie plate. Make sure there are no holes between the flattened rolls.
In a mixing bowl, mix the flour, brown sugar, cinnamon, butter, and pecans. Place the slices of pears on the prepared cinnamon roll crust. Spoon the streusel onto the pear slices.
Add 1 cup of water and a metal rack to the bottom of the inner pot. Lower the pie plate onto the rack.
Secure the lid. Choose the "Manual" mode and cook for 25 minutes at High pressure. Once cooking is complete, use a natural pressure release for 5 minutes; carefully remove the lid. Bon appétit!

544. Old-Fashioned Stuffed Apples

(Ready in about 25 minutes | Servings 4)

Per serving: 266 Calories; 11.5g Fat; 43.9g Carbs; 1.6g Protein; 36g Sugars

INGREDIENTS

4 baking apples

1/3 cup granulated sugar

1/2 teaspoon cardamom

1/2 teaspoon cinnamon

1/3 cup walnuts, chopped

4 tablespoons currants

2 tablespoons coconut oil

DIRECTIONS

Add 1 ½ cups of water and a metal rack to the bottom of the inner pot.

Core the apples and use a melon baller to scoop out a bit of the flesh. Mix the remaining ingredients. Divide the filling between your apples.

Secure the lid. Choose the "Steam" mode and cook for 15 minutes at High pressure. Once cooking is complete, use a quick pressure release; carefully remove the lid.

Serve with ice cream, if desired. Bon appétit!

545. Chocolate Mini Crepes

(Ready in about 40 minutes | Servings 6)

Per serving: 364 Calories; 12.5g Fat; 56.5g Carbs; 6.1g Protein; 29.6g Sugars

INGREDIENTS

1/2 cup all-purpose flour

1/2 cup rice flour

1 ½ teaspoons baking powder

1 teaspoon vanilla paste

1/4 teaspoon ground cinnamon

A pinch of salt

2 tablespoons granulated sugar

2 eggs, whisked

1 cup milk

1/4 cup coconut oil

1 cup chocolate syrup

DIRECTIONS

Add 1 cup of water and a metal rack to the bottom of the inner pot. Lightly grease a mini muffin tin with shortening of choice.

Mix the flour, baking powder, vanilla, cinnamon, salt, sugar, eggs, milk, and coconut oil until thoroughly combined and smooth.

Pour the batter into the muffin tin and lower it onto the rack.

Secure the lid. Choose the "Manual" mode and cook for 25 minutes at High pressure. Once cooking is complete, use a natural pressure release for 10 minutes; carefully remove the lid.

Serve with chocolate syrup and enjoy!

546. Puerto Rican Pudding (Budin)

(Ready in about 1 hour | Servings 8)

Per serving: 377 Calories; 18.4g Fat; 41.7g Carbs; 10.1g Protein; 24.5g Sugars

INGREDIENTS

1 pound Puerto Rican sweet bread, torn into pieces

1 cup water

1 teaspoon cinnamon powder

1/2 teaspoon ground cloves

1 teaspoon vanilla essence

1 cup brown sugar

4 cups coconut milk

2 tablespoons rum

4 eggs, beaten

A pinch of salt

1/2 stick butter, melted

DIRECTIONS

Place 1 cup of water and a metal trivet in the inner pot of your Instant Pot. Place the pieces of sweet bread in a lightly greased casserole dish.

Now, mix the remaining ingredients; stir to combine well and pour the mixture over the pieces of sweet bread. Let it stand for 20 minutes, pressing down with a wide spatula until the bread is covered.

Secure the lid. Choose the "Manual" mode and cook for 25 minutes at High pressure. Once cooking is complete, use a natural pressure release for 10 minutes; carefully remove the lid. Bon appétit!

547. Orange Cranberry Spritzer

(Ready in about 25 minutes | Servings 8)

Per serving: 103 Calories; 0g Fat; 25.6g Carbs; 0.8g Protein; 24.7g Sugars

INGREDIENTS

12 ounces fresh cranberries
1/2 cup granulated sugar
2 cups pulp-free orange juice
1 cup water

DIRECTIONS

Place all ingredients in the inner pot.
Secure the lid. Choose the "Manual" mode and cook for 5 minutes at High pressure. Once cooking is complete, use a natural pressure release for 15 minutes; carefully remove the lid.
Divide between eight glasses and fill with club soda. Enjoy!

548. Famous New York-Style Cheesecake

(Ready in about 45 minutes | Servings 10)

Per serving: 340 Calories; 20.1g Fat; 29.7g Carbs; 10.7g Protein; 18.1g Sugars

INGREDIENTS

4 tablespoons granulated sugar
4 tablespoons butter
10 large graham crackers, crumbled
3 tablespoons almonds, ground
1/3 teaspoon cinnamon

12 ounces Philadelphia cheese
1 teaspoon vanilla extract
1 tablespoon lemon zest
1 tablespoon arrowroot powder
1/2 cup golden caster sugar

3 eggs
1 cup creme fraiche
2 tablespoons golden caster sugar

DIRECTIONS

Place a metal trivet and 1 cup of water in your Instant Pot. Spritz a baking pan with nonstick cooking spray.
Next, mix 4 tablespoons of granulated sugar, butter, crackers, almonds, and cinnamon into a sticky crust. Press the crust into the prepared baking pan.
In a mixing bowl, combine the Philadelphia cheese, vanilla extract, lemon zest, arrowroot powder, 1/2 cup of golden caster sugar, and eggs. Pour the filling mixture over the crust and cover it with a piece of foil.
Lower the baking pan onto the trivet.
Secure the lid. Choose the "Manual" mode and cook for 25 minutes at High pressure. Once cooking is complete, use a natural pressure release for 15 minutes; carefully remove the lid.
Lastly, beat the creme fraiche with 2 tablespoons of golden caster sugar. Spread this topping over the cheesecake right to the edges. Cover loosely with foil and refrigerate overnight. Bon appétit!

549. Classic Chewy Brownies

(Ready in about 40 minutes | Servings 12)

Per serving: 264 Calories; 18.1g Fat; 24.2g Carbs; 4.5g Protein; 19.3g Sugars

INGREDIENTS

1/2 cup walnut butter
1/2 cup sunflower seed butter
1 cup coconut sugar
1/2 cup cocoa powder
2 eggs

A pinch of grated nutmeg
A pinch of salt
1/2 cardamom powder
1/2 teaspoon cinnamon powder
1/2 teaspoon baking soda

1 teaspoon vanilla extract
1/2 cup dark chocolate, cut into chunks

DIRECTIONS

Place a metal trivet and 1 cup of water in your Instant Pot. Spritz a baking pan with nonstick cooking spray.
In a mixing bowl, combine all ingredients, except for the chocolate; stir well to create a thick batter.
Spoon the batter into the prepared pan. Sprinkle the chocolate chunks over the top; gently press the chocolate chunks into the batter.
Lower the baking pan onto the trivet.
Secure the lid. Choose the "Manual" mode and cook for 20 minutes at High pressure. Once cooking is complete, use a natural pressure release for 10 minutes; carefully remove the lid.
Place your brownies on a cooling rack before slicing and serving. Bon appétit!

550. Old-Fashioned Chocolate Fudge

(Ready in about 15 minutes + chilling time | Servings 12)

Per serving: 223 Calories; 11g Fat; 27.7g Carbs; 3.2g Protein; 18.3g Sugars

INGREDIENTS

16 ounce canned condensed milk
2 tablespoons peanut butter
1/2 teaspoon ground cardamom
1/2 teaspoon ground cinnamon

1 teaspoon vanilla extract
8 ounces bittersweet chocolate chips
8 ounces semisweet chocolate chips

DIRECTIONS

Line the bottom of a baking sheet with a piece of foil.

Add the milk, peanut butter, cardamom, cinnamon, and vanilla to the inner pot of your Instant Pot; stir until everything is well incorporated.

Next, press the "Sauté" button and use the lowest setting to cook the mixture until thoroughly warmed. Now, fold in the chocolate chips and stir again to combine well.

Lastly, pour the mixture into the prepared baking sheet and transfer to your refrigerator; let it sit until solid.

Cut into squares and serve. Bon appétit!

FAVORITE INSTANT POT RECIPES

551. Creamy Mustard Chicken

(Ready in about 20 minutes | Servings 4)

Per serving: 413 Calories; 27.2g Fat; 3.3g Carbs; 37.5g Protein; 1.2g Sugars

INGREDIENTS

2 tablespoons olive oil, divided
1 pound chicken breasts, boneless
1 teaspoon dried basil
1/2 teaspoon dried oregano
1/2 teaspoon dried sage
1 teaspoon paprika

1 teaspoon garlic powder
Sea salt and ground black pepper, to taste
1 tablespoon Dijon mustard
1 cup chicken bone broth
1/2 cup heavy cream

DIRECTIONS

Press the "Sauté" button and heat the olive oil. Sear the chicken breasts until they are no longer pink.
Add the seasonings, mustard, and chicken bone broth.
Secure the lid. Choose "Manual" mode and cook for 8 minutes at High pressure. Once cooking is complete, use a natural pressure release; carefully remove the lid.
Lastly, add the heavy cream, cover with the lid, and let it sit in the residual heat for 6 to 8 minutes. Serve in individual bowls. Enjoy!

552. Holiday Chicken Bake

(Ready in about 20 minutes | Servings 4)

Per serving: 756 Calories; 34.9g Fat; 66g Carbs; 45.2g Protein; 4.7g Sugars

INGREDIENTS

2 tablespoons olive oil
1 pound chicken breast, boneless, cut into chunks
2 cups cream of celery soup
2 cups spiral pasta
1 cup Cotija cheese, crumbled

1 cup queso fresco, crumbled
1 ½ cups spiral pasta
1 cup salsa
1 cup fresh breadcrumbs

DIRECTIONS

Press the "Sauté" button and heat the olive oil. Now, brown the chicken breasts for 3 to 4 minutes.
Add the remaining ingredients in the order listed above.
Secure the lid. Choose "Manual" mode and cook for 6 minutes at High pressure. Once cooking is complete, use a natural pressure release; carefully remove the lid.
Serve warm.

553. French-Style Chicken Tenders

(Ready in about 25 minutes | Servings 4)

Per serving: 305 Calories; 13.1g Fat; 2.8g Carbs; 41.9g Protein; 1.7g Sugars

INGREDIENTS

2 tablespoons butter, softened
1 ½ pounds chicken tenders
1 cup vegetable broth
1 teaspoon shallot powder
1 teaspoon garlic powder

1/2 teaspoon smoked paprika
Sea salt and freshly ground black pepper, to taste
1 cup Cottage cheese, crumbled
2 heaping tablespoons fresh chives, roughly chopped

DIRECTIONS

Press the "Sauté" button and melt the butter. Sear the chicken tenders for 2 to 3 minutes.
Add the vegetable broth, shallot powder, garlic powder, paprika, salt, and black pepper.
Secure the lid. Choose "Manual" mode and cook for 8 minutes at High pressure. Once cooking is complete, use a natural pressure release; carefully remove the lid.
Stir in the cheese; cover with the lid and let it sit in the residual heat for 5 minutes. Garnish with fresh chives and serve immediately.

554. Mediterranean Chicken Wings

(Ready in about 25 minutes | Servings 4)

Per serving: 457 Calories; 26.3g Fat; 13.7g Carbs; 39.8g Protein; 3.1g Sugars

INGREDIENTS

2 tablespoons butter, room temperature
4 chicken drumsticks, boneless
1/4 cup all-purpose flour
1 teaspoon Italian seasoning mix

Sea salt and ground black pepper, to taste
2 bell peppers, deseeded and sliced
1 cup scallions, chopped

4 cloves garlic, smashed
1/4 cup Marsala wine
1 cup chicken broth
1/4 cup cream cheese

DIRECTIONS

Press the "Sauté" button to preheat your Instant Pot. Melt 1 tablespoon of the butter.

Dredge your chicken in the flour; season with spices and cook until slightly brown; reserve.

Melt the remaining tablespoon of butter and sauté the peppers, scallions, and garlic. Pour in the wine, scraping up any browned bits from the bottom of the pan. Add the chicken broth and secure the lid.

Choose the "Manual" mode and cook for 10 minutes at High pressure. Once cooking is complete, use a natural pressure release; carefully remove the lid.

Press the "Sauté" button to preheat your Instant Pot one more time. Add the cream cheese and cook for a further 4 to 5 minutes or until everything is thoroughly heated.

To serve, spoon the sauce over the chicken drumsticks. Bon appétit!

555. Greek Chicken Fillets

(Ready in about 20 minutes | Servings 4)

Per serving: 444 Calories; 12.2g Fat; 45.1g Carbs; 37g Protein; 4.5g Sugars

INGREDIENTS

2 teaspoons butter, at room temperature
1 pound chicken fillets, diced
1 onion, diced
1 sweet pepper, deseeded and sliced
1 red chili pepper, deseeded and sliced
3 cloves garlic, minced

1 teaspoon dried rosemary
1 teaspoon dried oregano
Kosher salt and ground black pepper, to taste
2 cups vegetable broth
1 cup dry couscous
4 ounces halloumi cheese, crumbled

DIRECTIONS

Press the "Sauté" button to preheat your Instant Pot. Melt 1 teaspoon of the butter. Cook the chicken fillets until golden brown. Set aside.

Then, melt the remaining 1 teaspoon of butter. Now, sauté the onion, peppers, and garlic until tender and aromatic.

Add the rosemary, oregano, salt, pepper, and vegetable broth.

Secure the lid. Choose the "Poultry" mode and cook for 5 minutes at High pressure. Once cooking is complete, use a quick pressure release; carefully remove the lid.

Add the couscous and stir to combine. Secure the lid. Choose the "Manual" mode and cook for 2 minutes at High pressure. Once cooking is complete, use a quick pressure release; carefully remove the lid.

Divide between four serving plates; garnish each serving with halloumi cheese and enjoy!

556. Simple Teriyaki Chicken

(Ready in about 30 minutes | Servings 4)

Per serving: 294 Calories; 13.3g Fat; 15.1g Carbs; 27g Protein; 9.8g Sugars

INGREDIENTS

2 tablespoons sesame oil
1 pound chicken drumettes, skinless, boneless, cut into bite-sized chunks
2 garlic cloves, minced
1/4 cup soy sauce

1/2 cup water
1/2 cup rice vinegar
1/4 cup brown sugar
1 teaspoon ground ginger
2 tablespoons rice wine

3 tablespoons Mirin
1 pound broccoli florets
1 teaspoon arrowroot powder

DIRECTIONS

Press the "Sauté" button to preheat your Instant Pot. Heat the sesame oil and cook the chicken drumettes for 3 to 4 minutes.

Then, add the garlic and cook for 30 seconds more or until fragrant. Add the soy sauce, water, vinegar, sugar, ginger, rice wine, and Mirin. Secure the lid.

Choose the "Manual" mode and cook for 10 minutes at High pressure. Once cooking is complete, use a quick pressure release; carefully remove the lid.

Add the broccoli florets and secure the lid. Choose the "Manual" mode and cook for 2 minutes at High pressure. Once cooking is complete, use a quick pressure release; carefully remove the lid.

Transfer the chicken and broccoli to a nice serving platter.

Press the "Sauté" button to preheat your Instant Pot again. Add the arrowroot powder and stir until it is completely dissolved. Cook for 5 to 6 minutes or until the sauce thickens slightly. Spoon over the chicken and serve.

557. Chicken Enchilada Sliders

(Ready in about 25 minutes | Servings 4)

Per serving: 504 Calories; 17.2g Fat; 49.1g Carbs; 36.3g Protein; 6.7g Sugars

INGREDIENTS

1 pound chicken breasts, boneless and skinless
Kosher salt and freshly ground black pepper, to taste
1 cup chicken broth

8 ounces canner red enchilada sauce
1 cup spring onions, sliced
8 slider buns

DIRECTIONS

Place the chicken breasts in the inner pot. Season with salt and pepper; pour in the chicken broth and enchilada sauce.
Secure the lid. Choose the "Manual" mode and cook for 9 minutes at High pressure. Once cooking is complete, use a quick pressure release; carefully remove the lid.
Place the bottom half of the slider buns on a baking sheet. Top with layers of the chicken mixture and spring onions. Put on the top buns and spritz with cooking spray.
Bake about 10 minutes in the preheated oven until buns are golden. Enjoy!

558. Family Chicken Sandwiches

(Ready in about 25 minutes | Servings 4)

Per serving: 452 Calories; 27.1g Fat; 25.2g Carbs; 26.1g Protein; 4.5g Sugars

INGREDIENTS

2 tablespoons butter, at room temperature
1 pound whole chicken, skinless and boneless
2 garlic cloves, crushed
1 yellow onion, chopped
Sea salt and ground black pepper, to your liking
1 teaspoon cayenne pepper

4 hamburger buns
1 tablespoons mustard
1 large tomato, sliced
1 Lebanese cucumber, sliced
1 tablespoon fresh cilantro, chopped
2 tablespoons fresh green onions, chopped

DIRECTIONS

Press the "Sauté" button to preheat your Instant Pot. Melt the butter and cook the chicken for 3 to 4 minutes or until slightly brown.
Add the garlic, onion, salt, black pepper, and cayenne pepper.
Secure the lid. Choose the "Poultry" mode and cook for 15 minutes at High pressure. Once cooking is complete, use a quick pressure release; carefully remove the lid.
Shred the chicken with two forks.
Spread the mustard on the bottom half of each hamburger bun. Top with the tomato, cumber, chicken, cilantro, and green onions; top with the remaining bun halves. Serve immediately.

559. Classic Roast Pork

(Ready in about 1 hour 10 minutes | Servings 6)

Per serving: 545 Calories; 35.4g Fat; 4.2g Carbs; 48.2g Protein; 1.5g Sugars

INGREDIENTS

2 garlic cloves, minced
2 teaspoons stone-ground mustard
Sea salt and ground black pepper, to taste
1 teaspoon freshly grated lemon zest
2 ½ pounds pork butt

1 tablespoon lard, at room temperature
1/2 cup red wine
1 large leek, sliced into long pieces
1 carrot, halved lengthwise

DIRECTIONS

Combine the garlic, mustard, salt, pepper and lemon zest in a mixing bowl. Using your hands, spread the rub evenly onto the pork butt.
Press the "Sauté" button to preheat your Instant Pot. Melt the lard and sear the meat for 3 minutes per side.
Pour a splash of wine into the inner pot, scraping any bits from the bottom with a wooden spoon.
Place a trivet and 1 cup of water in the bottom of the inner pot. Lower the pork butt onto the trivet; scatter the leeks and carrots around.
Secure the lid. Choose the "Manual" mode and cook for 50 minutes at High pressure. Once cooking is complete, use a natural pressure release for 10 minutes; carefully remove the lid.
Transfer the pork butt to a cutting board and let it sit for 5 minutes before carving and serving. Enjoy!

560. Creamy Pork Loin Roast

(Ready in about 45 minutes | Servings 6)

Per serving: 436 Calories; 22.8g Fat; 2.6g Carbs; 52.2g Protein; 2.2g Sugars

INGREDIENTS

2 tablespoons sesame oil
2 ½ pounds pork loin roast, boneless
Sea salt and freshly ground black pepper, to taste
1 teaspoon dried basil
1 teaspoon dried oregano

1/2 teaspoon paprika
1/2 lemon, juiced and zested
1 cup vegetable broth
1 cup milk

DIRECTIONS

Press the "Sauté" button and heat the oil until sizzling; once hot, sear the pork for 4 to 5 minutes or until browned on all sides. Work in batches.

Add the remaining ingredients.

Secure the lid. Choose the "Meat/Stew" mode and cook for 35 minutes at High pressure. Once cooking is complete, use a quick pressure release; carefully remove the lid.

Turn on your broiler. Roast the pork under the broiler for about 3 minutes or until the skin is crisp.

To carve the pork, remove the cracklings and cut the crisp pork skin into strips. Carve the pork roast across the grain into thin slices and serve.

561. Hot Paprika and Pork Omelet

(Ready in about 25 minutes | Servings 2)

Per serving: 449 Calories; 33.6g Fat; 4.3g Carbs; 32.2g Protein; 1.6g Sugars

INGREDIENTS

1 tablespoon canola oil
1/2 pound ground pork
1 yellow onion, thinly sliced
1 red chili pepper, minced
4 eggs, whisked

1/2 teaspoon garlic powder
1/3 teaspoon cumin powder
1 teaspoon oyster sauce
Kosher salt and ground black pepper, to taste
1/2 teaspoon paprika

DIRECTIONS

Press the "Sauté" button and heat the oil until sizzling; once hot, cook the ground pork until no longer pink, crumbling with a spatula.

Add the onion and pepper; cook an additional 2 minutes. Whisk the eggs with the remaining ingredients. Pour the egg mixture over the meat mixture in the inner pot.

Secure the lid. Choose the "Manual" mode and cook for 8 minutes at High pressure. Once cooking is complete, use a natural pressure release for 10 minutes; carefully remove the lid. Bon appétit!

562. Grilled Pork Spare Ribs

(Ready in about 45 minutes | Servings 4)

Per serving: 500 Calories; 28.6g Fat; 8.9g Carbs; 49.2g Protein; 6.1g Sugars

INGREDIENTS

2 pounds pork spare ribs, cut into 4
equal portions
1 tablespoon sea salt
1/2 teaspoon black pepper
1/2 teaspoon chili flakes

1 teaspoon cayenne pepper
1 teaspoon shallot powder
1 teaspoon garlic powder
1 teaspoon fennel seeds
1 tablespoon sugar

1 cup chicken stock
1 cup tomato ketchup
1/4 cup dark soy sauce

DIRECTIONS

Generously sprinkle the pork spare ribs with all spices and sugar. Add the chicken stock and secure the lid.

Choose the "Meat/Stew" mode and cook for 35 minutes at High pressure. Once cooking is complete, use a quick pressure release; carefully remove the lid.

Transfer the pork ribs to a baking pan. Mix the tomato ketchup and soy sauce; pour the mixture over the pork ribs and roast in the preheated oven at 425 degrees F for 6 to 8 minutes. Bon appétit!

563. Asian-Style Pork Medallions

(Ready in about 30 minutes | Servings 3)

Per serving: 355 Calories; 10.1g Fat; 13g Carbs; 51g Protein; 7.2g Sugars

INGREDIENTS

1 tablespoon sesame oil
1 ½ pounds pork medallions
1/2 cup tamari sauce
1/2 cup chicken stock
1/4 cup rice vinegar

1/2 teaspoon cayenne pepper
1/2 teaspoon salt
1 tablespoon maple syrup
1 tablespoon Sriracha sauce
2 cloves garlic, minced

6 ounces mushrooms, chopped
1 tablespoon arrowroot powder, dissolved in 2 tablespoons of water

DIRECTIONS

Press the "Sauté" button and heat the oil; once hot, cook the pork medallions for 3 minutes per side.

Add the tamari sauce, chicken stock, vinegar, cayenne pepper, salt, maple syrup, Sriracha, garlic, and mushrooms to the inner pot.

Secure the lid. Choose the "Meat/Stew" mode and cook for 20 minutes at High pressure. Once cooking is complete, use a quick pressure release; carefully remove the lid. Remove the pork from the inner pot.

Add the thickener to the cooking liquid. Press the "Sauté" button again and let it boil until the sauce has reduced slightly and the flavors have concentrated.

Serve over hot steamed rice if desired. Enjoy!

564. Cholula Sandwiches with Pork

(Ready in about 40 minutes | Servings 4)

Per serving: 516 Calories; 14.4g Fat; 37.1g Carbs; 56.7g Protein; 15.2g Sugars

INGREDIENTS

1 tablespoon olive oil
2 pounds pork shoulder roast
1/2 cup tomato paste
1/2 cup beef bone broth

1/4 cup balsamic vinegar
1/4 cup brown sugar
1 tablespoon mustard
1 teaspoon Cholula hot sauce

2 cloves garlic, minced
1 teaspoon dried marjoram
4 hamburger buns

DIRECTIONS

Add all ingredients, except for the hamburger buns, to the inner pot.

Secure the lid. Choose the "Meat/Stew" mode and cook for 35 minutes at High pressure. Once cooking is complete, use a quick pressure release; carefully remove the lid.

Remove the pork from the inner pot and shred with two forks. Spoon the pulled pork into the hamburger buns and serve with your favorite toppings. Bon appétit!

565. Classic Pork Chops in Mushroom Sauce

(Ready in about 30 minutes | Servings 6)

Per serving: 438 Calories; 25.8g Fat; 7.2g Carbs; 42.8g Protein; 2.7g Sugars

INGREDIENTS

2 tablespoons butter
6 pork chops
1 tablespoon Italian seasoning blend
1/2 teaspoon coarse sea salt
1/2 teaspoon cracked black pepper
1 pound white mushrooms, sliced

1 tablespoon fresh coriander, chopped
1 teaspoon dill weed, minced
2 cloves garlic crushed
1/2 cup double cream
1/2 cup cream of onion soup

DIRECTIONS

Press the "Sauté" button and melt the butter. Once hot, sear the pork chops until golden browned, about 4 minutes per side.

Add the remaining ingredients and gently stir to combine.

Secure the lid. Choose the "Meat/Stew" mode and cook for 20 minutes at High pressure. Once cooking is complete, use a quick pressure release; carefully remove the lid.

Serve over mashed potatoes. Bon appétit!

566. Authentic Sesame Beef

(Ready in about 45 minutes | Servings 5)

Per serving: 322 Calories; 17.8g Fat; 3.1g Carbs; 38.1g Protein; 1.6g Sugars

INGREDIENTS

2 tablespoons sesame oil
2 pounds chuck roast, slice into pieces
1/2 cup beef bone broth
1/2 (12-ounce) bottle beer
1 tablespoon mustard
1 tablespoon granulated sugar

Kosher salt and freshly ground black pepper, to taste
1 teaspoon onion powder
1 teaspoon garlic powder
1 teaspoon ginger powder
1/4 teaspoon ground allspice
2 tablespoons sesame seeds, toasted

DIRECTIONS

Press the "Sauté" button to preheat your Instant Pot. Heat the oil and brown the beef in batches; cook for about 3 minutes per batch.
Add the broth, beer, mustard, sugar, salt, black pepper, onion powder, garlic powder, ginger, and ground allspice.
Secure the lid. Choose the "Manual" mode and cook for 40 minutes at High pressure. Once cooking is complete, use a quick pressure release; carefully remove the lid.
Serve garnished with toasted sesame seeds. Enjoy!

567. Traditional Pot Roast with Garden Vegetables

(Ready in about 50 minutes | Servings 5)

Per serving: 425 Calories; 19.2g Fat; 15.5g Carbs; 48.8g Protein; 4.8g Sugars

INGREDIENTS

1 tablespoon lard, melted
2 pounds pot roast
Pink salt and ground black pepper, to taste
1/2 teaspoon ground cumin

1 teaspoon onion powder
1 teaspoon garlic powder
2 cups cream of celery soup
2 celery stalks
4 carrots

1 onion, halved
2 tablespoons fresh parsley leaves, roughly chopped

DIRECTIONS

Press the "Sauté" button to preheat your Instant Pot. Melt the lard and cook your pot roast until slightly brown on all sides.
Season with salt, black pepper, cumin, onion powder, and garlic powder. Pour in the cream of celery soup.
Secure the lid. Choose the "Meat/Stew" mode and cook for 35 minutes at High pressure. Once cooking is complete, use a natural pressure release; carefully remove the lid.
After that, stir in the celery, carrots, and onion.
Secure the lid. Choose the "Manual" mode and cook for 8 minutes at High pressure. Once cooking is complete, use a quick pressure release; carefully remove the lid.
Garnish with fresh parsley and serve immediately. Bon appétit!

568. Ground Beef Frittata

(Ready in about 25 minutes | Servings 2)

Per serving: 368 Calories; 24.1g Fat; 3.7g Carbs; 33.9g Protein; 2.4g Sugars

INGREDIENTS

1 tablespoon olive oil
1/2 pound ground chuck
4 eggs, whisked
A small bunch of green onions, chopped

1 small tomato, chopped
Sea salt and freshly ground black pepper, to your liking
1/2 teaspoon paprika
1/2 teaspoon garlic powder

DIRECTIONS

Press the "Sauté" button to preheat your Instant Pot. Heat the oil and brown the beef for 2 to 3 minutes, stirring continuously.
Lightly spritz a baking pan with cooking oil. Add all ingredients, including the browned beef to the baking pan.
Cover with foil. Add 1 cup of water and a metal trivet to the Instant Pot. Lower the baking pan onto the trivet.
Secure the lid. Choose the "Manual" mode and cook for 6 minutes at High pressure. Once cooking is complete, use a natural pressure release for 10 minutes; carefully remove the lid.
Slice in half and serve. Bon appétit!

569. Corned Beef Brisket with Root Vegetables

(Ready in about 1 hour 25 minutes | Servings 6)

Per serving: 563 Calories; 35.8g Fat; 19.5g Carbs; 39.3g Protein; 6.5g Sugars

INGREDIENTS

2 ½ pounds corned beef brisket
2 cloves peeled garlic
2 sprigs thyme
1 sprig rosemary
2 tablespoons olive oil
1 cup chicken broth

1/4 cup tomato puree
1 medium leek, sliced
1/2 pound rutabaga, peeled and cut into 1-inch chunks
1/2 pound turnips, peeled and cut into 1-inch chunks
2 parsnips, cut into 1-inch chunks
2 bell peppers, halved

DIRECTIONS

Place the beef brisket, garlic, thyme, rosemary, olive oil, chicken broth, and tomato puree in the inner pot.
Secure the lid. Choose the "Manual" mode and cook for 80 minutes at High pressure. Once cooking is complete, use a quick pressure release; carefully remove the lid.
Add the other ingredients. Gently stir to combine.
Secure the lid. Choose the "Manual" mode and cook for 4 minutes at High pressure. Once cooking is complete, use a quick pressure release; carefully remove the lid. Bon appétit!

570. Old-School Short Ribs

(Ready in about 1 hour 45 minutes | Servings 6)

Per serving: 655 Calories; 50.8g Fat; 3.3g Carbs; 43.7g Protein; 0.6g Sugars

INGREDIENTS

4 pounds beef short ribs, bone-in
Sea salt and ground black pepper, to taste
2 tablespoons olive oil
1 medium leek, sliced
2 cloves garlic, sliced

1 cup water
1 packet of onion soup mix
1 sprig thyme
1 sprig rosemary
1/2 teaspoon celery seeds

DIRECTIONS

Place all ingredients in the inner pot.
Secure the lid. Choose the "Manual" mode and cook for 90 minutes at High pressure. Once cooking is complete, use a natural pressure release; carefully remove the lid.
Afterwards, place the short ribs under the broiler until the outside is crisp or about 10 minutes.
Transfer the ribs to a serving platter and enjoy!

571. Mexican Drunk Ribs

(Ready in about 40 minutes + marinating time | Servings 8)

Per serving: 399 Calories; 29.2g Fat; 13.3g Carbs; 20.7g Protein; 5g Sugars

INGREDIENTS

2 racks chuck short ribs
2 shots tequila
Kosher salt and cracked black pepper, to taste
2 tablespoons honey
1 teaspoon garlic powder
1 teaspoon shallot powder
1 teaspoon marjoram

1 tablespoon Sriracha sauce
1/2 teaspoon paprika
1 cup apple cider
2 tablespoons tomato paste
1 tablespoon stone ground mustard
1 cup beef bone broth

DIRECTIONS

Place all ingredients, except for beef broth, in a ceramic dish. Cover with a foil and let it marinate for 3 hours in your refrigerator.
Place the beef along with its marinade in the inner pot. Pour in the beef bone broth.
Secure the lid. Choose the "Meat/Stew" mode and cook for 35 minutes at High pressure. Once cooking is complete, use a natural pressure release; carefully remove the lid. Bon appétit!

572. Margarita Glazed Chuck Roast

(Ready in about 1 hour | Servings 6)

Per serving: 348 Calories; 14.9g Fat; 10.3g Carbs; 42.7g Protein; 7.7g Sugars

INGREDIENTS

2 pounds chuck roast
1 cup beef broth
1/4 cup soy sauce
1/4 cup champagne vinegar
Sea salt and ground black pepper, to taste
1/2 teaspoon red pepper flakes

2 cloves garlic, sliced
Margarita Glaze:
1/2 cup tequila
1/4 cup orange juice
1/4 lime juice
2 tablespoons dark brown sugar

DIRECTIONS

Add the chuck roast, beef broth, soy sauce, champagne vinegar, salt, black pepper, red pepper flakes, and garlic to the inner pot.

Secure the lid. Choose the "Manual" mode and cook for 40 minutes at High pressure. Once cooking is complete, use a natural pressure release for 10 minutes; carefully remove the lid.

Meanwhile, whisk all ingredients for the margarita glaze. Now, glaze the ribs and place under the broiler for 5 minutes; then, turn them over and glaze on the other side. Broil an additional 5 minutes.

Cut the chuck roast into slices and serve the remaining glaze on the side as a sauce. Bon appétit!

573. Yummy Beef Round Roast

(Ready in about 50 minutes | Servings 6)

Per serving: 426 Calories; 11.4g Fat; 29.9g Carbs; 48.7g Protein; 2.8g Sugars

INGREDIENTS

2 tablespoons olive oil, divided
2 pounds beef round roast, cut into bite-sized pieces
1 white onion, chopped
1 garlic clove, sliced
1 bell pepper, sliced

1/4 cup tomato puree
1/4 cup dry red wine
1 cup beef broth
2 pounds whole small potatoes

DIRECTIONS '

Press the "Sauté" button to preheat your Instant Pot. Heat the oil and brown the beef round roast for 3 to 4 minutes, working in batches.

Add the white onion, garlic, pepper, tomato puree, red wine, and broth.

Secure the lid. Choose the "Meat/Stew" mode and cook for 35 minutes at High pressure. Once cooking is complete, use a quick pressure release; carefully remove the lid.

Add the potatoes. Secure the lid. Choose the "Manual" mode and cook for 10 minutes at High pressure. Once cooking is complete, use a quick pressure release; carefully remove the lid.

Serve in individual bowls and enjoy!

574. Sunday Blueberry Butter

(Ready in about 25 minutes | Servings 10)

Per serving: 230 Calories; 0.3g Fat; 59g Carbs; 0.7g Protein; 53.6g Sugars

INGREDIENTS

2 pounds fresh blueberries
1 pound granulated sugar
1/2 teaspoon vanilla extract
1 tablespoon freshly grated lemon zest
1/4 cup fresh lemon juice

DIRECTIONS

Place the blueberries, sugar, and vanilla in the inner pot of your Instant Pot.

Secure the lid. Choose the "Manual" mode and cook for 2 minutes at High pressure. Once cooking is complete, use a natural pressure release for 15 minutes; carefully remove the lid.

Stir in the lemon zest and juice. Puree in a food processor; then, strain and push the mixture through a sieve before storing. Enjoy!

575. Romantic Pots de Crème

(Ready in about 25 minutes | Servings 6)

Per serving: 351 Calories; 19.3g Fat; 39.3g Carbs; 5.5g Protein; 32.1g Sugars

INGREDIENTS

2 cups double cream
1/2 cup whole milk
4 egg yolks
1/3 cup sugar

1 teaspoon instant coffee
A pinch of pink salt
9 ounces chocolate chips

DIRECTIONS

Place a metal trivet and 1 cup of water in your Instant Pot.

In a saucepan, bring the cream and milk to a simmer.

Then, thoroughly combine the egg yolks, sugar, instant coffee, and salt. Slowly and gradually whisk in the hot cream mixture.

Whisk in the chocolate chips and blend again. Pour the mixture into mason jars. Lower the jars onto the trivet.

Secure the lid. Choose the "Manual" mode and cook for 6 minutes at High pressure. Once cooking is complete, use a natural pressure release for 10 minutes; carefully remove the lid.

Serve well chilled and enjoy!

Made in the USA
San Bernardino, CA
06 December 2019